DISTANT PARTNERS

Community Change Through Project Renewal

Ben W. Lappin
Morton I. Teicher

UNIVERSITY
PRESS OF
AMERICA

Lanham • New York • London

Copyright © 1990 by

University Press of America®, Inc.
4720 Boston Way
Lanham, Maryland 20706

3 Henrietta Street
London WC2E 8LU England

Library of Congress Cataloging-in-Publication Data

Lappin, Ben W.
Distant partners : community change through Project Renewal / by
Ben W. Lappin & Morton I. Teicher.
    p.   cm.
1. Project Renewal (Israel) 2. Urban renewal—Israel—Case studies.
3. Community development, Urban—Israel—Case studies.
4. Community development consultants—United States—Case studies.
5. Community development consultants—Israel—Case studies.
6. Sister cities—Case studies. I. Teicher, Morton I. II. Title.
HT178.I7L36   1990   307.3'416'095694—dc20   90–12037 CIP

ISBN 0–8191–7760–1 (alk. paper)
ISBN 0–8191–7761–X (pbk. : alk. paper)

HT
178
I7
L36
1990

Project Renewal

Table of Contents

PREFACE

For two intensive years, a community worker carried out the tasks of social development in Kfar Oranim, a distressed town in Israel. A detailed, day-by-day documentary account of his activities is the heart of this book.

One afternoon, the worker arrived in the town and was introduced at a meeting in the Mayor's office as the liaison-consultant, newly appointed by the Project Renewal Committee of Croydon, U.S.A. The appointment was part of Croydon's "twinning" agreement with Kfar Oranim, some seven thousand miles distant. This inter-community partnership was brought into being as part of Project Renewal, the country-wide urban rehabilitation program sponsored by the Israeli government in collaboration with world Jewry, acting through the Jewish Agency.

The Mayor of Kfar Oranim and the members of the town's Project Renewal Steering Committee who were sitting around the table were informed that, henceforth, the liaison-consultant would be spending two days a week, or the equivalent, in Kfar Oranim. The goal of his involvement, among other things, was to create what might be termed "a Croydon presence" in order to help convert the "twinning" arrangement between the two communities into a living social reality by attempting to bridge the great distance that separated them geographically. To create such a direct link, the liaison-consultant would keep his sponsors in Croydon fully informed on all aspects of community life in Kfar Oranim, especially the Project Renewal activities being financially supported by the Croydon Jewish Federation.

A representative of the Croydon Jewish Federation who happened to be visiting Israel at the time was present at the meeting but, since he did not speak Hebrew, the introduction was made by a senior executive of Project Renewal. The liaison-consultant had not met this individual nor, with the exception of the Croydon visitor, was he familiar with anyone else in the room. The general knowledge he had about Kfar Oranim was limited to a few facts about its population and its institutional structure. This information was of little use to him at the moment. All he could assume about the people in the room was that they were individuals of some prominence in the town, having been elected or appointed to serve on the Kfar Oranim Project Renewal Steering Committee.

The announcement of the liaison-consultant's appointment was received without comment. Since the liaison-consultant was not asked to respond to the introduction, he too remained silent. Yet, while this formal introduction was proceeding, members of the Steering Committee sent an occasional smile or approving nod across the table.

i

The liaison-consultant reacted in kind with amicable gestures of his own. On this unspoken note of geniality, the first steps were taken toward establishing a feeling of mutuality between the people of Kfar Oranim and the liaison-consultant.

At the same time, interaction of a more formal type was being initiated by the senior executive as he included in the presentation his definition of the circumscribed role of the liaison-consultant. Thus, the informal and formal components of the relationship were symbolically and actually present from the very outset.

The liaison-consultant had not expected the dual nature of the relationship to assert itself virtually on the heels of his arrival in Kfar Oranim. From the standpoint of timing, it was something of a surprise. However, he was sure that it was bound to come since the element of dualism is an inherent characteristic of community work.

The formal and informal aspects of community work complement each other. The informal role is aimed primarily at the natural community and is concerned with citizen morale, voluntarism, participation, community development, social and economic growth. The formal approach deals more often with the functional community and its agency or institutional structure, with needs and resources, social and fiscal planning, priorities, standards of service and criteria for measuring progress

While the exchange of friendly gestures was crucial to one type of relationship that was being initiated between the people of Kfar Oranim and the liaison-consultant, the formal introduction by the senior executive was essential to the entire role he was slated to play in the community. A community worker, unlike a physician or a lawyer, must have, in addition to his professional credentials, a publicly avowed sponsor who proclaims legitimation of the specific function that the worker is about to undertake. Accordingly, the introduction was, in fact, gaining the liaison-consultant his entry to the people of the locality which was "twinned" with the Croydon Jewish community, its distant partner.

The dual nature of the liaison-consultant's role and the legitimation by a recognized sponsor are two characteristics that are basic to all the liaison-consultants working within Project Renewal. Aside from these elements, there are marked variations in the performance and approaches of these workers. Differences begin with the title assigned to them in various communities. In Kfar Oranim, it is "liaison-consultant"; in some places, it is "community representative"; in others, it is "neighborhood communicator". None of these labels actually describe with any precision just what this functionary does in a given locality. For example, in Kfar Oranim, the "liaison" part of the title accurately describes the linking aspect of the role. However, the "consultant" part is deceptive as a designation since the liaison-consultant is often more directly involved in the affairs of the town as a link rather than as a consultant. The term, "consultant" may have been added to the title in order to indicate to all concerned that the liaison-consultant does not duplicate nor in any other way become directly involved in the work done by existing agencies and their staffs. To his sponsor in Croydon, the hyphenated name, "liaison-consultant", is in keeping with reality. The overseas community does indeed rely on his information and advice with regard to many aspects of its association with its distant partner in Israel.

In addition to differences in title, the liaison functionaries varied in the tasks they performed although there was a common thread running through their activities. Whether the particular undertaking was a lobbying action, a training course for neighborhood leaders or a campaign to clean the streets, there was an immediate objective rather than a longer range goal at stake. While the Croydon Federation would require some short range intervention from its liaison-consultant, it was fully aware of Kfar Oranim's fundamental problems as a depressed town with low morale. The quality of education had to be improved; social services had to be bettered; economic development was needed. These were problems of a deep-seated nature that did not lend themselves to superficial solutions. They called for the liaison-consultant to act as an enabler in helping to bring out the community's inner resources so that it could begin to tackle these long-standing difficulties. The liaison-consultant saw himself acting as enabler which was an integral part of his role and which symbolized the Croydon presence in Kfar Oranim. The enabling role was uniquely appropriate for someone representing a distant partner who, in accordance with his terms of reference, could not intervene directly in the affairs of the community in the same manner as the local professional workers.

Lists supplied by Project Renewal headquarters and by the Jerusalem Center for Public Affairs indicate that, as of August, 1985, there were 41 liaison functionaries active in 48 communities out of the 86 undergoing rehabilitation by Project Renewal. However, far more than 86 overseas communities are involved. Smaller communities which lack the means to sponsor rehabilitation programs on their own join several similar communities which are then collectively "twinned" with an Israeli neighborhood or town. There were 28 such clusters that included a total of 221 separate Jewish communities throughout the world, principally in North America. (1) Many sponsoring communities especially those combined with others, do not employ a liaison person.

Of the 41 individuals functioning in a liaison capacity in August, 1985, 22 were men and 19 were women. All were employed on a part-time basis. They range in age from 25 to 65 and they bring a great variety of professional backgrounds to the work. Four or five are qualified social workers but they have not all specialized in community work.

Facts about these liaison functionaries are not readily available. There is no established job category for them within Project Renewal, nor is there any official description of what they do. Reference is not made to them in the descriptions of Project Renewal published by the Jewish Agency or the Ministry of Housing which represents the Israeli government in Project Renewal. The 1985 brochure, *Guide to Project Renewal* (2) has no mention of the liaison functionary under any designation.

A history of Project Renewal, commissioned by the Jewish Agency, appeared in 1986; it contained only two brief references to the liaison functionary:

"Many communities sought to maintain contact with their neighborhoods on a year-round basis which they accomplished by periodic visits of community leaders or by hiring Israelis to serve as their local representative and liaison with the neighborhood and the authorities. This role has never been clearly defined and the results have varied considerably with the personality and the experience of the person who fills it."

"The representatives of the Diaspora communities developed active roles for themselves on the local level in their contacts with the neighborhood residents, the Local Steering Committee and project manager and local institutions such as the community center. At the national level, their inputs have been most strongly felt in contacts with the Agency Renewal Department, but they have not hesitated to knock on government doors from the ministerial level down if they felt that the interests of 'their' neighborhood warranted it." (3)

The mention of Israelis being appointed to serve as liaison functionaries refers to the fact that while they are indeed Israelis, most of them either came from the overseas sponsoring community before immigrating to Israel or from an English-speaking country. Those who are native-born Israelis speak English fluently.

As the quotation indicates, the liaison functionaries interact periodically with the Renewal Department of the Jewish Agency. Occasionally, their work brings them in touch with the Israeli government through the Ministry of Housing. When the need arises, these individuals can be quite effective in their representations either directly or through the local lobbying groups which they are apt to organize. However, as far as formal recognition is concerned, the Ministry of Housing is no more inclined to grant this than is the Jewish Agency. This stance is borne out in the publications issued by the Ministry. For example, in connection with the International

Project Renewal

Conference on Urban Revitalization which took place in Jerusalem in March, 1986, the Ministry of Housing produced an elaborate 96-page pictorial brochure which gives a full account in Hebrew, English and French of the background and current situation of Project Renewal. There is not a single mention of the part that liaison functionaries play in this renewal effort.

The closest that these workers come to being afforded recognition as a group is in the amenities they are offered by the Jerusalem Center for Public Affairs. This organization, headed by Professor Daniel J. Elazar, acts as host for monthly meetings of the liaison functionaries. Occasionally, Project Renewal officials come to the sessions to speak on such topics as fiscal matters, policy questions, urban renewal trends and impending changes in Project Renewal. The Jerusalem Center also serves as a clearing house where the liaison functionaries can exchange ideas and perhaps consult with a member of the Center staff regarding problems encountered on the job. The Renewal Department of the Jewish Agency takes a benign view of the services provided by the Center. From time to time, Project Renewal officials might consult the Center as to the progress a specific liaison functionary is making in a particular community. However, it is clearly understood by all concerned that the Jerusalem Center for Public Affairs is not an integral part of Project Renewal.

The Jerusalem Center for Public Affairs sponsored what was officially called *An International Conference on Urban Revitalization: Project Renewal and Other Experiences.* Israel was participant and host to nine other countries which sent representatives to this gathering. There were 87 papers given at the Conference. Fifteen were presented by participants from abroad; they dealt with general issues pertaining to urban populations and the city environment. Seventy-two papers addressed the subject of urban revitalization in Israel; 39 of these dealt specifically with Project Renewal. A careful reading of the abstracts of these papers and discussions with participants in the Conference revealed that there was no mention at all of community representatives, neighborhood communicators or liaison consultants. (4)

Clearly, in the formal sense, the community representative, neighborhood communicator or liaison-consultant is a worker whose services go unrecognized by the two sponsoring bodies of Project Renewal in Israel. Even the *Conference on Urban Revitalization* organized by the Jerusalem Center for Public Affairs which caters to the needs of these individuals was unable to take their work into account in the sessions of the Conference. In view of the marginal position that liaison functionaries are depicted as occupying in this national urban rehabilitation program, the reader may well wonder whether or not their role is of sufficient scope and significance to warrant the extensive treatment afforded to it in this book.

v

The position of the authors is that the role of the liaison functionary is far more important than meets the eye. Were the role given an institutionalized basis to achieve its full potential, the "twinning" process between Israel and Diaspora communities would be greatly enhanced. This is posited as a hypothesis to be proved or disproved by the material which follows.

Since this is a documentary which records the involvement of one particular liaison-consultant with one specific community and since there is such marked variance in the work of the liaison functionaries, the question inevitably arises as to the broader implications of the work of one liaison-consultant for other community workers and for other communities. It is the contention of the authors that the documentary approach used here portrays community work in action more comprehensively than the conventional case record and thus makes it possible for principles to be drawn which should guide community work in the future.

The liaison-consultant is a community worker practising within the framework of Project Renewal. The role extends the repertoire of community organization methods since it is singularly based on the special needs which have to be addressed because the sponsoring community and the assigned community are thousands of miles apart. The liaison-consultant carries day-to-day responsibilities which call for communicating with partners in two different languages, responding to different cultures, dealing with different traditions and relating to different orientations to organized community life. In the process, the worker copes with varying power structures and functions under dissimilar conditions of role legitimation.

Since the role emerged less than ten years ago, it is possible to examine it in its early formative stage. This will be done by means of the documentary account of the liaison-consultant role. The documentary is viewed by the authors as both the source of information and the instrument for examining and analyzing the liaison-consultant role. During the two-year period that the role was being carried out, a mass of material was accumulated which is too voluminous to be included in this book. Therefore, the documentary is drawn solely from the entries which record what occurred when the liaison-consultant visited Kfar Oranim or other places in the performance of his duties.

To determine whether or not carry-over exists, as well as to obtain data about the liaison functionaries as a group, interviews were conducted with senior officials of several organizations. These included the Ministry of Housing, Renewal Department, Jewish Agency, the Jerusalem Center for Public Affairs, the Israeli offices of Diaspora fund-raising groups and the International Committee for the Evaluation of Project Renewal. Since the last named organization is not including the liaison functionary's role in its evaluative research, the work presented here represents the first detailed study of the liaison functionary's role and should be useful in future research.

The interviews with senior officials provided information to supplement the documentary and the references cited in footnotes. Assurances were given that the names of those interviewed would be kept confidential. Accordingly, data gleaned from the interviews can only be acknowledged in part. Thus, in expressing appreciation to the people who provided such valuable information, the authors regret that their names cannot be mentioned. Similarly, the names of the communities and their residents as well those of the government and Project Renewal officials have all been disguised.

The term "documentary" deserves an explanation. Why not "case record"? This is the label ordinarily used by social workers for describing, illustrating and teaching their work.

It was pioneered by social caseworkers and subsequently emulated by social group workers and community workers. (5) What prompts the departure from this standard usage? Is this simply a stylistic nuance or is there a substantive change implied by the term, "documentary"?

Use of the term, "documentary" reflects the authors' dissatisfaction with the prevailing term, "case record". The social caseworkers who used this term originally were from the outset under the marked influence of medical practice in their search for a modality for their own professional intervention. This trend was prominent in the work of Mary Richmond whose writings at the turn of the century laid the foundation for social work as a profession. An example of her close identification with the doctor-patient model is evident as early as 1912 in an address she delivered that year to the National Conference of Charities and Corrections which she concluded with the following observation:

". . . while we have the right to expect our clients and our public to be patient, nevertheless it is a thoroughly good thing for *ourselves* (emphasis Mary Richmond's) to keep task number two in mind and to set ourselves about doing it just as soon as task number one is well under way. Let us choose deliberately, excluding one of two irreconcilable things for the time being, if need be, but let us take up the other task as soon as we possibly can. Such a policy of inclusion, even in minority of cases, makes for understanding, for resourcefulness and for flexibility, makes for these alike in the practice of the doctor and the social worker." (6)

Regardless of what Miss Richmond was referring to as "task number one" and "task number two", she presented a point of view in which the practitioner's mastery of role is an essential ingredient of professional practice. Her stance has gone unquestioned from the time she first began formulating her concept of social work nearly one hundred years ago. However, the medical model which guided her thinking with respect to work with individuals has never been a good fit for community work. Similarly, the "case record", echoing the medical record is not applicable to community work.

The community worker (7) functions in the public arena, relating to community leaders who are often vested with prestige, high status, influence and power with all of which the practitioner must cope as an aspect of practice. By contrast, the physician and the social caseworker relate to the patient or client in the privacy of the one-to-one or one-to-family environment. The focus is a disease or a personal dilemma which can, as a precondition of treatment, structure a relationship in which social rank, high or low, is set aside as being residual. Conceptually, this allows the need of the patient or client, regardless of whether or not it is affected by status in the community, to be the unimpeded focus of the helping relationship.

In the realm of community, neither the worker nor the community leaders can expect respective status endowments to be suspended since these are inherent in the working relationships between the community leaders and the community worker. This being the case, the community worker's own status which is often less substantial than that of the community leader, poses a problem. In such a situation, the worker cannot impose a structure which insures mastery over the practice role since the individual representing the community usually brings a higher status than that of the worker.

Accordingly, a community work record, if it is to convey an accurate picture of what transpires in the interaction between community worker and community leaders, must document the inherent problem of role mastery. Rather than rely on a selective recording that aims to include only those elements deemed relevant to a given problem, the authors decided to use the documentary method that depicts the total social situation out of which desired specifics may be selected. Whether or not a practitioner who is not in a position to exercise mastery over the role can claim to be functioning as a professional is another matter which will be examined in the concluding section where the implications of such a situation are considered.

The various discrete episodes of the documentary record are not unlike the individual entries in a diary. This term was used by the authors initially but it was discarded for the reason that diarists, as a rule, are bent on sharing their innermost thoughts with the reader. They are concerned with telling secrets either about the subjects they are discussing or about their own hidden impressions, feelings and attitudes.

The purpose of the documentary record is not for the recorder to indulge personal responses to a particular situation. Rather, the aim is to reflect episodes out of which a given aspect may be abstracted for examination and study. In this instance, emphasis is placed on the role of the liaison-consultant in the act of serving two communities thousands of miles apart which are linked in a partnership brought about by Project Renewal. The pivot here is a relationship in the public sector and not in the private arena of family or friendship groups.

The mass of detail in the documentary is a record of what actually happened. It contains the richness of human interaction in all its complexity; it mirrors reality. Matters are not selected for omission or inclusion nor are elaborate interpretations offered. As much as is humanly possible, the documentary truly describes what occurred. As part of the reality, the liaison-consultant's passing thoughts are occasionally recorded on the assumption that they are the basis of his activities. Also recorded are insights, impressions and intuitions which illuminate decision-making. Some thoughts are noted which subsequently fall away because they are either unproductive or irrelevant. The documentary thus reveals spontaneous idea formation as distinguished from the type of theorizing which belongs more properly to the later evaluative phase of intervention.

It may be argued that the recording was not an autonomous, mechanical phenomenon that proceeded without the recorder deciding what to include and what to omit. How can the reader know that subjective elements did not enter into the recording? In this sense, the limitations that affect all types of record-writing hold true for this presentation as well. Some screening of material almost inevitably took place. However, there were certain conditions that pervasively enhanced objectivity with respect to the selection of what is included in this documentary record. One of the most important of these was the factor that restricted the relationship between the liaison-consultant and the people of Kfar Oranim to the public sector. Since the liaison-consultant did not live in Kfar Oranim, he met the residents solely on what may be described as the community level and not in such roles as family heads, spouses, parents, children, siblings nor as members of kinship or friendship groups. This does not mean that there were no occasions for spending time casually with the residents nor that there were no home visits from time to time. However, these situations were not entered into for the purpose of cementing friendships. Such encounters were invariably a function of the liaison-consultant role in which the "Croydon presence" was being symbolized. The local residents were pleased to have it that way and the liaison-consultant understood this preference and was always ready to accommodate it.

Another point worth noting to substantiate the claim of impartial recording is the opportunity for the liaison-consultant to take full notes during interviews and meetings. Whether it was a meeting of the Town Council, a sub-committee engaged in reviewing a budget, a session with the Mayor or a passing chat with a neighborhood activist, notes were carefully and overtly taken. The liaison-consultant scribbled in his own version of shorthand what was transpiring during these encounters and, if there was some confusion in his mind about what was being said, he always requested clarification for the record. Indeed, at times, individuals would try to make sure that the burden of their statements was transferred accurately to the notebook by asking, "Did you get it all down?"

Frequently, note-taking can cause tension and inhibit free speech. For various reasons, people may become uneasy about being quoted. In Kfar Oranim, however, such reservations were minimal since the liaison-consultant was the link to Croydon, the source of sympathetic interest and support for the people of the town. Whether a point was being made at a meeting or in an individual conversation, the Kfar Oranim resident was nearly always interested in getting the message across to Croydon. The liaison-consultant was seen as the medium by which the message could reach the United States. Note-taking was facilitated from the time that the liaison-consultant was formally introduced as the appointee of the Croydon Jewish community who would keep his sponsor fully informed on an ongoing basis about life in Kfar Oranim.

Furthermore, there was the question of perspective. To say that the liaison-consultant saw himself as functioning in the public rather than the private sector and that the documentary would reflect events in the community and not the family was of some help in setting the direction of the recording even if only in a general way. The community is the focus of many sectors — cultural, religious, political, social welfare, etc. Moreover, each of these sectors is composed of various components — service agencies, policies, professions, organizations, etc. The true bearing of the liaison-consultant lay in the involvement with the social welfare sector and its agencies. Beyond that, the liaison-consultant took the view that, at the core, his interest was in the interaction of these agencies with other institutions and organizations in Kfar Oranim as they functioned within the framework of Project Renewal. Thus, this is not a narrative of triumphs and defeats, recording the deeds of saints and sinners, heroes and cowards, but, rather it describes people in the process of pursuing what is best for the community in accordance with their values and the doctrines and policies of their respective organizations. In bringing these outlooks and vested interests into the civic arena of Kfar Oranim, they inevitably choose sides, engage in strategies and tactics that create coalitions and oppositions, cooperation and conflict, problems, solutions and endless polemics.

For two years, the liaison-consultant was witness and participant in this process, testing each stipulated component of his role against the reality he encountered in seeking to implement it. The possibility of submitting the viability of the practice role in all of its components to a process of deliberate testing in the execution made the experience memorable. What was envisaged and what indeed took place was no haphazard exercise of random interactions but rather a deliberate process of engagement, informed by consideration of principles which guided the day-by-day practice.

For this unusual professional experience, the writers are deeply indebted to the people of Kfar Oranim and to the Croydon Jewish Federation. We owe thanks to Graenum Berger and Morris Latchman who read the manuscript and made many helpful suggestions. We appreciate the cooperation of Brian Bilzin who provided an office and a typewriter. We are grateful to Teddy Kollek who kindly invited one of us to spend a month in Mishkenot Sha'aninim, the Jerusalem guest house for artists and writers so that we could work together on finishing the manuscript. The staff of Mishkenot Sha'aninim was especially helpful and we owe them our gratitude. Finally, we express our deep appreciation for the tolerance, patience and forbearance of our wives, Adah Lappin and Mickey Teicher.

FOOTNOTES

1. *Guide to Project Renewal.* Jerusalem: Project Renewal Department, Jewish Agency, 1985.
2. Ibid.
3. Hoffman, Charles. *Project Renewal: Community and Change in Israel.* Jerusalem: Renewal Department, Jewish Agency, 1986. Pp. 111, 45
4. *An International Conference on Urban Revitalization.* See brochure entitled *Abstracts.* Jerusalem: Jerusalem Center for Public Affairs, 1986.
5. Ross, Murray G, with Ben W. Lappin. *Community Organization: Theory, Principles and Practice.* New York: Harper and Brothers, 1967
6. Richmond, Mary E. *The Long View: Papers and Addresses.* New York: Russell Sage Foundation, 1930. P. 342.
7. The term, "community worker" is used as a general designation synonomous with such names as "community development worker", "community organizer", or "community organization worker".

INTRODUCTION

Community development is the participatory process of improving the quality of life in a particular locality by using social and economic resources. The goal of community development is to raise standards and conditions by helping the developing community to help itself. Without the community's will to bring about change, no amount of external assistance can produce lasting betterment. Providing financial assistance may help in the short run but it cannot insure enduring change. Assistance needs to be tied to an overall community development strategy which aims to foster self-reliance. The ultimate goal is to develop a community in which the best qualities of people can be realized, where everyone can achieve maximum human happiness and where the greatest possible satisfaction is attained by the greatest number.

The community development approach to human enhancement through involving the participation of local residents and through simultaneously using external help has many antecedents but it came into its own after World War II. As the colonial system broke up, efforts were made to assist emerging Third World nations to modernize and to provide an improved life for their citizens. These efforts were seen as a way of helping societies which had long been dependent on colonial administrations to cope with the drastic changes that followed the dissolution of European imperialism. The relatively abrupt end to colonialism was typical of other causes of unplanned change such as war, invention, population growth, diffusion and the interaction of peoples. Cultural, social and technical change usually comes about in human history as an unforeseen consequence of uncontrollable and unpredicted phenomena. By contrast, in community development work, a conscious and deliberate effort is made to induce change on a systematic basis.

Although it is not generally thought of as a prototype for community development, the Marshall Plan illustrated the great potential for upgrading living conditions by its enormous success in facilitating the recovery of war-devastated Europe. A major feature of the Marshall Plan was its emphasis on combining the encouragement of self-reliance with the provision of material economic resources. Similarly, community development joins external aid with raising the consciousness of people through social animation, through securing broad participation and through building inner resources.

The colonial powers, especially Great Britain, recognizing the inevitability of independence, began to help their colonies to move towards self-government. The process through which this help was given was called community development. It was seen as "a movement designed to promote better living for the whole community with active participation and, if possible, on the initiative of the community, but if this initiative is not forthcoming spontaneously, by the use of techniques for arousing and stimulating it in order to secure its active and enthusiastic response to the movement." (1)

Community development was considered to be the "one movement which is growing faster than almost any other single social movement, captivating the imagination of the people of many countries and holding promise of bringing new life and hope to millions of persons." (2)

The repeated use of the word "movement" in these citations is noteworthy. Community development took on all the features of a movement as it swept along the developed countries through their bilateral aid programs and the United Nations with its multilateral aid programs. The idealistic concept that compassion should rule relationships with needy individuals was elevated to apply to relationships with needy nations. The latent strength of ordinary people was to enter the mainstream of national development.

Motivation for the developed countries to participate in community development was not altogether altruistic. Colonial powers wished to retain influence and were generally successful in doing so. Former British colonies tend to have membership in the British Commonwealth and former French colonies retain military, political, trade and language associations with France. For the United States, security concerns helped to stimulate foreign aid efforts. The Marshall Plan sought to re-establish stable democracies in Europe as a buffer against the Soviet Union. American assistance is often tied to winning friends for the United States in the rivalry between the Soviet Union and the United States. It is part of the continuing struggle between two opposed systems of thought. At best, motives for the donor in foreign aid are mixed with some blend of self-interest and altruism. (3)

Just as the motivations for community development efforts are mixed, so are the results. If, for example, one practical objective is to engender positive attitudes toward the donor nation as measured by votes in the United Nations and its specialized agencies, then American aid is a failure. Except for Israel, many recipients of American aid consistently vote against the positions espoused by the United States.

Obviously, this is too narrow a criterion for measuring the success of community development. A broader standard is the degree to which the poor people of a developing country realize better living conditions. Unfortunately, this objective is often thwarted because foreign aid funds sometimes provide income for elite rulers and not for poor people. An unanticipated consequence of American foreign aid is the creation of dependency relationships to the point where beneficiaries occasionally demand the aid as a matter of right instead of philanthropy in order to maintain their self-respect. The disappointing results of American foreign aid in the Third World have turned many Americans against the idea of foreign aid. (4)

In local communities, the high expectations which accompany the inception of a community development program are frequently frustrated. In a volume designed to be a textbook for community development, (5) most of the projects described achieved only limited success and a number were complete failures. The ingredients of the community development process which lead to success or failure are complicated and numerous. After analyzing 19 different community development projects, one authority indicated that "there are at least 17 different kinds of forces which impinge on the change process". (6)

Understanding and evaluating particular community development experiences is a difficult task. Individual projects are not experimental research programs with control group design. They are placed in a social setting and not in a laboratory. Community development projects have multiple variables, program changes, personnel turnovers and unanticipated consequences. In many ways, they are essentially ventures into the unknown, usually with little theoretical support. Very often, they are best assessed and understood in a descriptive, anecdotal fashion with emphasis on the craftmanship of the community development worker.

One good way to understand community development — its successes and its failures — is to examine specific illustrations. Even though each situation is unique, there are lessons to be learned and principles to be induced. This approach involves a long-term commitment and, preferably, the use of participant-observation which requires a high degree of inter-personal and analytic skills. One advantage of using particular instances with a participant-observer is that there is direct access to the events as they unfold so that there is no need to rely on the memory of others to reconstruct the narrative of what occurred.

In the documentary to be offered here, one author was involved as the participant-observer for a two-year period from 1981 to 1983. The second author has maintained an association with the project from its inception to the present. Thus the requirement of a long-term commitment to make a case study useful is well satisfied in this particular experience.

The participant-observer who served as liaison-consultant kept a careful record of his activity. Supplemented by reports, letters and documents, this record which is being called a "documentary" constitutes the nucleus of the case study. Since it was written day-by-day, the documentary is an actual, not a retrospective, account of a community development project. The material represents an unique description of human interaction consciously designed to improve the quality of life in a particular locality through the process of community development.

FOOTNOTES

1. *Report of the Ashridge Conference on Social Development, 1954.* Cited in *Community Development: A Handbook.* London: Her Majesty's Stationery Office, 1958
2. *Community Development and Community Organization: An International Workshop.* New York: National Association of Social Workers, 1961. P. 3.
3. For a brilliant discussion of the relationship between donor and beneficiary nations, see *The New Diplomacy: International Affairs in the Modern Age.* By Abba Eban. New York: Random House, 1982. Pp. 171-188.
4. Some of these problems have been spelled out in a book which claims that foreign aid is not only ineffective but that it is destructive. *The Destruction of a Continent.* By Karl Borgin and Kathleen Corbett. New York, Harcourt, 1982.
5. Niehoff, Arthur, editor. *A Casebook of Social Change.* Chicago: Aldine Publishing Company, 1966.
6. Ibid.

CHAPTER ONE

PROJECT RENEWAL

The documentary to be offered here deals with one part of a country-wide development effort in Israel known as Project Renewal. Some understanding of the entire project and its background is necessary to set the stage for the major focus of this presentation which is on one particular community development venture in one Israeli town which is called by its pseudonym of Kfar Oranim.

The need for Project Renewal may be traced to the early days of Israel's re-creation as a state in 1948. No sooner had the State been proclaimed than the armies of surrounding Arab countries attacked in a determined effort to push Israel into the sea. At the same time, while fighting for its very life, Israel fully embraced the urgent necessity of bringing to the country the survivors of the Holocaust.

Throughout the War of Independence and thereafter, vast numbers of refugees came to Israel. They were joined by a small stream of voluntary immigrants coming from free countries who wanted to help build a Jewish state. In the first three years of the reborn State, the Jewish population more than doubled. From 654,000 in 1948, it rose to 1,404,000 at the end of 1951. (1) In a similar period of mass immigration to the United States which began in 1880, it took 40 years until 1920 for the population to double.

This explosive leap in the number of inhabitants brought knotty problems and complex challenges. Temporary housing had to be built literally overnight. New towns had to be established to receive people who came directly from the ships which brought them to Israel. It was almost as though the Biblical days of creation were re-enacted. There was evening and there was morning and there was a town. And there was evening and there was morning and there was another town. All kinds of people came to these towns, eventually hailing from 79 different countries. Since, as a matter of firm policy, there was no selectivity exercised in determining which Jews could enter Israel, all Jews were welcome. This meant that thousands came with severe problems that interfered with their becoming productive workers. They were weak and worn out from struggling to survive the Holocaust and, in some instances, from months of languishing in the internment camps on Cyprus.

1

After 1948, with few exceptions, Jews could no longer live in the Arab countries and so hundreds of thousands of penniless refugees fled to Israel from North Africa and the Middle East. Forty-six thousand came from Yemen; 121,000 came from Iraq; 30,000 came from Egypt; 32,000 came from Libya; 36,000 came from Morocco; 10,000 came from Tunisia and Algeria. (2)

Many of the newcomers emerged from folk societies and were not equipped to enter the labor force of a country rapidly moving to industrialization. They were ethnically identified as Sephardim, different from the Ashkenazim with a European background who constituted the establishment. There were cultural differences reflected in language, customs, food preferences and family traditions. A substantial number lacked formal educational qualifications. Thousands of them were drafted to fight the War of Independence almost as they stepped on the shores of their new country.

Absorbing the new immigrants proved to be a monumental task. Most were housed in hastily-erected, temporary shelters — tents and tin huts. The crude short-term facilities which enveloped entire towns were called *ma'aborot*. The urgency faced by Israel in getting newcomers out of these structures soon led to single-story dwellings, strung out like railway coaches and which marked a second stage in housing the new arrivals. The permanent housing which they finally occupied consisted of large, multi-storied apartment blocks that were hurriedly built. Funds were limited and so the cost of this construction was kept to a minimum. The units soon deteriorated and became sub-standard. Most of the apartments were too small for the Sephardim who traditionally had ten to twelve children in each family. This was another characteristic differentiating the Sephardim from the Ashkenazim who followed Western patterns of family size. Small apartments in high-rise buildings were very different from the courtyard-centered family homes of their native lands.

Immigrants were settled in accordance with policies that called for planned distribution of the population all over the country. For several reasons, it was decided to disperse the people into new localities called "development towns". Many leaders in Israel took the position that the entire country could not be possessed if the population were concentrated in a few large cities. Inundating Tel Aviv, Jerusalem and Haifa was seen as a threat to economic viability because of demographic imbalances. National security was (and is) an important consideration which called (and calls) for a more even distribution of the population throughout the country.

There was also an ideological basis for the policy of population dispersal which harked back to the original Zionist dream that envisioned a state where Jews could be close to nature, working the land and engaging in agriculture. For the early pioneers, agricultural

2

labor was a sacred calling with Jewish nobility and normalization being derived from closeness to the soil. These ideas, influenced by Tolstoy through A.D. Gordon, an early Zionist thinker, had a quality of Rousseauean romanticism. They led to establishing the kibbutz as the fulfillment of an ideal that was to confer full freedom, dignity and economic security on each Jew as a member of a primary group, engaged in agriculture.

The visionary goal has been achieved only minimally. No more than two percent of Israel's residents live in kibbutzim. The population is primarily urban. However, the early aspiration helped to determine the policy in the 1950's of steering people away from the cities into development towns.

There was only marginal success in the physical and social planning of the development towns. In fact, there was no time to plan; the towns were often put up and peopled in a matter of days or less. Austere economic conditions meant that only limited amenities such as schools, synagogues and community centers could be provided. Most important, it was difficult to establish the kind of industries which could employ people who were unskilled and often illiterate.

Ambitious, able-bodied individuals left the development towns seeking opportunities in Tel Aviv, Jerusalem and Haifa. For the most part, they were successfully integrated into the urban areas. Those left behind in the development towns were poorly educated, untrained, elderly and dependent. Any jobs they managed to find were at low wages. A number of them became apathetic, bitter and cynical. Delinquent behavior, hardly known in the early days of the State, became a problem. Family breakdown, truancy, drop-outs and evasion of military service all emerged as previously unknown social problems. Some rudimentary protest movements made their voices heard but the country's preoccupation with its security problems took precedence. One important study of Israel's social problems appeared in 1973 but it was buried by the Yom Kippur War. (3)

By the time that Menachem Begin became the Prime Minister of Israel in 1977, the problems of distressed communities in Israel had become critical. He came to office with the support of the Sephardim who had become a majority of Israel's population. Despite their numbers, the gap between them and the Ashkenazim was large and social indicators showed it to be persistent. The large families and the low educational achievement of the Sephardim as contrasted to the Ashkenazim resulted in their being referred to as "the other Israel". With only a few exceptions, they have not yet broken into the economic, professional and power elites of Israel.

The problem of the social gap between the Sephardim and the Ashkenazim is exacerbated by the fact that it is not simply a problem of haves and have-nots, of rich and poor. What causes great anguish

3

and divisiveness is the concentration of "the other Israel" among the Sephardim, the Oriental communities of which the dominant group comes from North Africa. On the other side of the social gap are the Ashkenazim who are mainly of East European descent and who consititute the "establishment". The unfortunate situation breeds tension and prejudice.

Aware of his support from the Sephardim and genuinely determined to tackle the problem of the distressed communities, soon after he became Prime Minister, Begin called on world Jewry to join in a massive community development effort to rehabilitate and renew the slum neighborhoods and development towns of Israel. He proposed the expenditure of $1,200,000,000, half to come from the Government of Israel and half to come from Jews all over the world. American Jews were asked to be responsible for $400,000,000 of the $600,000,000 Diaspora share. These sums were to be used in a unified effort to close the social gap between the Sephardim and the Ashkenazim by focussing on the 160 distressed communities which had been identified in 1974 as needing rehabilitation and renewal. These communities contained almost 500,000 people, many with little or no formal education and with a variety of social problems.

The distressed communities and their residents had been by-passed in Israel's rapid economic development. Most of the country had achieved astonishing feats. Impoverished immigrants came to a land almost barren of natural resources and within a few short years built agricultural, industrial and service sectors comparable to much of Europe. These remarkable accomplishments took place despite continued threats to Israel's very existence by its hostile neighbors — threats which forced Israel to devote an enormous portion of its production resources and manpower to defense.

Prime Minister Begin challenged the Jews of Israel and the Jews of the Diaspora to launch a 5-year crash program in which their cooperative endeavor would raise the quality of life in the distressed areas of Israel. In 1978, through the Jewish Agency, world Jewry responded to this challenge by setting in motion a unified attempt to declare war on poverty in Israel. Project Renewal was born.

The Ministry of Housing was assigned governmental responsibility for the new program and a special Project Renewal Department was established in the Jewish Agency which is the organization that receives and disburses philanthropic funds contributed by Jews all over the world. A committee was formed with representatives of the Ministry of Housing, the Jewish Agency and other governmental units involved in the distressed communities. This Inter-Ministerial Committee was charged with overseeing Project Renewal. One of its first tasks was to determine which of the 160 distressed communities would be selected for inclusion in Project Renewal since it was clear that even with

4

the huge sums of which Prime Minister Begin had spoken, not all the distressed communities could be included, certainly not at the outset.

Criteria for choosing communities to participate in Project Renewal were developed by the Inter-Ministerial Committee. These included a number of social indicators such as overcrowded housing, unemployment, size of families, delinquency rates, educational levels, dependency on social services and age distribution. Other factors considered were the readiness of the community to participate and geographical location. (4) The criterion of location was particularly important if the distressed community was situated adjacent to a prosperous area, thus heightening tensions by visibly emphasizing the acuity of the social and economic gap. As we shall see, this was a significant factor in selecting Kfar Oranim for inclusion in Project Renewal.

As of 1987, 86 communities were identified as meeting the criteria established by the Inter-Ministerial Committee and the program was operating in each of them. By the beginning of 1987, Diaspora Jewry had spent $228,700,000, just half the sum that Prime Minister Begin had called for in 1977. (5)

An innovative feature of Project Renewal called for relating each Israeli Project Renewal community to a "twin" community in the Diaspora. This was designed to express the notion of partnership but it also provided for interaction between Israelis and Diaspora Jews on a level that had not been known in the past. Heretofore, Jews all over the world contributed large sums of money that were used by the Jewish Agency for immigrant absorption, health, welfare and educational purposes in Israel. A consequence of the prevailing arrangement was anonymity with no connection between donors and recipients. Project Renewal profoundly altered this state of affairs.

A new special relationship was established by Project Renewal between identified communities in Israel and the Diaspora. This relationship has an impact on a problem which has persisted since 1948. How can Zionism be reconciled with the continued existence of the Diaspora? The Zionist vision called for all Jews to be "ingathered" and to settle in Israel. However, the majority of the world's Jews continues to live outside of Israel. These Jews are often regarded by Israelis as having failed to live up to their moral obligation since their continued existence in the Diaspora thwarts the goal of Israel to "ingather the exiles". This issue contributes to ruffled relationships between Israelis and Jews elsewhere. Israeli Jews have considerable ambivalence toward Diaspora Jews. They simultaneously disdain and envy them. Some Diaspora Jews resent the frequent calls on them from Israelis to settle in Israel since they think of their native countries as home and they foresee no circumstances in which they will be forced to leave involuntarily. The Israelis, on the other hand, assert that what happened in Germany can happen in other countries and that, in any event, it is the solemn obligation of all Jews to settle in Israel.

Another issue which makes the relationship between Israelis and Diaspora Jews a nettlesome one is the question of the degree to which each should participate in the internal affairs of the other. Israelis, eager for continued support from the United States government, have often urged American Jews to support candidates for public office who will be friendly to Israel even though they may hold positions on other issues which American Jews disapprove. American Jews, concerned about possible harm to Jewish-Gentile relationships in the United States, have often urged Israel to be more forthcoming in its dealings with the Arabs.

Both kinds of interference have been strongly criticized. Israelis have told American Jews to hold their tongues on Israeli policy decisions since it is Israeli bodies which are "on the line" while American Jews enjoy their lavish lives. If they want to affect Israeli policies, say these critics, then American Jews should immigrate to Israel. At the very least, they should not voice their criticism in public. American Jews have told Israelis to stay out of American politics and especially to avoid endorsing candidates in American elections. Moreover, they insist that if they are true partners, they must be involved in the debates about the future and the direction of the Jewish state

These and similar issues keep plaguing relationships between Israel and Diaspora Jewry and there is no resolution in sight. They cause frequent irritation and occasional flare-ups of bitterness. How to handle the *intifada* by Arabs in the occupied territories is an illustration of a question that causes dissension and acrimony.

By contrast, Project Renewal offers a benign opportunity for cooperation between Israel and Diaspora Jews. It does not solve the intractable problems but it brings some Jews in Israel closer to some Jews in the Diaspora through the arrangement for "twin" communities. Project Renewal is far less laden with controversy than issues of Israeli policies and American elections although it certainly has its share of difficulties. There are differences of opinion in Project Renewal — often sharp and strident — but resolution of issues is more readily found. Project Renewal offers opportunities for genuine partnership and for a wholesome relation between Israel and Diaspora Jewry.

"Twin" communities interact with each other through a variety of connections. At least once a year, representatives of the Diaspora community visit their Israeli "twin" and engage in extensive joint review of proposals for expenditures and development as well as consideration of progress during the preceding year. During the year, visitors from overseas make a special point of spending time in the Israeli community which is "twinned" with their home town. In some instances, Israelis are invited to visit their "twin" community in the Diaspora. School children in each community are encouraged to become pen pals. Personal relationships develop and, for the first time, contributors begin to know the Israelis who benefit from their donations. They also have a good deal to say about how their money is to be spent. This is a major departure from the pattern of anonymity which characterizes control of donated funds by big, faceless bureaucracies. For the first time, Jews from abroad have open, heart-warming, face-to-face discussions with the Israeli man-in-the-street. They "follow the money" and develop considerable sophistication about Israeli politics and Israeli bureaucracy.

A significant aspect of Project Renewal is the involvement of local residents in identifying community needs, ranking them in order of priority and discussing their preferences with representatives of their "twin" community. (6) This second major feature of Project Renewal means that grass roots groups come together and engage in responsible social planning. Such participation by local residents in community decision-making is new in Israel which has a highly centralized governmental process that is traditionally paternalistic. Project Renewal gives the local residents a taste of direct democracy. It calls for their active participation in developing plans and programs. They take part for the first time in deciding what goes on in their own neighborhoods. Project Renewal legitimates the right of local residents to participate in critical decisions concerning the future of their community. Oddly enough, this aspect of Project Renewal recaptures the practice of communal decision-making which characterizes the kibbutz. Although, as previously noted, the number of Israelis who live in kibbutzim is small, their influence is large. It is not too fanciful to speculate that Project Renewal's insistence on community participation in decision-making is a descendant of the kibbutz tradition.

These two elements — direct involvement by Diaspora communities in Israeli communities through the "twinning" process and local participation in decision-making — are salient features of Project Renewal. They represent unprecedented by-passing of central government authority and democratic participation by local residents in decisions which affect them and the communities in which they live. These two innovations may ultimately have a profound effect on Israel-Diaspora relationships and on Israeli democracy. This impact may even outweigh the practical benefits of rehabilitating slum neighborhoods.

FOOTNOTES

1. Berman, Morton Mayer. *The Bridge to Life: The Saga of Keren Hayesod* 1920-1970. Tel Aviv: Shifrin and Na'aman, 1970.
2. Ibid.
3. *Prime Minister's Commission for Children and Youth in Distress.* (Summary of Recommendations). Jerusalem: Szold Institute for Research in the Behavioral Sciences. Publication #545, July 1973.
4. *Guide to Project Renewal.* Jerusalem: Project Renewal Department, Jewish Agency, 1984.
5. *Project Renewal Report to the Board of Governors.* February, 1987. Jerusalem: Project Renewal Department, Jewish Agency, 1987.
6. Moshe, Hill. *Project Renewal: How Successful a Strategy for Neighborhood Rehabilitation?* Lecture to Plenary Session of the International Conference on Urban Revitalization — March 4, 1986. Haifa: Technion, Israel Institute of Technology, 1986.

CHAPTER TWO

THE TWIN COMMUNITIES

In order to understand the community development process as it unfolded in one Israeli Project Renewal community, it is important to have some background information about the two "twin" communities, Kfar Oranim and Croydon. (1)

KFAR ORANIM

The town of Kfar Oranim is an outgrowth of Ma'abara Junius. (A *ma'abara* was a temporary residence for new immigrants.) It is located close to the ancient city of Junius, on the Mediterranean coast, half way between Tel Aviv and Haifa. Adjacent to the ruins of Roman Junius, there lies one of the wealthiest communities in Israel, consisting of large private villas and containing a luxury hotel.

In April, 1951, at the peak of mass immigration into Israel, fifteen families from Rumania were brought directly to Ma'abara Junius from the ship which carried them to Israel. They were followed by scores of families from Iran, Iraq, Egypt, Syria, Libya and Morocco. Before long, the ma'abara had a population of 2,000.

The newcomers lived in wooden or aluminum shacks that were hot in the summer and cold in the winter. There was no electricity, no drinking water and no comforts. Water was finally piped in from a nearby village but the pipe was laid above the ground so that it was hot by the time it reached the ma'abara. More and more immigrants arrived, mainly from North Africa. By the end of 1952, the ma'abara was overcrowded with 3,000 people, many of them children,

In 1953, the population of Ma'abara Junius reached 3,500. The people were living in shacks, barracks and quasi-farm dwellings. The Ma'abara Committee demanded self-rule and, after months of haggling with the Ministry of Interior, municipal status was granted. Ma'abara Junius became the town of Kfar Oranim. It followed the path of similar efforts to cope with the waves of newcomers who poured into Israel after the War of Independence in 1948. Fortunately, the ma'abara is now a past phenomenon.

The unfortunate conditions which existed in the ma'abara were slow to disappear and they contributed to many of the physical and social problems which now confront Kfar Oranim. These problems are compounded by the location of the town, sandwiched between

9

the old and the new roads that connect Tel Aviv and Haifa. This leaves little room for growth or development. Moreover, the town's proximity to the tourist areas of ancient Junius and to the lavish homes of modern Junius emphasizes the social and economic distance sensed by the residents of Kfar Oranim.

Demography

As of 1987, Kfar Oranim had 8,500 people, drawn from 19 different countries. The Afro-Asian group is the predominant population component. The two largest groups of residents come from Rumania and Morocco. The demographic composition is as follows:

50% North African — principally Moroccan
25% East European — principally Rumanian
20% Russian — Caucasus Mountains and Georgia
5% Israelis, Ethiopians and others

The Russians who came from the Caucasus Mountains in the late 1970's pose a special problem. They are known as "Kafkazim", mountain Jews who speak a Persian-based dialect with some Hebrew words. According to one legend, they fled from Persia to Russia about 2,500 years ago at the time of Queen Esther. In Kfar Oranim, they are a minority group, living in one section of the town with their children segregated into one school.

Of those persons in Kfar Oranim not born in Israel, 82% come from Asia and Africa as compared to the national average of 51%. About 55% of the population is under the age of 24 which is higher than the national average. The population mixture is characteristic of immigrant towns with low socio-economic status and with a high rate of problems.

Although the population has increased because of immigration and natural growth, Kfar Oranim tends to lose people. Toward the end of the 1970's, four times more people moved out of Kfar Oranim than moved in. A 1980 comparison of 63 towns in Israel with 5,000 or more people showed Kfar Oranim ranking ninth in population influx (20.1 persons per thousand) and seventh in departures (49.1 per thousand). The processes of influx and departure have not been kind to Kfar Oranim. Over the years, economically and socially stronger individuals tended to move out while new immigrants with many problems moved in. The result is a community with a concentration of social and economic difficulties.

There are about 2,000 households in Kfar Oranim with an average size of 3.8 persons. However, about 20% of the households have six or more people, as contrasted with the national average of 14%. There are more large families per household in Kfar Oranim than in Israel generally.

Education

The educational achievement of adults in Kfar Oranim is significantly lower than the national average. Sixty percent of the adults have less than eight years of schooling. In Israel as a whole, this figure is 32%.

For the children of Kfar Oranim, there are 29 educational institutions, starting with infant day care. There are 2,300 pupils and about 150 staff members, including clerical, maintenance and administrative personnel. Most of the teachers — about 75% of them — come to work from outside Kfar Oranim and leave the town at the end of the school day.

There are four elementary schools in Kfar Oranim, two religious and two secular. There is no high school and about 400 students travel each day to neighboring towns for their high school education. They are usually last in line after residents of these towns are looked after so that they often wind up in less advanced and less desirable programs. This feature, combined with the difficulties and the expense of commuting, leads to resentment which causes irregular school attendance and a high drop-out rate.

For the most part, the local educational system is characterized by low achievement goals and under-achieving pupils in comparison to national and regional averages. Although there are some devoted teachers, the over-all quality of the teaching staff leaves much to be desired. Kfar Oranim cannot compete for ambitious, skilled teachers with the large cities of Israel, especially since the salaries are the same throughout the country because education is a function of the central government. Salary supplements may be paid in "hardship" areas but Kfar Oranim is not considered to be in this category because of its location.

A serious problem in the educational system of Kfar Oranim is the segregation into one school of the children whose families come from the Caucasus Mountains of Russia.

Employment

There are three factories in Kfar Oranim which manufacture carpets, artificial fur and foam rubber. They employ about 800 people, half of whom commute from outside of Kfar Oranim. The factories employ unskilled, blue collar workers at relatively low wages. One indicator of the income level in the town is the rate of vehicle ownership. In Israel as a whole, there are 115 vehicles for every thousand people. In Kfar Oranim, the rate is 17 vehicles per 1000 people.

A study conducted by Technion in 1983 found that:

14% of male heads of households of working age are unemployed
79% of male heads of households are employed
29% of female heads of households are employed as compared
to the national average of 43%
46% of female heads of households of working age who are
not employed want to find a job
    In December, 1984, 450 job-seekers were registered with the Labor
Exchange. They constitute 18% of the local labor force.
    The basic factors in Kfar Oranim employment situation may be
summarized as follows:
On average, there is less than one earner per household
Most jobs are held by blue collar, unskilled, low income, non-
professional workers
Underemployment is a serious problem
Local factories offer jobs which require little training and which
are low paid.
There is lack of suitable vocational training
The employment situation results in low family income

Social Problems

1. Youth

    About 15% of Kfar Oranim's young people between the ages of
13 and 23 are neither working, studying nor serving in the army.
They are considered to be "alienated youth". They contribute in large
measure to the problem of juvenile delinquency in Kfar Oranim. Many
of these young people are involved in illegal activities. There is some
evidence of an increase in the violence and severity of crimes. In
1980, of 63 Israeli urban areas with populations exceeding 5,000, Kfar
Oranim ranked tenth in the male juvenile delinquency rate and fourth
in the female juvenile delinquency rate. Ten percent of all Kfar Oranim
youth were under the observation of the Youth Parole Board in 1984.
Personnel responsible for this work in the town were not qualified
by training for this complicated task.
    A special youth problem arises from the isolation of the "Kafkazim"
and their absorption problems. They have an exceptionally high
juvenile delinquency rate.

2. Welfare

    In 1980, Kfar Oranim was ranked first among 63 towns with
populations over 5,000 in rate of welfare recipients. About 650 families,
amounting to 32% of all Kfar Oranim households, are under the care
of the municipal Social Services Department.

3. Physical, Emotional and Mental

    Kfar Oranim has about 150 handicapped people, including 60 blind
persons. In 1979, the infant mortality rate in Kfar Oranim was 23.4
per 1,000 live births. This is the fourth highest infant mortality rate

among 63 Israeli towns with populations over 5,000. There are residents suffering from alcoholism, drug addiction and mental illness but the exact numbers are not known.

4. Aged

Of the 760 people in Kfar Oranim who are over the age of 60, 710 receive some kind of care from the Social Services Department. One hundred and ten require home care. Facilities to serve old people are grossly inadequate with only one tiny senior citizens center.

5. Housing

About three-fourths of the housing units in Kfar Oranim are more than 25 years old. They were not well constructed originally since there was great pressure to produce housing in a hurry in order to get people out of the ma'abara shacks. These units are deteriorating; most of them are small and there is a great deal of overcrowding.

Summary

In 1981, when the Croydon Jewish community decided to become "twinned" with Kfar Oranim, the Israeli town was clearly manifesting the consequences of what happened when many immigrants flooded Israel precipitously after the State was reborn in 1948. These immigrants, largely Sephardic, arrived in Israel with little money, meager education and few marketable skills. These limitations led to frustration, alienation, delinquency and feelings of hopelessness. There was a severe social gap between the citizens of Kfar Oranim and many other Israelis. The gap was intensified by the location of the town, adjacent to the very wealthy community of Junius. This juxtaposition accentuated the contrast between rich and poor.

The catalog of Kfar Oranim's social and physical problems included:

1. Housing needs were sorely neglected.
2. Infrastructure urgently needed repair and renovation.
3. Public services such as health and welfare were not up to the demand.
4. Retail shops were below par and created an eyesore.
5. Educational programs and facilities were inferior.
6. Lack of recreational opportunities, especially for youth, contributed to the growing problems of delinquency and alienation.
7. There was little opportunity for meaningful employment or for economic and social development.
8. Many families relied on public assistance; there was a great deal of underemployment as well as unemployment.
9. There was a negative community self-image and considerable out-migration. People had little incentive to move into Kfar Oranim.

10. The percentage of large families was higher than in the rest of Israel.

The very fact that Kfar Oranim was selected for inclusion in Project Renewal for rehabilitation and development inevitably stresses the community's problems and the disadvantages which its residents confronted in their daily lives. However, it would be less than fair to the town to leave the impression that Kfar Oranim was a place of unrelieved gloom. Its citizens observed the holidays and festivals with the same spirit of dedication and celebration that is found in the rest of Israel. Joyful occasions, formal and informal, some specific to Kfar Oranim, brought pleasure into the lives of its residents. When talented individuals from the town received recognition, the community as a whole was proud. This was particularly true of its first-rate music program for young people. There were and are many happier moments that mitigate the adversities faced by the people of Kfar Oranim.

CROYDON

Croydon is a large American metropolis with a Jewish population of more than 200,000. Its Federation has been in existence for more than fifty years. Each year, it raises several million dollars, half of which goes to Israel through the United Jewish Appeal. In Israel, the money is disbursed by the Jewish Agency.

Several Jewish community leaders from Croydon were present in 1977 when Prime Minister Begin proposed the establishment of Project Renewal. They were dubious about his offer to provide $600,000,000 in Israeli government funds to match a contribution of the same magnitude by Diaspora Jewry. Their experience in Jewish affairs led them to question the capacity of the Israeli government to provide this much money, knowing, as they did, the enormous portion of the Israeli budget which had to be devoted to defense. Accordingly, when Project Renewal began to function in 1978, the Croydon Jewish Federation did not participate, based on the recommendation of these individuals.

There was one community leader in Croydon who did not share the doubts of his colleagues. Phillip was an enthusiastic supporter of Project Renewal. His deep belief in the importance of the plan led him to assume the national chairmanship of Project Renewal for the United States.

As Phillip travelled across America to promote Project Renewal and to raise funds for it, his embarrassment mounted about the failure of his own community to take part. Finally, he succeeded in persuading the Board of Directors of Croydon's Federation to look into the possibility of adopting a "twin" community in Israel and, thus, to

14

become part of Project Renewal.

In 1980, the Board asked Solomon, one of its highly esteemed members, who was about to visit Israel on other business to stop at Kfar Oranim, the Israeli community which the Project Renewal officials had selected for "twinning" with Croydon.

On June 24, 1980, on his return to Croydon, Solomon made his report to the Board. He emphasized the problems of Kfar Oranim's school children. There were practically no supervised after-school recreational programs for them. There was a good deal of delinquency, although there were, as yet, no hardened criminals. Solomon stressed the need for well-organized and well-supervised after-school programs to help prevent the children from growing up to become criminals. He also commented on the poor physical conditions of the schools. Some of them were in shambles and the kindergartens lacked the ordinary equipment which is taken for granted in the United States.

What struck Solomon particularly during his visit was the personnel problem. There was no educational leader; there was a desperate need for social workers; the teachers needed training; all the human service personnel were poorly paid and most of them did not live in Kfar Oranim.

Moved by the needs he observed and the potential for remedying the situation, Solomon recommended that Croydon join Project Renewal by agreeing to spend a million dollars a year over a three-year period provided that the Israeli government matched this sum. The money should be used to employ teachers and social workers, to train them and to upgrade their salaries. High priority should be given to the establishment of after-school programs. In Solomon's opinion, this could not be a one-time grant. Continued support from Croydon and the State of Israel would be required to give the program continuity. Solomon urged that the Croydon Federation form a permanent Project Renewal committee to oversee and monitor the program.

The Board carefully considered Solomon's report and voted to approve his recommendations. It decided "to proceed with the immediate next steps in the implementation of the plan". However, nothing was done. The leaders who were not favorably disposed to Project Renewal originally maintained their reluctance to see Croydon become involved. Their influence was powerful enough to block any movement.

As time passed without any action, Phillip became increasingly restive; he was determined to change the situation. Early in March 1981, he called a meeting of those community leaders who felt more positive about Project Renewal. He arranged for Roger, the newly-appointed director of Project Renewal in the United States, to visit Croydon in order to attend this session and to clarify the issues which

15

were still of concern.

Roger urged that a small delegation from Croydon be appointed to visit Kfar Oranim. The purpose of the visit would be to listen to the Kfar Oranim Project Renewal Steering Committee as it presented its views about community needs and its sense of priorities. The delegation would also meet with Hanoch, the Israeli director of Project Renewal as well as with appropriate government officials. Based on what it learned during the visit, the delegation could make its own evaluation and formulate its own recommendations for the Board of the Croydon Federation

Roger's visit secured some vocal allies for Phillip and intensified the pressure for Croydon to commit itself to Project Renewal. As a result, the President of the Croydon Federation appointed a special ad hoc committee composed of the past presidents of Federation, those individuals who were interested in Project Renewal and those who had negative feelings about it. This committee identified the questions which had to be answered before Croydon could adopt Kfar Oranim as its "twin". The questions were:

1. Will the Israeli government actually provide funds to match those contributed by Croydon?
2. Are the people of Kfar Oranim involved in planning, assessing and ranking their community needs and in implementing the programs to be supported by Project Renewal?
3. How valid are the needs of Kfar Oranim?
4. What assurances are there that the money contributed by Croydon to Project Renewal will really be earmarked to meet the needs of Kfar Oranim?
5. What is the significance of the "twinning" process for both Croydon and Kfar Oranim?

The special ad hoc committee then selected a three-person delegation and directed it to visit Israel promptly in order to secure answers to these questions. The committee persuaded Melvin, one of Croydon's most distinguished citizens, to head the delegation. Accompanied by Mark, a senior staff member of the Federation, the delegation visited Israel from April 2 to April 8, 1981.

In Israel, before proceeding to Kfar Oranim, the delegation first saw Hanoch, the senior executive of Project Renewal in Israel. He gave them a general orientation to the program, stressing the importance of partnership between the "twinned" communities in each step of the planning and implementing processes.

In Kfar Oranim, the delegation met with the Steering Committee, the Mayor and other local officials. Marcus, an Israeli government representative, was present at some of the meetings along with Leah and Vered from the Jewish Agency. The delegation was assured by Marcus that the Israeli government was abiding by its commitment to share equally with the Diaspora in building up the Israeli communities selected for inclusion in Project Renewal. He acknowledged that the funds were not necessarily matched on a project-by-project, dollar-for-dollar basis but he claimed that the over-all contribution of the government to any given Project Renewal community at least matched and often exceeded the amount donated by its "twin" community in the Diaspora. The Jewish Agency representatives, Leah and Vered, told the delegation that all funds contributed by Croydon for Project Renewal would indeed be earmarked for specific projects in Kfar Oranim, as approved by the Steering Committee, Croydon, the Israeli government and Project Renewal headquarters in the Jewish Agency.

The local residents of Kfar Oranim impressed the delegation with their dedicated involvement and with their frustrations in getting the various units of the Israeli government to meet their needs. The Steering Committee presented a long list of needs with estimates of the cost of meeting them. It was apparent that Leah and Vered, who were very vocal throughout the visit, had influenced and assisted the Steering Committee in drawing up its list of proposals and in providing cost information.

Based on its meetings, discussions and site visits, the delegation reached the following answers to the questions posed by the Croydon special, ad hoc committee:

1. With regard to participation by the Israeli government, it seems that the matching of funds may not be fully in effect but there is certainly a substantial contribution, some of it in kind rather than in cash. Regardless of the degree of government sharing in Project Renewal, the delegation believes that Kfar Oranim should not be penalized.

2. The delegation had a number of opportunities to see the deep degree of involvement in Project Renewal by Kfar Oranim residents, especially its local officials. It can give an affirmative answer to the second question concerning the participation of Kfar Oranim residents in Project Renewal.

3. With regard to the question of needs, the delegation believes that it saw clear evidence as to the validity of those needs. Schedules were prepared by the community and presented to the delegation. Discussions with the Steering Committee resulted in tentative agreement (subject to Board approval) on an expenditure of $1,100,000 in 1981. The delegation concluded that the needs unmistakably exist.

4. The delegation is satisfied that Project Renewal funds are used for planning, implementing and administering Project Renewal. There are sufficient safeguards through reporting and monitoring to make certain that funds are not diverted for other purposes.

The delegation feels that there is accountability to insure the appropriate use of Croydon funds in Kfar Oranim.

5. The "twinning" arrangement will show Kfar Oranim that a community in the Diaspora cares and will assist in developing a community identity that will enable Kfar Oranim to become a full-fledged member of a strengthened Israeli society. For Croydon, the "twinning" process will make it possible for its residents to relate to Kfar Oranim residents on a people-to-people basis, thus furthering links with Israel. Inspiration and stimulation will benefit the Croydon Jewish community as it deepens its involvement with the people of Israel through participation in Project Renewal.

6. The delegation was struck by the opportunity which Project Renewal provides for participatory, grass roots democracy in the local community. This is in contrast to the centralized decision-making which is prevalent in Israel. Project Renewal requires that local residents take an active role in identifying community problems, designing programs to resolve them and setting priorities. This may prove to be an historic innovation in Israel.

On June 1, 1981, the delegation made its report to the Board of Directors of the Croydon Federation. It recommended that Croydon accept "twinning" with Kfar Oranim in Project Renewal and commit up to $1,000,000 a year to Kfar Oranim for the next five years, beginning on July 1, 1981, subject to the following conditions:

a) The first year's allocation should be used for projects discussed with the Croydon delegation during its April, 1981 visit, with quarterly progress reports submitted to Croydon by the Kfar Oranim Steering Committee.

b) A liaison-consultant is to be hired by Croydon to assist Kfar Oranim in developing its priorities and to act as a bridge among the two "twinned" communities, the State of Israel and Project Renewal headquarters. The continued flow of dollars beyond the first year is to be contingent on the progress made and on recommendations provided jointly by the liaison-consultant and the Kfar Oranim Steering Committee.

c) The Croydon special, ad hoc committee should be made a permanent committee of the Croydon Federation.

The Board of Directors approved and accepted the report and recommendations of the delegation, emphasizing the necessity to make sure that funds raised in Croydon for Project Renewal are actually used by Croydon.

On June 23, 1981, the Croydon Project Renewal Committee, now an established committee of the Croydon Federation, interviewed an Israeli professor who was visiting the United States and unanimously agreed to engage him as its liaison-consultant in Kfar Oranim. His responsibilities were described as follows:

18

1. Interpreting to Kfar Oranim the participation of Croydon in Project Renewal.
2. Facilitating the exchange of information between the two communities.
3. Assisting Kfar Oranim in operating its Steering Committee.
4. Establishing accountability among the agencies and organizations involved in Project Renewal in Kfar Oranim.
5. Assisting Kfar Oranim in assessing needs and determining priorities.

Other expectations were discussed such as the basic responsibility for helping to improve the quality of life in Kfar Oranim, monitoring all financial expenditures and serving generally as Croydon's representative.

The problems set by these expectations will become apparent in the documentary record which follows, especially in the very first entry.

FOOTNOTES

1. Factual, historical and descriptive material about Kfar Oranim is drawn from interviews by the authors with residents as well as from numerous typewritten Project Renewal reports. These include a profile of the town prepared in 1983 and an analysis by the Economic Development Officer in 1986.

    The Croydon material is based on reports, records and minutes in the files of the Croydon Jewish Federation. It is supplemented by notes and recollections of one of the two authors who was a member of the special, ad hoc committee and of the delegation which visited Kfar Oranim.

    Specific citations are not given in order to maintain the disguise under which the material is presented.

CHAPTER THREE

THE DOCUMENTARY

July 23, 1981 — Initial Visit to Kfar Oranim

The visit is timed to coincide with Mark's trip to Israel. A senior staff member of the Croydon Jewish Federation, he carries responsibility for Project Renewal. I am answerable to him and will send reports to him. I am not scheduled to begin my assignment until September 15, 1981, but we are taking advantage of Mark's presence to go to Kfar Oranim today. Our visit jibes with a meeting of the Kfar Oranim Project Renewal Steering Committee which recommends expenditures for physical and social development to Croydon and to Project Renewal headquarters.

We are late because we have trouble locating Kfar Oranim. The entrance to the town is not off the main highway but through a two-lane side road which has few identifying signs.

There are fifteen people in the modest civic chamber where the meeting is held. The room is also the Mayor's office. He presides in his capacity as chairman of the Committee. After introducing Mark whom he remembers from the Croydon delegation's visit in April, 1981, the Mayor calls on Hanoch to introduce me. I have not met Hanoch and Mark whispers that he is a senior executive in Project Renewal, based in Jerusalem. He is reputedly a tough administrator who is busy with the national and international aspects of Project Renewal but who takes time to visit the distressed communities to keep an eye on things. I heard he proposed an individual of his choice for the liaison-consultant position but Croydon insisted on making its own selection.

Hanoch hardly looks like an aggressive administrator. He is dressed informally with his white shirt open at the throat in Israeli fashion. I judge him to be in his middle forties. He speaks softly and nothing about him suggests the firebrand. His introduction barely deals with me as a person. Rather, Hanoch focuses on the role of the liaison-consultant as he sees it. He says I am to be considered a staff worker and not a representative of Croydon. He asserts that Croydon is expected to deal with his office and not rely on the liaison-consultant for representation. Finally, he perfunctorily acknowledges me, saying he understands I have an interest in social services and that I could make a contribution by improving social services in Kfar Oranim.

21

As Hanoch speaks, I hark back in my mind to the discussion with the Croydon Project Renewal Committee a month ago when I was interviewed for the job. My role as defined there conflicts with what Hanoch is propounding. The Croydon people indicated I was to serve as their representative by checking on the funds they allocate to Kfar Oranim and by letting them know what happens once the money reaches Israel. In addition to being their representative, as I clearly understood it, they want me to act as a community development worker to improve the quality of life in Kfar Oranim. They expect me to generate joint activities by both communities, encourage voluntarism in community work by the local residents and raise the level of community morale.

Discussions with the Croydon leadership emphasized my role as their representative in all aspects of Project Renewal. Now, Hanoch is plainly expressing a contrary view. He specifically excludes responsibility for my serving as a representative. I don't know how his remarks are being received and I am painfully aware of Mark's inability to understand Hanoch's Hebrew. He is challenging Mark's legitimation of my role. For me to respond without involving Mark will increase doubt as to my status. How do I switch to English without bewildering members of the Steering Committee who speak no English? Should I allow Hanoch's statement to proceed in Hebrew with Mark kept in the dark? As I struggle with these questions, the opportunity to intervene slips by. Hanoch has moved to another topic.

I realize I have just been confronted with my first problem in this assignment. Conflict looms between how Hanoch and Croydon define the role of the liaison-consultant. I am so preoccupied with this issue that I cannot apply myself to the agenda which, fortunately consists of routine matters. The meeting soon ends.

Mark and Hanoch engage in spirited conversation (in English). I join the local people who receive me warmly. Shaul, the Mayor and Eitan, the Executive Secretary of the Steering Committee, amiably introduce themselves and say Croydon and Kfar Oranim need direct links. They hope I will deepen the connection between the communities. I assure them I share their hope and I will address myself to this matter as soon as I start my work in Kfar Oranim.

I return to Mark and Hanoch who continue their pleasant conversation. Presently, Hanoch turns to me and I say I am eager to meet with him as soon as possible to discuss Project Renewal in Kfar Oranim, especially the budget and finances. He says a meeting can be arranged if I call his office. He is rather distant and though he is not curt, the cordiality in his conversation with Mark has noticeably faded. I take no personal umbrage. His attitude is obviously conditioned by the policy he had enunciated about my role.

On our way to the hotel, Mark and I review the meeting. It is apparent that in their animated chat, Hanoch did not tell Mark what he said about my role as liaison-consultant. I decide not to raise the issue. Our relationship has started on a warm, collegial note and I want to keep it that way. I don't yet know Mark well enough to predict his reaction to my sounding contentious so early in the game. Besides, I wonder if there is something between Mark and Hanoch that I need to know. Why did Mark agree to Hanoch's introducing me when Hanoch felt snubbed by Croydon's rejection of his offer to name a candidate in order to appoint me? A better way to insure an introduction without complications could have been to arrange a preliminary meeting with the Mayor so that he could have presented me.

Anyway, Mark has little time left in Israel and he would not be able to do much about the problem even if he wanted to. Raising it now would only leave an unresolved issue. While I have no illusions about replicating with Hanoch the easy-going relationship that I have quickly established with Mark, I am loathe to start with him on a quarrelsome basis. After all, he is the senior official in Project Renewal.

The burdened wisdom of hindsight brings pointers about making proper arrangements after the fact. Hindsight examinations of actions and reactions can also guide future behavior. In any event, right or wrong, I decided not to start a dialogue with Mark that required his availability to intervene with Hanoch and also to serve as my regular consultant. The distance separating us makes this impossible.

September 15, 1981 — Kfar Oranim
Today is the official beginning of my work in Kfar Oranim. It coincides with a meeting of the Steering Committee. Eitan, the Executive Secretary, serves as chairman in the absence of the Mayor. Others present include Aryeh, a paraprofessional who works with neighborhood committees, and Vered, a Project Renewal official, based in the Regional Office, who assists Kfar Oranim. She is in charge of preparing budgets and drawing up plans. Tamar joins us a few minutes late. She is a small, quiet person who is introduced as the new community worker. Her place in the hierarchy and her sponsorship are unclear. She is understandably uneasy since this is her first day on the job.

Eitan opens the meeting. He is a former school principal who is responsible for all aspects of Project Renewal in Kfar Oranim. Although Eitan speaks forcibly and zestfully, he delivers a cheerless report on the mutually negating decisions and directives which come from the Ministries of Interior, Housing, Labor and Social Affairs as well as from Project Renewal headquarters. These contrary instructions block the Steering Committee from carrying out approved programs. Hearing about this for the first time, I find it hard to keep track of all the bottlenecks and I get a sense of frustrating confusion. I

23

make a mental note to follow up with Vered.

Eitan pauses and Vered interjects that she is depressed by what she heard. She and Eitan worked hard to produce a 120-page manual-report which has detailed information about the renewal programs that were ratified by the Steering Committee. Also, progress reports flow regularly into the government ministries and Jewish Agency offices, designed to keep the authorities up to date on plans and activities in Kfar Oranim. Despite this volume of communication, funds are not forthcoming. She leafs through the report and repeats she is depressed. I comment that we must keep our pessimism in check to leave some despair for the lay members of the Steering Committee. Vered laughs and the mood lightens. Eitan's report ends inconclusively because no one present can do anything about the situation he describes in such melancholy terms.

We consider two projects I want to propose to get the most out of the partnership between Kfar Oranim and Croydon. I assure everyone I realize how much effort has gone into planning the 1981-1982 Project Renewal program. My suggestions are intended to be complementary. Perhaps, they will help us to begin dealing with the problems raised by Eitan.

I summarize the proposals. One is designed to provide vocational opportunities for alienated youth in Kfar Oranim, involving some Junius residents. The other has to do with developing a "living bridge" between Kfar Oranim and Croydon through pen pal programs and exchange visits. I promise to present detailed plans in writing next week. Aryeh is enthusiastic about my suggestions and Vered also seems favorably inclined. Eitan reacts in a mildly affirmative manner. He is removed and restrained, still under the influence of the gloom created by his report.

I say I am eager to meet with the new Director of the local Welfare Department which provides family casework services, financial aid and community work. Eitan says that we will all go to the Welfare Department as soon as we finish the next item.

This is an announcement that Reuven will visit Kfar Oranim tomorrow. Recently appointed Deputy Minister of Housing, he is in charge of Project Renewal for the State of Israel. Eitan and Aryeh want to use Reuven's visit to raise tough questions about the subjects Eitan identified at the beginning of our meeting. They insist it is important for me to be present when Reuven comes. I agree to appear but I say I will have to leave by 2 P.M. to keep an appointment with Hanoch. This date was scheduled soon after my first visit to Kfar Oranim when I was introduced by Hanoch. Since the appointment has been delayed, I am determined to let nothing interfere with it. Eitan assures me Reuven's stay in Kfar Oranim will be over long before 2 P.M. since he has to attend a meeting elsewhere later in the day.

We now proceed to the office of Uri, the new Welfare Department Director. He is an American social worker in his early thirties who recently settled in Israel. He is very harassed, having been on the job for only a few days. He doesn't know what to make of our unannounced visit and so I arrange to return later. Uri is still conditioned by the American value of setting appointments. He resents this sudden foray and he is irritated by people taking liberties with his time.

We return to Eitan's office and I review the fiscal aspects of Project Renewal programs in Kfar Oranim with Vered. She skillfully relates social problems to programs designed to deal with them and the budget. She traces the funding sources, delineating the contribution of each government ministry. I ask about the relationship of governmental funds to the money from Croydon. I want to know if Croydon's money makes up the deficit when government funds are used up. My question irks Vered. She doesn't want Project Renewal funds to be mistakenly viewed as covering the deficits of other funding sources. I ask whether the State of Israel and Project Renewal constitute a partnership which finances the programs listed in the manual-report she and Eitan prepared. Or, I want to know, are Project Renewal funds applied to activities that would ordinarily not be funded in Kfar Oranim's regular municipal budget? I tell Vered I am genuinely seeking answers to these questions which are also being raised by the American communities involved in Project Renewal. Vered declares that Project Renewal funds are used for community rehabilitation in both its physical and social dimensions. She suggests a visit to some of the agencies which use Croydon's funds; on-site observation will give substance to her explanations. I agree this is a good idea and we arrange to meet after I see Uri. I tell her I am grateful for this opportunity because the tour will help me prepare for tomorrow's session with Hanoch. I look forward to learning the principles which underlie Project Renewal fiscal policies and after I see some of their beneficiaries, I will be better able to comprehend them.

At the Welfare Department, Uri is calmer than when we descended on him earlier. He says he started working in Kfar Oranim a few days ago and he is trying to make sense of what is going on. I mention that I am also new and I explain my task in Kfar Oranim. He immediately seizes on my identification as a professor of social work to ask if I can help locate caseworkers for his department. If I could possibly find qualified workers to serve pre-school children, I would take a load off his shoulders. I say I will try but I have little hope of success since the larger cities of Israel are constantly recruiting social workers. A small place like Kfar Oranim has trouble competing. I try not to stress my doubts and I assure him I will do all I can.

I tell Uri I plan to visit Kfar Oranim at least twice a week and we could get together from time to time to examine ways in which I might be of assistance. He is amenable to the suggestion. As I leave, I reiterate my intent to help him recruit caseworkers.

As I walk to keep my appointment with Vered, the thought occurs to me that perhaps I can help Uri to get some volunteers to fill in until he is able to appoint professional staff. I decide to contact some community workers I know in neighboring towns who might be in a position to locate volunteers. Since I will be seeing Uri tomorrow when I return for Reuven's visit, I make up my mind to discuss with him this idea of volunteers.

Vered and I begin our tour in the area near the municipal offices. This unprepossessing spot is the town center. There are vague plans for improvements but no definitive decision. Vered suggests that lack of progress in beautifying the area reflects Kfar Oranim's poor leadership. She thinks the Mayor is ineffectual and Eitan is inept. According to her, lack of leadership is responsible for Kfar Oranim's reputation as a problem community.

We visit one of the two religious elementary schools. It is a hodge-podge of wooden huts in a poor state of repair. Vered says the principal is a gifted man, devoted to the school. Her assertion is borne out by decorations on the walls of the huts. But, for all this attention, the buildings are still firetraps which urgently need replacement. I wonder whether the work is the responsibility of Project Renewal or the Ministry of Education. I hope the Croydon delegation on its next visit can sort this out in a manner that combines realism with compassion.

We return to where we began and enter the Community Center, situated close to the municipal offices. I am introduced to Rafael, the conductor of the Youth Orchestra. He talks enthusiastically about the group's development and about how nice it would be if they could make an overseas tour. He claims it would be good for Kfar Oranim as well as for the members of the Orchestra. I think to myself that an expensive trip abroad would need far more justification than group or community therapy but I merely respond that it is too early in my work to react to such an idea. He presses his case, pointing out that the Youth Orchestra performs at a very high level of competence. I am saved from further pressure by the arrival of the drummer who immediately starts to play loudly. It is obvious that he is mentally handicapped. Rafael assures me that the drummer plays well and that his participation in the Orchestra is good for his ego and for his family's morale. It appears that rehabilitation has been achieved in this instance.

The conductor states that the drummer is one of 100 students studying music at the Community Center. The excellence of instruction and the fine quality of the teaching staff assures progress towards establishing Kfar Oranim as a regional center which would teach music not only to local residents but also to people in the surrounding areas. According to Rafael, accreditation by the authorities will come soon.

Such recognition will boost community morale. Life in the town will take a turn for the better when the Community Center has a conservatory to attract students and audiences from neighboring communities. The music program is supported by Project Renewal funds and has high potential for improving the social and cultural life of Kfar Oranim.

Our tour ends, leaving me with a better feeling than I had after Eitan made his bleak report. His disheartening analysis is not reflected in the day-to-day life of the town, judging by what we saw. Both the Youth Orchestra conductor and the school principal are unquestionably trying to brighten the spirit of Kfar Oranim. Their efforts suggest that I need to help local leaders emphasize local projects in order to reduce the feelings of helplessness that arise when they deal with officials of the government or Project Renewal.

Vered and I stop at Eitan's office to say good-bye. He says Uri seems a promising addition to Kfar Oranim. What Eitan likes particularly is Uri's determination to help people without becoming enmeshed in local politics. Eitan tells us that when Uri was appointed, he told the Mayor he doesn't care about people's politics. Aryeh differs emphatically with Eitan. Politics are important and individuals who work for the community need to be politically astute. No one responds to Aryeh. I tell Eitan I agree with his estimate of Uri. However, I point out, he needs support. He has considerable potential but his job is tough and he requires encouragement, especially in these early days of his tenure.

Later, at home, I call some friends to ask about volunteers for Kfar Oranim. I find several possibilities and I promise one of my contacts to get information about supervision for the volunteers.

September 16, 1981 — Kfar Oranim

I arrive at the Mayor's office for the meeting with Reuven, Deputy Minister of Housing and the Israeli cabinet member carrying the government portfolio for Project Renewal. Eitan informs me that plans have changed. Reuven is at the airport to greet the Prime Minister who is returning from the United States today. We will just have to wait for him. The room slowly fills. A man is introduced as Yuval, the newly-appointed Director of Kfar Oranim's school system. Ariela enters and is showered with attention. A resident of Junius, she and Noam, her husband, take great interest in Kfar Oranim. As people come in, I am introduced as the "link" between Croydon and Kfar Oranim. Aryeh sits down and loudly asks whether any one has seen the newspaper story about attempts to clarify the tasks of the Jewish

Agency and the Ministry of Housing in Project Renewal. According to him, this clarification will lead to smoother functioning of the two organizations. His statement receives a mixed response of weak enthusiasm and mild cynicism.

Reuven finally arrives. He is poised and surprisingly young. As he checks the agenda with the Mayor, conversation flows among the people crowded into the room. Aryeh speaks up to say that a new day has dawned in Israel with the election of Reuven's party. He makes negative comments about the previous Labor Party governments.

At last, the Mayor opens the meeting, asking people to identify themselves by their names and organizations. More than half are paid workers, not volunteers. Ariela draws laughter and applause by introducing herself as a resident of Kfar Oranim Bet (Kfar Oranim #2).

The Mayor makes a half-hour speech, lauding the government and particularly our guest, Deputy Minister Reuven. He lists Kfar Oranim's complaints, emphasizing the government's failure to grant official status as a "development town". This technical classification which would provide tax benefits to investors was denied to Kfar Oranim because of its location. He points out that Kfar Oranim has no proper beach even though it is close to the sea. The partly prepared shore now used is hazardous. Drownings occur every year. Just two months ago, a soldier about to be released from the army after his military service, was swept away by the treacherous currents and killed. Such fatalities could be prevented if Kfar Oranim had a beach just a fraction as good as Junius' which is open only to Junius residents.

The Mayor calls on people to speak, selecting mainly those involved in physical planning. Reuven listens quietly, asks an occasional question and takes notes assiduously. He is scheduled to respond later.

After the presentations, everyone accompanies Reuven on a planned tour. The strung-out crowd engages in conversation unrelated to the business of the day. I talk with Tamar, the new community worker and with Marcus, the chief official in Project Renewal under Reuven. Tamar asks about admission to the MA program in my university to study community work. I promise to make inquiries. I talk with Uri, the Welfare Department Director, about using volunteers since the likelihood of finding qualified caseworkers is slim. I tell him that my discussions concerning volunteers indicate they are reluctant to come to Kfar Oranim. I get information about supervision of volunteers and Uri asks me to keep trying to find some.

The procession reaches one end of town where a Ministry of Housing planner points to land which he says can be used for a sports area. A similar piece of land in Junius is just across the boundary, separating the two communities. This leads to an argument about segregating

Kfar Oranim from Junius. There is confusion about what the planner means but an undertone of hard feeling between Kfar Oranim and Junius is in the offing, if not already present.

The tour ends and I leave to keep my appointment with Hanoch. While I missed the remainder of Reuven's visit, I saw enough to realize that an opportunity was lost for discussing Kfar Oranim's real problems in his presence. Whether this was the fault of Kfar Oranim's leaders or whether there was external pressure to avoid basic issues is something I need to ascertain. Failure to confront an elected political leader on behalf of Kfar Oranim was a disappointment. Who can tell what constrained the Mayor? Aryeh also held his peace. Although he has no use for the Mayor, he can't attack without alienating Reuven since all three belong to the same political party. Strong neighborhood spokesmen could have compelled Reuven to face Kfar Oranim's problems. But, Aryeh and the Mayor stifled grass roots voices. I learn this through the grapevine to which I am hooked up. I shall soon know where these two stand since I will be working closely with them.

September 16, 1981 — Jerusalem

Hanoch invited two staff members to be present at our session. One is Judith whose responsibilities appear to be those of a junior executive, judging from her prominent part in the discussion. The other is Menashe, a new senior aide in Project Renewal and a former student at my university whom I know from his previous social welfare employment. Hanoch is surprised we are acquainted.

I tell Hanoch that it would help in my work if I had a better understanding of Project Renewal's fiscal affairs and procedures. Vered's help is limited to Kfar Oranim. I need a more general orientation. Hanoch replies he has already dealt with this subject today and he does not want to go into it again. He looks tired. He invites me to a workshop on finances to be held next week and I indicate I will try to attend if I can re-arrange my schedule.

Hanoch says my understanding of Project Renewal finances may help me report to Croydon but more is needed from me. He remarks that I could make a real contribution if I could bring Kfar Oranim's youth into the job market. I agree with him that my assignment goes beyond filing reports to Croydon and I tell him I am getting into community work in Kfar Oranim.

I describe a project I conceived for the alienated youth of the town. It has two related features. First, a cooperative will be created through which the young people will do home improvements and repairs or produce a simple product that is readily marketable. Members of the cooperative will develop skills for producing, marketing, selling and delivering the service or product. Collective ownership through the cooperative will stimulate the incentive to succeed and bypass the problem of one individual facing an impersonal job market alone and with little understanding.

The second feature calls for teaching and overseeing personnel to help the cooperative become viable and productive. These people will be volunteers who will guide the cooperative and provide financial support, especially at the outset. They will promote the cooperative's services and products. I envisage the volunteers as consisting of Junius businessmen. Hanoch and Judith are interested. They name people in the Ministry of Education who might help. However, on second thought, Hanoch questions the project. It is too expensive and it does not integrate alienated youth into established industries. He argues that my plan will baffle and frighten the youth. I feel this is not the time to debate these issues. I conclude this part of the conversation by assuring Hanoch I will consider his views. I want to forestall opposition to my plan which seems to be crystallizing in his mind even though I gave him only a skeleton outline. I don't want anything to interfere with the favorable reception the idea received in Kfar Oranim.

Hanoch asks how things are developing in Kfar Oranim. I share with him my tentative impression that Kfar Oranim officials, both elected and appointed, have much to learn about leadership. He retorts that the town's problem is ineffective people in all community positions. He is remarkably familiar with individuals and specifics of Kfar Oranim. Judith and he identify others elsewhere who would do a better job in Kfar Oranim and he says it is time to think about replacements. Judith slows this trend by wondering if it is realistic to dismiss incumbents and expose others to the hardships of Kfar Oranim. Hanoch does not comment and I surmise that his outburst is more a result of fatigue and frustration than a clear-cut decision to fire people who displease him.

As our conference ends, Judith repeats it is a serious step to fire the town's workers. I agree it would probably be counter-productive. It occurs to me later that these workers ought to improve as a result of all the consultation they are receiving from me and the two Project Renewal staff members, Leah and Vered. Our combined efforts should start producing some results.

The discussion confirms my emerging conviction that a basic problem in Kfar Oranim is the quality of its leadership. No particular individual is at fault but they all need help in playing their roles effectively. Ways must be found to energize the community leaders. The tradition of passivity and fatalism which seems to be at the root of Kfar Oranim's problems needs changing. I plan to proceed on this premise - at least, for the time being.

September 22, 1981 - Kfar Oranim

Tamar, Eitan and Aryeh and I meet to discuss my proposal for alienated youth. They scan my written descriptions of the plans. We

30

consider the pros and cons of vocational training and the aided self-help approach. Aryeh feels we should concentrate on men recently discharged from the army. Eitan and I agree although he seems preoccupied with other matters. Tamar quietly conveys her concurrence. Having reached consensus, we turn to ways and means for achieving our goals. We decide to ask Ariela and Noam, as avowed friends of Kfar Oranim, to invite some local industrialists to their home for a discussion of the project. We telephone but there is no reply. We are disappointed but decide to keep trying. Aryeh is eager to move quickly and says he and I should meet with the industrialists. He reluctantly accepts my view that this would vitiate our decision to start by securing Ariela and Noam's support.

Aryeh then informs us that the Neighborhood Council has rejected the idea of building a swimming pool in favor of focusing on developing the beach. We all see this as a sensible judgement. Aryeh enthusiastically invites me to see the beach area. I accept since I do not want to reject his second initiative.

Before we leave, I tell Tamar I checked at the university for her and learned she is ineligible for the MA program but she can take a special certificate course. She says she will look into this possibility and she expresses her appreciation.

I stop at the Welfare Department to ask Uri about assigning one of my community organization students to him for field experience. He expresses interest and we agree to pursue the matter. As we prepare to visit the beach, I tell Aryeh that there may be a contradiction in seeking the cooperation of Noam, Ariela and other Junius residents in the alienated youth project while at the same time pressuring the Junius Land Corporation about the beach. Aryeh insists there is no problem since permission to develop the beach has already been granted. Eitan disagrees, holding that the question of beach development is still to be settled with the Junius Land Corporation. I remain concerned that simultaneous approaches on both the beach and the alienated youth project may be self-defeating. Accordingly, I ask Aryeh to invite me to the next meeting of the Neighborhood Council so that I may judge for myself the strength of its determination about the beach project. He promises to invite me.

We drive to the beach. Aryeh voices his hope that differences between Kfar Oranim and Junius can be narrowed soon. I express my doubts. The two communities are truly separate worlds. Aryeh doesn't argue but I sense that he has not dropped his vision of quick change.

We look at the two beaches which I see as "Gold Coast" and "Slum", side by side. I think that Israel's early pioneers with their egalitarian ideology would be aghast at the sharp contrast between rich and poor symbolized by the two beaches, a developed one belonging to the wealthy community of Junius and an undeveloped one which is dangerous to use. When we finish, Aryeh insists we stop at the Junius Planning Office and I reluctantly assent. The impromptu visit is in vain since the Director of the Planning Office is too busy to see us. We decide to call for an appointment.

Despite our failure to see the Director, Aryeh is happy with the visit. He says it is important to include Kfar Oranim residents in all official visits. He asserts that the Planning Office is especially consequential since it arranges tours and archaelogical trips which exclude the people of Kfar Oranim. They lose out on the enrichment offered by these activities. I assure Aryeh I am primarily interested in Kfar Oranim's residents and I add that it is part of my job to broaden their contacts with the resources in the area. I conclude the visit by telling Aryeh I will keep trying to arrange for us to see Ariela and Noam.

I recognize that Aryeh is using my status to get into places previously denied to him. I have no objection so long as his efforts do not interfere with my access to these places.

October 6, 1981 — Kfar Oranim

My day begins with Aaron, the new youth worker. He has been on the job for six weeks. The first four were spent in learning about Kfar Oranim's youth. I met him earlier at a Steering Committee meeting and I tell him that I was impressed by his performance on that occasion. He strikes me as energetic, yet easy-going. He looks younger than his age of 29. He has a BA in sociology and political science and is studying for his MA in sociology. He worked as a volunteer in Kfar Oranim before taking this paid job. His predecessor apparently left much to be desired.

Aaron shares his findings about the youth of Kfar Oranim:
1. Of 2,446 gainfully employed young people, 1,524 (62%) work outside of Kfar Oranim.
2. Jobs in the town are generally low-paid with few prospects for advancement.
3. Most jobs in Kfar Oranim are in the textile industry which is considered "laggard" rather than a "growth industry".
4. 469 out of 700 youths (67%) between the ages of 14 and 17 are attending school. The rate for Israel as a whole is 76%.
5. Only 8.4% of the 700 youths are enrolled in academic courses as compared with 17.2% for the rest of the country.
6. Between 1971 and 1978, 1,050 young people came to live in Kfar Oranim and 2,495 left.
7. From 100 to 158 youths are temporarily or permanently out of school, They wander in the town and the surrounding areas.

Aaron read my proposal regarding the cooperative work enterprise for alienated youth. He agrees with my suggestion that Kfar Oranim needs a teaching center to prepare youth for higher-paying jobs but he does not see Malachti, the local trade school, as meeting this need now or in the future. It trains youth for low-paying jobs and keeps them off the streets. However, it has a negative image, being perceived as an institution that works with failures, offering them a low level of vocational training. Youth are loathe to go there. Aaron's appraisal of Malachti contradicts the praise which Eitan and Aryeh voiced when they recommended it be the corner stone of the job opportunity program in my proposal. I take Aaron's view seriously. He confirms my own observations of trade schools in Israel. Most function in a vacuum, turning out graduates who compete for jobs without any help. Few, if any, of these schools work with recognized business people to create links with potential employers of the graduates.

We discuss Aaron's ideas about work with problem youth. He enunciates two principles: upgrading education and upgrading vocational training. In the absence of these two approaches, Kfar Oranim youth are stuck in low-paying jobs or look to illegal ways of earning money.

Aaron has spent the last two weeks with the youth and I ask him to tell me about his experiences. He has been mingling with them in the streets, trying to form groups. He needs leaders for these groups. Out of 30 ex-soldiers he tried to recruit, only three volunteered. I think to myself that I might get a student to take over one group but I don't mention this since I want to make sure that it is a real possibility.

Aaron complains he has no meeting place which means the program cannot function. I ask if he would like me to discuss this with the Mayor. He enthusiastically accepts my offer.

As we finish, Aaron asks that we meet regularly even though he already has two supervisors. One is from the Ministry of Labor and Social Affairs and the other from the Ministry of Education. Aaron is unimpressed with both. I say I would like to maintain contact with him, especially in connection with job opportunity programs.

I keep my appointment with Mayor Shaul. Our session is short. A group of Croydon visitors is coming to Kfar Oranim soon and the Mayor asks me to work with Eitan on plans for them. We set a date to consider the outline which Eitan and I are to formulate.

I report briefly on my activities and I mention Aaron's problem of a place for his program. The Mayor has heard from Aaron and has asked the government housing corporation to provide two apartments. This will give Aaron a meeting place and an office. I tell the Mayor that I was not aware of his involvement and I ask if I may relay this information to Aaron. The Mayor has no objection. He presents me with a diary for the new year. His gift is in keeping with his kind, gentle personality.

I return to Aaron to tell him about my conversation with the Mayor.

33

He is not pleased with the Mayor's solution to his problem since the space to be provided is in an apartment house. His program will disturb the residents and cause friction. I urge that he start with the space being offered. His office work should create no problem for the residents. Formal group meetings may also be free of difficulty. I understand his concern about noisy recreational programs and I suggest a site might be found for them in one of the schools or in the Community Center. We agree to explore the matter further when we next meet since I have to keep my appointment with Uri, the Welfare Department Director.

Uri and I talk first about the student being assigned to his Department. He will work out a list of possible tasks. I move to the question of volunteers, saying that money may be needed to pay for their transportation. Uri says he has no funds for this. I turn to Eitan who has just joined us and I put the question to him. He is sure money can be made available by Leah, the Project Renewal Regional Office supervisor. He suggests I talk with her and offers to write a letter, if she needs it. I thank him, saying that I will raise the question with her after we locate our first volunteer.

I go to see Tamar who declares she decided not to enroll in the university's certificate course because she feels it is more suitable for prospective community center directors rather than community workers, which is her interest. I refrain from correcting her. She adds that, in any event, the heavy time requirements preclude her from taking the course.

Tamar explains the sponsorship under which she works. Project Renewal denied the original request from the Steering Committee to create the position she now fills. The Ministry of Labor and Social Affairs established the position and provides supervision. Since the local Welfare Department represents the Ministry in Kfar Oranim, she reports to Uri and also to Eitan as the Project Renewal Executive Secretary. She finds Uri to be marginally related to community work, being preoccupied with the family aspects of social welfare.

Tamar has begun to organize a group of recently released soldiers. She wants to enroll them in a three-months program which she calls a "school for activists". This idea was recommended by her Ministry supervisor, who also has some say about about her work, in addition to Uri and Eitan. The "school" will offer instruction on running a meeting, community organizing and strategies of change. She believes this course will develop well-prepared, active-minded people who can follow an advocacy approach to community work.

According to Tamar, there is little hope of any change in the town with the present leadership in control. She includes Aryeh in this category even though he is a paid community worker. He is supposed to represent the street blocks and neighborhoods on the Steering

Committee but his position is confused because he receives a salary for his work. In her opinion, he suffers from a conflict of interest. Moreover, his situation is complicated by his desire to become the Mayor or Deputy Mayor of Kfar Oranim. Tamar says that he has no chance to realize this ambition, basing her assessment not only on her professional judgement but also on her knowledge of the local political scene as a long-time resident of Kfar Oranim. I ask if there is any duplication between her and Aryeh in their community work. She thinks this is not a problem at present since Aryeh is working primarily in the neighborhoods while she is interested in her ex-soldiers group.

I do not share my thoughts with Tamar but our conversation stimulates me to think about working more closely with her and Aaron. They may be able to bring new strength to Kfar Oranim through their work with young adults. Our discussion also makes me think about the necessity of bringing the professionals together to coordinate their efforts and to make a more effective contribution as resource persons to the Steering Committee and its sub-committees. I will discuss this with Uri when we get together again.

Aryeh comes to the Welfare Department where I am waiting for Tamar to reach Ariela and Noam. We have been trying in vain for a week and I am hoping for success today. If they can see us, then Aryeh and Eitan will accompany me which is why Aryeh is here now.

While we wait, Aryeh tells me that the Ministry of Housing has promised Kfar Oranim 63 million shekels but that the money was frozen until Deputy Minister Reuven visited. He got the Ministry to release 19 million shekels but this was probably arranged as a political tactic before he came. According to Aryeh, this shows that Project Renewal is a force to be reckoned with since Reuven is now the chief governmental leader for Project Renewal. Before Project Renewal, there was no way of pressuring the ministries or the political parties. They were all kingdoms unto themselves and the ordinary man in the street had nothing to say about their policies and decisions. This is changing because of Project Renewal. The neighborhoods now have real muscle.

I listen to Aryeh without commenting. I have no idea on what he bases his observations but they certainly give a good picture of his own thinking. He goes on to talk about the Mayor, accusing him of being a weakling. Aryeh believes that the Mayor is worn out and will not seek re-election, having already served for six years. This is for the best, asserts Aryeh, since Kfar Oranim needs strong men at the top if it is to prosper within the framework of Project Renewal with its fresh opportunities for constructive change.

Tamar interrupts to say that she has Ariela on the phone. I ask if we can come over to see her about a project we wish to propose for Kfar Oranim. She cannot make it today but we fix an appointment for tomorrow. She asks that I come alone so that she can see the proposal and study it with one person for clarification. After that, the others from Kfar Oranim can join us. Aryeh accepts this with good grace.

I go over to see Eitan who appears to be distressed. He is writing a letter to Hanoch in Jerusalem asking that funds be released for those projects approved by the Steering Committee so that they can be started. He asks me to intervene with Hanoch and I agree to do so. I tell him that I am ready to help in any way that he wishes. He says that he will speak with the Mayor to determine the best way to approach Hanoch. Eitan's concern about funds is at odds with what Aryeh has just told me.

I turn to the question of the forthcoming visit of a group from Croydon on October 27, 1981. Eitan immediately tries to phone various officials in Jerusalem to get more details about the visit. He cannot reach anyone and so we talk in a preliminary way about plans for receiving the guests. He thinks we should have a tour of the town, informal meetings with Kfar Oranim families and a performance by the Youth Orchestra. He recommends that we avoid any final decisions until we have more information and instructions from Jerusalem. We decide to keep trying to reach the appropriate officials and to confer by telephone so that we can come to the October 18, 1981 planning meeting with a firm proposal. I am uneasy about this loose approach but Eitan is confident that the visitors will be pleased with their reception. He assures me that he has had lots of experience with such visits.

October 7, 1981

I telephone Ariela from my home and she apologizes that our meeting will have to be called off for the time being. Since the assassination of President Sadat (about an hour after I called her yesterday) her household has been in a turmoil. People are coming at all hours to discuss the outlook for Israel following this grave event. She and Noam are about to leave for Tel Aviv to sign the book of condolence. Then, they must go to Cairo after Yom Kippur. After that, they have to be in Europe for a few days. We postpone our meeting indefinitely.

October 25, 1981 - Kfar Oranim

The planning meeting originally scheduled for October 18, 1981 was put off until today because several participants had to be elsewhere at the time. We meet in the Mayor's office — an hour later than the slated time. The following are present: Mayor, Deputy Mayor, Eitan, Vered, Uri, Aryeh, Tamar and I. Eitan reads the plan he has prepared:

a) The group is received at the Community Center.

b) Each Croydon visitor is presented with a flower.
c) The Youth Orchestra plays welcoming music.
d) The Mayor extends brief greetings, stressing Kfar Oranim's pressing needs.
e) The visitors are divided into two groups for a tour to observe places that have been selected to give a balanced view of achievements and failures.
f) The visit ends at the Community Center where the Youth Choral Group performs.

Amos, the Deputy Mayor, forcefully objects to the long guided tour in Eitan's plan. Eitan vigorously defends it as necessary to give Croydon supporters a picture of Kfar Oranim's needs. Most people agree with the Deputy Mayor but their lack of robust support for his position angers him. He stalks out of the room in a huff. I express my opinion that time could be saved with a shorter tour and Eitan reluctantly agrees to eliminate some stops. We are all in accord on Vered serving as translator. I am pleased about this decision because I feel it is important to involve the local people. Vered's English is not bad and what is lost in translation is gained in hearing first-hand from a native Israeli. For missions such as this one, a sense of direct contact with Israeli society is provided. Besides, Vered will gain extra recognition and added satisfaction. The Mayor who has been passive throughout the meeting indicates that he will keep his remarks brief.

Many of the same people who were at the planning meeting now reconvene in Eitan's office to review budgets. These will have to be ready for submission to Project Renewal headquarters before the end of December, 1981. Our session today is the first in a series that will take place in November and December. Information for the meeting today has been prepared by Vered and Eitan.

Before we start, two women come in to ask that something be done about their institution, Ramit. This Orthodox day care center is about to be enlarged. Its premises must be vacated during the renovation and the women are concerned about the hardships this will cause the children. Eitan offers several possible solutions but none are acceptable to the women because they do not include kosher food to meet their requirements. Eitan indicates that he will talk to others and find a solution. The women have to be nudged out of the room to permit consideration of the budgets to begin.

Eitan, as chairman of the meeting, calls on Vered who gives an expert and detailed explanation of the budget process. Comments are invited and there is an immediate loud response by many people claiming simultaneouly that the proposed equipment allocation is grossly inadequate. Other items are also seen as under-budgeted. Eitan tries to make some order out of the chaotic uproar. From time to time, there is a moment of calm. Vered, who has been patiently waiting, seizes these opportunities to elicit decisions before the shouting begins again.

I see no way of my contributing to this raucous process and so I slip Uri a note about a prospective applicant for a job in the Welfare Department. He writes back in appreciation since he is carrying practically the entire load of his office by himself and he is sorely in need of help.

Uri is one of several professionals in attendance. Lay people are present as advocates for their agencies. Most of them appear not to understand the complicated budget process. It is easy to get lost in the maze of multiple funding sources and in the differences between Project Renewal programs and those which are on-going government responsibilities.

Finally, this meeting which has been dealing with pre-school children ends and the Sub-Committeee on the Aged enters. There is a great deal of overlap in the membership of these sub-committees, especially among the professionals.

Before the meeting begins, there is a disturbance caused by a man who noisily insists that the Sub-Committee on the Aged is sheltered from what goes on in the real world. He contends that the Ashkenazim in Kfar Oranim are dominated by the Sephardim and that this skews the participation of the synagogue delegates on the Sub-Committee. Eitan skillfully turns the man's wrath aside by inviting him to sit in on the meeting. The man takes a seat at the door and quietly follows the proceedings with surprising passivity.

This meeting is less strident than the preceding one but it is equally undisciplined. A general discussion about the plight of poor people in Kfar Oranim is the starting point. Complicated eligibility requirements for financial assistance block many people from getting the help they need. Many of the poor live in houses which are in bad repair but the various agencies which are involved are not providing the money to fix them. Eitan acknowledges the problem and tries to explain the funding complexities of the different ministries. His explanation is too intricate for most people and only adds to the air of cynicism in the room.

Vered brings the discussion around to the budgets. Meals for the aged are considered. It is reported that hot meals are no longer being provided because the mandatory charge of IL 75 is too high for the aged. Eitan argues for reducing the required payment to IL 50. His proposal is easily approved. However, the main point of restoring the provision of hot meals is not discussed. Eitan may know some way to accomplish this but the matter is not pursued. The next item is the allocation of IL 80,000 for repairing teeth and for dentures. Thirty old people are receiving this service, their eligibility having been established by a means test. Approval is given. Home repairs in the amount of IL 7,000 are also approved. Seven houses are presently benefiting from this program. Leisure activities are discussed. It is reported that the aged women prefer to meet on their own; they feel inhibited in joint programs with the men.

The conversation veers to the fear among old people about violence at the hands of young delinquents. Two old people cite instances of such violence. I ask whether there is really an outbreak of violence or a fear of it. No one can throw any light on the subject. Those who have the information are away, one on military reserve duty and one for reasons unknown. There must be some police records but nobody has the facts. The old people are put out by this discussion. What's the difference between actual violence and the fear of it? They maintain that this fine distinction is neither here nor there.

The meeting tapers off with many questions left unanswered. Vered is satisfied with the quality of the discussion. She feels it is a definite improvement over the first meetings of this Sub-Committee. I have no reason to doubt her but I believe that much more is needed if these sub-committees are to function properly. There is much confusion because people do not grasp the variance between general policy issues and immediate budget decisions.

As the buget reviews move from sub-committee to subcommittee, the lack of understanding among a number of members is a problem that repeats itself. It is also clear that these people cannot reveal their ignorance without injury to their sense of worth. A few try to hide it behind irrelevant comments. Most sit passively and silently. Even if Vered had time, these sessions are not the occasion for singling out poorly informed members for special tutoring. It would be more logical and more considerate to offer a budgeting course but this will not come overnight. Tamar is the person to give such a course but she is too new on the job. Besides, she may not see the need. However, there is no one else. At the appropriate time, I will raise this with her.

October 26, 1981 - Kfar Oranim

We meet at 6 P.M. to continue the meeting of the Sub-Committee on Day Care which was not completed yesterday and which meets now to permit attendance by lay members who work during the day.

There is much shouting about unserved children. Vered tries vainly to direct attention to the budgets of existing services but there is more shouting. Considerable time is used for examples of unmet needs. Finally, several people leave and the clamor subsides. Vered finishes the rest of the budget without much discussion.

There is a break before the meeting of the Sub-Committee on Community Services. Uri tells me that he talked with the person whose name I gave him as a possible staff member. She has reservations about working in Kfar Oranim because of its bad reputation. He will try to convince her to take the job but he is worried that the very name of Kfar Oranim dissuades people from working here. I say we must improve the town's image. We should bring the agency directors together to discuss the issue. Their lack of interaction contributes to the problem. I hope we can ask the student to organize the professionals to figure out what can be done about Kfar Oranim's notoriety, especially among prospective employees. Uri agrees to discuss this when we meet to plan the student's assignment.

He reverts to the potential worker and tells me that the woman I referred to him is more interested in administrative work than in casework. He would welcome her involvement in community work. Tamar is doing a fine job but needs help. I hope this is a sign that Uri is developing a more accepting attitude toward the community dimensions of his role.

He returns to Kfar Oranim's poor reputation. He feels the problem rests with a few residents who will not stop at violence to get their way. Some are Welfare Department clients who frighten him and his staff. He plaintively asks, "How can you deal objectively with a client who threatens you?"

I try to interpret the implications of his question. Fear undermines a professional helping relationship. I sympathize with him and indicate he cannot cope with this problem alone. The Town Council and the police must be involved.

Uri is unhappy about the situation. I worry that an accumulation of these irritants will provoke him to leave Kfar Oranim. This would be unfortunate since he is a definite asset to the town. I have been told he is a vast improvement over his predecessor. I resolve to continue with this matter.

We come back to the room where Eitan calls the session to order. He makes an appeal on behalf of Ramit, the Orthodox day care center which must vacate its premises during renovations. He addresses his remarks to the representative of an agency which presumably could make temporary arrangements for Ramit. His suggestion is rejected and it becomes clear that Eitan will have to do a lot of wheeling and dealing to solve Ramit's problem. He senses that no one else is disposed to help and so he drops the subject.

The Sub-Committee on Community Services handles its business quickly. There is discussion about the slow pace of improvements. Some members declare that social betterment is harder to discern than readily observable physical improvements. The forthcoming training program for neighborhood leaders is mentioned. Tamar interjects that a complication has arisen. Those who take the course to qualify for employment as paraprofessionals need 100 hours of training by an approved instructor. Tamar is unacceptable because her degree is in sociology rather than social work. Eitan asks what can be done to break the impasse. I suggest the matter be referred to Tamar and me. We will find a solution. My suggestion is gratefully accepted and the meeting ends.

October 27, 1981 - Kfar Oranim

Before the Croydon group arrives, I have sessions with Eitan, Tamar and Uri.

I want to review final plans for our visitors. Eitan greets me by triumphantly announcing he solved the problem of temporary quarters for Ramit. He located a day care center which is not used to capacity. He is greatly relieved because he can now avoid difficult negotiations. The stony reception he received on his first stab at solving the problem made him wary of further efforts. Eitan explains the need for renovations. Ramit's capacity will be doubled and conditions for the 43 youngsters currently served will be greatly improved. The work is financed by Project Renewal and I make a mental note to report on this to Mark.

Eitan and I conclude our conversation by going over the final plans for the visit. Everything seems to be in order.

Next, I see Tamar to follow up on yesterday's meeting at which her lack of formal qualifications to conduct the training was discussed. I tell her I am prepared to act as her supervisor for purposes of meeting the requirements. I have no qualms about my offer because the course will be rudimentary. Insistence that the instructor have a special university degree seems to me to be bureaucratic humbug, resting on a false notion about paraprofessionals. The course content has little bearing on their responsibilities in the neighborhoods. "Certifying" them brings an unrealistic self-image and engenders groundless hopes among those who take the training. The small remuneration for para-professionals obscures their standing as natural leaders. In Kfar Oranim, residents look on paraprofessionalism as a means of changing altruism from an ideal into a source of extra income.

I go to Uri's office and he tells me the candidate for the vacancy in his department rejected his offer. She is planning a visit abroad and will not consider job offers until she returns. Uri will approach her at that time. I give him another name and he assures me he will follow up.

Uri is baby-sitting for his youngest child while his wife is at work. Their child care arrangements have gone temporarily awry. Combined with his regular tasks, this keeps him hectically busy. Everyone pitches in to help. A secretary takes the six-months old child to be changed. Others stop to play with the baby. Israelis easily accept what elsewhere might be seen as a bizarre intrusion. It is the kind of incident which brings out their attractive qualities.

Our visitors from Croydon arrive. They are affluent, sophisticated people, committed to Kfar Oranim. Their good will is reciprocated by the residents with a genuine desire to please. The visitors are impressed by the performances of the Youth Orchestra and the Choral Group which show that Kfar Oranim is not lacking in talent. The agency tour provides useful insights into Kfar Oranim's needs. However, the visits drag because Eitan is determined to drive home the needs of the community. Also on the negative side, the Mayor prattles on far too long, losing any effectiveness his message may have had. The visitors' reactions vary. Some show irritation as they view with distaste the dirty streets. Others are too tired to react one way or another. The rousing performance of the Choral Group brings the visit to an upbeat close.

This is my first experience with such a visit. I want to be identified with Kfar Oranim's residents but I don't want to be seen as an easy conduit for requests to Croydon. Having managed to dispel that notion in my first week on the job, I am determined to avoid any change in the course of this visit.

Vered thinks my role in the visit should center on the schedule. She holds me responsible for our visitors' late arrival. Moreover, she thinks I must pressure them and the agencies to adhere to the schedule. She is an expert on budgets, but she is naive about the time tables of tourists. Between visitors and hosts, bus drivers and guides are driven to distraction. This is no tour of an archaeological site which can be inspected in a fixed time. Overseas partners come a vast distance to be with their "twin" community. Who is to say, "Okay, folks it's time to leave! The next agency awaits you!", when the visitors are sitting on the floor accompanying kindergarteners in a sing-song? Or, who is to ask the guests to leave in the midst of the Youth Orchestra's concert to catch the bus for the next stop on the itinerary? There are best-laid plans which are fated to go astray. The Croydon mission visit belongs to that category.

October 28, 1981 - Kfar Oranim

Edith, a Croydon community leader, is spending a day in Kfar Oranim, seeing professionals and attending a sub-committee meeting. She is interested in concrete projects but is also alert to the intangible factors which affect the "twin" relationship. She has been to Junius where she met with Adah who, along with Ariela and Noam, supports efforts to help their neighboring community. I have not met Adah but I plan to and Edith gives me the telephone number. She also provides a list of projects Croydon has agreed to pay for and this is most helpful. She asked Dan, the Director of the Community Center, to send her an enumeration of equipment needed by the agencies in Kfar Oranim and I promise to follow up on this.

November 2, 1981 - Junius

I visit Ariela in her home. A socially aware person, she is irked by the snobbishness and indifference manifested by most Junius residents to Kfar Oranim. She readily agrees to work with me and the students I am bringing to Kfar Oranim.

Kfar Oranim

Uri and I review the plans for the students. Eitan provides further clarification about the funds for Ramit, the Orthodox day care center.

November 9, 1981 - Kafar Oranim

We have more visitors from Croydon today but first I talk with Vered and Dan about the students. I get a mixed response, especially from Dan. He has a protective attitude toward the Community Center which he directs. He puts its interests above the general community good and I decide to work through the Junius volunteers rather than through Dan.

The Croydon group is much smaller than the last one and the visit is less draggy. Unfortunately, the Youth Orchestra is not up to snuff partly because the conductor was just released from military reserve duty for a few hours to lead the group. Even without rehearsals, the Orchestra makes a fair impression. The agency visits are shorter with the highlight being a stop at the dental clinic where a Croydon dentist who is in the group shows special interest.

The visit culminates with a reception at the home of Ariela and Noam which I arranged on short notice to show that there is a host at the Israeli end and not just a petitioning beneficiary. Noam's comments reflect his brash individualism but also his genuine concern for Kfar Oranim. The gracious hospitality he and Ariela show make the visit a positive experience for the Croydon group.

We clearly need to provide regular opportunities for such thoughtful encounters between Croydon visitors and residents of Kfar Oranim and Junius. I increasingly feel we must foster a collaborative relationship between Croydon and Junius in a strategy of aided self-help in Kfar Oranim.

November 17, 1981 - Kfar Oranim

I meet with Mordecai, Secretary of the Kfar Oranim branch of the Labor Party. I want to get his organization to help enlarge work opportunities for Kfar Oranim youth.

I point out that even though Labor is no longer in power, it still commands tremendous resources in its banks, health organization,industries, supermarkets, etc. Just as its affiliate, Na'mat, participates in day care programs in Kfar Oranim so should the Labor Party branch concern itself with the vocational outlook for youth. Mordecai listens quietly and then tells me that, in the last election, 2,200 Kfar Oranim citizens cast their ballots for Likud, as compared with 900 who voted for Labor. Despite this, he agrees his Party should play a role along the lines of my suggestion. He will discuss the matter with the manager of the local Labor Party-controlled bank. We agree

43

to keep in touch and he offers to arrange an appointment with his boss, the head of the Labor Party branch. We set a tentative time. I see Eitan to tell him of my meeting with Mordecai so as to avoid conjecture about my involvement in local politics.

I spend time with Micha, a volunteer from a nearby kibbutz. He visits Kfar Oranim to tutor youngsters who have trouble with school work. We get together for me to learn about this activity.

November 22, 1981 - Kfar Oranim

The students and I meet with Ariela in Uri's office. She knows one who directed an organization in which she was a volunteer. Ariela emphasizes practical work over theory. She identifies programs in which the students could help. One is a used clothing store which she, Adah and other volunteers operate. Another is cleaning up Kfar Oranim's streets. After two hours, we plan a second meeting to include other volunteers. Since Ariela will be abroad for the coming three weeks, we decide to await her return inasmuch as she is an influential person in both Kfar Oranim and Junius. Meanwhile, the students will try to recruit volunteers in Kfar Oranim.

November 29, 1981 - Kfar Oranim

A budget meeting is convened by Vered to decide on priorities among the items approved by the sub-committees. Only professionals are present and disappointment is expressed about the absence of lay people. Eitan suggests we postpone the meeting to a time when lay people can attend. Vered agrees but she wants those who are here to do their own priority rankings. We go over the items and everyone feels each one is of the highest importance. The exercise strikes me as a poor example of setting priorities.

November 30, 1981 - Kfar Oranim, Junius

Eitan and I visit three day care centers and the technical "high school". We inspect the renovations in the day care centers and we learn about the educational program in the technical "high school", all financed by Project Renewal funds from Croydon.

I proceed to the home of Adah and Myron in Junius. This visit was arranged following my conversation with Edith on October 28, 1981. I hope to interest Adah and Myron in joining Ariela to serve as a leadership core in helping with Kfar Oranim's development.

We discuss the involvement of Junius volunteers in Kfar Oranim. Adah and Myron emphasize tennis and golf projects to teach youngsters sports skills, thus building their self-image and sense of self-worth. Other scattered projects are mentioned and it becomes clear that an organized approach is needed. Adah is glad to hear about the assignment of students to Kfar Oranim. She hopes they will help the Junius volunteers.

I must leave to keep an appointment with the Mayor. Reference to the Mayor evokes critical comment by Adah and Myron. They

44

know a lot about Kfar Oranim politics even though they insist they do not want to be involved in political hassles. Adah hints that Kfar Oranim politics are on the unseemly side.

December 6, 1981 - Junius

I return to the home of Adah and Myron to continue last week's discussion. I introduce the idea of Croydon and Junius cooperating in Kfar Oranim and they are receptive. Adah, who is more active than her husband, says we should wait until Ariela returns before launching any activity. I agree. I tell Adah and Myron about my conversation with Dalia who uses her house in Junius weekends. Dalia called to urge that I interest Croydon in erecting a tennis facility in Kfar Oranim, similar to one in Keren Malka. Dalia asked Dennis, the Director of the Keren Malka Tennis Center, to get in touch with me. She cannot be at our meeting because she is leaving for the United States. The constant traveling of affluent Junius residents makes it hard to bring them together for planning purposes. Since Adah and Myron are pleased at the prospect of a tennis center in Kfar Oranim, I ask if they would join my meeting with Dennis. They demur because their main interest is the used clothing store. Also, they give high priority to Kfar Oranim's sanitation problem. Adah reiterates her readiness to recruit Junius volunteers to help Kfar Oranim.

Kfar Oranim

I meet with Aaron, who is in charge of work with problem youth, and with his two supervisors — one from the Ministry of Education and the other from the Ministry of Labor and Social Affairs. Before the meeting, Aaron told me the supervisors are interested in setting up an enterprise in Kfar Oranim that will be built by the youth. Our meeting does not bear this out. The supervisors disagree about handling problem youth and, in any event, the resources they command are negligible. I come away hoping their supervision is more effective. Clearly, Aaron cannot look to them for help in the youth program.

December 7, 1981 — Kfar Oranim

Officials from the Ministry of Health are here to inspect Project Renewal programs. Eitan and I accompany them on their rounds. We go to a day care center in a relatively new building which has a leak that creates a one-inch pool of water through which the children have to wade to carry on their activities. We are told there is no money for repairs. To cover the dry part of the floor, which is too cold for the children to sit on, Zalman was asked to contribute a rug. He owns the Scopus Manufacturing Company which makes rugs in Kfar Oranim and he is also a member of the Knesset. The request was turned down.

This center is in a neighborhood populated by families from the Caucasus Mountains of Russia, the "Kafkazim", along with some immigrants from Arab countries. One Ministry of Health representative comments that this day care center is at the end of the world. It does appear isolated but more people are expected to settle the area in the future.

We next visit the Tandor School in a new building that is not yet occupied. The Ministry of Education refuses to equip the building until burglar bars, now on the first floor, are installed on the second floor as well. Ministry officials fear that furniture will be hoisted out of the windows by Kfar Oranim's innovative thieves. The attractive building has no classroom walls, having been erected with the pedagogical idea of open classroom space. There is no money for portable partitions which are to be used as needed. The air raid shelter has been designed to double as a theater in order to save money.

Our final stop is a well-baby clinic which stresses education for mothers on how to engage their babies in play activities. The clinic is housed in a cottage too small for its health functions, let alone for the well-conceived educational program.

December 13, 1981

I attend a day-long seminar of Kfar Oranim residents and professional workers in a nearby resort. There are 103 participants of whom 63 are lay people. The rest are professionals and other functionaries. This is a most impressive turnout.

The Mayor opens the seminar. Marcus then gives an overview of Project Renewal. He is the Ministry of Housing official in charge of Project Renewal and is the counterpart of Hanoch in the Jewish Agency. These two men direct Project Renewal. Hanoch cannot be present. The Jewish Agency is represented by Yonatan who gives a clear description of Project Renewal's five-year plan. Yonatan acknowledges the difficulties of the first years, seeing them as indispensable learning years. He says the remaining years will be different because the residents themselves will decide what is going to happen. Such a comment would have been inconceivable prior to the advent of Project Renewal.

The discussions are actively guided - even directed. The lay people listen quietly to the experts but speak up in the small groups. As I move around, the most worrisome problem I hear mentioned is the presence in Kfar Oranim of the ghettoized "Kafkazim". They are virtually cut off from the rest of the community. One participant asks, "Why don't they send American immigrants? Why only 'Kafkazim'?"

Everyone is asked to rank needs and problems in order of concern. The chairman promises to tabulate the results and report at another community meeting. The final session consists of summaries from the small groups. Unlike the morning presentations, these reports are given by lay people.

There is general satisfaction with the quality of the discussion and the size of the turnout. I have reservations because I see too much domination by professionals. It would be preferable to have the lay people arrive at priorities without control by the professionals.

December 21, 1981 - Kfar Oranim

I meet with Yuval, head of the Kfar Oranim school system. He is a 36-year-old man who has been on the job for three months. He is relaxed, good-humored and open to suggestions. Before coming to Kfar Oranim, he was in the United States for three years, serving as a Jewish educator.

I share with him my hope to improve the self-image of Kfar Oranim's residents. I indicate that I have made little headway and I attribute this, at least in part, to the lack of cooperation among the local agencies. I ask Yuval to break the impasse by forming a central council of the parents' associations in Kfar Oranim's elementary schools.

Yuval asserts that he too is concerned with the low state of morale in Kfar Oranim. However, he can't do anything at the moment. The parents' associations are caught up in the election campaign, supporting Yehuda, an opponent of the incumbent Mayor. Yehuda claims the Mayor withholds school funds and he implies that there has been misappropriation of funds. The Tandor School principal openly charges that school funds are being misused. The authorities in Jerusalem have frozen the funds pending an investigation. As a result, money for needed improvements and for cultural enrichment is not available and the children are suffering.

I tell Yuval I understand why this is an inopportune time for my idea and I suggest we form a council of students instead. Maybe, they could teach their parents a lesson. Yuval likes this idea and we agree to think about next steps. I promise to set down some guidelines for the student council as a basis for our further consideration.

December 23, 1981 — Kfar Oranim

Today, the whole town is at the Community Center for Mother-of-the-Year awards. My wife was invited to attend and we are greeted warmly. The hall is full although the program won't start for another half-hour. To avoid the crush, we go to the rear but are summoned to sit in front with all the notables. I see this as expressing my personification of Croydon among the people of Kfar Oranim. During my visits, many residents ask if I know their friends or relatives in the United States. The warmth they show expresses their characteristic friendliness, a feeling that is palpable in the hall today. The Kfar Oranim Youth Orchestra starts the festivities. They seem louder than usual, perhaps because we are sitting up front. Chanukah candles are lit to observe the holiday and Ariela is called to the podium. Her remarks are brief and gracious. She and her husband, Noam, are the sponsors of the affair. Prizes are distributed to the Mothers-of-the-Year. A summary is given of each woman's remarkable

47

achievements. Despite their modest circumstances, they have seen their children through to successful careers as doctors, lawyers and teachers. The evening closes with a fashion show which I find boring, even though Israeli clothes are stylish. The crowd enjoys the performance of presentations, entertainment and rituals. The affair is certainly good for Kfar Oranim.

December 30, 1981 — Kfar Oranim

The Sub-Committee on Formal Education meets to discuss budgets but the members pull the session in another direction. Two principals quarrel about the complaint which led the Ministry of Education to freeze school funds pending an investigation. Eitan and Vered remind the principals that the meeting is going to waste. Their agenda is budget review but they are ignored. The poor quality of education in Kfar Oranim becomes the subject for discussion. One principal complains that Kfar Oranim is a forsaken place. Another echoes his sentiments. The teachers are good, they insist, and they work harder than teachers elsewhere. However, they can't get results because the low cultural level of the students is too big an obstacle.

The Parents Association representative pleads passionately for the principals and teachers to rise to the challenge presented by Kfar Oranim. As a lay person, she spares no effort to help the town. She expects no less from the professionals. Vered loses patience with the discussion and a shouting match results. A few minutes later, the meeting ends in disarray.

Yuval and I talk about my student council suggestion. I give him the outline I had promised. We are joined by one of the university students assigned to Kfar Oranim for his field placement. He asks about the possibility of working with the "Kafkazim". He learned of their living in a ghetto with their children concentrated in one school. He understands that pupils attend their neighborhood school but he would like to tackle this and other problems of the "Kafkazim". Yuval says the difficulties are too deep-seated for part-time intervention by a student. The student accepts Yuval's statement and indicates he is ready to help organize the student council.

January 4, 1982 — Kfar Oranim

Since I could not be at the meeting when Aaron presented his budget proposal to the Sub-Committee on Problem Youth, he makes a special presentation to me. I tell him I understand he wants me to get Croydon's approval but I say that he will have to follow the established procedure. Approval by the Steering Committee must precede communication with Croydon. Also, I make it clear that I will need Vered's advice about the reaction of Project Renewal, Jerusalem to the budget. Aaron's notion of getting budget approval is simplistic. I wonder why he is not getting supervision on this matter.

I tell Aaron he needs an advisory committee of influential persons

48

from Kfar Oranim and Junius to give his program legitimation. It is a mistake for him to act alone. The status and guiding presence of an advisory committee are essential. He is eager to establish such a leadership group and he asks if I will serve on it. I promise to help and we make another appointment to continue the discussion.

Aaron has ability and energy but he is under a shadow because he antagonizes people by his independent approach.

Yuval has read my memo on the Student Council and is ready to proceed with the project. I remind him that one of the university students is prepared to assist. Yuval says this will give him the help he needs; he is pleased. Moreover, since the student is experienced in community work, Yuval can spend less time in supervision than would be required were the student a beginner. I assure Yuval that I will be available for consultation or for any other needed assistance.

January 11, 1982 — Kfar Oranim

I meet with Ephraim, head of the Labor Party branch in Kfar Oranim to follow up my session with Mordecai, secretary of the Labor Party branch.

Ephraim is a hearty man in his mid-forties. We talk about the Labor Party in Kfar Oranim. He is cautious since his Party is now the opposition in Israel. I point out that it still commands enormous resources and could play an important part in Kfar Oranim's economic development. I am eager to get him to help in the work opportunity program which I have proposed to bring jobs to the town's youth. He is wary, hinting that he needs direction from his superiors in Tel Aviv and Jerusalem. He implies this is not a good time for his Party to become involved. The recent election resulted in bad feeling between supporters of the country's two main parties. Ephraim assures me that he is willing to cooperate but I am convinced he will take no initiative.

January 17, 1982 — Kfar Oranim

I get together with Tamar who tells me a clean-up program has started. She is working on this with Yuval.

I ask Tamar's opinion about the assignment of the student who wants to work with the "Kafkazim" despite Yuval's discouragement. It has been suggested that one way to get their participation is through a synagogue building project. Tamar feels it is important to help the "Kafkazim" become active in the community. She sees the need for them first to develop their own leaders. However, she questions the value of the synagogue project for achieving these ends. Only the older "Kafkazim" will be interested and Tamar asserts that the younger and middle-aged ones have to be brought in. A recreation center would have a better chance of attracting their support. She adds that the town's future depends on fostering leadership capacities of young people. I tell her I will relay her excellent ideas to the student.

49

I go to the Mayor's office to discuss the "Kafkazim". He chairs
a committee charged with integrating them into the community. It
is supposed to focus on the ghettoization of the "Kafkazim" in one
neighborhood and one school. So far, nothing has been done. I tell
the Mayor that a university student will be available to help the
committee. He is pleased and says he will work with the student.
I declare that his leadership is crucial if integration is to be achieved.
His limited interest in the matter is shown when he abruptly changes
the subject to ask how I feel about my work in Kfar Oranim generally.
I reply appropriately but briefly and I come back to the student who
will be seeing the Mayor soon. He assures me of his cooperation
but I am dubious.

January 26, 1982 — Kfar Oranim

Yuval informs me progress has been made in forming a student
council along the lines of my proposal. The university student has
effectively interpreted the idea to the principals but Yuval had to
intervene before they all accepted the plan. They were reluctant to
take on another chore, insisting they already have more than enough
on their hands. Youngsters in one school are engaged in helping old
people as their civic work. Other pupils are engaged in clean-up activity,
giving a "summons" to persons not maintaining cleanliness. Most
people take it nicely and are stimulated to clean their area. Yuval
told the principals that the work under way needs broadening and
coordinating through a student council. He succeeded in winning their
approval and they finally agreed to send representatives to the first
meeting with the university student.

I attend a session of the Steering Committee. The Mayor expresses
regret about recent newspaper articles which criticize Project Renewal.
He asks Committee members to avoid interviews with reporters since
they are slanting the stories to emphasize the negative aspects of Project
Renewal.

The meeting becomes contentious. The neighborhood representatives
ignore the Mayor and demand instead that the Steering Committee
stop work to protest the failure of the Ministry of Housing to make
physical improvements. While social programs are proceeding
reasonably well, there has been one delay after another in physical
rehabilitation work. Demands are vigorously voiced by the
neighborhood representatives who constitute one-third of the 21
Steering Committee members in attendance.

The militancy of the residents is due in part to their having gained
national press and TV attention with their demonstration against
Zalman, owner of the Scopus Manufacturing Company. The dispute
was about land next to the factory which the residents claim was
set aside for community expansion but which Zalman is acquiring
to enlarge his enterprise. The land was quickly transformed into a

forest of home-made signs, proclaiming that the Scopus Manufacturing Company is seeking to increase its holdings at the expense of Kfar Oranim's growth potential. Zalman threatened to move his factory and a sullen truce has set in. Having tested their strength, the residents are now militantly demanding that the Steering Committee cease work as an act of protest.

The Mayor asks that the decision be postponed until Eitan, the Committee's Executive Secretary, returns from military reserve duty. Several people speak up noisily. Hanoch, from Project Renewal headquarters, is present as a guest. He captures the floor long enough to try persuading the community representatives not to go through with their demand. His efforts fall on deaf ears and the din resumes.

Suddenly, the Mayor stands up and announces he has to leave to greet important out-of-town guests who are here for the theater performance that will take place in the Community Center. He reminds everyone to come to the show, turns the chair over to the Deputy Mayor and makes a speedy exit.

The demand for a stoppage peters out and Vered is asked to give her report. She summarizes the recent community conference, highlighting the problems which were identified as troubling Kfar Oranim. She is lauded but Shulamith, the representative of Na'mat, tempers the praise for Vered by asserting that neither the chairmen nor the sub-committee members know what is really going on in the programs they consider. Vered and others respond by pointing out that, if people only took the trouble to read the material which is sent to them, they would understand everything. Before there can be further dispute, the Deputy Mayor stops the meeting, saying it is time for us all to go the Community Center. We file out.

The disjointed nature of this meeting suggests that Shulamith's charge is valid. I am glad that Hanoch witnessed the poor quality of deliberations. I plan to follow this up with him and his staff in Jerusalem.

Before we enter the auditorium, I have a brief, cordial chat with Hanoch concerning the youth work opportunity project. He is preoccupied these days with newspaper attacks on Project Renewal and with the dissension this is causing. Ariela and Noam appear. I tell Ariela that Dan talked with me about a tour of the United States for the Youth Orchestra. She doubts the value of such a tour, saying it could turn the heads of the youth to thoughts of emigrating. I promise to bring this issue to Dan's attention.

We enter the overflowing auditorium. The play is amateurishly written with much blustery, slow-moving rhetoric. However, the youngsters tackle their roles virogously, much to the delight of the audience. I find the play dull but the residents hang on to every word. The play saddens me because it implies contempt for the Jewish pioneers who built Israel. They are perceived by Kfar Oranim's youth as part of a resented, unfeeling establishment.

January 29, 1982 — Junius

I go to Adah's home where she, Dalia, Ariela and I discuss a tennis program for Kfar Oranim similar to one in Keren Malka.

That successful program has established branches elsewhere in Israel. The idea for consideration is setting up a branch in Kfar Oranim. Dalia is sure the Keren Malka people will cooperate if Kfar Oranim takes the initiative. She believes she can muster support in Junius and she proudly announces she has a promise from Israel's former women's tennis champion to volunteer as a coach. Dalia turns to me and tells me I need to investigate the availability of land for tennis courts, preferably close to the Community Center. I promise to check this out. Ariela interjects that the residents of Kfar Oranim must approve before we proceed. I concur, adding that we are only discussing possibilities at this time. Nothing is said about financial support from Croydon, although this is implicit.

Ariela asks if I spoke with Rafael, the Director of the Youth Orchestra. He talked with her, urging that an American tour be arranged for the Orchestra. Dan, the Community Center Director, is also pushing the idea. Dalia and Adah are opposed. They doubt the Youth Orchestra will be a drawing card in the United States. I remember Ariela's concern that a tour might lure the youth into emigrating and I refrain from expressing an opinion, saying I have no expertise to judge the appeal of the Youth Orchestra to American audiences. This is a decision for Croydon since it will be asked to foot the bill.

Before the meeting ends, Adah produces a copy of the 1981-82 Project Renewal budget for Kfar Oranim. Among the items Croydon agreed to support is an allocation of $250 for preliminary investigation of a tennis project.

February 1, 1982 — Kfar Oranim

I talk with Yuval to make sure the meeting of the university student with representatives of the four schools will take place as planned. He assures me it is all set. He invites me to attend a meeting he has scheduled with the principals. I know how touchy the principals are and I wonder if I would be intruding. Yuval insists that, as Croydon's representative, I have a right to attend all community meetings. Besides, he says I will not interfere with their deliberations. I indicate I will try to come for at least part of the meeting but I have several other appointments scheduled. One is with Aaron, the youth worker and the other is with Tamar, the community worker.

Yuval tells me that both are suspect in the eyes of the Major who believes they are supporting Yehuda who wants to unseat him. Aaron complicated matters by going over the head of the Mayor to appeal to the Deputy Minister of Labor and Social Affairs for help with his program for alienated youth. The Mayor is incensed about Aaron's trotting off to see a high government official without clearance. According to Yuval, the Mayor is finished with the matter even though he has received a call from the Deputy Minister with whom Aaron spoke.

I see Tamar who tells me about a survey she is doing with the help of Richard, one of the university students. The aim is to ascertain how young couples feel about their future in Kfar Oranim. I make some suggestions about the study.

I tell Tamar some people see her as on the side of the Mayor's rival in the forthcoming election and I point out that non-involvement of professionals in politics is important. She knows about this, having been alerted by Dan, the Director of the Community Center. She is careful to keep out of politics, but her parents are known supporters of Yehuda, the Mayor's opponent. This may be so but I heard her tell Aaron to invite Yehuda to serve on the sponsoring committee which I recommended as a way of strengthening Aaron's hand in the community.

Politics in Kfar Oranim are pursued with great intensity. The professionals are constantly scrutinized by the Mayor to make sure of their neutrality. It is considered ethically improper for civil servants to take sides in the campaign.

I meet with Aaron, the youth worker, to discuss the program he presented at the last meeting of the Steering Committee which called for an expenditure of IL 4,850,000. Hanoch, the head of Project Renewal, who was at the meeting, suggested that Aaron visit other towns to look at youth programs before decisions are made about such substantial expenditures. Aaron claimed he already made such visits. His proposal is based on a successful program which he saw in Haifa. I had urged him to make his peace with Hanoch. Since I agreed to try to help Aaron without becoming a member of his sponsoring committee, I arranged today's get-together to pursue these matters.

Aaron is still angry. He cannot get money for his program and he hints it is being misappropriated. I don't want to get into this colloquy, since I know the money is being held back because of lack of confidence in Aaron. He is not fully aware of this. I am determined to discuss the matter with Eitan when he returns from military reserve duty. I am anxious for the issue to be resolved as soon as possible.

I drop in to ask the Mayor if the university student has been to see him about the integration of the "Kafkazim". He tells me he saw the student and advised him as to how best to launch the activity.

I mention the negative newspaper articles about Project Renewal. I am concerned that these articles will reach Croydon and raise questions among contributors to Pro]ect Renewal. I suggest a letter from him setting the record straight insofar as Kfar Oranim is concerned may be helpful. The Mayor and his Deputy who is in the room, agree such a letter makes sense. They assert, not too convincingly, that it will be forthcoming.

By this time, it is too late to attend Yuval's meeting with the principals. I arrive barely in time for the session of the school representatives with Ehud, the university student. About 20 youngsters between the ages of 14 and 15, representing Kfar Oranim's four schools, show up. Ehud opens by asking them to identify themselves. He then skillfully leads the students into a discussion of Kfar Oranim's problems. They cite many of the same issues as are identified by adults: cleanliness, ghettoization of the "Kafkazim", low morale, etc. The young people enthusiastically indicate their readiness to work on these problems. Ehud agrees to convene them again to make plans but they will need to wait a month while he is away for reserve duty.

February 3, 1982 — Kfar Oranim

On Eitan's return from military reserve duty, we meet to review several matters. First, I fulfill my commitment to the Junius volunteers by asking about land for the tennis courts.He tells me provision has been made for tennis courts in the sports area being planned near the Tandor School. This is far from the Community Center and I say I will talk further about this location with Dan, the Director of the Community Center.

Next, I inform Eitan that I received from Croydon a "Working Paper for Kfar Oranim, 1982-1983", showing items budgeted at a total expenditure of $855,000. I ask why I have to rely on Croydon for such information. Eitan is baffled. He has not seen the paper. All he had was a phone call from Jerusalem, giving a budget of $750,000 for 1982-1983. He breaks into a smile, realizing that my paper shows an increase of $105,000 over the figure he was given. This is unclear and we decide to ask Vered for an explanation.

Eitan introduces the subject of a music conservatory. Kfar Oranim received permission to establish the program and a building is now needed to house it. Do I think a donor could be found in Croydon for whom the building would be named in recognition of such a gift? I ask how much money is needed. After some quick calculations, he comes up with a figure of $400,000. I tell him the subject should be raised with the Croydon delegation when it visits in the near future.

February 11, 1982 — Kfar Oranim

Tamar, Richard and I meet to discuss their study of young couples. After we finish, Richard tells me Tamar fears her days on the job are numbered. She has been identified as a partisan in the mayoralty race on the side of Yehuda, the "sworn enemy" of the incumbent. Even if there is any truth to the rumor that the present Mayor has decided not to run again, he will undoubtedly name a candidate to oppose Yehuda and Tamar's situation will remain unchanged. Richard knows enough to steer clear of local politics because of our discussions about Kfar Oranim as a seething cauldron of political intrigue.

I go to see Dan about his cherished wish to have the Youth Orchestra tour the United States. He sees this as good for the youngsters and as bringing pride to Kfar Oranim. He thinks Croydon need not be the sole support for the trip. The parents and the Town Council can provide some funds. Dan mentions that there are 33 members of the Youth Orchestra.

I say Ariela is supportive of the Orchestra but has doubts because the trip might give the youngsters ideas of emigration. The conductor tried to dissuade her from this fear. He told her of the successful trip to Germany by a similar group from another town. I suggest that since the Choral Group made a hit with the Croydon visitors and that since it has 18 members, maybe a trip for this smaller group should be considered, substantially reducing the cost. We agree to talk about this with the conductor when I am next in Kfar Oranim.

February 14, 1982 — Keren Malka

Dalia and I visit Keren Malka to discuss a tennis program in Kfar Oranim under the supervision of the Keren Malka Tennis Center. We meet with Naomi, the director of public relations for the Keren Malka Tennis Center and with Dennis, an ardent supporter. He is a prosperous dental surgeon who came to Israel 8 years ago from South Africa. Bitten by the tennis bug, he advocates it as a sport and also as a way of socializing youth to community responsibility and to civic graces.

I ask the cost of four tennis courts. Dennis says it would range from $30,000 to $60,000 per court, depending on the soil and the topography. If there are no unusual problems, he estimates the total cost as between $250,000 and $300,000 for four courts and showers. Dalia asserts this amount is in the Kfar Oranim Project Renewal budget for 1982-1983. This is not in accord with my information but I decide not to contradict her.

Naomi and Dennis are planning to visit Croydon soon to meet with American supporters of tennis in Israel. I mention that Phillip who lives in Croydon and who is United States chairman of Project Renewal as well as an avid supporter of tennis in Israel will probably be at the meeting. I suggest they consult him regarding a tennis program in Kfar Oranim.

Dennis wants evidence that Kfar Oranim will support a tennis program, showing us letters from other Israeli towns, asking the Keren Malka Tennis Center to start the program. Dalia replies that we recognize a tennis program cannot be imposed on Kfar Oranim. I say I will ascertain the feeling in the town about a tennis program.

If the idea is acceptable and if Phillip agrees to get financial support, then I am ready to develop leadership for the program among Kfar Oranim residents. Dennis candidly tells us that their trip is designed to raise money for existing tennis programs in Israel rather than to start new ones. I reiterate that it would be important to consult Phillip and Dennis agrees to do so.

February 15, 1982 — Kfar Oranim

Eitan and I discuss the problem of Aaron's credibility. I say I don't want to interfere in local politics but I need to know what the situation is since Aaron's program is financed by Croydon. I sense Eitan's impatience. He asserts that Aaron is too aggressive, demanding complete autonomy for his work with alienated youth. This is impossible since Aaron must be accountable to Project Renewal and to the Steering Committee just like all other professionals in the program. Eitan tells me that Aaron's predecessor, who he thinks was more capable than Aaron, was dismissed because he refused to work within Project Renewal policies. Eitan alludes to Aaron's seeing the Deputy Minister of Labor and Social Affairs without clearance. Aaron's presumption has made an enemy of the Mayor. Moreover, Aaron is asking for an excessively large portion of the Project Renewal budget. He ignores all other needs. It is not right to spend so much money on an untried program.

I ask Eitan why Aaron is being kept on with so much doubt about him. Eitan responds that many people think Aaron's ideas are sound and they hope he will become less aggressive and more cooperative. I tell Eitan that Aaron is waiting to hear about our meeting. He is non-committal.

I go to Aaron's office and I say that while there is respect for his ideas about alienated youth, people resent him because he is perceived as overly-aggressive. I mention his approach to the Deputy Minister of Labor and Social Affairs. Aaron's anger verges on despair. He is not mollified by respect for his ideas. Kfar Oranim's leaders are just toying with him.

I ask if he can reduce the cost of the work opportunity program by viewing it as a pilot project. He replies by querying me as to how he can reduce the cost of a truck — even an old one. The truck is essential to get the youth started on contract work involving earth removal, sanitation, and land fill. He is confident this cooperative venture will be financially viable and would benefit the youngsters.

He cites an incident in which he was led to believe he could appoint part-time group leaders in his program. After he invited candidates for interviews, he was told there is no money for salaries. I ask him point-blank why he stays on the job in view of his frustration and his sense that he has no support from Kfar Oranim's leaders. He answers that he will soon decide whether to leave or to stay. He wants to start the work opportunity program because he cares for the young people in his charge. If he decides to leave after the program is initiated, at least he will feel he has accomplished something. I wish I could stand up for him but he has antagonized too many people and I reluctantly tell him I cannot go to bat for him. He is undoubtedly disappointed but he maintains his pleasant demeanor and says he understands my position. His response indicates that he feels little can be done to reverse the negative attitudes toward him.

I wonder about his two supervisors from the Ministry of Education and the Ministry of Labor and Social Affairs. There is no evidence of their helping Aaron with his impulsiveness, his aggressiveness and his poor personal relationships. As we part, Aaron says the leaders in Kfar Oranim disapprove of his political views. He claims this is at the root of his difficulties. However, he insists that his politics are his private business and there will be absolutely no give on his part.

I return to Eitan. He and Vered are busy with the contractor who is enlarging the day care centers, using Project Renewal funds. I stay with them for a half-hour as they carefully review every item but then I need to leave to keep my next appointment.

On my way out, I am stopped by two neighborhood leaders who want to explain their demand for a cessation of activities at the last meeting of the Steering Committee. Not only were they upset by what they termed a "land grab" by Zalman, the owner of the Scopus Manufacturing Company, but they were also incensed by what occurred before the Steering Committee met that day.

Twenty neighborhood representatives went to Jerusalem to protest the transfer of Kfar Oranim's town planner to another locality. They were infuriated by this action since they saw her as a good town planner. Sending her elsewhere symbolized the indifference of the Ministry of Housing to Kfar Oranim's needs. Their visit to Jerusalem was a failure since they could not get to see any top officials in the Ministry. They were received by a bureaucrat who was powerless. This experience showed their lack of clout. It helped to make them more militant when they attended the Steering Committee meeting where they tried to demonstrate strength by demanding a stoppage of Steering Committee activities.

Since I was already late for my next appointment, I delayed it further to see the Mayor. He says nothing about the letter to Croydon to counteract the bad press which Project Renewal is receiving. I do not raise the issue and I am sure that it will rest there.

Amos, the Deputy Mayor, tells me that he is leaving to resume his profession as an engineer. His decision is wise since he has been ineffectual as Deputy Mayor. He has virtually been forced to resign since he refused to relocate from Haifa to Kfar Oranim.

I finally get to the Community Center where Rafael and Dan are waiting. Dan has a new idea. He wants the 33 members of the Youth Orchestra *and* the 18 members of the Choral Group to make the trip to the United States. Rafael doesn't agree because it will mean asking Croydon for too much money. Also, he feels the skits and songs of the Choral Group in Hebrew would be meaningless to most American audiences. The performance of the Choral Group, he argues, would have limited appeal. Dan is adamant. He cannot choose one group over the other without hurting the youngsters and their parents. He points out that I told him the Croydon visitors enjoyed the Choral Group even though they performed in Hebrew. Since Croydon is asked to bear only part of the cost, he feels they will agree to sponsor the trip. Rafael comes round to Dan's position. I say they will be presenting Croydon with a sizeable request and I cannot predict the reaction. Neither can I guide them since I honestly do not know how either or both groups will be received in the United States. I tell Dan and Rafael I have written to Croydon to ask that time be set aside for the delegation to audition the groups during its visit. They agree this is a fair suggestion. Rafael says he will immediately start on rehearsals for the audition. I caution him that preparations should not be based on the assumption that either the audition or the trip are assured. He picks up my warning, saying that no one should know of our discussion since loose talk about an American tour will cause ill feeling if it does not materialize. I am surprised by their lack of judgement in expecting Croydon to pay for this costly junket.

The meeting ends and I tell Dan about Dalia's efforts to start a tennis program in Kfar Oranim. He is most enthusiastic and when I say Dennis wants proof of Kfar Oranim's support for the project, he immediately dictates a letter to his secretary which is to be signed by him, Eitan and the Mayor. As soon as the letter is typed, he dashes off to get the other signatures so that I may present the letter to Dennis before he leaves for the United States.

February 28, 1982 — Tel Aviv

I meet Vered at the Jewish Agency for a budget briefing. The printed copy is not ready yet so I talk about Aaron, the youth worker, who is having so much trouble. I tell her I am concerned about the alienated youth program. Eitan's preoccupation with other matters gives the program low priority. Since she can pressure Eitan, I ask her to help get the matter resolved. She thinks the problem of alienated youth is perhaps Kfar Oranim's toughest challenge. I point out that lack of faith in Aaron has brought work to a standstill. A decision is needed about his future. Vered concurs. She reviews the situation, adding some interesting background information.

Before Aaron came to Kfar Oranim, alienated youth work was divided among five different authorities. Aaron's predecessor tried to unify the work and eliminate the confusion. However, he was a radical who set the Ashkenazim and the Sephardim against each other. Stirring up conflict in order to bring about change led to his dismissal. When Aaron came, the work was centralized. People would like to give Aaron responsibility for the program but they are put off by his insistence on complete independence.

Vered describes a meeting she attended between Aaron and his two supervisors which had increased her ambivalence about him. Given her supervisory experience in a technical high school, she anticipated a disciplined discussion about specific programs. Instead, there was vague conversation about nothing in particular. While this wasn't all Aaron's fault, his ideas are experimental and he insists that they be launched immediately. He is impulsive and his personal relationships are deplorable. Yet, he is creative so there are pluses as well as minuses. I indicate that this ambivalence makes Aaron bitter. He winds up sounding like an ideologue rather than a professional. Vered feels he must be accountable to a group in Kfar Oranim; his demand for total autonomy is unreasonable. I suggest the group should include Uri, Dan, Eitan and Yuval. They could develop terms of reference with Aaron to guide his work. She likes this idea and will press for it tomorrow when she sees Eitan. She wants to tell him that I will also sit with the group and I agree.

As we end, I tell her that Croydon has asked for pictures to use in fund-raising but I have no money for a photographer. She promises to add this to her agenda for the meeting with Eitan and I indicate that I will pursue it too.

March 3, 1982 — Kfar Oranim

A protest demonstration against the Scopus Manufacturing Company is scheduled but it does not take place because of the heavy rain. There is a sign at the town entrance which says,in Hebrew, "The children of Kfar Oranim grew up in ma'aborot (temporary shelters) and Zalman (owner of the Scopus Manufacturing Company) has come to reap the fruit."

At the Welfare Department, I run into Yael, a Moroccan who represents a national organization working in the interest of large families. She is a devoted volunteer who is studying for her BA at the Labor Party college. In her typical hearty manner, she invites me to a Purim celebration. I accept since I welcome opportunities to meet the town's everyday residents.

In the heavy rain, I go to the Community Center to see Dan. Since he is unsure of his English, he asks me to help compose a reply to a letter from Croydon proposing a joint venture for old people. I promise to look after this. He feels he knows me now and he is more comfortable with me. I take advantage of the congenial feeling to raise a question which I had mentioned soon after I began my work. The town square where the Community Center sits is a barren place devoid of physical beauty. As a consequence, it is not used. Dan says if I saw it on a Friday evening or on a holiday when it is thronged with people. I would change my mind. I grant this but assert the town square should be a focal point on ordinary days as well. If the place were fixed up, it would tone up the town. I am leading to the possibility of bringing together people with physical and social planning skills to turn this expanse of bleak pavement into a human resource for Kfar Oranim. Dan points out that my idea would cost money. I can't deny the additional costs but I fear the transformation I would like to see is as distant as the work opportunity program for Kfar Oranim's youth.

I return to the Welfare Department. Tamar and I are meeting with Richard, the university student assigned to Kfar Oranim. As we wait, she tells me she has discussed with the Mayor the accusation that she is politically aligned against him. She assured him it is her parents who support his opponent, not she. He accepted her statement but warned her to stay away from Yehuda's campaign headquarters. This poses a problem since the place is frequented by the activists she needs to keep in touch with. Cutting herself off from them may only enmesh her more deeply in politics.

Richard enters and tells us he saw smoldering tires on the lot where the protest demonstration was to take place. After we finish, as I leave town, I see charred remains of tree trunks with curls of smoke rising from them, the rain having failed to extinguish the embers completely.

March 11, 1982 — Kfar Oranim

I see Yuval who welcomes me cordially although he is very downcast. He says he may be out as head of the school system. He talks about the three components of his job: administering the four elementary schools and the technical "high school", overseeing the enrichment programs for culturally deprived students and supervising the innovative educational programs which are financed by Project Renewal. When he started on the job six months ago, he was prepared to give it his all. "What went wrong?" I ask. He is not sure but he speculates. There is resentment about his not being a resident of Kfar Oranim; he is an Ashkenazi in a town dominated by Sephardim; the Deputy Mayor is gathering complaints from the workers under him. Yuval is worried because the labor market is tight and he has to support his wife and three children. He is anxious about his livelihood being so precarious. I urge he not yield to pessimism but this is of no help. I promise to inquire about job possibilities. I doubt he would be unemployed for long. Inquiring into other job opportunities is designed to give him some alternatives if required. He is grateful.

Yuval was informed that the Mayor objects to an expenditure of

IL 99,000 which Yuval approved and spent. This adds to his burdened feeling. I suggest he try to clear this up. He telephones the Mayor and insists that everything was done properly. The Mayor says the expenditure will need to be reviewed by the Town Council at its next meeting.

I go to the Community Center to give Dan the letter I wrote for him concerning the proposed venture between older adults in Kfar Oranim and Croydon. I translate the letter and he is pleased. He is eager to know when the Croydon delegation will arrive for budget discussions and I promise to let him know just as soon as I hear.

I meet with Aaron who wants to write to Croydon to complain that the money allocated for work with alienated youth is being denied to him. This is only partly true since his salary comes from Croydon Project Renewal funds. However, it is true that money for his activities is being held up. I say that writing a letter is his privilege but, in my judgment, it will worsen his already fragile position with the leaders of Kfar Oranim. Also, it will puzzle the people in Croydon. They will ask me to look into the situation. If he is determined to send a letter, I suggest he give it to me for transmission. He says he doesn't want to get me into trouble. I assure him he need not worry about that. We leave things inconclusively. I am not sure he will write the letter so I do not pursue the matter.

I return to Yuval's office and I mention that I have just come from Aaron whose mood is similar to his. Yuval wonders why Aaron has trouble with people. I point out that Yuval's situation is not much better than Aaron's even though he has no problems in his personal relationships. Yuval observes ruefully that this had not occurred to him.

When Hanoch originally introduced me to the Steering Committee on July 23, 1981, he said I might contribute to improving the social services in Kfar Oranim. Little did he or I anticipate what course this might take. By coincidence, Uri, Yuval and Tamar assumed their positions at the same time as I while Aaron preceded me by several weeks. Now all four face serious problems. Their situation amounts to a crisis in Kfar Oranim which is being ignored by everyone else. For me, this crisis is a point of entry, not so much to improve the social services as simply to insure that they keep functioning. As for Aaron, the only solution is to help hasten his departure.

Retaining the services of the others is crucial. If they leave, there is no way for this depressed community to replace them with better workers. I shall do all I can to keep them at their posts to avoid the disruption which the town can ill afford. On further thought, I see Aryeh, the part-time neighborhood worker, as joining the threatened group. He and Tamar are moving on a collision course, of which neither is yet aware as they pursue their interests in the neighborhoods.

March 15, 1982 — Tel Aviv

I meet with Stephen at the Jewish Agency. He is a senior executive in Project Renewal. We talked a number of times on the telephone but this our first face-to-face meeting.

We discuss Croydon's request for photos to help in fund-raising. Providing a photographer is one of his tasks, along with making arrangements for visiting missions, public relations, preparing budgets, overseeing expenditures and working with local steering committees. He tells me who to see for various services. Much of this is known to me. I say it is strange that I cannot deal directly with Croydon's request for photos but I am on my own when it comes to community problems.

Our discussion moves easily as he asks how things are going generally. I reply frankly that my effectiveness could be improved if his organization were a resource for community development. I assure him I am aware of the difficulties and the intricate politics which go beyond this one community. However, I assert that the Jewish Agency's power on budgetary matters could be used positively to resolve many issues. Such influence need not interfere with Kfar Oranim's autonomy.

I cite as an illustration the possibility that Yuval may be fired, thus wasting the six months he has spent in Kfar Oranim and delaying things for another six months while his successor is oriented. Such impulsive and politically inspired hiring and firing is detrimental to Kfar Oranim. My influence is limited since I am alone and the source of my authority is thousands of miles away. By contrast, if he and his colleagues were to exercise influence, Kfar Oranim's leaders might be persuaded to avoid an obviously counter-productive step.

Another example is the Steering Committee. Joint action by his office and Croydon could improve its deliberations. I am asking Stephen for cooperation in matters of central importance to his organization. He is sympathetic but says that he can't do much about my suggestions. He will look into Yuval's situation but there is little likelihood of his being able to accomplish anything.

March 17, 1982 — Kfar Oranim

I begin my meeting with Eitan and Vered by asking whether or not anything has been done about Yuval. Eitan replies that Yuval is a nice person. In fact, he claims he had a great deal to do with Yuval's appointment. However, he has picked up disturbing information since I first told him that Yuval might be fired. Some of the town's leaders feel Yuval lacks initiative. Moreover, he is tardy in submitting reports to the Ministry of Education and this hurts Kfar Oranim's budget.

Vered changes the subject. She asks us to accompany her to a nearby town to observe a youth project which Hanoch has urged us to see. She thinks Aaron should come along and I agree. I express my regret that I will be unable to join them since I have to teach at the time scheduled for the visit.

The photographer who is to take pictures for Croydon to use in fund-raising is discussed. We talk about times for him to come and places to photograph. Eitan will set a date and will call me. He angrily adds that he will have to call from the Community Center since the Ministry of Housing cut off outgoing calls on the suspicion that too many unnecessary calls are being made from his office.

I see Yuval who says he feels left out. The Mayor asked him to arrange with Dan a joint program between the schools and the Community Center for Israel's Independence Day. He has been unable to reach Dan. An assistant finally told him Dan is taking care of everything and there is nothing for Yuval to do. In fact, Dan refused to organize a program unless the Town Council provides funds.

March 18, 1982

I talk with Dennis on the telephone. He returned from the United States where he met Phillip and another Croydon leader. Both objected to a tennis program in Kfar Oranim since there is one in a neighboring town and in Junius. They are willing to provide travel money to these places but they do not want to duplicate what is close at hand. I tell Dennis the lack of amenities in Kfar Oranim has an adverse effect on the town's morale. While swimming facilities, good shopping and educational opportunities are all close by, the fact that Kfar Oranim residents have to travel to reach them has, over the years, built up a sense of inferiority. To be told about tennis courts that are available nearby will only reinforce their negative self-image. At the same time, I indicate I understand Croydon's reluctance to spend money for tennis courts when they can be used in a neighboring community.

March 28, 1982 — Kfar Oranim

I report to Eitan and Dan the decision about the tennis courts. As I anticipated, they insist that traveling to nearby communities, even if the costs are met, will only deepen Kfar Oranim's low morale and hasten the out-migration of its youth.

I meet with Tamar who tells me an advisory committee to Aaron has been formed along the lines of my suggestion. The membership is as I proposed: the heads of the school system, the Community Center, the Welfare Department and the local Project Renewal office — Yuval, Dan, Uri and Eitan. Vered will serve as chairperson. They are to meet regularly with Aaron for reports on his work. Tamar is optimistic that this accountability will solve the problem of Aaron's credibility. I am less sanguine since I learned from Eitan that the Mayor is determined to get rid of Aaron. Also, for this reason, I have given up the idea of a citizen's sponsoring group.

March 29, 1982 — Kfar Oranim

I visit Malachti, the local trade school, to see it for myself. I have heard different opinions about this school. Eitan and Aryeh consider it to be a praiseworthy institution. Aaron and Tamar have a contrary view. They say Malachti keeps youngsters off the streets but its reputation is so bad that parents won't send children there to learn a trade.

Avram, the principal of the school greets me. After some preliminary wariness, he warms up. He is a concentration camp survivor who, ironically, learned to be a mechanic under the Nazis.

Avram tells me that there are 50 students in the school. They come from culturally deprived homes; their parents are only interested in the money they bring home. Many are delinquents with police records. All are school drop-outs. Their initial adjustment to Malachti is hard because Avram insists on discipline in attendance and studying. While some do not succeed, Avram is proud of those who do. He would be pleased to arrange for me to visit the work places where his graduates hold jobs and earn a living. He says that some machine shops in the area send work to the school and the money earned is given to the students. He is pleased by the space and equipment he has managed to acquire. He hints broadly that Croydon should support the school. I tell him I will let Kfar Oranim's friends in Croydon know about Malachti but I cannot recommend singling it out for special attention.

At this point, a young soldier in a neat, clean uniform comes in. Avram introduces me and we chat briefly. After he leaves, Avram proudly tells me that the soldier comes from a family of "Kafkazim". He typifies the graduates who think of Malachti as their home and visit whenever they can.

Avram has a problem because the Town Council put Aaron's program in one of his buildings. Aaron's older teen-agers are disruptive and Avram does not believe that Aaron is rehabilitating them. Moreover, there was a recent theft of Malachti equipment and Avram's teachers suspect Aaron's group of alienated youth. As we part, I assure him I am interested in the school and in his invitation to visit its graduates.

On the way out, I meet Aaron. He still doesn't know where his job stands but he is more optimistic since he received permission to buy two expensive machines for his program. He shows me a brochure describing them but I have no time to absorb the capability of these electronic pieces of equipment because I am rushing to my next appointment. I promise Aaron I will talk with him soon about the machines and his plans for rehabilitating alienated youth. I also want to know more about what makes him hopeful about his future in Kfar Oranim.

As I drive to my next appointment, Tamar, who is with me, says there is considerable conflict between Avram and Aaron.

I meet with Vered and Eitan who confirm the formation of an advisory group to Aaron. However, Vered just saw the Mayor and he insists Aaron be fired. Eitan verifies this. I ask what it means for the advisory committee. Vered maintains it will work with Aaron for four months during which time he will be on probation. Eitan is dubious. Legally, the Mayor has the power to hire and fire. Eitan feels that the die has been cast and he no longer wishes to work with Aaron.

Vered asserts that the Mayor cannot ignore a decision by the Trustees of Educational Institutions and Cultural Organizations Committee which has the final say over Project Renewal in Kfar Oranim. She claims Aaron must be given a chance for the stipulated period of four months. After that, a decision can be made. Eitan shrugs his shoulders, indicating the matter is out of his hands.

Aaron comes in and the entire discussion is repeated. Eitan spells out the reasons why the Mayor is angry. Aaron denies the charge that his behavior is inappropriate. He reviews his visit to the Deputy Minister of Labor and Social Affairs, saying that the Deputy Minister called the meeting. Furthermore, Aaron claims it was cleared with the Mayor; it took place in a nearby town, not in Jerusalem as alleged; his supervisors accompanied him. In short, there was nothing irregular. He is prepared to work with the advisory committee but he sees no point to it in view of the Mayor's non-negotiable stance. The meeting ends on this undecided note.

I drop in to see Yuval who says that nothing has changed in his situation. Dan informed him it is not the Deputy Mayor who is the source of his troubles. Rather, it is the Mayor himself. Yuval believes Dan is right since the Town Council refused to approve the expenditure he told me about when we met on March 11, 1982. He is being dunned for payment. He is sure that the Town Council will finally have to pay but it may take a court order. Meanwhile, his life is being complicated by the Mayor. He is carrying out his responsibilities despite the difficulties. He completed plans for an Independence Day program and has prepared his budget for next year. He repeats that his work is proceeding despite all the uncertainty.

April 1, 1982 — Kfar Oranim

Eitan and I tour facilities supported by Project Renewal. The day care centers are greatly enlarged and improved to provide better service. We look at streets and apartment buildings where new gardens have been planted and new pavement has been laid. Some of the work was done by the government housing corporation and some by the Ministry of Housing.

We come to a neighborhood square where people are sitting and chatting, oblivious to the garbage which surrounds them. Stray cats and dogs wander about, sniffing at the garbage. The pleasantries in the midst of these sordid conditions depress me. I ask Eitan why something can't be done about getting the filth off the streets. He deflects my question by assuring me that if I went into the apartments where these people live, I would find clean, well kept homes.

We finish our tour and I ask Eitan about Aaron's purchase of expensive machines. How come this was approved if there is uncertainty about his future? Eitan explains that the technical "high school" is to become a training facility for high-paying trades and will use the machines. Whether or not the new equipment will fit into its plans is unclear. Yuval may know.

We go to a meeting of the Steering Committee. Despite the unruliness of the session, Eitan manages to get approval for his budget proposals.

Aryeh insists more day care centers are needed. He is less boisterous than usual, partly because the Deputy Mayor, as chairman in the Mayor's absence, is quite conciliatory. Vered says the Steering Committee cannot approve funds for more day care centers unless the Sub-Committee which has jurisdiction over this matter makes this recommendation. Leah, the Regional Director of Project Renewal, supports Vered. People just cannot make spur-of-the-moment suggestions after so much time was spent in the sub-committees on preparing their parts of the budget. This gets her into a row with Ephraim, head of the Labor Party branch in Kfar Oranim. He insists the Steering Committee is the final authority. It can and should make corrections when members agree they are needed. He maintains that the professionals should not impede decision-making with "games" which is his characterization of Leah's intervention. She answers Ephraim politely and a confrontation is avoided.

Aryeh demands to know why his comments on physical rehabilitation were omitted from the minutes of the last meeting. Leah suggests formal ratification of the minutes to catch such omissions and the Chairman agrees. He instructs Eitan to amend the minutes of the last meeting to include Aryeh's comments.

Physical renewal problems are discussed. Aryeh and his supporters express resentment about the failure to publish tenders in the press. This would give local residents a chance to bid for the work and make sure that the lowest possible prices are obtained. He urges that the Ministry of Housing and the Jewish Agency be given until April 25, 1982. If they don't respond, he argues, Croydon should be asked to join Kfar Oranim in a protest strike to stop all Project Renewal activities.

The Chairman answers obliquely by asking for the schedule of the Croydon delegation. Leah says it is not known yet but it will undoubtedly include a meeting with the neighborhood representatives where Aryeh can make any proposal he wishes.

The meeting ends, having lasted barely an hour. Everyone wants to get quickly over the unpleasantness of these chaotic encounters. Lack of clear terms of reference adds to the confusion. I have the impression that the meetings are called to satisfy official requirements rather than to produce results.

Before we leave, Aryeh and Marcus, the government official in charge of Project Renewal, get into a loud argument. As it rages, a young man asks me for an opportunity to talk with the Croydon delegation. He wants to describe his problem in getting utility services for his new house. He is distraught, calling everyone in authority a liar. I say I cannot promise intervention in his situation but he can feel free to speak up when the delegation meets with the neighborhood representatives.

Marcus stops the argument with Aryeh and rides with me on my way home. He asks why there is so much bitterness against the Ministry of Housing. He knows the Ministry has not lived up to its obligations but things are not so bad as to warrant this powerful hostility. I tell him that, as I see it, anger against the Ministry of Housing symbolizes animosity toward all authorities for cynically disregarding their assurances to Kfar Oranim. I mention the actions of the Israel Land Authority, the continuing failure to do anything about the beach and the frustration about the ineffectiveness of the Steering Committee as examples of what the residents see as indifference to Kfar Oranim. He knows these complaints and he asks why nothing has been done about the beach. I turn the question back to him and he promises to help. He asks me to gather the facts which establish Kfar Oranim's right to the beach and I promise to do so.

Marcus returns to the deep enmity for the Ministry of Housing which poured out at the meeting. He cannot get over this and he keeps referring to it throughout our drive. I confirm that these stored up feelings are held with great passion. I have been asked more than once to bring Croydon in to help Kfar Oranim get from the Ministry of Housing what has been promised. Marcus becomes agitated. He says this is purely a domestic affair. If Kfar Oranim brings in outside elements, even as well-meaning as Croydon, to serve as reinforcements in its arguments with the Ministry, he will make short shrift of such tactics. I do not respond even though I know that there have been several instances in which other Project Renewal communities used the "twinned" relationship with their distant partners for support in confronting the power structure, I plan to follow this approach in spite of Marcus' view — one which has echoes of the opposition to any interference by Diaspora Jews in Israeli policies.

April 6, 1982 — Kfar Oranim

The advisory committee to Aaron holds its first meeting. Vered outlines the committee's function. It is a clearing house for the Steering Committee which has the final say. The advisory committee will advise (Vered makes it sound more like "approve") on hiring and firing group leaders, on running the program and on purchasing equipment. Aaron is to report to the committee monthly and Vered asks that he start by describing what he has done during these past six months.

Aaron makes a report on which Yuval comments favorably, saying Aaron is clearly a gifted and imaginative worker. He hopes the relationship problems which dog Aaron can be resolved. He should continue his promising approach to the problems of alienated youth. I think to myself that his sympathetic reaction reflects Yuval's identification with Aaron as fellow-sufferers at the hands of the Mayor.

The meeting is poorly attended. Uri is on reserve duty. Dan is absent even though we are meeting in the Community Center. Eitan leaves early. I am present in my liaison-consultant capacity, not as a full member of the committee.

Soon after Yuval completes his comments, Dan enters and asks that I come with him to meet Ariela who has just arrived. I excuse myself to accompany Dan. Ariela, Dan and I consider how best to present to the Croydon delegation the idea of an American tour by the Youth Orchestra and Choral Group.

We complete our discussion and I start back to the advisory committee meeting. Dan stops me to say he deliberately stayed away from the session because he cannot work with Aaron. He wrote a letter saying he refuses to serve on the advisory committee.

I do not intend to boycott the committee's meetings, but I am not inclined to serve as a member. For all her ability, Vered fails to see the futility of a committee to hold Aaron accountable when the Mayor is determined to get rid of him. Vered is working at cross purposes with the Mayor who sees the feud as beyond negotiation. Aaron has entered into a mindless political contest, the outcome of which was predictable from the moment he went over the Mayor's head to the Deputy Minister. Eagerness to keep Tamar, Uri and Yuval in place relegates me to the sidelines as far as Aaron is concerned. When I suggested an advisory committee to Aaron, his precarious position was not common knowledge. Now, when he is on the verge of dismissal, the committee only provides a useless forum for airing a hopeless situation. It really cannot help; for all intents and purposes, the committee is irrelevant.

My return to the meeting is further delayed by Martha, one of Aaron's volunteer group leaders. She asks me to arrange for her and the other group leaders to meet with the Croydon delegation. They want to tell Croydon about their accomplishments under Aaron's leadership. I tell her I will try to work this out and I finally get back to the advisory committee.

Aaron's problem with the Mayor is under discussion. He says he can't continue on the job without some assurance of permanence. He claims the Mayor is uninterested in work with alienated youth and is rigid about dismissing him. Aaron seems incapable of winning support for his program. His supervisors who have joined the meeting are not helpful. One is new to the job and asks antagonistic questions that betray his ignorance of what Aaron is doing. The other is supportive, praising Aaron for not making a craven appeal to the Mayor. Vered concludes the meeting, fixing the date for our next session.

April 18, 1982 — Kfar Oranim

A large group meets to plan for the visit of the Croydon delegation. In attendance are: Hanoch and two assistants who have come from Jerusalem, Eitan, Leah, Vered, Dan, Uri, the Deputy Mayor, Ephraim and a representative of the Israel Education Fund, equipped to provide information about medals, plaques and other honorific presentations for the visitors.

The schedule is drawn up. Hanoch says he has several questions, starting with where things stand in physical development. While this is primarily a government rather than a Jewish Agency responsibility. Hanoch says it would help if he had the facts as seen by Kfar Oranim. The Mayor and Eitan take the lead in telling of the town's frustration with the Ministry of Housing. The Mayor is bitter about the impact of the delays on his credibility. Tenders are supposed to appear but they do not come out. Anger is mounting because people feel the government is just playing a game.

Hanoch asks if anything at all has been done. Eitan replies that one street was paved, ten houses were enlarged and the appearance of twelve houses was bettered. Some apartments have been improved by the government housing corporation but, all in all, the Ministry of Housing and the government housing corporation have failed to make good on promises of physical renewal. The Mayor adds he is particularly disappointed with Reuven, the Deputy Minister of Housing, who is a long-time friend. His negligence has magnified the Mayor's bitterness.

Hanoch moves to the social component of Project Renewal. Eitan reports improvements in the schools and day care centers. He mentions work with alienated youth and Hanoch indicates he is aware of the difficulties between Aaron and the Mayor. The Mayor says he knows Aaron's capabilities and imaginative approach. However, Aaron's poor relationships nullify any possible contribution. Moreover, few youth are involved in the program. The Mayor is supported by his Deputy and by Ephraim who points out that the Mayor has the right to choose his staff. He says he personally disapproves of the Prime Minister but he has to abide by his authority as the head of government. This draws laughter because everyone knows that, except for Ephraim and the Deputy Mayor, the leadership of Kfar Oranim is drawn totally from the Prime Minister's party.

Leah talks about the recommendation that Aaron be given a probationary period of four months and she tells of the advisory committee. This angers the Mayor who says his power to hire and fire municipal employees is being thwarted. He then abruptly adjourns the meeting, saying he must go to a funeral.

Aaron comes into the room and Hanoch tells me he is going to inform Aaron that he has lost his job. It is interesting that the Mayor, who is insistent on his right to hire and fire relies on Hanoch to deliver the final blow. Hanoch carries out this task, ignoring the plea which Leah, his own deputy, has just made to let the advisory committee work with Aaron on a four-months trial basis. Speak about coordination! The manner of this misguided worker's dismissal burdens the soul.

I am upset by Hanoch's opening an escape vent for Kfar Oranim residents to air their fury at the Ministry of Housing. This was plainly a ploy to create an invidious distinction between the Jewish Agency and the government in fulfilling Project Renewal obligations. This may be clever politics but it is ethically questionable from the value perspective of community organization and community development as practised by the helping professions.

April 19, 1982 — Kfar Oranim

Eitan, Vered and I meet to make detailed plans for the Croydon visitors. I see Aaron outside Eitan's office and he says Hanoch told him he is as good as through in Kfar Oranim. He calls this absurd because Hanoch acknowledged Aaron's ability and offered him a job with Project Renewal. Furthermore, Aaron demands, how is it that Yuval who is such a quiet fellow is also being sacked? He looks as though he expects me to unravel this mystery. I observe that effectiveness on the job is not a guarantee against being fired. In his case, the critical factor is relationships that have become politicized. I say I don't know if there was a way to have prevented this turn of events but, in all frankness, I feel he has not done much to calm the stormy waters. I point out that a powerless professional worker seals his doom if he tries to confront a powerful political leader unless he has strong community backing. I do not accept this division between Aaron as a capable worker and Aaron as someone with relationship difficulties. Both are important aspects of effective professional endeavor. I put it to him directly that, if he wants to continue as a professional youth worker, he ought to get training. I inform him he will have a chance to describe his work when the Croydon delegation meets with community representatives. We part on good terms although I have no doubt that Aaron has many reservations about my views regarding his role in youth work.

I enter Eitan's office and, before we get to plans for the Croydon visitors, I tell Eitan and Vered about my conversation with Aaron. Eitan is annoyed that I told Aaron he will have a chance to speak with the delegation. The community meeting is for town residents and Aaron is not a resident. I say the meeting is open to everyone. Eitan is worried about the Mayor's reaction when he learns that Aaron was granted a forum to make his views publicly known to the Croydon visitors. There is no point in pursuing the argument. I declare that what I told Aaron is based on my understanding of the community meeting and I am not prepared to withdraw what I said. Eitan drops the subject and we work on the schedule.

April 23, 1982 — Junius

My wife and I have been invited to spend the Sabbath with the Croydon delegation before it conducts the annual budget review of Project Renewal activities in Kfar Oranim.

We settle in our room and I telephone Mark to exchange greetings. We arrange to meet in the lobby where the four-man delegation is seated. My wife and I are cordially welcomed by Melvin who is very much the host and obviously the leader of the group. Although he is now in his seventies, I recognize him as an important American Jewish leader whom I first saw in 1948 at the dramatic conference of the Council of Jewish Federations and Welfare Funds when he helped to provide a platform for Golda Meir as she asked American Jews to assist Israel when its very survival was threatened by the surrounding Arabs.

I remind him about this historic episode and he recalls it with much satisfaction, pleased to have been personally involved in so momentous an occasion.

Our preliminary chit-chat starts us off on a nice note. Departing from generalities and nostalgia, Melvin gets down to business. He wants to know my impressions about Project Renewal in Kfar Oranim now that I have been on the job for eight months. It is the sort of question I hoped for and I pounce on it. I begin by dealing with the meager diversity of job opportunities in Kfar Oranim. After a few moments, I notice that the members of the delegation are struggling to absorb what I am saying. They are clearly exhausted from their long flight and are suffering from jet lag. I terminate my remarks and I express the hope that we will pick up this theme, among others, at a later time. I add that there will be plenty of opportunities for us to be together during the course of their visit.

I hope this is accurate. I need to discuss the question of community morale in Kfar Oranim. It can't be an overnight strategy, decided in a few moments by people who are exhausted by their trans-Atlantic journey. Community morale is a problem for community development and aided self-help not in money but in terms of social support. What is required more than a few individual volunteers is influential people working in an organized manner to help attract business ventures to the town. I cannot look to Project Renewal, Jerusalem for cooperation. I see a possibility of bringing Junius into the picture with encouragement from Croydon. I broached this to Mark in our correspondence and I wonder why there was no reaction. I have to know whether Croydon backs such a move, since much work and a long time will be necessary to bring it to fruition.

I worry that the heavy schedule will prevent examination of the liaison-consultant role as it is emerging. The work is falling into three categories: 1) Providing services such as monitoring and relaying information. 2) Sustained advocacy such as supporting the professionals facing interference from local politicians. 3) Organizing tasks such as fostering citizen participation in the neighborhoods and involving Junius as a source of aided self-help for Kfar Oranim.

The need to discuss these three categories with the delegation is not simply a matter of providing orientation. I must mobilize Croydon's support if it comes to a confrontation between the politicians and the workers in the social agencies. In such a situation, I would be on the side of the workers and I would need backing. Similarly, I need Croydon's help in my efforts to foster interaction between Kfar Oranim and Junius. This change process requires a community development approach in which I envision Croydon playing the role of sponsor. I need explicit reaction from the delegation to this strategy.

April 24, 1982 — Junius

The delegation and I meet with Hanoch and Leah. The visitors are interested in all aspects of life in Kfar Oranim but are focused on last year's expenditures and the estimated budget for next year. They are mindful of their responsibility to report to the Croydon Federation Board and to bring recommendations for its consideration. They ask for fiscal information and Hanoch replies with specifics on a line-by-line basis. He obviously did his homework and he is a fund of data, facts, figures, insights and projections which he gives with great authority. As the discussion proceeds, his impressive ability to deal with the observations, questions and comments of the visitors conveys the scrupulous sense of accountability which they are seeking. Much of what is examined will be given detailed consideration during the next few days. This preview persuades the visitors that they are dealing with at least one dependable authority who knows what he is talking about.

After Hanoch and Leah leave, I sit with the delegation. They express their low opinion of the Mayor. I say there will be no change until the next election, if then. They ask about the professionals in the town. What can be done about them? I am curious as to the source of their negative judgment about Kfar Oranim's personnel. I suspect they have heard from Hanoch who is contemptuous of the town's paid workers. He would like to see them all fired, starting with Eitan, the Steering Committees's Executive Secretary. I caution the delegation that changing workers is easier said than done. Raising salaries would not bring about a change. Salaries are uniform throughout the country and Kfar Oranim cannot compete with the big cities nor even with other medium sized towns in attracting professional workers. It is fated to make do with third and fourth-rate functionaries. One delegation member asks if anything can improve the personnel situation. I reply that little can be done at the local level. If the Ministry of Education would offer incentives to bring good teachers to small communities, that would help. A new breed of motivated professionals living and working in Kfar Oranim would insist on high quality education for their children. They would not tolerate the present inadequate standards.

Attracting new people is part of the challenge to endow Kfar Oranim with better community spirit. Among other things, this requires economic development. The town square symbolizes Kfar Oranim's plight. It is a sorry, neglected area with two small ice cream parlors, a scruffy kiosk serving barbecued meats, a deteriorating, closed-down theater and a couple of wearing apparel stores that look like used clothing depots run by a volunteer organization. Kfar Oranim residents will continue to shop in neighboring towns and look elsewhere for leisure-time enjoyment unless there are radical improvements in the town square, including attractive stores run by energetic entrepreneurs.

The members of the delegation listen but remain quiet. I am not sure what their silence implies. Finally, one member of the delegation with experience as a human service professional seizes the idea of community development, obviously acquainted with the concept. In his opinion, emphasis on carrying out community development is needed. I am encouraged by this statement. We can return to this point when and if the time comes for more concrete proposals.

Since I am eager to foster cooperation between Junius and Croydon, I arranged for Junius' three leading volunteers to meet the delegation. Each woman is interested in Kfar Oranim generally but also has a specific idea to advocate. Dalia wants tennis courts in the town to create civic graces among young people as they learn to play the game. I know from previous conversations with her that she thinks it would be odd if the delegation fails to support her recommendation. Another Junius volunteer, Ariela, wants the delegation's support for the idea she has now embraced that the Kfar Oranim Youth Orchestra be invited to visit Croydon and tour the United States. The other two women do not share her enthusiasm for this notion.

By previous agreement with Mark, I invited Dalia, Adah and Ariela to come to the hotel in the early evening. They arrive and I make the introductions. After refreshments and some preliminary chatter. Ariela tells the delegation about her close links to Kfar Oranim. She indicates that this relationship gives her much satisfaction. She is especially pleased by her association with the Community Center. Its Youth Orchestra and Choral Group improve Kfar Oranim's image by appearing in towns and cities all over Israel. If these youngsters were accorded recognition outside the country, it would do the community a world of good. The members of the delegation are attentive and cordial but their unspoken response suggests they are not buying Ariela's proposal.

Melvin handles the situation with great aplomb. Since I wrote to Mark about the idea of the tour, he must have briefed the delegation. They are prepared for Ariela. Melvin lauds the good work of the Community Center and says that Ariela's proposal will receive serious consideration. He won't predict how the decision will go and he does not want to build up false optimism. The notion of an American tour will be examined by hard-headed, practical people who will ask whether performances by the Youth Orchestra and Choral Group will be attractive enough for fund-raising to justify the expense.

Dalia follows Ariela with her recommendation for a tennis facility. She evokes the same response from Melvin as he gave to Ariela. Despite his expert handling and dignified courtesy, the women look sorry about their visit with the delegation. Ariela seems to be more adversely affected than Dalia.

I tell myself this is only a first, indirect step in my efforts to nurture cooperative activity between Croydon and Junius. However, I wish it had come closer to cementing a working relationship between the Croydon delegation and the Junius volunteers. The meeting ends as I try to estimate what it implies for my attempt to initiate a three-way affiliation and support system encompassing Kfar Oranim, Junius and Croydon.

April 25, 1982 — Kfar Oranim

The Croydon delegation comes to the Town Hall where many residents and professionals are waiting. Mayor Shaul greets the delegation, peppering his words of welcome with talmudic references nicely geared to the partnership between the two communities. He says their linkage is rooted in the unchanged ancestral fate shared by both communities. He is an educator by profession, devoutly Orthodox, shy, sensitive and rather learned. As I listen, I can't help wondering how he got caught up in the rough and tumble of local politics. I am convinced Kfar Oranim would be better off if he found the way to self-expression in his profession rather than in politics where his leadership is uncertain and where he lacks the armor to slug it out.

Leah translates the Mayor's greeting, leaving out the talmudic spices.

74

To do justice to his remarks requires a Biblical background which she lacks. She reports on Project Renewal in Kfar Oranim, emphasizing the services provided by the national and regional offices. These services go far beyond consultation. They reflect a comprehensive and controlling involvement more akin to the relationship between the local municipalities and the highly centralized government of Israel.

Vered reviews the budget process, emphasizing her work with the sub-committees. She describes how each sub-committee develops recommendations for the Steering Committee where she plays another key role in guiding its consideration of the submissions by the sub-committees. The Steering Committee's recommended budget is sent to Project Renewal headquarters where it is vetted before it is sent to Croydon. Like Leah, Vered excels in discussing the connection between Croydon's funds and the welfare of Kfar Oranim's chiidren, youth and aged. She stresses the participation of the man-in-the-street who previous to Project Renewal had little opportunity to become involved in community affairs.

The presentations by Leah and Vered skillfully reinforce each other and impress the delegation. I would have preferred less horn-blowing about their own contributions. Vered redeemed herself by referring to participation in decision-making by the everyday citizen. Her expertise in budgeting is enhanced by her background as a teacher. I admire her patience in the sub-committee meetings, her acceptance of people struggling to master the intricacies of a budget and her efforts to maximize opportunities for self-expression.

While Vered works closely with Leah, she is not on the Project Renewal staff. She is employed by a consulting firm which has a contract with the Ministry of Housing which holds government responsibility for Project Renewal. Vered was assigned to Kfar Oranim to help encourage local participation. She is accountable to Marcus in the Ministry of Housing.

Vered works at being on good terms with everyone. I'm not sure whether this is a function of her personality or whether it is an approach encouraged by Marcus. Perhaps it is both. In any case, it makes for good professional relationships. I have been able to exchange mutually helpful opinions and information with her. It took me a long time to sort out the complicated bureaucratic structure which brings her to Kfar Oranim.

When this meeting ends, we set out on visits to agencies aided by Croydon's funds. This direct experience reassures the delegation as to the value of Croydon's contribution. The professionals we meet are engaged in meeting the needs of youth, children, aged, disabled, disadvantaged and deviants of Kfar Oranim. They give living progress reports which are more vivid than anything Hanoch, Leah, Vered or I can convey verbally. They provide rich testimony to the worth of Project Renewal.

The visits produce demographic and cultural sidelights which reveal some of the strengths and problems of Kfar Oranim. For example, we see children who can only speak Hebrew. Their parents are mostly bilingual, speaking Hebrew and Arabic. A declining minority speak Yiddish. These are the people from Rumania who arrived with the earliest Sephardic pioneers.

Language differences come to the fore when we reach the Senior Citizens Center where lunch awaits us. The worker explains that the people who use the Center are Ashkenazim who speak Yiddish and Hebrew. Efforts to integrate old Sephardim with old Ashkenazim have failed. Members of the ethnic groups are more comfortable among themselves just as the women would rather meet without the men.

The delegation is greeted by the old people who drift over in small clusters. There is an implicit feeling that fellow Ashkenazim are meeting. However, only one member of the delegation speaks Yiddish but his ability is rusty and I am pressed into service to interpret. Language is no barrier to the warm feeling that is quickly generated between the delegation and the old people.

One wiry man comes to our table and the others call on him to entertain with a Yiddish song. He is no shrinking violet but he wants a sign from the delegation. Receiving affirming nods, he launches into a tune that once resounded on the Yiddish stage of New York's Second Avenue. In his prime, he must have been a professional entertainer. He is still good and, at first, he has the riveted attention of the visitors. It wanes as he sings many stanzas, each accompanied by a chorus that becomes increasingly familiar with repetition. Finally, the song ends and the old actor is ready to favor us with another. I must tell him we have to move on. Although I do this gently, he sends out the hurt glances of an unrequited artist who wasn't granted an encore.

We move to a meeting with neighborhood representatives which is taken over by Aryeh who sees himself as a leader out to right the wrongs of the disadvantaged. His position is anomalous since he is a part-time employee of the municipality with a minimal stipend, assigned to serving the neighborhood residents. He basks in the approval of the visitors, finding their accepting response very different from the hostility, sometimes snide and sometimes explosive, which he draws and returns in kind to his opponents. There will be no squabbling while the delegation is in town.

For Aryeh, Project Renewal is more than a country-wide plan to rehabilitate deprived localities. In his eyes, it is a movement designed to liberate the bereft Sephardim from the dominating *"poritz"*, a Yiddish word he picked up which describes a member of the Polish landed nobility who once ruled Jews with an iron fist. This is Aryeh's playful allusion to the Labor Party which he loathes, and which, to his delight, was defeated by the Likud Party. Although Kfar Oranim's leaders are followers of Likud, Aryeh sees little to choose between them and the Labor Party. These veiled references are incidental to the eloquent and deeply felt tribute which he asks the delegation to take back to Croydon. Leah has trouble recasting Aryeh's flights of oratory into English.

The translation gets easier when Aryeh launches into a tirade against the Ministry of Housing, stressing its broken promises. According to Aryeh, the Ministry disdainfully snubs the families who were encouraged to join the Build-Your-Own-Home scheme but who now remain without essential utilities.

What was supposed to be a money-saving plan has put these families into debt as they had to pay large sums to connect these services to their homes. Aryeh is on solid ground and others echo his complaints. A climax is reached with the revelation that Ministry bureaucrats have turned a deaf ear to pleas that open culverts with sewage flowing through them be covered in accordance with Project Renewal plans.

The delegation is aroused by learning that such a health hazard has been ignored. Melvin asks that details be provided promptly since the delegation is scheduled to meet with the Ministry of Housing later in the week. He asserts that if the information bears out the report, he and his colleagues will insist on corrective action. Mayor Shaul promises to have the facts in Melvin's hands before the meeting. A positive mood is created by Melvin's forthright declaration. The residents feel good about their "twin" community's readiness to go to bat for them with the Ministry of Housing.

Aoril 26, 27, 28, 1982 — Kfar Oranim

The rest of the delegation's visit is devoted to more tours of agencies, sub-committee meetings, a Steering Committee meeting, discussions with individuals and the session with representatives from the Ministry of Housing.

The Ministry must have learned what happened when the delegation met with neighborhood representatives since they sent senior officials to see the Croydon delegation. Armed with the facts Shaul provided, Melvin adamantly maintains that the open stretches of the town's sewer system must be put under ground without delay. The delegation is indignant at the Ministry's negligence in leaving this foul-smelling sore run through a large section of the town. Explanations and excuses make the members of the delegation angrier. They demand that the government representatives come to see the open culverts and elicit a promise that the sewers will be covered in a few weeks. Melvin takes a picture of the culverts and puts the officials on notice that Croydon will keep watch through its liaison-consultant who is charged with advising Croydon as to progress on fulfilling the commitment that has just been made.

Sub-committee meetings show the fiscal and social backgrounds of programs receiving Project Renewal support. The members get a heady feeling that they are receiving feedback directly from the grass roots. This is only partly true because Leah and Vered carry a disproportionate share of the decision-making responsibility. Vered shows the skill and sensitivity of an excellent teacher but she is not a community development worker. Moreover, her time in Kfar Oranim is limited since she works in several other towns.

The sub-committees demonstrate some ability to present budgets and the reasoning behind the figures. The principals and the day care workers who compete keenly for funds show the effects of Vered's coaching. They list needs, refrain from speeches, deal adroitly with questions and avoid enmity. Unintentionally, they reveal their primary roles in budget preparation, albeit with much help from Leah and Vered. The neighborhood representatives are outnumbered by professionals and have little aptitude for navigating through budgets. Too shy to show their lack of understanding, they remain passive. Decision-making is left to the professionals. An invidious distinction is made between the "slow ones" and the "elite" who are at home in the rare art of budget-making.

Though troubled by professional domination, the delegation comes away with some sense of a grass roots response to needs and priorities. Vered participates actively but tries to give the impression that she is only clearing up ambiguities. Her interventions keep the meetings moving along.

I must make sure that the training Tamar is planning for neighborhood representatives will include agency finances and budgets. The knowledge they need can be better acquired in training geared to their level than in the sub-committee meetings where the atmosphere is often charged with mental acrobatics. They are no place for an uncertain learner.

Aoril 29, 1982 — Kfar Oranim

On the last day, after a closing assembly in the office of the Mayor, the delegation and a group from Croydon which is in Israel on a Young Leadership mission have a ribbon-cutting ceremony with music and speeches, to dedicate a Family Health Center, built with Project Renewal funds. The ritual gives reality to the partnership of the communities. The festive mood is marred by some residents who are too alienated and too deeply afflicted by their own misfortunes to be touched by the prevailing happy spirit. They call out, asking why the world is indifferent to their problems. Some attach themselves to the promenading phalanx of visitors but their complaints and cat calls in Hebrew, are not understood. After a few paces, they drop away and are forgotten.

The young people leave to continue their visit to Israel and the delegation goes to Jerusalem to meet Hanoch and his staff. Kfar Oranim has a flushed feeling of triumph at having hosted the delegation successfully. It will be felt for some time before the town settles down to business as usual.

My hoped-for discussion with the delegation did not materialize. We were sped along by the rush of meetings, visits and events. Time ran out before we knew it. I regret the loss of this once-a-year chance. The discussion would also have given the visitors an overview of my progress. However, there is compensation of sorts in the good relationship that developed between members of the delegation and me. Their positive appraisal of my work was no doubt heightened when the Mayor described me as a *"ben beit"*, a member of the household. The delegation caught the mellow feeling of mutuality that is implicit between its representative and its distant partner.

May 10, 1982 — Kfar Oranim

I arrive to see the Mayor but he is not in his office. Aryeh and Eitan are there, engaged in a loud discussion which Aryeh stops in order to direct his complaints to me. He says nothing has been done to keep the promise about covering the open drains. Aryeh warned the delegation not to be taken in by the assurances of the Ministry of Housing officials. He was not fooled. Now, Croydon is being let down.

Half insisting and half pleading, Aryeh says I must cable Croydon at once to report that nothing has been done. Eitan winces but he does not want to arouse Aryeh further so he suggests I check with the new head of Project Renewal physical planning in Kfar Oranim, Ovadiah. He will know the situation and I should get his information first. I agree with Eitan and Aryeh reluctantly acquiesces.

He abruptly drops the subject and produces a statement signed by twenty Neighborhood Council members. The Deputy Mayor who has entered the room busies himself with some computer print-outs but it is obvious that he is listening very carefully. The gist of the statement which Aryeh reads aloud is that the signatories object to the appointment of the Deputy Mayor as Chairman of the Trustees of Educational Institutions and Cultural Organizations Committee which is the local outlet for transmitting Project Renewal funds from the Jewish Agency to Kfar Oranim. Their objection is not directed against the Deputy Mayor personally but rather is based on the principle that leadership responsibilities should be distributed. The statement concludes with the recommendation that Aryeh, rather than the Deputy Mayor, should be appointed Chairman.

I am not sure what Aryeh expects of me by way of a response, especially with the Deputy Mayor in the room, studiously noting what is going on. I look at the statement and then I remind Aryeh that

79

even though we have talked about it several times, he has still not invited me to a meeting of the Neighborhood Council. He agrees that it is high time I be invited and we fix May 25, 1982 as the date for me to come to a meeting. Aryeh then turns to the Deputy Mayor, having ignored him up to now, and asks if the meeting of the Neighborhood Council can take place in the Mayor's office. Wanting to be conciliatory, the Deputy Mayor agrees to Aryeh's request. I don't want to be seen as taking sides in this interplay and so I state that I am ready to come to wherever it is that the Neighborhood Council regularly meets. Aryeh will have none of it. He asserts that the Mayor's office is the proper place for the meeting and that's it.

As I walk out with Aryeh, I tell him that I am pleased at the prospect of meeting with the Neighborhood Council but I wish it were a regular meeting rather than one called for the express purpose of meeting with me. I tell Aryeh that, at the meeting, I will expect to hear about Project Renewal activities since that is why I am in Kfar Oranim.

I continue my conversation with Aryeh, saying that in order to build a political career, one must demonstrate solid achievement in meeting community needs. Somewhat preachily, I add that, in the final analysis, we judge others not by their rhetoric but by their accomplishments. Aryeh defensively replies that what he says is accompanied by a "pathos" (his word) which he cannot help. I decide to abandon my unsubtle attempt to kindle Aryeh's insight and we part on a friendly note as Aryeh assures me that I will find the forthcoming meeting of the Neighborhood Council to be an interesting occasion.

I return to the Mayor's office where Eitan and the Deputy Mayor are working separately and quietly. I break the awkward silence by commenting that it is my responsibility to be in touch with all segments of the community. I sense this to be a superfluous comment as the Deputy Mayor says that he appreciates what I am doing as the link between Kfar Oranim and Croydon. He asks if I know what a millstone Aryeh is. He hurriedly adds that Aryeh will continue to receive his salary as a paraprofessional since it is against Jewish tradition to deny a man his livelihood. But — Aryeh isn't making it easy and he has had a report from at least one expert who recommends that Aryeh be fired. Eitan says that it is time for us to go to his office, thus ending the discussion.

We are joined by Ovadiah, the newly appointed director for Project Renewal physical planning. I ask about Aryeh's charge that no progress has been made in covering the sewers. Ovadiah says that he has been unsuccessful in getting any information. He is embarrassed and he asks me to come to his office where he will make another effort to find out what the situation is.

He telephones the Ministry of Housing and I am taken aback by his saying that he has the Croydon liaison person in his office with a cable from Croydon, demanding to know what is happening about covering the sewers. I surmise that he is being referred to someone else. Before dialing again, Ovadiah tells me that he is unhappy about the run-around he gets from petty bureaucrats. He says that he really doesn't need this aggravation because he has a decent pension as a retired colonel. It hurts him to admit that he hasn't earned his salary in Kfar Oranim this week. He seems to be an honest person but I am not sure he is capable of cracking the bureaucracy. He makes his call only to learn that the person he wants is away because of illness. Ovadiah promises that he will keep trying to get an answer but, meanwhile, I can write to Croydon that nothing has been done to cover the drainage ditches.

May 11, 1982 — Kfar Oranim

Since my meeting with Eitan yesterday was interrupted when I went off with Ovadiah, I return today to tell him that the Croydon delegation insists that cleaning up the town and maintaining proper sanitation is an absolute requirement. Members of the delegation told this to the Mayor, insisting that they cannot campaign for funds to meet Kfar Oranim's health needs when the community itself is so indifferent to public health. Outsiders inevitably take away negative impressions when they see the foul-smelling piles of garbage that litter Kfar Oranim's streets. Eitan is uneasy but he tells me that a beginning has been made in dealing with the problem. The Mayor has asked the Town Council secretary to become overseer of sanitation. I suggest that we go see him immediately in order to learn his plans for cleaning up the town. Eitan telephones but gets no reply. Suddenly, he remembers that it is a holiday and the municipal offices are closed. I ask how it is that he is at work. He says that he has some things to look after but he hints that he really came in to keep our appointment. He promises to arrange for me to see the Town Council secretary on my next visit.

I move on to the question of the beach, saying that Marcus has made a commitment to do something about it but that he first needs information about Kfar Oranim's access rights to the beach. Eitan indicates that the best person to provide this information is the Mayor. He will arrange an appointment with the Mayor for the same day that I come to see the Town Council secretary. Considering the state of Kfar Oranim's records, I have a premonition that it will not be easy to secure the information for Marcus.

We return to the question of sanitation and Eitan declares that new machinery will be needed. I suggest that we wait to hear the plans of the Town Council secretary. Eitan agrees, satisfied that he has made the point that Croydon's ultimatum about sanitation means the allocation of funds.

Eitan goes on to the subject of the music conservatory which is to be built next door to the Community Center. He says that Croydon will need to put pressure on Hanoch to get the work done. I tell Eitan that Croydon expects me to act on its behalf in such matters since I am on the scene. He says that it is simply a matter of getting things under way since approval has already been granted. I am not sure as to whether approval was given for planning or for actual construction and I make a note to clarify this with Croydon.

Eitan says that we should talk with the Jewish Agency architect who is working on the music conservatory plans. He calls for an appointment without waiting for my concurrence. As it turns out, the architect is too busy to see us for a month and Eitan says that he will call back in a couple of weeks to set a mutually convenient time for us to get together. He informs me that there will be a battle with the architect who wants to design a multi-purpose building while Eitan is determined that it be a music conservatory only.

Eitan invites me to have tea with him. He chats about all manner of things as he prepares the tea. We are seated and Eitan lifts a cookie to his mouth but changes his mind about biting into it. He waves it back and forth as if to lend greater emphasis to the confidence he is about to impart. Yuval is not going to be fired after all. He has it on the highest authority that the Mayor has decided to allow Yuval to remain in Kfar Oranim. I let him relish his feeling of being at the center of the town grapevine.

In fact, the information about Yuval is old hat. I have already received it from the Mayor himself. After telling me about his decision, the Mayor added, "I am doing this for you." He said it with unassuming pleasure as though he were genuinely gratified that he was able to do something which he was sure would give me satisfaction. The personalized touch he brought to his message took me by surprise. My first impulse was to say that, with decent supervision, Yuval could make a pretty good public servant. But — it might have sounded as though I were pleading Yuval's case as my personal concern. Instead, I said that he made the right decision. It was in the best interest of Kfar Oranim to retain its personnel and to provide good supervision.

Yuval is to be shifted from his present position as Director of the school system to head of the Department of Cultural Development. This means that he will administer that part of the educational program which helps children who come from families that lack the capacity to give their children the preparation they need to enter the school system. In this job, Yuval will be working in one of the social programs financed by Croydon. While, in one sense, this is a demotion for Yuval, I have learned through my association with him that the job of Director of the school system is far less impressive than the title implies. In accordance with the centralization that characterizes Israeli governmental processes, the principals of the local schools do not report to the local Director but rather to "Inspectors" in the Ministry of Education. Yuval may even be better off with his new assignment.

May 17, 1982 — Kfar Oranim

I am to meet with Rani, the Town Council secretary, to find out what he is doing about the sanitation situation. We have difficulty in finding a place where we can talk privately. On the way to the Community Center where we hope to find a room, Rani is stopped by a woman with a complaint. He tells me to go on and that he will join me as soon as he takes care of the woman's problem.

In the Community Center, Dan welcomes me and seizes the occasion to talk about his becoming a candidate for Mayor. He says he was encouraged by two members of the Croydon delegation during the visit. I doubt this since the members of the delegation had all indicated to me their determination to keep out of Kfar Oranim's politics but I let the matter rest. Dan tells me that Noam and others have offered to support him. I think to myself that it might be a good thing for the town if a young man like Dan — he is 29 — became Mayor but I maintain neutrality in our conversation.

Rani comes in and says that he knows I want to discuss plans for cleaning up Kfar Oranim. First, however, he has some exciting news about the beach to share with me. The Junius Development Corporation wants to build a yacht club, hotel, restaurant and sports area along the shore where Kfar Oranim has some rights. If the Town Council will cede the rights, the Junius Development Corporation will provide compensation by building a beach for the residents of Kfar Oranim with all the necessary amenities and with the right of access to the new facilities.

The proposed construction will provide jobs for Kfar Oranim residents as well as solve the problem of swimming facilities. I restrain my enthusiasm and suggest that we need some expert advice. Perhaps we should talk with Noam since he lives in Junius and is also a friend of Kfar Oranim. Rani agrees and goes on to say that the shoreline development is complicated by the presence of sunken Roman ruins in the waters off Junius and Kfar Oranim. It is unlawful for building contractors to damage these antiquities.

Rani has already made some preliminary investigations and he believes that we are now ready for a group to look further into the matter. He asks if I would be willing to join such a group and I assent. He plans to bring the idea to tonight's meeting of the Town Council and he will let me know what happens. He also says that a story about the offer from the Junius Development Corporation will appear in the next issue of Kfar Oranim's newspaper so that all residents can be in on the matter from the very beginning. We turn to the question of sanitation and Rani says that he plans to contract for sanitation services, replacing the present arrangement where the town hires its own cleaners. He figures that it will cost about 600,000 shekels ($27,272) a month for this service. I am surprised by the high cost but he assures me that the price is in line with what other towns are paying. I point out that contracting for sanitation services may be fine but that the residents need to cooperate. If they keep throwing garbage in the streets and if the shopkeepers continue to junk their trash outside their shops, then the contractor won't be able to do much good. Rani refuses to be deflected from his preoccupation with cost. He does not know whether or not the Ministry of Housing will foot the bill. I do not pick up his implication that Croydon should help but rather continue to insist that community awareness and a sense of community pride are essential if sanitation standards are to be raised in Kfar Oranim. Rani neither agrees nor disagrees with me. We set a meeting for next week to follow up on both the beach and sanitation. I still need the material for Marcus and I think that Rani may be able to get it for me more quickly than the Mayor.

May 25, 1982 — Kfar Oranim

I attend a meeting of the Sub-Committee on Informal Education and Culture. The first item on the agenda is the proposed budget for a cultural week on the folkways and customs of Libyan Jewry. A similar activity for the Moroccan community which makes up 50% of Kfar Oranim's population has taken place. It is agreed that programs to deal with the cultural roots of Kfar Oranim residents are beneficial. Similar events on the Rumanians and the "Kafkazim" should follow, in the opinion of the Sub-Committee members. This expresses a relatively sophisticated valuing of cultural pluralism over the "melting pot" approach.

The budget is carefully scrutinized and intelligent questions are raised. The expenditure is approved in principle, subject to examination by experts on Libyan culture. The next item is a proposal to spend 380,000 shekels for the soldiers' recreation center. Sub-Committee members are sympathetic but feel the need for more information. The proposal is deferred until a detailed budget with explanations can be brought before the Sub-Committee.

Three members of the Kfar Oranim football team who have been waiting are now invited to speak. First, however, Eitan reminds everyone that we have limited time since most of the people present are expected at the Neighborhood Council meeting which is scheduled to begin shortly. The football team delegates present their needs in general fashion, arguing that they deserve support from Project Renewal. They are not prepared to answer specific questions from members of the Sub-Committee. Their request is deferred until further information can be provided.

I intervene to point out that this is the second time a decision has been deferred for lack of knowledge. In my view, the Sub-Committee has a responsibility to guide those who are to appear before it with outlines of what specific information is required. The Chairman approves my suggestion but I have to leave to attend the Neighborhood Council meeting and so I do not know what action, if any, is taken to comply with my recommendation.

Most of the people who were at the meeting of the Sub-Committee on Informal Education and Culture are present for the session of the Neighborhood Council in the Mayor's office. Aryeh calls the meeting to order. Eitan introduces me as the liaison between Kfar Oranim and Croydon. He is gracious and articulate in his presentation. As I listen to him, I wonder about his presence. Is he here to smooth the way in my first meeting with the Neighborhood Council? Or, is he a watch dog for the Steering Committee to see how I will respond to pressure from this group?

Aryeh takes over, speaking with his usual forcefulness. The mood is peaceful and warm as Aryeh announces that everyone will have a full opportunity to be heard. First, however, he wants to make some introductory remarks. He says that other Project Renewal towns are making better progress than Kfar Oranim and that we should visit them in order to learn from them. He then recommends that the Community Center which controls the budget of the Neighborhood Council should be asked for space and for a half-time secretary to facilitate the work of the Council. Someone tries to make a comment but Aryeh insists on finishing his remarks before anyone else speaks.

Aryeh's final comments have to do with the sanitation problem. He suggests that the Town Council appoint someone with authority to fine people who throw garbage into the streets. He claims that this arrangement has worked well elsewhere. He does not follow up any of his suggestions and recommendations but rather turns to the main agenda item which is the open drains. He asserts that nothing has been done by the Ministry of Housing to fulfill the commitment it made to the Croydon delegation. Croydon is being treated as shabbily as Kfar Oranim. With this statement, he turns to me.

I tell the group that Aryeh has asked me to send a cable to Croydon about the open drains. I am reluctant to do so because it would be difficult to explain the situation in a few words. Our Croydon friends would only be confused. I suggest that it would be better to send a letter from the Neighborhood Council, giving a full explanation of the situation and I offer to translate and post it. I promise to add my own message about the bitter resentment which this delay is causing in Kfar Oranim. I will suggest in my message that if the work is not started in two weeks, then the Croydon Project Renewal Committee should protest directly and vigorously to the Minister of Housing.

Aryeh now opens the floor for comments and each member recites a lengthy litany of woes about the crude neglect of the Ministry of Housing.

Finally, after everyone has made complete use of his time, I tell the group that I have already informed Croydon about most of the items which they have reported. Now — I need a letter from the Council. Who will write it? Aryeh is singled out as the person for this task.

To conclude the meeting, Eitan announces that Aaron, the youth worker will be leaving soon. Two candidates are under consideration for the position. The new person will report to Uri, head of the Welfare Department. This should prevent the problems caused by Aaron and his predecessor in going off on their own.

May 27, 1982 — Kfar Oranim

I meet with Uri to discuss the university students who are assigned to Kfar Oranim for their field experience. The BA student has had a good learning experience but this has not been the case with the two MA students. Uri is sorry that Richard, the BA student, has decided not to accept the summer job which has been offered to him. He has shown much promise. Our plans for his placement have worked out well. We did not have a chance to plan adequately for the MA students and their situation was complicated by Uri's five months absence for military service. We counted on Yuval for back-up but his difficulties interfered. We agree to plan more carefully for next year.

Uri introduces the subject of Aryeh who is being paid by the Town Council for his services as secretary of the Neighborhood Council. Uri is expected to administer the salary and to be administratively responsible for Aryeh. Officially, Aryeh is responsible to Tamar but he refuses to recognize her as his supervisor since he sees himself as the leader of the Neighborhood Council and not just as a secretary. Uri admires Aryeh and his potential for leadership. He has suggested to Aryeh that he get a job that would enable him to serve as a volunteer leader. His small stipend confuses the role of paraprofessional and community leader. Uri is obviously burdened by Aryeh. He wishes he could be free of the supervisory responsibility which the Town Council has assigned to him. I offer to see if I can come up with a suggestion but it appears that Uri is less interested in figuring out how to work with Aryeh than in having nothing at all to do with him.

Aryeh is the man who may be credited with bringing a fierce argumentative tone to public debate in Kfar Oranim. If the Steering

Committee meetings often take on the character of a large feuding family, it is in no small measure thanks to him. I do not join the censure he evokes so as to avoid giving him the feeling that I agree with his foes. However, in our private conversations, I question his stance as a would-be leader. Our relationship is by now solid enough for him to know I bear him no grudge and am primarily concerned about the effect of his aspirations on the quality of public life in Kfar Oranim. Whether or not this will get us anywhere remains to be seen.

I try to see Rani to discuss the proposal of the Junius Developoment Corporation but he is away on reserve duty. This means I must put plans for cleaning up the town on hold.

I run into Mordecai, the secretary of the Labor Party branch. I tell him I hear his cultural program is going well. He says it is but he has a problem because the program takes place on Friday nights. This violates the Sabbath and perturbs the Mayor who is observant and who wants the program shifted to Saturday night. Mordecai fears the change will cause trouble with Dan since it will compete with Community Center recreational programs. At present, there is no conflict because the Center is closed Friday nights. Mordecai will let a vote by his members decide the issue.

June 3, 1982

I have been unable to arrange a meeting with the Junius volunteers since their unsatisfactory encounter with the Croydon delegation. I decide to talk with them on the phone.

I first call Ariela who is abrupt. She tells me she is very busy. When I mention the Junius Development Corporation proposal concerning the beach, she says this is not a matter for volunteers. She almost seems hostile.

I wonder about this as I call Dalia. I say I am sorry we haven't been able to arrange a meeting of the volunteers. I appreciate their individual efforts but I hope for more coordination. I cite the need for job opportunities for Kfar Oranim's youth as requiring collective action. Dalia says lack of progress on the tennis project is due to factors other than the disinterest shown by the Croydon delegation during its visit. There are additional possibilities for launching the project but she isn't free to tell me about them. Ariela can provide the details. I think to myself that this is hardly likely in view of the frigid reception I have just received from Ariela.

With regard to job opportunities, Dalia says this is a government responsibility but she reminds herself that two wealthy neighbors talked about setting up a business in Kfar Oranim. They are reluctant to proceed because they fear the Scopus Manufacturing Company will oppose them. She says the Kfar Oranim Town Council knows about this. I indicate that I will discuss it with the Mayor but it might be useful if I first meet with her two neighbors. She agrees to arrange it.

I call Adah to tell her about my previous conversations. She says she will be in touch with Dalia. She remarks that Junius needs leadership to get people started. I say that I will telephone her from time to time as the need arises.

June 7, 1982

I call Dalia about the meeting with her neighbors. She has not had the heart to talk with them in view of the fighting in Lebanon. One neighbor's son is in the midst of the attack and he is understandably worried. I tell her I understand fully since my son-in-law is in the fighting too and I hesitated before calling her. She assures me that she will arrange the meeting as soon as the military situation eases.

Kfar Oranim

Israel is at war this morning. I have trouble getting to Kfar Oranim because of the military traffic. I wonder about the mood in Kfar Oranim. Aryeh and I meet as planned.

Although the fighting is on his mind, he declares it will give the government an excuse not to cover the drainage ditches. In a determined voice, he says, "War or no war! The bureaucrats will have to deliver on their promise to the people of Kfar Oranim." I am taken aback by this local twist to a national emergency and, somewhat clumsily, I ask if he has the letter which the Neighborhood Council asked him to prepare. He has it and he wants to discuss it so that I can translate it properly. We agree to meet later.

First, we visit Motti who is working on his house under the government's Build-Your-Own-Home plan. He and a hired worker show me what Motti has to do at his own expense. He incurred extra costs for hooking up the public utilities — costs which he claims should be borne by the town. Since the town refused to pay, he had to go into debt. Motti and Aryeh aim barbs at the establishment in Kfar Oranim and in the national government. Not a word about Lebanon!

I go to see Uri. Outside his office, some people are listening to the radio and arguing about the fate of a pilot who was shot down and captured by the PLO. Some say it would have been better had he died because the PLO will torture him to death like a trapped butterfly. Others disagree and I move past them.

Uri tells me he has decided to end his relationship with Aryeh. He told the Deputy Mayor his decision. He recognizes that Aryeh has followers and there may be repercussions but he must take a stand. I question Uri's decision but I am not prepared to debate it. Uri tells me he was embarrassed by Aryeh's loud and aggressive behavior during the visit of the Croydon delegation. I assure him the delegation was composed of experienced people who could size up Aryeh. Moreover, he played a useful role in forcing the issue of the culverts.

I go to see Rani who expects to be called up for the army at any moment. He shows me the local newspaper with the news about the Junius Development Corporation's offer and with coverage of the Croydon delegation's visit. We discuss the beach situation and he tells me he broached to the Town Council my suggestion that friends such as Noam be lined up. The idea was rejected in favor of hiring a Tel Aviv lawyer. I am not surprised since legal advice is essential but I am disappointed by this lost opportunity to involve residents of Junius.

I meet Aryeh who insists on going to the Junius Hotel for our chat. He drives us in his small car and I muse about how he can afford the car on his tiny stipend. I also wonder how it is that this Kfar Oranim self-proclaimed local patriot chooses to go to posh Junius for our conversation.

After a sandwich, we sit on the porch to talk. Tourists are discussing the war in Lebanon and this keeps Aryeh from giving play to his natural exuberance. He reviews the letter to Croydon and then goes beyond the problem of the culverts. He asserts his commitment to Project Renewal. It is a major innovation created by the Begin government. Labor Party governments never made available such an opportunity for ordinary people to take hold of their own community. While it is important to fight the outer enemy, it is equally important to fight the inner enemy which stalks poor people as they try to fulfill themselves. His preoccupation today when Israel is embattled proves that he means what he days.

June 14, 1982 — Kfar Oranim

I drop in to tell Uri that a Croydon dentist will visit in August to see about arrangements for volunteer dentists to work in Kfar Oranim. Uri is disappointed since he hopes for something more concrete and immediate. He is pressured by the mounting demand for dental services. I also tell Uri about a possible $50,000 donation from a Croydon resident for work with disadvantaged youth. A proposal is required. Uri is not interested. He says money is not the problem. The need is for skilled and experienced workers. The group counselors who remained after Aaron was fired need supervision. One was unable to work independently and Uri had to let him go. It seems that Uri's vision is limited to the family dimensions of social welfare. I decide to drop the matter. At an appropriate time, I'll talk with Dalia about it.

Others I want to see are away on military service. Rani is not in the army yet but he is in Tel Aviv conferring with the lawyer about the Junius Development Corporation proposal. The Mayor and his Deputy are in and I describe my meeting with the Neighborhood Council. I want them to know that a letter is going to Croydon regarding the sewers. The Mayor may be offended if this occurs without his knowledge. He listens without comment but the Deputy Mayor launches into a tirade against Aryeh, saying he is a trouble-maker.

The Mayor seems uninterested in this conversation so I change the subject to sanitation. The Mayor proudly tells me of his efforts to clean up the town. He hired thirteen part-time street cleaners even though this may cause trouble with the Ministry of Interior which will have to pay their salaries. There is a noticeable difference in the appearance of Kfar Oranim's streets. However, the Mayor says a mechanical sweeper is needed. I ask its cost and the Mayor instructs his Deputy to have the information for my next visit.

June 25, 1982 — Kfar Oranim

Since most of the people I ordinarily see on my rounds are in the army, my focus is switched to the municipal office where the Mayor, the Deputy Mayor and the Town Clerk are on duty. The Deputy Mayor is indignant about Aryeh's insistence that a scheduled meeting of the Trustees of Educational Institutions and Cultural Organizations Committee proceed even though most of its members are on military service. At the meeting, Aryeh tried to have a vote taken for the chairmanship, hoping to be elected over the Deputy Mayor who had only a few of his supporters present. Aryeh contends that life must go on despite the war. The Deputy Mayor succeeded in postponing the vote but he is still very angry at Aryeh.

Our discussion takes place just before the funeral of a Kfar Oranim soldier killed in the Lebanese war. The anticipation of this sorrowful duty adds to the Deputy Mayor's irritation. The Mayor listens quietly to his Deputy's outburst. I gather a response from me is expected. I ask how Aryeh got into this confused role which has him functioning partly as a natural leader and partly as a paid worker. Until this is straightened out, I say, little can be done about the dilemma of Aryeh's involvement in community activities.

The Mayor nods, saying a solution must be found to the issue of Aryeh's dual role. The Deputy Mayor is disappointed not to get a response which clearly shows my stance. I state that Aryeh may be a problem but he does have official duties in the community. I add that my recognition of his position may help since our relationship is free of the tensions in Aryeh's interactions with Kfar Oranim leadership. The Mayor accepts my comments but I feel that I am not getting across to the Deputy Mayor and so I leave off.

We talk about sanitation until the time for the funeral. People are standing around in small groups, lamenting and weeping. Police are present to guide the funeral procession. The presence of police in Kfar Oranim is an unusual sight.

July 1, 1982 — Kfar Oranim

Eitan is back from the army and, in accordance with his pattern, he plunges right into business. The election at the Trustees Committee was held two days ago and Aryeh was chosen Vice-Chairman. He defeated the Deputy Mayor who is incensed and is planning to protest to Project Renewal officials. The chairmanship of the Committee was assigned for three months to an employee of the Jewish Agency who is charged with straightening out the financial affairs of the Committee.

No one is suspected of illegality, according to Eitan. However, the records are sloppy and must be put in order. After three months, Aryeh will become chairman. Another option might be possible but this is not clear. Eitan speaks with finality and, even though the arrangement makes no sense, I have come to know Eitan well enough to recognize when a subject is closed.

He moves to the budget. Have I heard anything about its approval? I tell him I received a copy of Croydon's letter to Project Renewal headquarters. It has the recommendations of the delegation which recently visited us. Eitan is to discuss the budget with Leah tomorrow and he will be better prepared if I share my information with him. His request is reasonable and I go over the letter, translating it into Hebrew.

Eitan then asks for my help in extending his contract as Executive Secretary of Project Renewal in Kfar Oranim. He originally came for a year, planning to return to his school principalship in another town. However, there is difficulty about his reclaiming the post and so he would like to stay in Kfar Oranim for one more year. He wants me to make this recommendation to Marcus, at the Ministry of Housing. I am surprised to learn that this is a government rather than a Jewish Agency appointment but I agree to call Marcus to urge that Eitan be retained.

I meet with Tamar who tells me that her course for community activists started off well. There were 27 participants and they were enthusiastic about learning how to lobby, how to run a meeeting, how to organize, how to engage in social action, etc. Unfortunately, by the third session, the coordinator, the lecturer and ten participants were called up for the Lebanese war. The remaining male students anticipate their orders any day now so Tamar has postponed further sessions until conditions return to normal.

We are holding our discussion at an outdoor cafe. Mordecai, who works for the Labor Party in Kfar Oranim, stops at our table. He tells me his Friday evening entertainment and cultural program which was the source of dispute because it was held on the Sabbath, was stopped because so many people have been mobilized. He hopes to resume the program when the fighting ends. He tells me about a group of engineers who are interested in opening an electronics plant in Kfar Oranim. However, they too are in the army so nothing can be done now. I say I want to know more about his possibility and we agree to meet next week. providing he is not in unform.

July 7, 1982 — Kfar Oranim

I see Yoram, a social worker who deals with alcoholics in the town. He identified 35 men with this problem; twenty are now in his case load. Most are heads of large families. Some are in and out of mental hospitals for treatment. Others can't keep a job and still others go on periodic binges. Yoram got a few to Alcoholics Anonymous. He also makes referrals to a Haifa treatment clinic. His worst cases are "Kafkazim" who were formidable drinkers in Russia before coming to Israel. Some are from families in which they are the second, third or fourth generation of heavy drinkers.

Yoram says an institution for alcoholics is being built in a nearby town but Kfar Oranim residents may not be eligible for treatment. I will take this up with Uri to whom Yoram is responsible. We agree to keep in touch.

I meet with Aryeh who makes a point of telling me he appreciates my telephoning to arrange this session. He wants to discuss a problem and he hopes I can get our Croydon partners to help solve it. Something tells me he is referring to the chairmanship of the Trustees Committee. I make it clear that I called him to make sure I am included in the trips to other Project Renewal communities. I learned of one trip just a day before it took place and it was too late to rearrange my schedule. Aryeh is pleased I want to accompany the neighborhood representatives. He promises to give me ample notice.

He praises what they saw in Rafaela and he tells me a return visit is planned. He hopes I can go on that one as well as another which is being considered. In Rafaela, activists are getting things done. Backed by a young, energetic mayor, they have established a power base which makes the national leaders of Project Renewal listen. Among Rafaela's accomplishments is the dental clinic which is a model for other communities. Also, they worked out a contracting cooperative which does building improvements and renovations under Project Renewal. Contracts go to local residents and they employ problem youth who used to wander the streets as trouble-makers. This approach to physical improvement has the extra value of reducing delinquency. Aryeh hopes the return trip to Rafaela will inspire Kfar Oranim to adapt these programs for use at home.

He shifts to the matter he wants to discuss. As I suspected, it is the election at the Trustees Committee. He denounces what he calls a travesty of democratic procedure even though he was elected Vice-Chairman. He resents the Jewish Agency representatives who came to the meeting and engineered the election so as to install their man as provisional chairman. He is determined to fight these tactics and he asks me to induce Croydon to join his battle for justice. I reply that the Trustees Committee which links Kfar Oranim to the Jewish

Agency is the counterpart of the Town Council in its relationship to the national government. These matters are internal Israeli organizational affairs removed from the Project Renewal partnership between Kfar Oranim and Croydon. I don't see how Croydon can intervene in his struggle with the Jewish Agency. Aryeh doesn't respond. He is undeterred at the prospect of carrying the fight by himself. He is ready to pay the price of non-conformism.

Although we are alone, Aryeh holds forth as though he were addressing an audience. He sees himself in the unenviable position of having to inspire and goad people out of their apathy. I ask whether he has thought of returning to his trade of television technician. I figure I know him well enough to confront him with this question. He seems baffled and I explain that his way of fulfilling his mission confuses people. He summons them as a leader but they respond to him as a paid functionary. I ask if he couldn't achieve more as a volunteer, earning his living in his trade rather than as a paraprofessional. Aryeh replies that what needs to be done in Kfar Oranim cannot be accomplished on a part-time basis. If he worked all day on another job, he would have neither the energy nor the time to be involved in the community. His stipend is small and this poses a problem for him and his pregnant wife but he is determined to carry on.

July 14, 1982 — Kfar Oranim, Junius
I meet Aryeh to pursue an idea he raised on the phone. He wants to arrange an outing for the neighborhood representatives. This would show appreciation for their volunteer work and add an element of recreation. He would like the party to be held at the Junius Hotel and he hopes to secure the facilities without charge. He asked me to accompany him to make this request.

At the Junius Hotel, we are received nicely even though we have no appointment. The man with whom we talk is introduced by Aryeh as someone who was born in Kfar Oranim. He shows a barely veiled indifference to Aryeh's request to see the manager. She is not available. We make an appointment to see her on July 20, 1982.

July 15, 1982 — Kfar Oranim, Junius
The Steering Committee meets to learn about the approved budget for 1982-1983. In the Mayor's absence, his Deputy presides. Eitan goes through the budget item by item. Questions are asked and the meeting proceeds smoothly.

The Deputy Mayor calls on representatives of the Kfar Oranim football team and things begin to heat up. The first representative complains his organization has no money for paid workers. They are dependent on volunteers even though they provide constructive sports activities for the youth which prevent delinquency. His invidious distinction between paid and unpaid workers creates resentment. A

second representative takes over as the Deputy Mayor reaches for
a mallet-sized gavel. The man argues for a budget allocation from
Project Renewal. His organization's work is as important as any now
supported by Project Renewal and it is high time they receive funds.
A member of the Steering Committee asks for a specific proposal.
This request is dismissed by the football team representatives as mere
humbug. A shouting match ensues and the Deputy Mayor pounds
the meeeting into some semblance of order. The football team
representatives leave on a surprising note of good cheer, waving good-
bye and shaking hands with everyone in reach.

The next item is Na'mat's request for funds to enlarge its day care
center. Shulamith, Na'mat's representative, says demands for service
outstrip the available facilities. A new center is badly needed. Eitan
asks me to comment. I say that the budget for 1982-1983 is set. I
am prepared to help frame a special request to Croydon and the
Deputy Mayor quickly appoints a committee to work with me.

Eitan is angered by a comment from Shulamith. He bawls her
out for making a request which is out of order. The Steering Committee
spent months wrestling with the budget. It is improper to make demands
on the spur of the moment. Shulamith gives as good as she receives
and they are both soon on the verge of hysteria. Half out of his
seat, the Deputy Mayor works his gavel and finally succeeds in restoring
relative calm. Uri sarcastically says there is an agenda item called
"miscellaneous" which can be used for matters such as the one raised
by Shulamith. The Deputy Mayor ignores Uri's sarcasm and voices
his assent.

The next item is Eitan's problem concerning Aryeh. Since the Town
Council is no longer Aryeh's employer, salary checks cannot be issued.
The Deputy Mayor adds apologetically that he was forced to write
to Aryeh on behalf of the Town Council, dismissing him because
of budget cuts. He implies that his hands were tied. Uri is angry
about Eitan's announcement but before he can speak, Dan proposes
referring the matter to the Trustees of Educational Institutions and
Cultural Organizations Committee. He is sure arrangements can be
made to pay Aryeh out of Project Renewal funds rather than the
government funds which now provide his salary. The Deputy Mayor
is relieved by this suggestion and wants to move on but Aryeh speaks
up. He says he has been trying for six months to get transferred
to the Project Renewal budget. The Deputy Mayor interrupts to ask
Aryeh to refrain from participating. He says he should have asked
Aryeh to absent himself from this discussion but did not do so out
of consideration for Aryeh. Ignoring the Deputy Mayor, Aryeh
continues to shout. The meeting deteriorates until Uri is finally
recognized on a point of order. He has trouble suppressing his rage.
Uri reminds Aryeh that he has expressed admiration for Aryeh's

leadership abilities. However, he is being dismissed for objective reasons which he does not spell out. He clearly does not want to publicize his reasons for recommending Aryeh's dismissal. Aryeh yells that he rejects everything Uri said. Moreover, he questions Tamar's role in his having been fired. She stands up and says she is leaving since this issue does not belong here. She will not take part in this discussion and she will not be forced into answering Aryeh's unfounded allegations. She runs out of the room and confusion reigns.

The Deputy Mayor uses his gavel and two supporters of Aryeh speak on his behalf. Their remarks are not those of followers extolling a leader. They sound more like laymen's evaluations of a paid worker. As the meeting ends, there appears to be implicit understanding that an arrangement will be worked out for Aryeh to get his job back.

July 19, 1982 — Kfar Oranim

I talk with Uri about Yoram, his worker with alcoholics. I also mention my worry about the suspension of work with alienated youth. I note that these two programs require sound planning to avoid a haphazard approach. There is need for setting priorities and for a social planning structure. Uri agrees and we decide to ask the MA students to organize a planning group. I am ready to ask Croydon for funds to continue the work if the students' efforts prove successful. I tell Uri I will prepare an outline, suggesting how we should proceed and I promise to have it ready shortly.

I meet Mordecai at the Labor Party office. He says it may be possible to see the engineers who are interested in opening an electronics plant but he wonders if we should wait until the battle in Lebanon ends. We can't do anything now but I say it might be helpful to begin discussions. Mordecai is pessimistic about the venture's chances of success. However, he suggests we talk with his boss, Ephraim. We see Ephraim and tell him about the possibility of an electronics plant in Kfar Oranim. We urge him to join the Mayor to meet the engineers and encourage them. Ephraim becomes enthusiastic about the idea and agrees to see the Mayor. He promises to include me in meeting the engineers.

July 20, 1982 — Junius

Aryeh and I see Deena, the manager of the Junius Hotel. She is a pleasant woman who greets us cordially and offers refreshments. Aryeh appreciatively and politely refuses. He introduces me and persuasively presents his request for hotel facilities to provide an outing for Kfar Oranim's neighborhood representatives. I add that her compliance with the request will be a source of encouragement to Kfar Oranim's distant partner in Croydon. Deena says the hotel has always been forthcoming to Kfar Oranim but its last good-will effort was repaid with violence. A few months ago, Kfar Oranim held a fashion show at the hotel with little or no cost for the facilities. During the affair, a waiter was slapped and a glass door broken. A Kfar Oranim representative promised to pay for the door but no money was sent and no one has had the decency to apologize. I sink into despair. What can I say? Aryeh explains that many Kfar Oranim residents grew up in *ma'aborot* — the temporary transit camps for new immigrants. This experience has taken its toll. Deena gently dismisses this excuse, saying that many of her senior staff also grew up in the *ma'aborot*. I say even if Aryeh has a point, his explanation cannot absolve the town from its responsibility.

Aryeh asks which Kfar Oranim organization sponsored the show. I add that we need to know the cost of repairing the damage. She asks an assistant for the file but the information is not available. She says that she will send it to me. Aryeh asks if the sponsoring organization was Na'mat and if the responsible person was Shulamith. Deena isn't sure but says that may be right. Aryeh promises to follow up.

I say that I can no longer support Aryeh's request until we pay the repair costs. I feel we have no right to ask more favors while this matter is pending. Deena accepts our intent to resolve the matter. She is ready to let Aryeh's group use the facilities without charge. Her decency makes me feel more responsible for restitution. We are pleased by her response and I come away determined to clear this matter up.

August 2, 1982 — Kfar Oranim

I ask Tamar and Uri for advice about Aryeh's offer to set up a meeting with Yehuda, candidate for Mayor against Shaul, the incumbent. I don't want to get snarled in local politics but Aryeh has advanced another reason for meeting Yehuda. It turns out that Na'mat was not responsible for the damage at the Junius Hotel. It was Yehuda and his followers who sponsored the affair. Aryeh wants me to get Yehuda to reimburse the hotel. While I want to meet Yehuda about this matter and also since he may be the next Mayor, I am not sure that Aryeh should arrange it. This was discussed at length in several telephone conversations before today's meeting and I finally told Aryeh that I have to think about his suggestion.

I ask Tamar if she believes my relationship with Mayor Shaul would be adversely affected if I meet his rival at Aryeh's instigation. She firmly advises against Aryeh's involvement. If I want to meet Yehuda, then she, not Aryeh, should arrange it. The meeting will have to be outside Kfar Oranim. I am troubled by the idea of a clandestine rendezvous and I tell her to hold off. Uri agrees with Tamar, recommending I not meet Yehuda on Aryeh's initiative.

He changes the subject to his troubles with the Town Council. Between the Mayor's feeble leadership and the Deputy Mayor's trivial input, Uri doesn't know where he stands one day to the next. There are no policies and no predictable financial decisions. Uri is particularly upset since he has a good candidate for the alienated youth work position that has been vacant for some time. He fears that the candidate will be put off when he negotiates with the Mayor and the Deputy Mayor. Uri's complaints have been mounting and I ask whether he is planning to leave. He tells me he was offered another job elsewhere but turned it down. He would like to stay. I am relieved because I believe he is an asset.

I see Ovadiah who is in charge of physical planning to persuade him to organize a cooperative similar to the venture in Rafeala which Aryeh described. Ovadiah has little interest in the idea.

August 5, 1982 — Kfar Oranim

Although I decided not to let Aryeh arrange a meeting with Yehuda, I seek Eitan's advice about the wisdom of such a meeting. He doesn't want to dirty his hands in local politics but says I should feel free to see Yehuda.

Eitan asks me to accompany him to inspect the dental clinic and the Ramit Day Care Center. We see both buildings and I hardly recognize them. They were cramped little structures before renovations were made and they look entirely different. Workers are installing the obligatory iron bars on the windows and I am saddened by the extra work, the extra cost and the extra equipment which is necessary to make the buildings safe from vandalism and burglary.

I see Ovadiah to press again the contracting cooperative to do work under his jurisdiction. This time, he is more responsive. He tells me he has been thinking about my proposal since we talked about it three days ago. His problem is lack of funds to pay for the work. The municipality has no money and cannot be counted on as a reliable employer.

August 11, 1982

Aryeh phones me at home to say Yehuda has been called up for military service. Our meeting will have to be postponed. He also cancelled the Rafeala visit because the neighborhood representatives are busy with condolence calls to friends and relatives who are mourning the men killed in the Lebanese war. The people in Rafeala are similarly engaged and are not disposed toward having visitors now. I agree with Aryeh that it is inadvisable to push a good idea at the wrong time.

He talks about the election at the Trustees Committee meeting where he was made Vice-Chairman instead of Chairman, as he expected. His voice goes up in pitch and he shouts that he will not let matters rest. He is going to kick up a storm of protest the likes of which the Jewish Agency has never before experienced. After a few moments of this harangue, he asks me to take the issue up with Leah since he holds her responsible for this miscarriage of democratic procedure. I repeat my promise to bring the matter to the attention of Leah's supervisor in Project Renewal headquarters. However, this official is overseas at present and I will have to wait until he returns.

Kfar Oranim

I see Ovadiah to discuss again the contracting cooperative to do physical rehabilitation work. The government housing corporation is interested in the idea and is prepared to get it started. The plan to employ problem youth has special appeal. The Ministry of Labor and Social Affairs also likes the idea but Ovadiah is skeptical about their support. We decide to proceed and I go to the Welfare Department to tell Uri our decision since he is responsible for work with alienated youth. However, he is not at work today.

At the Community Center, I tell Dan about a suggestion made by Ovadiah. He thinks we should arrange for local young golfers to visit Croydon for friendly competition. These men once served as caddies at the Junius golf course. They are now good golfers, supported and trained by sponsors in Junius who want to do more than exploit the youngsters for caddying. Ovadiah believes a visit by these golfers to Croydon will enliven the partnership between the two communities. Dan is surprised that the idea originated with Ovadiah since it is completely outside his realm of responsibility. I too was non-plussed by Ovadiah's initiative. In any event, we agree it is a good idea. It would provide for interaction between the two communities on a basis other than giving and receiving.

Dan says several "twinned" Project Renewal communities have exchanged visits. He is disappointed that Croydon has neither invited Kfar Oranim residents to visit nor has it sent volunteers. He is obviously still unhappy that nothing came of his idea for the Youth Orchestra and the Choral Group to make an American tour. I say I will write to Croydon about the golfers' visit, indicating that it has Dan's support.

August 19, 1982 — Kfar Oranim

I meet with Rani, the Town Clerk. I ask if he has seen the letter sent by a Croydon leader after visiting Kfar Oranim. He said that he would not contribute to Project Renewal because the unsanitary conditions he saw mark Kfar Oranim as a place without any desire to improve itself. Rani can't find the letter.

He says there is a problem with the sidewalk-cleaning machine which the town was to have purchased. During the trial period, it did not perform in accordance with the promises in the brochure. He is worried about the deficit being piled up because of the high cost of cleaning the streets and sidewalks. He thought the Croydon delegation indicated, during the recent visit, that money would be forthcoming to help Kfar Oranim tackle its sanitation problem. I promise to inquire but I tell him that, as I understood it, one member of the delegation asked about the cost of an effective sanitation program without making any commitment. Rani says that he will give me the required cost information for the mechanical sweeper. He will also provide an account of the deficit now being incurred for the sanitation program.

I try to see Mordecai to tell him about my conversation with an industrial consultant concerning the electronics plant but he is in the army. I reach his boss, Ephraim, by phone and tell him the consultant's name was given to me by a Croydon leader during a recent visit as someone with experience in economic development and in raising overseas capital. He seems cooperative and ready to help. He would like a prospectus before meeting the engineers and Ephraim promises to get it.

I was planning to see Vered today to give her books on problem youth which were donated by a member of the Croydon delegation in the hope that they might help in formulating plans for Kfar Oranim's alienated youth. However, Vered is ill and our meeting has to be postponed. I use the free time to telephone Deena, manager of the Junius Hotel. I ask about the information she was to send concerning the cost of damages. She apologizes for not having written. This is a busy time at the hotel. She will try to get word to me soon.

August 23, 1982 — Kfar Oranim

Five of us are scheduled to meet this morning to discuss the youth work project but three are unable to come. We talk briefly about the plan which involves putting teenagers to work on physical improvements as a means of rehabilitating them. There are complications and unknowns but it appears worth going forward.

I am told that Tamar received a dismissal notice. I am distressed to learn this since she is a reliable community worker, dedicated to the well-being of Kfar Oranim. Her dismissal must be related to town politics since she is supposedly a backer of the Mayor's rival in the coming election.

Eitan, Shulamit, Dan and I talk about Shulamit's request for funds to enlarge the Na'mat Day Care Center. This item caused dissension between Eitan and Shulamit at the last Steering Committee meeting. We are sitting as an ad hoc committee for me to get the facts I need to send the request to Croydon. I ask for background information which is provided by both Shulamit and Eitan.

Three and one-half years ago, a decision was made to enlarge one of the two day care centers which Na'mat runs in Kfar Oranim. For several reasons, there were delays in getting the work done. The present roadblock is the architect-builder. I ask why he has not been dismissed and I am told that this would cause further delays because it would mean seeking new bids.

As the discussion proceeds, anger mounts against the architect-builder and, on the spur of the moment, Eitan telephones the man in Haifa. An angry conversation ensues in which Eitan accuses the man of being unreliable and dishonest. We gather the architect-builder is attributing the delay to the problem of a building permit. He wants Eitan to bring the permit to his office. Eitan makes an appointment to bring the permit. Shulamit takes over the phone and gives the man a piece of her mind. When she finishes, a residual outrage remains from this stormy telephone conversation. Eitan reiterates that the delays are being caused by the uncaring and disorganized architect-builder.

We turn to the question of the second day care center run by Na'mat which Shulamit claims also needs enlarging. Eitan reminds her that approval was given for the work to proceed during the coming fiscal year. It becomes clear that there is no need to involve Croydon. One piece of work is being held up by the architect-builder and we made some progress toward solving that problem. The other project has been approved and, a different firm will no doubt be selected to do the job. We come away from the meeting with a sense of accomplishment. I am glad that my request for background data seems to have restored perspective to Shulamit and Eitan.

We move to the Mayor's office for a Steering Committee meeting. Thirteen people are present of whom eight are paid functionaries and five are volunteers. Marcus, the government official responsible for Project Renewal, is present. The Mayor and the Deputy Mayor are absent. Eitan presides.

He begins by saying we must activate a committee composed of all sub-committee chairmen to evaluate Project Renewal programs in the town. This committee is mandated by Project Renewal. It is functioning in other communities but, for some reason, it was never established in Kfar Oranim. People ask if evaluation is the task of the Steering Committee. I state that evaluation is certainly a function of the Steering Committee. Perhaps, it should be assigned to an executive committee of the Steering Committee. Eitan insists the committee must be formed precisely as he indicated since legal requirements permit no options. No formal decision is made but there is unvoiced consensus to follow Eitan's dictum and the matter is closed.

Ovadiah reports on physical planning and rehabilitation. He followed up on the promise to the Croydon delegation to cover the open sewers. He believes there is some progress as a result of his pressure. He talks of plans to build a decent market-place, replacing the present jerry-built stands which are an eyesore. Ephraim points out that the owners of the stands will demand restitution and temporary accommodations for their businesses while the new market-place is built. There is little sympathy for the Mayor and the Town Council who will have to confront these people. Steering Committee members claim that confrontation is long overdue and that intimidation by the stand owners should not be tolerated.

Ovadiah continues his report, telling about plans for a new entrance to Kfar Oranim to replace the drab turn-off which now provides access to the town. The plans envision part of the industrial area being set aside for small workshops to be used by self-employed residents. This will bring industry to the Russian immigrants who are segregated in a fenced area across the highway. They are newcomers, not to be confused with the "Kafkazim". The development will reduce their isolation. Approval is voiced but Ovadiah is warned to be on the look-out for an under-the-table land deal by the Scopus Manufacturing Company.

Eitan raises a point not on the agenda, confident that no one will object. He states that Tamar has received a dismissal notice. The Town Council blamed its action on the drastic budget cuts imposed by the Ministry of Interior. Eitan recommends the Steering Committee rescind this letter. His proposal is unanimously supported since everyone recognizes Tamar as a valuable neighborhood worker.

Next is a request to increase grants to families with large numbers of children so that they may buy school books. Project Renewal is one of three funding sources for these grants. A noisy discussion ensues with many opinions stated as to the size of the grants and the idea of such a subsidy. Finally, sensing no agreement, Eitan recommends a special committee to look into the matter and his recommendation is quickly approved. The advocate of increased grants is disappointed. I surmise that there are unmentioned difficulties beetween him and Eitan that go beyond the book subsidy.

Eitan turns to the dental clinic, holding that a choice must be made between two possible sponsors: the Ministry of Health or Kupat Holim, the trade union health organization. An intensive discussion follows with impassioned speeches by partisans of each organization. Marcus joins the discussion. Eitan finally says he perceives a majority for Kupat Holim. To make sure his view prevails, he makes a brief foray into health care politics, saying that Kfar Oranim should avoid getting caught as a pawn between the Ministry of Health and Kupat Holim. He sees Kupat Holim as the preferred choice because of its experience in small communities. There is no vote but Eitan's statement wins the Committee's support. I have the impression that politics figured in the debate as much as concern for dental care.

As the meeting ends, Ephraim tells me he has not yet obtained the prospectus for the electronics plant but he is working on it and he expects to have it soon.

This meeting was a bit less raucous than other Steering Committee sessions. Maybe, Marcus' presence helped.

August 26, 1982 — My Home

Aryeh asked to see me outside of Kfar Oranim and I invited him to my home. He tells me the outing for the neighborhood representatives will take place in Magar rather than in the Junius Hotel. He hopes to use the hotel for a future outing but more time will be needed to make restitution for the damage during the fashion show. He says Yehuda is being demobilized and will pay for the repairs. Aryeh repeats his offer to arrange a meeting with Yehuda and I finally accept. I worry that Aryeh may be wrong about Yehuda's readiness to pay for the damage and I want to learn his intentions from him. I am eager to clear this matter up since Kfar Oranim's good name is at stake.

Aryeh's real reason for seeing me is the election at the Trustees Committee meeting. He is still angry about what he sees as manipulation in making him the Vice-Chairman rather than the Chairman. I tell him I spoke with Leah's supervisor, as promised. He feels the matter has to be settled by Hanoch but Hanoch is in the United States and we will need to await his return. Aryeh waves his hand in futility. He is put out by the new delay but he also dismisses Hanoch as a typical bureaucrat who pushes ordinary people aside. Aryeh bitterly declares that the old, hard-nosed establishment is collaborating with the local power structure in exploiting people.

He shifts the conversation to let me know he has taken in the drift of our discussions about the confusion caused by his being both a community leader and a paid paraprofessional. He says his small paraprofessional stipend is not the sole source of his income but he wants the money as public testimony of his connection to Kfar Oranim's leadership. This link gives him status and helps to maintain his influence in championing the neighborhoods against the establishment. I am delighted that Aryeh is paying attention to my opinion. I intend to keep this subject as a live matter.

August 31, 1982 — Kfar Oranim

Six of us meet in Ovadiah's office to discuss the alienated youth work project. He brings everyone up to date on efforts to launch the project as an experiment. The representative of the Ministry of Labor and Social Affairs agrees to provide financial support and identifies a long list of individuals and organizations to be recruited for assistance. I notice that Ovadiah is worried by the prospect of dealing with unfamiliar bureaucracies.

Ilan, a Community Center youth worker, asserts that no one in town is truly responsible for working with alienated youth. He challenges the group to say how youth will be selected for the project. Ovadiah replies that we will rely on Uri as head of the Welfare Department. It is suggested that we start with youth not too deeply mired in delinquency.

Ovadiah tells us he has in mind a trustworthy person to serve as contractor for the work which is to be paid for by the government housing corporation. There is no response. The representative of the Ministry of Labor and Social Affairs says we should look at other communities to observe their work programs. He thinks there are better ones than the Rafaela model. Ovadiah asks me to accompany him on an observation trip. I agree.

As the meeting ends, I make a mental note to slow the pace of development to suit Ovadiah. He seems confused by the speed at which there is a piling up of ideas, suggestions, cautions, advice and doubts, all voiced by people and organizations he knows nothing about. His basic job is physical planning and rehabilitation, not the social rehabilitation of alienated youth. When the complexity peaks, he is apt to say he is a military man and this talk is getting us nowhere. He may wash his hands of the project. I want to prevent this by limiting the planning group to a few people whom Ovadiah can get to know and trust.

I meet with Uri who is upset about the dismissal letter to Tamar. He protested to the Mayor who agreed not to fire her. Despite this, the letter was sent. Uri feels that the Mayor reneged on his promise. He says nothing good can come of this game-playing. If the dismissal letter to Tamar is not withdrawn, he has no alternative but to leave Kfar Oranim.

I meet Shulamit who tells me she fights a constant, uphill struggle to protect the interests of Na'mat's day care centers. She sees the problem as being purely political. Eitan is a member of the Religious Zionist Party and he protects that organization's day care center. The Mayor has no appreciation for Na'mat's work since it is affiliated with the Labor Party to which he is steadfastly opposed. She often feels like throwing up her hands in despair. I say submission would only harm the mothers and children of Kfar Oranim. She invites me to visit the day care centers and the other Na'mat programs in Kfar Oranim. Such inspection will give me an idea of the fine work done by her organization as well as a first-hand view of their problems. We agree to examine the Na'mat facilities next week even though I am by now well acquainted with their work.

I go to the Mayor's office. He tells me the Junius Golf Club thinks it would be good to send five golfers to Croydon for a tournament. The idea Ovadiah originally proposed which I passed along to Dan has now gained wider support. The Mayor favors the trip as a way of enriching the relationship among Kfar Oranim, Junius and Croydon. I say my conversations with Ovadiah and Dan gave me the impression that we were talking about a trip by teenagers and I wrote to Croydon accordingly. The Mayor disabuses me of this notion. The proposed golfers are in their thirties and are nationally known. The Mayor says we should meet the Director of the Junius Golf Club and he calls for an appointment. He is anxious to get this project underway and he will accompany me to Junius.

I see Tamar to tell her Ovadiah's report to the Steering Committee about physical changes was abstract for me because I have not seen the places he mentioned. She volunteers to take me on a tour. We start where the new Russian immigrants live. It is a trailer camp surrounded by a wire fence which cuts them off from the rest of Kfar Oranim. The poor housing and the fence sadden me. I ask why there is a fence since the road already separates these people from the town. Tamar doesn't know. We look at the site for the new entrance and the area with open sewers. In anticipation of the sewers being covered, people are putting up houses under the Build-Your-Own-Home scheme. Once the sewers are covered, this will be a pleasant residential neighborhood.

September 8, 1982 - Kfar Oranim

To my embarrassment, I mistakenly listed appointments scheduled for September 7 for today. One was with the Mayor and the Director of the Junius Golf Club. The Mayor forgives my absent-mindedness. He accepts it as part of my vocation as an academic. He calls for another date but the line is busy. He assures me he will arrange the meeting for September 13. I make a big show of writing an entry in my diary to make sure there will be no further mistake.

Fortunately, Shulamit who was to take me to see Na'mat facilities yesterday is available and we proceed on the tour, a day late, to my chagrin. Shulamit also laughs off my mistake. As we drive to the first stop, she complains about the hostility towards Na'mat because of its association with the Labor Party. I say I don't understand her feeling of helplessness. Even though the Labor Party doesn't form the government at present, it is still powerful with its kibbutzim, health organization, trade unions, cooperatives, banks, etc. She thinks for a moment and grudgingly agrees with me. My reservation about her sense of desolation reflects my frustration about being unable to use these substantial resources to help establish a work opportunity program for the problem youth of Kfar Oranim.

At the first day care center, seventy children are engaged in play activities. Shulamit shows me the small kitchen that could hardly serve one family let alone seventy children. For 3½ years, there has been talk about enlarging the kitchen, fixing the roof and making other repairs but nothing has been done. We go into the yard where a foul smell assails our nostrils. A bubbling geyser sends out small waves of water. The children avoid the growing puddle as they play around it. A worker explains with great distress that a bulldozer accidentally broke a sewer pipe yesterday. The filthy water is churning up in the yard of the day care center, creating a dreadful odor. Shulamit wants to know why no one has come to fix the sewer. The worker says the sanitation department has been called innumerable times with no results. Shulamit says she will see Ovadiah about this. We are taken to see the broken sewer. A few feet away, a hill of garbage blocks the view. It must have been piling up for a long time but no one seems to be upset. Attention focuses on the broken sewer.

The second day care center has 30 children in a crowded room. The care is conscientious but there is no room for anyone on the waiting list in these cramped quarters.

Shulamit asks why empty wires hang from the ceiling. She is told that the electrician who did the repairs was paid and it's impossible to get him back. Eitan has been apprised with no results. I am outraged by the wires and the broken sewer and I make up my mind to get these problems solved.

September 13, 1982 — Kfar Oranim, Junius

I pick up Charles at this hotel. He is a Croydon dentist who is in Israel volunteering at a kibbutz. He wants to see about having volunteer dentists from Croydon come to Kfar Oranim. We have been in touch by phone and I am encouraged by his enthusiasm. Volunteer dentists would help fulfill the goal of providing direct contact between the two communities.

Charles is active in the American dental fraternity that organizes volunteer dentistry in Israel. He tells me the program requires a local person for the preventive work that he and other volunteers insist on as part of their approach to dentistry. Proper housing will also be required. He is considering accommodations outside of Kfar Oranim because he fears the volunteers may find it difficult to live in such a small, lackluster community. He recognizes it would be better if they lived in Kfar Oranim and I promise to look into this. In Kfar Oranim, the volunteer dentists might take a broader interest in the town. They could attend some committee meetings and contribute to a more orderly decision-making process. Charles agrees with having them live in Kfar Oranim but he is worried about this because he remembers how garbage-laden and grubby the town was when he visited two years ago.

We arrive at Eitan's office where Charles is warmly greeted by Eitan, Uri, Ovadiah and Vered. Uri talks about budget limitations and supervision by Kupat Holim. Charles says Kupat Holim has a lot to learn about modern dentistry. However, he is confident that American volunteers will have an impact on dentistry in Israel. As we go to the dental clinic, Charles is pleasantly surprised by the improvement of sanitary conditions on the streets. I caution him that while there is improvement, Kfar Oranim has a long way to go.

We reach the clinic which Charles scrutinizes carefully. He is pleased and says there is potential for preventive and rehabilitative dentistry. As we leave, he takes pictures of the new facility and the adjacent hut which formerly housed the dental clinic to give Croydon a before and after view.

Our tour continues until we arrive at the Mayor's office. The Mayor calls Shmuel, the Director of the Junius Gold Club. He tells us that Shmuel is waiting for us.

Before we leave, there is an ugly scene. A young man desperately threatens to remain in the Mayor's office until he gets an apartment for his family. Ovadiah vainly tries to mollify him. We leave with the argument still raging.

On the way to Junius, we stop at the temporary dental clinic for children. The tiny waiting room is crowded. The dentist, a Russian immigrant, stops working to show us the equipment and tell about the program. She does not speak English so Uri and Vered translate. Charles says the equipment is faulty. He understands we are looking at a temporary, improvised arrangement but he comments on the clinic's slummy building by contrast with the new clinic which we inspected earlier. He takes a picture to show this disparity to his Croydon colleagues.

The Junius Golf Club is a posh scene of affluence. As we look at the well-kept grounds, I can't help but comment that we have the "Golf Coast" and the "Slum" cheek by jowl. Uri disagrees, pointing out that no one in Kfar Oranim is starving. Basic needs are met and it isn't a slum. I grant that he is right in one sense. The difference between Kfar Oranim and a poor village in a Third World country is greater than the gap separating Kfar Oranim from opulent Junius. I maintain, however, that the concept of relative want characterizes comparisons in welfare societies between the rich and the poor. Based on that concept, the three minutes in time and the few hundred yards in space which separate Junius from Kfar Oranim have no counterpart in the enormous socio-economic distance which exists between them.

Our debate ends when Shmuel, the Director of the Junius Golf Club, welcomes us. He is an enthusiastic man of thirty who immediately spots Charles as the overseas visitor. He directs his remarks to Charles, showing off a computerized machine that enables him to locate any trouble spots on the golf course. "As a golfer", he says to Charles, "you will recognize the value of this machine in keeping the course in good service". We watch the machine while Shmuel extols its wonders and then I suggest we talk about the recommendation to send golfers to Croydon.

Shmuel is eager to get into the subject. He wants us to understand its implications for Kfar Oranim, Junius and Croydon. I tell him I have received several different versions of the proposal so my reports to Croydon may not be accurate. Shmuel, who apparently originated the idea, explains that the golfers are in their twenties, except for one man who just turned thirty. He happens to be the Mayor's brother but he is also one of Israel's leading golfers. He deserves to be included as a matter of merit, not because of nepotism. The golfers selected for the trip started as caddies but the Club encouraged them to become golfers in hopes of closing the status gap between them and the Club members. Shmuel feels it is high time for people who grew up in poverty in Israel to be recognized as achievers. Maybe poverty needs emphasis to motivate donors to give generously but this approach should be changed to show how rehabilitation can improve the lot of poor people. The Kfar Oranim golfers personify this accomplishment. He is certain a tournament between Croydon and Kfar Oranim golfers will raise interest in Croydon and will help fund-raising.

Charles indicates he will bring the idea to Croydon and lend it his personal support. However, he wants us to know that Croydon's leaders are tough-minded veterans in community affairs. They will need to be convinced the proposed tournament will have a positive impact on fund-raising. Shmuel says he understands but he hopes Charles, as a golfer, will bring authority to the idea. A non-golfer could not do so. Charles nods understandingly and shifts to the question of the volunteer dentists. Can they have visitors' privileges at the Golf Club? Shmuel promptly promises that they will be welcome as guests and he hopes other Croydon residents will visit the Club. This would strengthen the bridge with Junius and Kfar Oranim. He presents Charles with an emblem of the Junius Golf Club and invites us to the Club dining room for coffee and sandwiches. He is a keen advocate for the Golf Club and for the idea of sending Kfar Oranim golfers to Croydon. We leave in a good mood.

On the way back, we tour Junius and Charles is impressed by the large well-kept homes. We return to Kfar Oranim to survey housing for volunteer dentists. Eitan takes us to an apartment house at the end of town which looks out on a weed-choked field. The area is deplorable and when Eitan unlocks an apartment, Charles politely calls it barely suitable. I am upset and I say that it will not do. If the other places we are to see are of the same caliber, I tell Eitan we should cut the tour short. He gets the message in my irritation and in Charles' disappointment. He says he will need to rent a house in the center of town. He takes us to a better street and points to a house but he has no key.

What started out on a high note of optimism bogs down at the prospect of volunteer dentists disappearing for want of appropriate housing. I insist we stop this fruitless trek and return to Eitan's office. As we go, Charles comments again on how much cleaner the streets are. I relish his comment and I wonder if I am over-reacting to the housing problem.

We reach Eitan's office. He assures me decent housing will be obtained. He has another meeting but he stops to wish me a safe journey. I notified him and others in Kfar Oranim that I am leaving for a six-week stay in Canada. The rest of the group joins Eitan in wishing me a safe trip.

Uri and I are left with Charles. Uri says that much as he would like to see the volunteer dentists living in Kfar Oranim, it wouldn't be so terrible if they resided in a neighboring town where proper housing would be available. I hark back to my earlier comment about the "Gold Coast" and the "Slum" but Uri maintains we should keep our eyes on the goal of providing dental care and not be distracted by the secondary question of where the volunteer dentists stay. I repeat my hope that they will live in Kfar Oranim and say I understand what is needed to make this possible. Charles kindly says he will trust my judgment. We leave Uri who expresses his desire to see the early arrival of volunteer dentists.

On the way to the hotel, Charles says he is aware of the difficulties in the dental volunteer program but he remains optimistic. I find his opinion bracing but I cannot free myself from a wait-and-see attitude. I'll believe it when the first volunteer dentist arrives in Kfar Oranim.

November 4, 1982 - Kfar Oranim

Following my six-week absence, I have a long agenda for today:

1. Housing for volunteer dentists — Eitan
2. Proposed marina for Junius and beach for Kfar Oranim — Eitan
3. Informal social planning group — Uri
4. Volunteers for Kfar Oranim — Uri
5. Election of the Chairman of the Trustees Committee — Tamar
6. Meeting with Yehuda — Tamar
7. Youth work program — Ovadiah

I get a warm welcome and a cup of coffee from Eitan. The Deputy Mayor passes Eitan's office and he stops to greet me. Eitan asks him about the marina project. He replies that the Town Council originally opposed the idea, seeing it as simply a ploy to bilk Kfar Oranim out of the beach for which it has been fighting over a period of years. The Council is willing to go along with the proposal providing ironclad guarantees are given that the beach will be built simultaneously with the marina. Eitan interjects that a story appeared in the newspapers describing the plans for a marina and a beach. A meeting is scheduled with the Director of the Junius Development Corporation to consider next steps and the Deputy Mayor offers to include me.

The Deputy Mayor leaves and Eitan tells me about the visitors from Croydon who came during my absence. One group of fifty was led by the President of the Croydon Jewish Federation. The visit coincided with the opening of a day care center built with Project Renewal funds and it was a highly effective occasion. The group stayed four hours rather than two, as had been scheduled. They enjoyed listening to the Youth Orchestra.

On October 14, 1982, the Youth Orchestra was part of a grand march in Jerusalem, honoring 1,200 community leaders from the

Diaspora, including several from Croydon. They were in Israel for an emergency fund-raising mission.

On October 27, 1982, a Croydon group of 100 came to Kfar Oranim. This too was a successful affair although Eitan could not comply with a request from Project Renewal headquarters to feed the visitors. He received insufficient advance notice.

On November 3, 1982, sixteen members of Croydon's Young Leadership Group came for what proved to be another auspicious occasion. The stay in Kfar Oranim ran two hours over the time that had been allotted for the visit.

Eitan's report is interrupted by two women who need his signature, authorizing one of them to receive dental work. The woman with her is a social worker. The client only speaks Yiddish which neither Eitan nor the social worker understand. I serve as the translator and, after some initial abruptness, Eitan signs the forms. He then gives me a meeting schedule.

I was welcomed back by Uri and Tamar when I dropped in to say hello before seeing Eitan. I return to Uri's office and we get right to business. I tell him I will be unable to assign an MA student as planned since an unexpectedly large number of students were forced to withdraw because they could not pay the increased university tuition fees. The idea we discussed several times about a student developing a coordinating structure will now be impossible. Uri is not overly disappointed since he sees coordination as a two-edged sword. While it can help the agencies get a better picture of the community's over-all needs and their roles in meeting those needs, it can also give revelations to agencies which they can use to the advantage of their programs. He cites as an example Yehuda's efforts to organize volunteers without any interest in coordinating with others. He wants the volunteers to support him for mayor and, according to Uri, he would only exploit a coordinating structure for his own "vested interest".

I agree that Uri's example has cogency since agency duplication is not seen in Israel as the serious problem Americans consider it to be. There are no social planning councils and no unified fund-raising for voluntary agencies in Israel. Uri is willing to try for a coordinating structure but he is not convinced it will benefit Kfar Oranim. Since no student is available for the project, I suggest that I approach Yuval to try to persuade him to lead the endeavor. Uri agrees Yuval would be a good choice if he would accept the assignment.

This effort has been preceded by attempts on my part and others to introduce into Israel a measure of coordination in the provision of social services. In the mental health field, efforts to achieve coordination came to naught because clinic directors resisted joint planning. There is no role model in Israel for social planning and coordination. The tiny attempt to create an informal information exchange in Kfar Oranim has some chance of success since there is a "twin" community with years of experience in social planning and agency cooperation.

Uri says he hopes we will soon have volunteer dentists in Kfar Oranim. He feels Eitan can solve the housing problem.

I tell Uri I received a letter from the volunteer coordinator in Croydon, offering to send 12 youth volunteers. Uri says there are tasks for volunteers but they must be able to speak Hebrew. He thinks volunteers will need rapid language training before beginning work. Uri identifies three possible assignments: aiding disorganized families, tutoring students with their English lessons and providing transportation for handicapped individuals. He recommends that I talk with Dan about other possible tasks in the Community Center.

Uri says I should meet Ralph who has just been made Director of Volunteers in Kfar Oranim. He has a six-month trial appointment and Uri hopes the Town Council won't wreck it. Uri is bitter about the Town Council. He tells me the Ministry of Interior is investigating the town's fiscal affairs. Many discrepancies are turning up and the Ministry is considering a special committee to run the town, replacing the Mayor, the Deputy Mayor and the Town Council. Uri would welcome such a development since he regards the elected officials as calamitous bunglers. I ask him to arrange a meeting for me with Ralph and he promises to do so.

I meet with Tamar and ask how Aryeh is coming along. He is reponsible to Tamar for his work as a paraprofessional, an arrangement he regards with scorn and disdain. She says Aryeh's mother died recently and nothing has been heard from him since. Her death was a great blow to him. However, Tamar isn't sure Aryeh's withdrawal from community work is entirely due to his grief. He may be reassessing his situation. There is a rumor to the effect that Aryeh is associated with his brother in a Tel Aviv store. I hope Aryeh has actually withdrawn from community activities even though it is hard to picture public life without his stentorian input. I will have to check Tamar's story. If true, it would be a welcome turn of events since Aryeh has become a serious disruptive force. I wonder if our conversations had any effect on him.

I ask Tamar whether she knows if Aryeh has been in touch with Yehuda about paying for the damage at the Junius Hotel. She does not know but is ready to arrange a meeting with Yehuda to ask him. We do not pursue the subject. I say I will see her later at a meeting on the youth work project that has been called by the representative of the government housing corporation.

Uri drops in and I am introduced to Chaya, a new worker with responsibility for dealing with large families. She sees to it that children in these families get the reference books needed for their school work by arranging for the libraries in the area to be stocked with such books.

Uri confirms Eitan's account of the visits by Croydon groups during my absence. He missed one because of reserve duty but he helped to host the others. He believes that the visitors received a positive impression. They noted the clean streets and generally felt that Kfar Oranim is progressing.

I go to the municipal offices to ask the Deputy Mayor if he has set the appointment with the Director of the Junius Development Corporation. He has been trying vainly to reach the man. He dials again and gets through. He declares that he has in his office "the representative from the Croydon Jewish community who is closely following the developments with regard to the marina and the beach for Kfar Oranim". This skillfully formulated statement gets a quick response. An appointment is made. I hope that the Director won't think that I have come all the way from Croydon to see him.

The Deputy Mayor now launches into a tirade against the Ministry of Housing. Fifteen young couples desperately need homes and want to rent since they can't afford to buy. There are many empty houses in Kfar Oranim and they are subject to ceaseless pilfering but the Minister of Housing who controls them won't hear of renting. He insists they are for sale and not for rent. The Deputy Mayor, who has no love lost for the Minister of Housing since he belongs to the opposition party, fears the needs of these young Kfar Oranim couples will never be met. The Likud government spends millions on the West Bank, he says, and can't spare a pittance to enable these couples to start their families. If only the government wouldn't be so rigid . . . if only the small sum needed could be made available to fix up the houses . . . if only . . . if only . . . I chime in with a vague expression of understanding. On this exchange of "if onlys . . .", I change the subject.

I ask what happened with the Chairman of the Trustees Committee. My question touches off a familiar harangue about Aryeh. The three-month trial period is over. An election was held and a man named Yishai was elected. Aryeh's status is unclear. He did not get to see any senior Project Renewal official in Jerusalem. He is the author of his own problems. Though they belong to the same political party, he despises the Mayor, and this is the key reason for his problems. As I leave, the Deputy Mayor reminds me of our appointment with the Director of the Junius Development Corporation.

Shimon, from the regional office of Project Renewal, is in Kfar Oranim to talk with me. He is Tamar's supervisor and he wants to discuss her difficulties with Aryeh. After some banter, we get to the purpose of our meeting. Aryeh refuses to be supervised by Tamar. He won't take a course for people in his category of work. He is not abiding by conditions set for part-time neighborhood workers. I refer to Aryeh as a paraprofessional. Shimon disputes this designation. I say I am just following everyone else in using the term. Shimon ignores my comment and keeps complaining about Aryeh's lack of discipline. I respond that Aryeh feels humiliated by having to be supervised by Tamar. He sees himself as a community leader. Shimon wonders why Aryeh lets himself be put in this position for a trifling stipend. I repeat the explanation Aryeh gave when he said he perceives the money as showing his recognition by the town's power structure. I quickly add that I think Aryeh is mistaken since the money confounds his status as a volunteer leader. However, he is adamant in his interpretation and brooks no argument.

Shimon thinks the money is important. He believes Aryeh is using it to supplement his income from a store he runs in Haifa. This is Shimon's version of the rumor Tamar mentioned to me. Shimon tells me consideration is being given to providing Aryeh with a monthly stipend of 5,000 shekels, not for his work but for his personal needs. This would encourage his bent for leadership. Shimon holds that this is the way things are done in America. I argue that it may be OK to encourage impoverished people in alienated racial ghettos but Aryeh is not impoverished and Kfar Oranim is not a racial ghetto in the sense of Black ghettos in the United States. Aryeh sees his neighborhood work as the stepping stone to a political career. I cannot understand the proposed monthly allottment. Since it is not a salary for work performed, is it some kind of politically motivated pay-off? It does not square with my understanding of leadership development. The money would only help to preserve an illusion that is causing turmoil. I must find out if there is substance to Shimon's talk about a grant to Aryeh. I must also check on Tamar's report that Aryeh is removing himself from public life.

I attend the meeting called by Zipporah of the government housing corporation. Some of her colleagues are present along with officials from the Ministry of Labor and Social Affairs. From Kfar Oranim, there are Tamar, Chaya, the worker with large families whom I met earlier, and Ilan from the Community Center. Uri alternates between this and another meeting. Ovadiah, who by now feels he personally initiated the youth work project, is not present, thus tempering my satisfaction with this impressive turnout of key people.

Zipporah talks about a neighborhood beautification project which concluded with a gala affair where prizes were awarded to those who excelled in dressing up their gardens. A film was made and Ilan offers to show it to us later. He asks about the youth work project and I am relieved that he raised the question.

Zipporah says the proposal was awaiting my return. Undirected discussion follows concerning an earlier meeting with Ovadiah. I break in to suggest the time has come for us to spell out a clear proposal instead of talking about vague ideas. We need to specify the work scheme, indicate what was tried elsewhere, describe the possibilities in Kfar Oranim, draw up a budget and recommend a three-year pilot project. Approval is expressed and I press on to ask who is going to write the proposal. Anticipating that I will be nominated, I say I will be glad to help with the writing but the author has to come from those present.

Shimon recommends Tamar. The group readily agrees. She is quiet. I doubt she has the background and the knowledge to produce the well-documented proposal which I envision but I say nothing. Ilan then announces he cannot screen the film that was mentioned earlier. I am pleased to be released from the group and the babble that passes for its proceedings.

November 11, 1982 - Kfar Oranim

I get together with Tamar to discuss her writing up the pilot project for youth work. Her idea is to prepare a document concerning housing and neighborhood organization aimed at creating a link between the government housing corporation and the Ministry of Labor and Social Affairs. She wants to omit references to youth to avoid angering the Youth Sub-Committee since the matter has not been raised with it. Uri drops by, listens to Tamar's statement and voices agreement. I am baffled by this surrealistic turn of events. Maybe I should have consulted the Youth Sub-Committee before talking with Ovadiah and Zipporah. I kept Uri informed since he is professionally responsible for youth work. He never mentioned the need to deal with the Youth Sub-Committee. Indeed, I received from him the impression that the Youth Sub-Committee is in a state of suspended animation with its budget frozen until an acceptable program is presented, approved and a worker hired to carry it out. I urged Ovadiah several times to report his idea of youth work to the Steering Committee. I am puzzled about where we are now and I tell Tamar I think she needs clarification from Zipporah. I plan to see Ovadiah but I wonder if he too has lost sight of what we set out to do before my trip.

I see Ralph, new Director of Volunteers for Kfar Oranim. He is a recent immigrant from Canada who seems to be moving into his work well. He gives me a run-down on his activities and asks that I put him in touch with a student who was in Kfar Oranim last year so that he can follow up on a pen-pal program that the student started. I agree to do so.

When I called Aryeh to convey my condolences on his mother's death, I got the feeling he was cutting his ties with community activities. As a result, I asked Tamar to arrange for me to meet Yehuda. I remain anxious to clear the slate with the Junius Hotel.

Tamar accompanies me to Yehuda's splendidly furnished home. He

113

welcomes us graciously and makes a fine impression. After some pleasantries, I tell him I am eager to resolve things with the Junius Hotel. He assures me that he has the same objective.

First, he shows me banners commemorating the annual walking competitions which he organized for Kfar Oranim and surrounding communities. He talks about a scholarship fund for needy students which he developed with the aid of donors in Junius.

Yehuda tells me that Ralph, the Director of Volunteers, came to see him for aid in enlisting volunteers. Yehuda complied with Ralph's request but if the town's ruling clique discovers this, Ralph would be fired. This is a symptom of the separate paths followed by the Town Council and Project Renewal. As a Town Council member, he is kept in the dark about Project Renewal. He comes across as a deeply involved community leader.

We discuss the Junius Hotel incident. He details what happened. His volunteers were running a fashion show when the damage occurred. It was caused by two Kfar Oranim men who had nothing to do with his group. They intruded, got into an argument with a waiter and, in the resulting fracas, a glass door was broken. His group was victimized by the trespassers as much as the hotel and Kfar Oranim collectively should not be blamed. He plans to see the hotel manager shortly and he hopes to persuade her that his group is not responsible for two rowdies who happen to live in Kfar Oranim.

I tell Yehuda his story is new to me. I would like to know what happens when he meets the manager. He promises to keep me informed and we exchange telephone numbers. I ask him to give my regards to the manager. He tells me she is being transferred to Jerusalem to become manager of a hotel there. This means I won't be able to resolve the discrepancies between Yehuda's account of what happened and hers.

Tamar and I leave by way of the garden which Yehuda proudly shows us. I thank him for our pleasant visit. I see Tamar looking furtively at a nearby house. She wonders if we have been spotted at the home of the Mayor's hated rival. I regret the split caused by this long-running fued.

November 18, 1982 - Kfar Oranim

I arrive early in order to have a chat with Ovadiah before our meeting with Zipporah and Tamar. I want to ascertain if he is still committed to the youth work project. I gladly learn he has not undergone the same puzzling metamorphosis as Tamar and Uri. He is ready to go ahead though his inquiries suggest scaling the project down from 15 youngsters to 8 or 10. We agree to see what we can do to proceed.

Tamar and Zipporah are accompanied by Amit, a neighborhood worker for the government housing corporation. Zipporah wants to take me on a tour after our meeting to show me the dramatic changes achieved by Amit in one neighborhood. She explains the confusion about our November 4, 1982 meeting. Its purpose was not to discuss the youth work project as I had anticipated but rather to coordinate the neighborhood work which is being done by different organizations. I am pleased to hear her explanation and relieved to know that the youth work project has not fallen apart. I am also delighted to know of her interest in coordination.

Tamar insists that the Youth Sub-Committee must be involved in the youth work project. I know Ovadiah is wary of bureaucratic entanglements especially with a committee that is still on paper. I observe that the Youth Sub-Committee should be kept informed for purposes of coordination. Ovadiah is simply planning to hire 8 or 10 young people to work on needed physical improvements. The fact that they are to come from Kfar Oranim rather than from outside should not require a complicated decision-making process. However, they need equipment which will cost about $2,000. Ovadiah feels this should come from Project Renewal. Tamar maintains her stance. She says the request for an allocation of $2,000 must go to the Youth Sub-Committee before going to the Steering Committee. We all agree. She also wants to report on the youth work project at a meeting of experts on alienated youth. Again, we all agree. Apparently, Tamar has activated the Youth Sub-Committee during my absence.

Two late-comers join the discussion. They are Dan, the Community Center Director, and Ranan who supervised Aaron, the dismissed youth worker. They caution us. Dan recently attended an all-day session on work with alienated youth in Project Renewal. He learned that all efforts either failed or ran into serious trouble. Amit supports this view, asserting that our project is almost sure to fail. The kind of youth that Ovadiah will be employing are not reliable. Ovadiah is annoyed by this pessimism and he leaves to get Uri's list of youth who are prospects for the project. I ask which course is better. We can heed the dire warnings and do nothing or we can take a chance and risk failure. I favor the latter choice since there is little to lose. The work has to be done and the equipment could be used by the school groups Ovadiah has recruited to clean up their school yards.

Ovadiah returns with a roster of fifty youths. He says we can surely find 8 to 10 willing workers from this list. Dan scans the names. He doesn't know everyone. Of those he does know, some have potential but most are too far gone in their delinquency to be included. He suggests a small, carefully supervised program and this provides enough legitimation for Ovadiah to proceed. I am pleased because I hope Ovadiah's enthusiasm will carry the project to success. I am glad it will be under his jurisdiction rather than under those whose determination to play it safe would lead them to do nothing.

The meeeting ends and Dan invites us to see the film that Ilan wanted to show on November 4, 1982. Zipporah insists we first view the results of Amit's work. The two apartment blocks on which he has concentrated are indeed clean and aesthetically pleasing. More apartment blocks are expected to join the beautification band wagon soon since Amit is working with 43 apartment block committees. We go to the Community Center but no one can get the complex TV contraption to work.

I see Rani, the Town Clerk, who says there is a problem with Leah which requires my intervention. With her encouragement, the Town Council rented a tractor to clean the streets. Now, she refuses to release money to pay the contractor, declaring this is not an appropriate charge against Project Renewal. Ovadiah stops at Rani's desk and is asked for confirmation of the story. He confirms her approval of the clean-up. Renting the tractor was a key component. If the bill is not paid, the contractor will refuse to deal with Kfar Oranim in the future. Leah is out of the country and I suggest that we await her return. Both men strenuously disagree. The town is paying interest on an overdue debt and we should appeal to Leah's supervisor without delay. There is nothing wrong with going over her head while she is holidaying abroad. The town deals with Project Renewal as an organization and not with one individual in the bureaucracy.

I reluctantly agree to call Project Renewal headquarters but I need all the details in writing along with whatever documentation they have. Rani promises to have a memo ready before I leave today. I need this material to be sure that I am dealing with more than subjective impressions or rumors.

Rani makes another request. Morris, a wealthy Junius resident, is interested in contributing a swimming pool to Kfar Oranim. He does not speak Hebrew and Rani asks me to get in touch with him. I am disinclined to take this seriously, having heard unfounded gossip in the past about prospective donors for a swimming pool. Rani is persistent and I phone Morris. We arrange an appointment at his home.

As I leave, I meet Ralph who takes advantage of this chance encounter. He has trouble with Ovadiah and Eitan. They are impatient with him even though he tried to ingratiate himself by moving into a portable van for immigrants in Kfar Oranim. He feels their pressure. I sympathize with Ralph. He is a '60's radical who returned to his Jewish roots. He is anxious to make a new start in Israel. I offer to put in a good word for him. I invite him home for dinner since he obviously needs support. He accepts willingly.

November 22, 1982 - Kfar Oranim, Junius

Leah brings together local youth workers and national organizations dealing with alienated youth. The center of attention is Gil from

"Eighteen Plus", a new set-up recommended by Project Renewal. It gives vocational training to youth over the age of eighteen and helps them find jobs.

Reports by the local workers open the meeting. Two women tell of their work with troubled young women and older teenagers. Tamar reports on the youth work project that Zipporah, Ovadiah and I have been trying to start. There is no report on work with male youth since there has been no male youth worker for the past six months. Kfar Oranim is low on the list for capable candidates to fill the vacancy.

Gil describes the "Eighteen Plus" program. It is like other vocational training efforts in Israel although it is aimed at a different age group. Several local workers express their doubts since factories are closing and youth are losing jobs. They want to know the source of new jobs. Gil asks for specifics about the factories they say are closing. He will bring together important people representing labor, management and government to see what can be done. Dan wonders about the coordination of this new program with existing national agencies in the same field. Gil tries to assure everyone that his organization will avoid duplication. He receives a polite reception. It is clear that Kfar Oranim workers are not convinced his organization can avoid stepping on the toes of the workers and agencies already in the field.

The meeting ends inconclusively. Vered asks several of us to remain. She introduces a young man as an applicant for the youth worker job in Kfar Oranim and she asks one of those who remained to interview the candidate. He is startled by Vered's request. After a few questions, he invites everyone to join the hiring committee. I don't envy the candidate who has to field questions from all over the room. He seems to know little about the work. He is asked to step out and we learn he was recommended by a Town Council member. Vered is outraged that so obviously unqualified a candidate was recommended. Someone suggests he be given a trial appointment during which he can be assigned to the youth work director in a nearby community. If he can learn the job, he should be hired. Otherwise, the trial appointment would terminate.

I drive to Junius with Rani, the Town Clerk, and Amos, the Deputy Mayor, to see Morris and his wife, Stella. We waste a half-hour trying to find their house and we are cordially received even though we are late.

Morris tells about his frustration in trying to build a pool for Kfar Oranim's children. There are many obstacles. The Orthodox don't want a pool open on Saturdays. Others are opposed because they see the pool as a pay-off to prevent the development of a beach. Still others point out that President Navon has promised a pool to

Kfar Oranim. And so on and so on. Amos insists all these objections belong to the past. I say the President's promise has no financial backing. Morris and Stella listen carefully. They heard this before but they are still open to building a pool. They express appreciation for my participation.

Morris asks about Project Renewal. I explain Croydon's connection to Kfar Oranim. He and Stella ask who will maintain the pool once it is built. Amos replies that an independent authority will be established to receive funds from the Town Council and, perhaps, from Project Renewal. Also, it will collect admission fees. Morris wants the pool to be free for Kfar Oranim residents. Amost quickly amends his statement to say that fees will be charged only to non-residents. We agree to meet at the Mayor's office to look at plans that have been drawn up. Rani promises to have the architect present as well as a representative of the construction company. The meeting is set for November 28, 1982 to accommodate Morris and Stella who are leaving three days later for a long trip abroad.

They will delegate responsibility to people authorized to act on their behalf. They hope the pool will be ready next summer. I echo their hope but Rani and Amos doubt the pool can be built so rapidly. We fall back on the old cliché that this is Israel where things take time. As we leave, I suggest that Morris and Stella invite Dalia to the meeting and I describe her helpfulness with the tennis project which, unfortunately, did not get off the ground. They know her and they readily agree to ask her to join us.

November 28, 1982 - Kfar Oranim

We assemble in the Mayor's office for the meeting on the pool. The Mayor, Deputy Mayor, Dan, Rani, Ovadiah, the architect, and Zev, representing the construction company, are present. Morris and Stella have brought Nadav who will represent them while they are away. He lives in Junius and has an office in Tel Aviv. Dalia is present as is Phyllis, Junius' representative on the Kfar Oranim Town Council. I talk with her before the meeting to placate her anger at Rani who, she feels, went over her head by meeting with Morris and Stella without notifying her. We ended our conversation pleasantly. Now that I meet her in person, I remind her of our telephone chat. I say I hope we can keep in touch. She agrees, saying many good things can come from a cooperative relationship among Kfar Oranim, Junius and Croydon. I hope this contact will be more productive than my first failed effort with Junius volunteers.

Morris asks for assurances that the objections mentioned when we met in his home are indeed behind us and will not plague future negotiations. I explain Morris' fears to the Mayor who says the objections are finished. He is ready to put the assurances in writing. Morris is satisfied. He turns to the architect who produces sketches of an athletic area, including a restaurant and facilities for tennis, soccer and other sports. The pool is to be half the size of an Olympic pool. Dalia objects, saying a half-size pool will limit its usefulness since only a few people will be able to use it. Also, lack of an Olympic-size pool means Kfar Oranim will be unable to hold swimming competitions with other communities. The architect asserts that an Olympic-size pool requires prohibitive maintenance costs. Stella agrees with Dalia but is aware of the costs and she suggests that we compromise by building a pool that is three-quarters of the Olympic size.

Morris asks for estimates. The architect replies that the entire development will cost $535,000. Morris says this figure is way out of line. Moreover, it entails a large-scale project which he says is nothing but a luxurious dream. What will the pool itself cost? The architect says the pool will cost $90,000. Morris claims he knows of Olympic-size pools that were built for $80,000. Why should this half-size pool cost $90,000? I break into the discussion to ask Zev if he can help with the price. He says he will submit an estimate in two weeks. Until then, he won't venture an opinion. Morris asks the architect to submit plans for a larger pool with realistic cost estimates and without the other features. He wants the plans and estimates in two weeks. The architect unwillingly agrees to provide new sketches and a revised estimate. I tell Zev we need his price in two weeks as a basis for comparison. He promises to have it and he announces that his company will cooperate on a non-profit basis. We agree to meet in two weeks. I exchange telephone numbers with Nadav to keep him informed during the absence of Morris and Stella. They hope we are getting somewhere despite the architect's cost estimates.

Phyllis says she sees Morris and Stella paying for the pool with others in Junius funding the remainder of the architect's comprehensive plan. I agree that this would be great and we all part with a nice feeling.

Ovadiah comes over to say the architect was high with his estimates. He tells me he is planning to ask the government housing corporation for funds to get the youth work project started. I urge him to go ahead while I seek money from Croydon or the Ministry of Labor and Social Affairs.

November 30, 1982 — Kfar Oranim

A new committee, set up while I was away, is meeting today. It is a response to the desire for more direct relationships with Croydon and the dissatisfaction with the limited relationships that now exist. These are confined to the short visits of Croydon missions, the brief annual visit of the Croydon delegation and individual visits by Croydon residents. There is interest in the idea of pen pals among school groups in the two communities and it was suggested that Croydon students in the High School in Israel be invited to visit Kfar Oranim.

All twelve people present are paid functionaries. Shimon, Tamar's supervisor, says we cannot proceed because the professionals cannot plan home hospitality. Finally, about a half-hour late, six volunteers straggle in and one reluctantly agrees to serve as chairman.

I recommend we focus on the visits by the High School students and think about two activities: home hospitality and a community reception. There is general agreement. Ralph says there will be a new group of students every three weeks. The volunteers say there will be no trouble in arranging home hospitality and a community reception. Furthermore, they assert this can easily be done for each group of students. A sub-committee is appointed to look after the arrangements.

The differentiation of responsibilities between Ralph and Tamar with regard to the High School students is unclear. The next day, I telephone Ralph who tells me he and Tamar agreed to divide the responsibilities. One will look after the community reception and the other will arrange for home hospitality. We make an appointment for next week. I am eager to learn his plans to get the supervision he so badly needs.

December 8, 1982 — Kfar Oranim

There is a general strike of Israel's civil servants. My scheduled meetings have been called off. Nevertheless, I go to Kfar Oranim because Ralph wants to keep our appointment.

We discuss the High School students. Plans are coming along satisfactorily and I see no reason to interfere. I suggest the students be encouraged to bring wine as a gift to their host families but Ralph disagrees and I do not press. I comment that he seems to be making headway with volunteers but he denies it. He doubts his employment will be extended beyond the six-month trial period. The Town Council is short of funds and he expects no sudden burst of enthusiasm for his efforts. His work on the visits of the High School students won't cut any ice because it is not what the agencies want. They need permanent volunteers to tutor students and help handicapped people with transportation. He has volunteers for single tasks but not for steady assignments. He claims the trouble lies with the residents who are not conditioned to this type of volunteer work. When the agencies ask for a regular volunteer, he cannot deliver and so they think he is a failure. I ask if he has thought of inviting agency representatives and leading volunteers to discuss the problem. Perhaps, they could proclaim as "Volunteer Week" to create a new awareness of volunteering. Ralph promptly rejects the idea, saying it wouldn't work, given the town's attitudes.

I ask how these developments affect his plans to settle in Israel.

He says he is determined to stay. If necessary, he will get a job in a local factory. We agree to meet again and Ralph is grateful that I am willing to keep in touch with him.

Eitan appears in the Community Center and says some Steering Committee members have decided to hold the scheduled meeting despite the strike. We assemble in the Mayor's office which was unlocked for us. About half the group is present. Eitan reports the decisions of the sub-committee which distributes grants to Kfar Oranim students attending university. The Steering Committee ratifies the recommendations.

Plans to receive the High School students are reviewed. Steering Committee members confirm what Ralph told me. They are sure that the reception of the students will maintain Kfar Oranim's sense of pride as a host. The Mayor agrees to participate and makes some suggestions which are accepted. A good spirit is engendered by this decision.

The feeling of amity is broken when a member requests funds for transporting boys from large families and from families where the father was killed in military service. The boys and their families are going to Jerusalem to celebrate their bar-mitzvahs at the Western Wall. The Mayor is angered by the request. He says the Steering Committee does not grant funds to small groups such as this. Someone shouts that if this allocation is approved, he will expect money for his group. The Mayor exclaims that the request intrudes politics into the work of the Steering Committee. His anger stirs in me the recollection that Yehuda was somehow involved in holding bar-mitzvah celebrations at the Wall for these boys. This explains why the Mayor is so furious. He refuses to go on with the meeting and he storms out of the room. Those left behind fall into squabbling groups.

I follow the Mayor into the outer office. He talks so pleasantly, I cannot believe he is the same man who strode out of the room in such rage a few moments ago. I tell him we need to convene the people who recently met to discuss the swimming pool. He says he is prepared to do so whenever the Junius group is ready. I go back to the meeting and ask Rani, the Town Clerk, whether or not the architect has the plans and the estimates he promised to provide when we met with Stella and Morris. Rani shrugs his shoulders and it becomes clear that the matter has been allowed to slide. I insist that the architect must be contacted. Rani doesn't react.

He changes the subject to the question of paying for the rental of the tractor. I tell him I learned from Project Renewal in Jerusalem that it is up to Ovadiah to request payment. Rani says he will get after Ovadiah.

December 14, 1982 — Kfar Oranim

My wife and I attend the annual "Mother of the Year" festival.

The Community Center audtorium is filled as it was last year. Dan welcomes us and escorts us to reserved seats in front of the overcrowded hall. After group singing and other entertainment, the master of ceremonies finally introduces the "Mothers of the Year". He describes their prowess in raising children with love and care, no easy task since they have large families. A rabbi offers a spiritual message, followed by the Mayor whose speech is filled with Biblical allusions.

Noam and Ariela are present. Appreciation is expressed to Ariela for getting firms to donate prizes for the winning mothers. She speaks warmly to the mothers and her comments are well received. I cannot help wondering if their participation is related to Noam's recent announcement of his candidacy in the coming Knesset elections.

After entertainment and a fashion show, the evening finally ends. People linger in the lobby to chat. I believe more imagination might have been shown in the planning.

December 15, 1982

I meet with Ruth at my university office. She is a liaison-consultant in a Jerusalem slum area, representing an American metropolis. She asked to meet me although she has no special issue to discuss. Ruth feels isolated. She tells me what she is doing. She asks if I attend the meetings of liaison-consultants, convened by Martin in Jerusalem. I say the times conflict with my lecture schedule. Also, I think the meetings aren't for the liaison-consultants but are designed to help Martin with his study of Project Renewal. It would be better if we met on our own to compare notes. Ruth likes this notion and offers to arrange a session.

December 21, 1982 — Kfar Oranim

The sub-committee planning for the High School students meets tonight and I attend at Ralph's request. I want to see him in action. Seven volunteers and four teenagers are present, a good turnout in view of the heavy rain.

Ralph handles the meeting poorly. He fumbles with papers and produces fragmentary bits of information. The teenagers sit silently while the other participants limp through the meeting. I get the impression that, one way or another, with or without Ralph, the visitors will be received. I have to make sure of this and I wonder to myself how I formed even a mildly positive impression of Ralph when we first met.

Decmeber 23, 1982 — Kfar Oranim

I want to follow up with Rani on the offer to build a pool. Other people I usually meet on a "drop-in" basis are not available. I bump into Gil, the representative of the "Eighteen Plus" organization. He is at loose ends because his scheduled meeting with Vered was canceled since her daughter is ill. I have time before my session with Rani and we chat about work with alienated youth. I tell Gil I am

122

disappointed with the lack of progress. I tie this to the absence of a youth worker for six months. He tells me the candidate interviewed last month was rejected. There is another candidate and Gil thinks he will get the job.

I begin my meeting with Rani by saying that Nadav who is representing Morris and Stella while they are away is waiting for the plans and estimates which the architect promised. I also tell him that I have learned from Nadav that Morris and Stella are not interested in the elaborate sports area which the architect planned. They only want a pool and they think that the architect's cost estimate is far too high.

Rani produces a letter from the architect with the same estimate he originally offered. I say that I think Morris and Stella will not accept this price. Rani is annoyed. "Then — let them not contribute," he says. He sees the price as fair. I am no expert but the price seems high to me. I ask what we can do to reduce it. He telephones the architect and listens for quite a while without speaking. He hangs up and says the architect is angry. He will submit no more sketches since he was not paid for the first ones. He doesn't care any more about Kfar Oranim's swimming pool.

Rani tells me the state of Kfar Oranim's treasury makes it unlikely that the architect will be paid. The construction company cannot provide estimates without the plans. I say the problem must be conveyed to Nadav. Rani is too embarrassed to do so and it becomes clear that I will need to talk with Nadav.

Rani says there is a new development. President Navon is to visit Kfar Oranim on February 16, 1983. During the visit, he will ask Junius residents to donate money for the pool. The government promised 25% of the cost and it is anticipated that the remainder will be raised by President Navon. I ask where this leaves Morris and Stella. How come they were not informed? Rani lifts his hands in a gesture that could mean he wasn't informed himself or he had not been free to talk about the President's visit or it just slipped his mind. His attitude is evasive. As I leave, he says that, of course, Morris and Stella will be invited to meet the President.

I see Yuval who doesn't seem very busy. I remind him we were going to talk about his organizing a coordinating body to bring about a systematic approach to the health, education and welfare activities in the town. He points out that the Town Council and the Steering Committee see themselves as fulfilling this role. However, he adds there are activities which are independent of both the Steering Committee and the Town Council. As an illustration, he cites the work of Yehuda, the Mayor's rival, in scholarship grants, public bar-mitzvah celebrations, the annual Kfar Oranim march and so on. Yehuda has wealthy supporters in Junius but his name is anathema to the officials in Kfar Oranim. Any municipal civil servant seen with Yehuda is summoned to the Mayor's office and warned to stop such contacts. Yuval himself was hauled on the carpet for talking with Yehuda even though the conversation was related to Yehuda's being an elected member of the Town Council. Yuval expects Yehuda to unseat the present Mayor.

I say this is interesting but neither the Town Council nor the Steering Committee can fill the coordinating role. My idea is for Yuval to convene the agency heads informally to discuss common problems such as the lack of centralized staff development programs. If this initial step could be nursed along until it became a regular opportunity to think jointly about common problems, the agencies will have moved toward planning and coordination. I assure him I discussed the idea with most of his colleagues and I will work closely with him every step of the way. However, the initiative for starting must come from within the group. I want to avoid their reliance on an outside prodder to launch the activity. Yuval sees my logic and states he would be pleased to help in establishing and maintaining the forum.

The conversation turns to Ralph. Yuval says people are dissatisfied. They think he is ineffective. Yuval doubts that Ralph will be kept on. I say I am aware of the problems. We set a date to talk more about the coordinating body.

December 25, 1982

I call Nadav to let him kow the architect's decision to discontinue his relationship with Kfar Oranim because he was not paid. I tell him as diplomatically as I can about the President's visit and the intent to use the occasion to raise money for the pool. He knows Kfar Oranim's pauperized situation. Morris and Stella may have to get their own architect. He will discuss this with Morris when they talk on the phone. As for the President's fund-raising affair, Nadav will be pleased to attend. He doesn't think Morris and Stella will be back in time but they will undoubtedly want to know their position as contributors in relation to any financial support the President is able to muster. I am relieved by his response. We agree to keep in touch.

December 30, 1982, December 31, 1982, January 1, 1983

Since the general strike is continuing and since my car is not available, I cannot get to Kfar Oranim to attend the reception for the High School students. Ralph and I have several telephone conversations before and after the meeting. The visit had its ups and downs. Only a few students came; the Mayor didn't show up for the community reception as he had promised; there was awkwardness between the visitors and the Kfar Oranim hosts. However, things improved as the visit progressed. Ralph feels it wasn't too bad for a first effort. I tell him we will have to review what happened to learn from the mistakes. I promise to call the High School principal to see if the visits can be put on a more predictable basis.

January 10, 1983 — Kfar Oranim

The strike is finally over and I go to Kfar Oranim to see Rani. I tell him about Nadav's mild reaction to the architect's refusal to provide further sketches and to the information about the President's visit. He is pleased and says we should discuss the matter with the Mayor. After that, we can see Nadav. I don't know what else we can tell him but I agree to call to see if he will meet us.

Rani suddenly asks why Croydon doesn't invite Kfar Oranim's leaders to visit the United States. Why is it a one-way street with Croydon representatives coming to Kfar Oranim but no traffic the other way? I say there would need to be a purpose for such visits, not merely the desire to travel to the United States. Rani conveys his disagreement by shaking his head dubiously.

I stop at the Welfare Department to see Uri. This day is set aside each week for people to see the "boss" about their complaints, questions and appeals. Uri is busy but he wants to talk with me. We sandwich our conversation between clients. He is concerned about Ralph whose six-month trial period is about over. While he is in many ways a disappointment, Uri would like to keep him, not as Director of Volunteers but as a worker with one job — recruiting volunteers to help the social workers and teachers. Uri is convinced the Town Council will not put up its 25% share of Ralph's salary. The balance now comes from the Ministry of Labor and Social Affairs. Uri wants me to support his request for Project Renewal to provide the 25%. I am hesitant since I have doubts about Ralph. We leave the subject with no clear decision.

Uri says he almost quit last week. The Town Council notified him that his travel allowance and his overtime pay were being discontinued. Uri lives at a distance from Kfar Oranim and often has to remain in the evening for meetings. He cannot rely on public transportation and he needs this subsidy to meet his car expenses. He wrote to the Town Council, threatening to quit and he was told some way would be found to continue the travel allowance and the overtime pay. I give a half-kidding, half-serious ultimatum "forbidding" him to leave. His going would be a sad loss for the town. He smiles appreciatively but says he is serious about quitting if the Town Council's commitment is not honored.

The conversation turns to alienated youth. Uri tells me about two lathes ordered by Aaron, the youth worker who has fired a few months ago. The lathes cost thousands of dollars and they are now gathering dust. This drives him up the wall. He suggested the lathes be sold but there is a legal impediment. The transaction took place while Uri was away on military reserve duty. He does not know who authorized the purchase. I decide to talk with Leah as soon as I get a chance.

Uri and I finish and I try to talk to Eitan about the lathes but he is away on reserve duty. I had once asked Eitan about buying lathes when Aaron was about to be fired. He said the machines would be absorbed by the technical "high school" which was to be converted into a training center to prepare people for high-paying jobs. For Kfar Oranim, this option was as important as the original purpose for which the lathes were bought. Eitan's keeping secret the complications which arose about diverting the equipment for other purposes is disturbing and surprising. He is a smooth operator in local politics. He is also a keeper of secrets which he shares or withholds based on a provincial sense of the importance he garners from his fund of undercover knowledge. He does not grasp the idea of sharing information on the basis of professional confidentiality. Ordinarily, what he tells me is reliable. The only way I see to make sure he retains credibility with me is to confront him directly. He must understand that this is not one of his secrets which he can decide to keep from me. A further complication is his having shared the secret with his colleagues. I realize I am not dealing with seasoned professional workers faced with a community problem. They are more like a conspiracy of cronies who feel guilty. Now that I know their secret, they will no doubt want to see what I do. I have made no decision but I am sure if I let it pass, they will conclude that I am a "soft touch". The problem has surfaced as a challenge. It offers an opportunity to drive home a lesson about the ethics of professional behavior based on a live situation rather than on an abstract discussion of morals.

I drop in to see Yuval and I ask if he knows anything about the lathes. He tells me it is common knowledge among the senior personnel in the town. The speculation is that Aaron was getting even with Kfar Oranim for firing him.

We discuss the coordinating group idea. Despite our earlier conversation about the inadvisability of an outside prodder, Yuval thinks pressure from Croydon might help get the group started. I say I will look into this. Meanwhile, I convince him that we should develop the idea ourselves.

Tamar and I talk about the upcoming session on the youth work project. I want to make sure that officials who can fund the project are present. Tamar says she will see to it.

January 11, 1982, January 12, 1983

To find out more about the lathes, I talk on the phone with Leah and Stephen in the Project Renewal office. I assert that this is a grave matter, involving misuse of funds. I did not know of the expenditure, nor did Croydon. I indicate that I shall report to Croydon and that I hope to get more information from Eitan. I intend to put him on notice that he has to do better in keeping me informed. Stephen agrees with me. He promises to back me completely since Project Renewal's credibility is at stake.

Leah shares my concern. She will arrange a meeting at which she, Eitan and I can go into the affair in detail. She tells me the new youth worker has not been appointed. In any event, he may not have the necessary background to use the lathes. I state that I am determined to see them as part of a genuine vocational training program in accordance with Eitan's assurances.

January 13, 1983 — Jerusalem

Although I told Ruth that I did not attend Martin's meetings of Project Renewal liaison-consultants, I arranged to be present today. About ten of us are in attendance. The discussion consists largely of a long report by the Rafeala liaison-consultant who enthusiastically describes his use of volunteers. He introduces two of them for presentations. They are followed by conversation about the preferable age of volunteers. Some members of the group support using youngsters and others say that more mature individuals are better. The discussion ends inconclusively.

January 16, 1983 — Givat Malka

I visit the High School in Israel to meet the people in charge, Rabbi Cohen and Oren. Rabbi Cohen describes the program's background. Originally, it was known as the Croydon High School in Israel. Since students and support now come from all over the United States, the Croydon designation has been dropped. However, 50% of the students still come from Croydon. The students are in Israel for two months, not three weeks as Ralph led me to believe. Both men were pleased with the students' visit to Kfar Oranim and they would like to see visits scheduled regularly. I mention that the first visit had a shaky start but things righted themselves. Both hosts and visitors felt their coming together was worthwhile. Two students showed up two weeks later to maintain the link with their host families.

Oren says Ralph's inexperience was evident but he tries his best. Oren plans to keep in touch with Ralph about future visits. I tell him I am not sure he will stay on the job. If he leaves, we will find some other way of making plans. I cannot fill that role since I don't live in Kfar Oranim. I am maintaining the contact in the absence of anyone else to do so.

I ask if the High School program includes volunteering by the students. Rabbi Cohen tells me that each student spends a month on a kibbutz as a volunteer. He is beginning to think it might be better to assign them to the communities "twinned" with their home towns in America. This would help Project Renewal, something Rabbi Cohen would like to do now that he has become familiar with Project

Renewal as a member of the Givat Malka Steering Committee. I tell him I recently heard a report on volunteers in Rafeala which bears out his views. Although I prefer American adults as volunteers, I recognize the value of having the High School students become a bridge between Israel and America. We agree to maintain contact. I am pleased by the positive and friendly tone of the visit.

January 17, 1983 — Kfar Oranim

Zipporah, Ovadiah and I have been talking about the youth work project for six months but there is no progress. Support was promised by the government housing corporation and the Ministry of Labor and Social Affairs but new officials of those organizations appear at each meeting and we start all over again, listening to stories about the failure of similar projects elsewhere. The meeting today is no exception. To make matters worse, Ovadiah, who is an avid supporter of the project, is delayed.

We start without him, discussing another subject — cooperation between the government housing corporation and Kfar Oranim. A workshop is scheduled to teach the residents home maintenance. There are now 30 apartment house committees and the plan is to have 100 in operation by the time the workshop takes place. I say this is a tall order but Zipporah is confident it can be done. Her worker has been effective in organizing these committees. Ovadiah finally comes in and the topic is dropped with good feeling about the progress, thanks to Zipporah's leadership.

Ovadiah says he is still interested in the youth work project despite the delays. He outlines what he needs to get going: a) assignment of 30 apartment houses for inclusion in the project; b) money to pay the participating teenagers; c) money for tools and supplies; d) a group worker to develop solidarity and a sense of purpose among the youth. His statement elicits vague assurances of cooperation. Then, almost as though on cue, one official echoes the chronic scenario of these meetings by telling about a similar project elsewhere that failed the day it started because the teenagers showed up not to work but to investigate the project. They decided the proposal was demeaning and left. I assert that the illustration just demonstrates lack of planning although I concede that the possibility of failure in Kfar Oranim exists. If all the doom stories are true, maybe we should drop the idea. It is suggested that we go ahead on a smaller scale — 15 apartment houses instead of 30. The Ministry of Labor and Social Affairs representative says he is ready to recommend financial support but he wants to know why the money can't come from Project Renewal. I inform him the Project Renewal budget for youth work is frozen until a sound program is developed and a professional worker appointed to direct it. Meanwhile, I am ready to urge Croydon to permit us to spend $2,000 for tools and supplies.

More suggestions are made. I interject that these good ideas will go the way of previous ones unless we find someone to take charge of the project. All eyes are fixed on Tamar. She says someone must do it and that she can't say no. I promise to work with her. We decide that the minutes of our meeting will constitute a request to the Ministry of Labor and Social Affairs for financial support. I get agreement from Ovadiah to meet regularly with Tamar. I press for a starting date for the project and we decide on April 1, 1983.

Ovadiah says he will need a group worker immediately. Giora, the representative of the Ministry of Labor and Social Affairs, offers to send a trainer-supervisor. Ovadiah retorts that's not what he needs. He wants someone to work with the youth. I ask Giora whether or not Ari can take care of this. He is baffled. "Who is Ari?" he asks. It is my turn to be astonished. I say, "Ari works with you at the Ministry. His department has a budget for work with alienated youth and he represented the Ministry at previous meetings." I assumed he was unable to come today and that Giora is here in his place.

Giora doesn't know what I am talking about. He came today at Tamar's invitation. He works in the Labor section of the Ministry. Apparently, Ari is in the Social Affairs section. These men don't know each other even though they work in the same Ministry and they both administer programs for alienated youth. I had heard that the two divisions of the Ministry were poorly coordinated but this is amazing. Tamar saves the day by saying that one of her youth leaders is not busy and she offers to have him do the work that Ovadiah says is needed. The meeting ends on a slightly more positive note than our previous sessions.

I go to Eitan's office where we are joined by Vered, Uri and Ovadiah. We fix dates for meetings of the sub-committees that must make budget decisions before the Croydon delegation arrives. Vered worries we won't have enough time because we lost a month due to her absence when her daughter was ill.

We finish the scheduling and I raise the question of the lathes. I have been waiting for Eitan's return from reserve duty. Now, we must act expeditiously since there is widespread gossip and everyone's reputation is at stake.

Uri reiterates his suggestion that the lathes be sold. Ovadiah wants to start a training program, using the lathes. Earlier in the day, Giora told me he tried to get the lathes transferred to a training institute in another town. However, the Jewish Agency lawyer said no, just as he vetoed Uri's suggestion. Uri argues for his proposal as the soundest and most honest one. We should admit that we made a mistake. He believes Croydon will respect such a stance. I assure Uri I want to find a sound and honest answer but his proposal was rejected by the Jewish Agency lawyer. Legal reasons prevent selling the lathes or transferring them. Even if it were possible, such actions are not so honest as Uri says. Recovering some money or having the lathes used elsewhere would only enable those responsible for the purchase to get off the hook. No one would have to account for the actions which led to this extravagant and wasteful expenditure. I believe the best solution is to use the machines in Kfar Oranim's vocational training program. Uri remains stubbornly opposed and I assure him I will report his views to Croydon. Eitan and Vered agree with me.

I ask Eitan for his help in answering the questions the Croydon delegation will undoubtedly raise. He assures me I will have his full cooperation. I don't ask why he didn't tell me about this matter earlier although I am puzzled by his reticence. Instead, I ask how come the lathes were bought with the youth work budget frozen. Eitan hastens to correct me. The lathes were bought on last year's budget and were ordered by the worker who was subsequently dismissed. I ask who authorized the purchase. On whose expert advice was it decided to buy expensive lathes? Where are they now? The last question is answered first. Ovadiah says one lathe is still in its original packing, well protected from deterioration. He can use it to train some youth for a useful trade. He needs a place to set it up. He adds that the machinery is too sophisticated for unskilled youth. The other lathe is being used by Malachti, the training school for youngsters with complicated family problems. Eitan is ready to take me to see the machine in use. As for the asnwers to my other questions, Eitan says they are available in minutes of the sub-committees. He will have the information for me when I return to Kfar Oranim.

January 20, 1983 — Kfar Oranim

Eitan gives me copies of minutes and letters pertaining to the lathes. I cannot trace the steps which led to the purchase decision. Knowing about record-keeping in Kfar Oranim, I suspect that much of the decision-making was done orally.

Eitan takes me to Malachti to see the lathe that is in use. On the way, he invites me to join him and Leah in interviewing a candidate for the youth work director's job. Eitan says it is important for me to be present. Also, we can talk further about the lathes. The appointment is scheduled for January 24, 1983. I agree to come.

At the Malachti School, the teacher and principal praise the lathe and contrast it with an old one that is no longer used. The new lathe is smeared in oil for protection. They tell me it will be available for others in the community besides their students. This complicated piece of machinery clearly requires considerable mathematical knowledge. It seems to be underused because few people can master its intricacies.

As we return to Eitan's office, he says that Malachti's pupils have such pronounced difficulties that everyone who makes a life for himself can be viewed as having been rescued.

I meet Yuval who tells me he has been working with Uri on the meeting of the professionals to exchange information as a first step to planning and coordination. He repeats his belief that a letter from Croydon urging this approach would be helpful and I promise to try to get it.

At the Welfare Department, Uri exudes pessimism. He has problems with the Town Council which he sees as totally hopeless. He vainly tried to interpret his work to the Deputy Mayor who thinks the Welfare Department is a waste. I ask if it might be helpful to talk with the Croydon delegation during its visit. He is dubious. A public discussion would add to the friction between him and the Town Council. I say it need not be done publicly. If it were raised privately and sensitively, he might be able to get some help. In any event, it could not add further problems since his views are well known. Uri insists nothing can change with the present Town Council. He is fixed in his view that the collective brain-power of its members is too low to run a town.

Uri shows me his recommendations to the Town Council for financial assistance to people in dire need. All have been rejected. I come back to my suggestion that he talk with the Croydon delegation. Conceivably, it might be of use. I point out that our discussions have not produced concrete results but I believe he has found them helpful. Talking with the visitors might give him a sense of support. It is my impression that Uri is moving towards leaving Kfar Oranim. I feel this will not be a good development for the town.

I ask if he has heard the rumor about the Ministry of Interior sending in supervisors to work with the Town Council to help Kfar Oranim live within its budget. Uri has heard the story. He thinks the only solution is for the Ministry to give the Mayor and the Town Council their walking papers.

January 24, 1983 — Kfar Oranim

In accordance with Eitan's invitation, I show up at the appointed time for the meeting with the candidate for the youth work director's job. Leah comes in, not with the candidate, but with Dan. She says something to Eitan and he tells me she wants a confidential meeting with him and Dan. They go into another room. After waiting a half-hour, I leave in irritation. I shall certainly take this up with Eitan and Leah. This is another example of boorishness surrounding the use of secrecy, similar to the incident of the lathes. Eitan's response to Leah was predictable. She is disliked and feared for her authoritarian ways by no one more than Eitan.

January 26, 1983 — Kfar Oranim

A series of sub-committee meetings is scheduled for today to prepare the budget for presentation to the Croydon delegation. I want to attend as many as I can to see if there has been improvement in their work over last year and because they provide useful information about the town's problems.

Now that her daughter has recovered, Vered is the animating spirit of these meetings. She prepares questions, provides background information and reduces issues to their essentials so that the sub-committees can reach their recommendations. I plan to attend two of the meetings.

First is the Sub-Committee on Community Social Welfare. Proceedings have just begun as I enter. Only one person is a volunteer; the others are paid workers. Eitan greets me and immediately apologizes for having kept me waiting yesterday. He reports that the idea of considering alternate sponsorship of the dental clinic is not feasible. Kfar Oranim is tied to the Kupat Holim network and is too small for anything else. This subject produced spirited and heated controversy at an earlier meeting but there is no discussion today.

The next item is disorganized families in which parents are unable to care properly for their children who come to school ill-clad and poorly fed. The parents need to learn the rudiments of homemaking but no money is available for teachers. The problem is noted but no action is taken.

The discussion moves to the laundry club. The existing one does not meet the demand. Someone says we should help large families buy washing machines rather than establish new clubs. Again, the issue is noted and no decision is made.

The Town Council's straitened finances clearly make it an unlikely source of funds for essential social programs.

A recommendation that tuition fees be paid for the neighborhood leaders who are taking BA courses is approved.

The worker who deals with "Kafkazim" reports progress in their response to Hebrew language courses. Her optimism is received with skepticism.

The budget for neighborhood development is presented by Tamar and accepted with little discussion. The meeting ends.

Next is the Sub-Committee on Informal Education. Dan delivers a gloomy report, forecasting severe cuts in the Community Center program. The ministries which provide funds had their budgets drastically slashed and are reducing support for local cultural and recreational activities. Project Renewal is now the major supporter of Community Center programs. Fund shortages will affect the community theater program, sports and the TV study group. The day camps will be scrutinized for possible savings. Neighborhood clubs will also face serious reductions.

Dan stresses the music programs which have nation-wide recognition. He thinks an economical approach will enable them to continue and even increase their effectiveness. It is vital to maintain these programs because Kfar Oranim is about to receive conservatory status based on the town's high standards of excellence in teaching music. However, a conservatory needs 5 million shekels a year. The Steering Committee and the Town Council will be confronted with hard decisions. Dan is a strong advocate of the music program and conservatory since he believes they will put Kfar Oranim on the map.

A suggestion to offer math courses to parents to enable them to help children with their homework is readily accepted.

January 27, 1983 — Kfar Oranim

The Steering Committee meets to review the budget. Eight of the 12 members present are paid workers.

The first item is a proposed modification to take into account inflation and a new policy that requires all employers to give a half-time appointment to any worker engaged for 8 or more hours a week. The Community Center is severely hit by this ruling and will need more money for personnel. Figures are presented by Eitan and there is lively discussion. No vote is taken as Eitan waits to discern consensus. He follows the same procedure with all other proposals. As soon as he detects agreement, he records approval.

After the budget review, other matters are taken up. Dan is concerned about Community Center programs for next year and the proposed conservatory. The Committee listens attentively but the responses are inconclusive.

Uri needs 200,000 shekels for poor families. He says this sum should be taken from the alienated youth budget which was not used this year. I remind him that the alienated youth budget was frozen by Croydon but Uri and Eitan assure me that the money to which Uri is referring comes from the government and not Croydon. Seeing nods, Eitan records a postive vote.

Shulamit says she isn't sure the budget, as modified, has been formally approved. She asks this be done forthwith because she wants the rest of the meeting to concentrate on a group of 50 or 60 children who attend school but who are illiterate. She asserts that this issue is more important than anything discussed thus far, including the conservatory. Sarcastically, the Mayor asks if it is more important than day care since Shulamit's organization operates two day care centers and she is a fierce advocate of their support. She responds defiantly that, yes, this issue is more important than day care. It is agreed that a special meeting of the Steering Committee will be called to discuss the problem. Shulamit prods the Mayor to schedule the meeting soon.

A committee member complains that many homes in town are afflicted with leaky plumbing systems. Ovadiah recasts the problem as one of leaking faucets. He says homeowners and tenants should look after this type of repair on their own.

The Mayor reports that President Navon will visit Kfar Oranim on February 16, 1983. He will host a meeting at the Junius Hotel to raise money for Kfar Oranim's swimming pool and sports field. The Town Council will have to appropriate funds for the visit since the town must be scrubbed clean. Some Junius residents associated with the "Beautiful Israel" organization were asked to help defray the street cleaning costs in preparation for the President's visit.

The Mayor's statement, especially the part about Junius residents, evokes a shrill response from Shulamit. The meeting degenerates into a screaming match. She bellows that inviting the Junius residents to participate opens the door to heaping another honor on Noam and Ariela who are always at the center when public recognition is handed out. She shrieks that the honorees should be local residents such as the volunteers who head large families. She wants it understood that she is not looking for recognition for herself. Ovadiah tries to enter the fray to quiet the storm. He wishes to explain Ariela's role. Shulamit yells that she doesn't want to hear from him. He quietly states that he is entitled to explain matters in his area of jurisdiction. Shulamit hollers that she doesn't want to hear from him no matter what his capacity is. He is a retired colonel with plenty of experience in action but he is obviously taken aback by this new kind of bombardment. He is effectively silenced.

The Mayor asks rhetorically, "What's wrong with asking Ariela and her friends to help make the town presentable?"

Shulamit slowly calms down. Eitan says we wouldn't need to rely on outsiders if we had our own volunteers. Ovadiah recently requested people to help plant trees. Not a single person turned out. Someone responds that the project was inadequately publicized. The matter is set aside.

Dan now introduces a subject which quickly becomes the most controversial one of the meeting even though it doesn't lead to a screeching confrontation. The Choral Group has been invited to tour South African Jewish communities. He thinks the invitation should be accepted. It will bring Kfar Oranim to the attention of Jews everywhere and it will bolster the youngsters. The cost of the tour is high but help is being requested only for the air fares — $20,000. The Mayor enthusiastically supports Dan's request. Uri says there are many more urgent needs. Tamar agrees with Uri. She claims that the Kfar Oranim leadership reacts on an ad hoc, unplanned basis. There is no vision of a good community and no planning to improve the quality of life. She refers to the proposed trip as "whipped cream" and maintains that we cannot substitute "whipped cream" for planning.

Project Renewal is suggested as a possible source for the fares and several people turn to me. They know I can't force Croydon's hand but they want to hear what I have to say. I indicate that I know this trip would be the chance of a lifetime for the youngsters and it would undoubtedly lift community morale. I mention the comments I invariably receive when I offer Kfar Oranim soldiers a lift. They always tell me that they will move just as soon as they finish military service. I tell Tamar I don't regard the trip as "whipped cream". It would help some residents and it would improve the town's self-image. A community does not live by welfare services alone. I conclude that, in principle, I support the trip.

Uri understands my point but he still disagrees strongly. Tamar holds fast to her negative opinion. Shulamit says the arguments pro and con are both valid. She cannot choose and she will abstain. Most of the others favor Dan's request. The Mayor hesitates to call for a vote. I say that nothing earth-shaking will happen if some negative votes are cast. The Mayor is looking for unanimity; he continues to stall. Eitan sails in to make things easy for the Mayor. The matter should have been cleared by a sub-committee before coming to the Steering Committee. The Mayor looks at Eitan with a sheepish smile, obviously relieved at this intervention. Eitan doesn't return the Mayor's look. He stares at his papers with the self-satisfied air of a fast thinker. Uri turns to me with a discomfited gaze. The Mayor adjourns the meeting.

January 30, 1983 — Kfar Oranim

I tell Eitan that one reason I am here today is the inadequacy of the information he gave me about the lathes. The material fails to show the origin of the decision to buy the lathes. Eitan says he will see a representative of the Ministry of Labor and Social Affairs who can trace the decision to its source. He will let me know by the end of the week.

I tell Eitan how annoyed I was last week when I was left waiting in his office for a half-hour. He is uneasy and blames Leah who asked for the confidential meeting. He will talk to her. I tell him I can talk to her myself. What I want is a clear understanding that if a meeting is cancelled, he will notify me. He says that what happened will not recur. I feel strongly because there is too much sloppiness about meeeting notices and cancellations. Unfortunately, this is a familiar phenomenon in Israel, not confined to Kfar Oranim, but I feel it is important to let my displeasure be known.

I meet with Ralph who is busy arranging for the next contingent of High School students. Some will be from Croydon but other American communities will also be represented. He hopes the visit will be successful since he has learned from the mistakes last time. The confusion about the Mayor's welcome will not be repeated. I learn for the first time that a reception with refreshments was awaiting the visitors in the Mayor's office while Ralph kept them in the

Community Center. I listen to his tale of the mix-up for which he was to blame. I express my hope that it will not happen again.

Ralph must have read my despairing thoughts about him and the mess he caused since he hastens to change the subject. He shows me albums of drawings, brochures and pictures which he prepared when he did community work in Canada. I see parts of the ghetto in which I was raised, the street where I lived and the school I attended thousands of miles away and years ago. I shake myself loose from this nostalgic interlude and we go back to business.

We talk about Ralph's future in Kfar Oranim. He says a decision will be made soon. I tell him I can't recommend a permanent appointment but I will suggest that he be kept on a month-to-month basis until this year's visits of the students are over. He says the town needs a Director of Volunteers, whether or not he gets the job. I ask his view of my suggestion. He is evasive but he registers no strong objections.

I make my recommendation to Eitan. He sees it as reasonable and will urge Ralph's employment for three months.

I report to Ralph my conversation with Eitan. He doesn't reject the idea but he is not wild about it.

February 6, 1983 — Kfar Oranim

I am late for the meeting of the Sub-Committee on Informal Education because of bad weather. Eitan interrupts the meeting to welcome me. The point being discussed is the responsibility of the Community Center for arranging municipal celebrations at the behest of the Town Council. The problem is the Town Council's difficulty in funding these events rather than whether they are an obligation of the Community Center. The discussion is unfocused and unresolved.

The activities and budget of the Community Center are reviewed in detail. The members go over the material with zest even though it was considered at the previous meeting. Several people present today were not at the other meeting.

Mordecai reports on the Friday evening programs sponsored by the Labor Party. About 50 to 60 young adults attend each week. Project Renewal has reduced its support for the program. There is unvoiced competition between the Labor Party and the Community Center with regard to this activity but the discussion omits reference to this feeling.

February 10, 1983 — Kfar Oranim

Many people I want to see today are away for one reason or another, mostly for military reserve duty. I hoped to explain to the Deputy Mayor that I must miss part of the President's visit since I have a prior commitment to deliver an address elsewhere on that day. However, the Deputy Mayor is not available.

Ralph is here and he tells me he is ready for the High School visitors. He had to ask that the number be reduced since he was not notified in sufficient time to prepare for the larger group the High School wanted to send. He made a schedule but he is worried about getting copies because the has difficulties with Kfar Oranim's nit-picking bureaucracy. I get this done and he is grateful.

Ralph says he could stay in Kfar Oranim with the Ministry of Labor and Social Affairs, providing that Project Renewal pays the 25% of his salary which the Town Council will no longer pay. However, he is uncertain since both Uri and his supervisor at the Ministry are down on him for not producing more volunteers. He perseveres in his view that Kfar Oranim badly needs conditioninng to the idea of volunteering. He sees the visits of the High School students and the used clothing shop he is trying to organize as promising starts. I ask why he does not ask the organizations he is trying to interest in the shop to consider the agencies' needs for volunteers. He evades an answer and he doesn't remember that we discussed this approach several times in the last few weeks. He has to distribute the schedules so he takes off.

I go to the Community Center to see Dan. We discuss an invitation to send two Kfar Oranim youngsters to Croydon as camp counselors. He likes the idea but picking two youngsters will be hard because those not selected will be disappointed. He says we have to plan the selection process very carefully. We decide to wait for the Croydon delegation to get more information about the proposal.

I introduce the notion of a meeting between agency heads and the Croydon delegation. They could provide a picture of the needs, problems and issues which confront Kfar Oranim. Dan likes the idea and agrees that Yuval would be a good one to convene a preliminary, planning meeting. Dan recommends we include the Mayor. I have no objection but I doubt he would be interested in the details of social problems. Dan accepts my comment and we consider others who might be invited. We quickly identify four people and then we decide to give more thought as to who else should be included. Meanwhile, I will give the names to Yuval so that he may call the meeting.

February 13, 1983 — Kfar Oranim

I meet Tamar to check on progress in forming a youth work group under Ovadiah as discussed often. Ovadiah was on reserve duty but has now returned. The Mayor was away this past week. He has to release the funds and approve the apartment blocks chosen to receive service. I tell Tamar I will see Ovadiah next time I am in Kfar Oranim to make sure that arrangements are complete. He is away today on town business. Tamar invites me to an all-day institute for community activists which will take place next month in a nearby town. Kfar Oranim's neighborhood workers will attend. I agree to come.

I tell Yuval that Dan approved the plan to convene the agency heads. I give him the names we chose. He promises to schedule the meeting and will report to me in a few days.

Yosef, an official in the Ministry of Housing, telephones to say he is about to go into a meeting of Jewish Agency and government representatives. He wants to know if there is anything I have to tell him about Kfar's Oranim's fiscal situation since the Project Renewal budget is to be considered. I am confused by his request. I tell him as casually as I can that the Croydon delegation will visit in three weeks to review the proposed budget for 1983-1984. I ask the connection between the budget session he is going into and the delegation's impending deliberations. He replies that he has heard nothing about a budget review by the Croydon delegation. He has neither time nor interest in coordinating his committee with the Croydon delegation. I am loathe to go into budget details and so I talk generally about the Community Center and the Welfare Department. The Town Council cannot support these agencies adequately and I ask him to do what he can to get them the money they need. He has no time for further discussion before his meeting and he is satisfied with my abbreviated response. He ends by saying he plans to visit Croydon soon. I give him some messages and I say I look forward to seeing him on his return. He agrees that we should keep in touch. I am astonished by the contradiction between his interest in visiting Croydon and his readiness to ignore its representatives in budget decisions.

February 16, 1983 — Kfar Oranim, Junius

President Navon is welcomed in the Community Center library where a hundred people are jammed together. He is serenaded by the Youth Orchestra, greatly reduced in size by the limits of the packed room. The Mayor introduces him to some of the functionaries. On hearing one name, the President asks how a man with such an Ashkenazi name manages in so Sephardic a town as Kfar Oranim. This sally is greeted with laughter. The President turns to the leader of the Youth Orchestra and asks about its repertoire. He is told it is big enough for a two or three-hour concert. The President mops his brow and states that's too much for him. Again, there is much laughter. He shall invite the Orchestra to play in the President's residence. He thanks the Mayor for the warm reception and says that he will speak at greater length later in the day

The Mayor and the President tour the Community Center. A large entourage follows them. Many of us wait in the foyer where people from Junius and Kfar Oranim mingle. Myron introduces me to Percy, the Junius resident who arranged for the Choral Group to tour South Africa. He tells me that all costs in South Africa will be met by Jews there but the air fare has to be paid in Israel. Ariela joins us and participates actively in the conversation. She is alone; Noam is away on business. She wants to meet the Croydon delegation during its visit. Since the Choral Group is going to South Africa, she hopes to persuade the delegation to pay for a trip to America by the Youth Orchestra. I promise to send her request to Croydon. She keeps making the case for the trip, saying it will be good for the young people and for the town. Her advocacy is undoubtedly the result of Dan's success in convincing her that the trip is a good idea, overcoming her earlier reservations. She is cordial and pleasant even though she was curt in our few exchanges since the last visit of the Croydon delegation. I am sure she is still disappointed about the lack of results from that session.

The tour finishes and the President enters the foyer. Eitan introduces me as Croydon's Project Renewal liaison-consultant. We chat for a few moments and the President asks if I have seen any progress in Kfar Oranim since I began to work in the community. I want to give him a qualified "yes" but the entourage is moving rapidly and my "yes" sounds more firm than I intended it to be. The Mayor catches my "yes" without the qualifications and he is pleased.

The President goes outside where people are waiting, straining to reach out and touch him. He approaches the barriers, shaking hands while moving along. The women begin to ululate in accordance with Sephardic custom. This adds to the outpouring of great affection for the President.

The next scheduled stop is the Washington Club for senior citizens. As I walk to the Club, I pass the market area which is usually a mess with discarded vegetables, chicken feathers and garbage strewn in the street. Today, the area is clean. I arrive at the Club where people are waiting for the President. Across the street, work is proceeding on the renovation of a group of apartment houses.

I take a look at the job which is supported by Project Renewal funds. The gleaming new stucco just applied to some houses distinguishes them from the untouched buildings. The gardens surrounding the houses are being dug. In some places, enough work has been completed to reveal what an attractive, well-planned area this was before it was allowed to deteriorate. I wonder how long it will retain its improved appearance before going to pot again. These apartments suffer hard wear and tear because they are too small for the big families that occupy them. Project Renewal has no plans to enlarge them.

The President arrives and people rush to shake his hand. He is obviously much-loved. Uri leads him into the building where he spends ten minutes. On the way out, a man addresses him in Russian and, to everyone's surprise, the President responds in Russian. Uri tells me that, inside, the President spoke to the Ashkenazi old people in Yiddish.

Uri and I walk to our cars to drive to the Scopus Manufacturing Company for a luncheon in honor of the President. The luncheon is there because Zalman, the factory owner, is footing the bill. As we walk, Uri tells me that an informal survey turned up 90 alcoholics in Kfar Oranim. This is a high figure for a small town. The alcoholics are mostly "Kafkazim". Uri tried to get help for them from an alcoholism treatment center. However, it is far from Kfar Oranim. By public transportation, it takes three-and-a-half hours and three buses to get there. Uri asked that a branch be placed in Kfar Oranim but his request was rejected for lack of funds. The head of the center offered to train one of Uri's workers and he was thinking about sending Yoram, the man I interviewed some time ago. However, Yoram is recuperating from a heart attack and, in any event, Uri is not impressed with his work.

Uri bemoans the lack of resources for Kfar Oranim. He talked with the heads of neighboring welfare departments who share his concern for their communities. On behalf of ten of them, he wrote to the Ministry of Labor and Social Affairs official who is responsible for this area. He asked the man to come and meet with the department heads to discuss opening a clinic for family counseling with young couples. He got a brusque reply saying that if they want to meet, they can come to the area headquarters. But — it will be no use; there is no money for such a clinic in their area.

As we near the cars, a woman stops Uri. She speaks anxiously but they are out of my hearing. Shulamit comes over and says she is disenchanted by the President raising money for a swimming pool and sports area when there are so many more pressing needs. We are back to the discussion at the Steering Committee meeting. Shulamit repeats her complaint that too many honors are heaped on Ariela and Noam as well as on other "people of the villas", her derogatory appelation for Junius residents. I restate my view that we need to go beyond the needy population so as to avoid making the entire town an extension of the Welfare Department. Uri joins us and she looks to him for support. He tells us that the woman who stopped him is the wife of a man who began a hunger strike this morning in the town square to protest against the lack of help from the Welfare Department. He chose this time, during the President's visit, to increase his chances of getting public attention. Uri says the man has justification but he has refused all offers to help him write the necessary letters for a review of his case. Uri thinks that the man is emotionally disturbed and the fast is hokum.

We arrive at the factory where Uri and Shulamit get out. I have to go to the meeting where I am speaking today.

I return at 5 P.M. in time for the closing ceremony in the Community Center auditorium. People are trying to enter the packed hall. I slip in just as the Mayor introduces the President who says that instead of giving a speech, he would like to chat with high school students in the audience. With a sly smile, he says the rest of us can listen. He asks the students to address two questions: what is good about Kfar Oranim and what needs improving? Three attractive and articulate girls of 16 or 17 deal in turn with the issues. One says that the town offers a great social life to young people but it is bare when it comes to recreation, entertainment, and leisure-time activities. The Community Center doesn't meet their needs and there is no movie theater. As the girls speak, the President injects levity by insisting they use the guttural sounds which befit their ethnic background. He is clearly at home in the Sephardic dialect, to the audience's delight. The girls make a gulping effort to work in the glottal stops to sound like Sephardim and the people roar with laughter.

A man rises and makes harsh comments about the Build-Your-Own-Home program, claiming people worked hard on their homes only to be denied municipal services such as sewage, water and electricity. The President asks the Mayor and other municipal officials to respond. Then, switching the subject to wind up on a positive note, he says that Kfar Oranim students do well on exams and that other good things have come to Kfar Oranim of which the best is Project Renewal. To my surprise, the President locates me in the audience and points to me, saying that a representative of Croydon which supports Project Renewal is present. He bends to the Mayor, asking to be reminded of my name which he then announces aloud. My reaction is that this man is thoughtful, benign, — and he is a real professional.

The man unhappy about the Build-Your-Own-Home program sits down and the woman who stopped Uri tells her tale of woe. She says she is speaking for her husband who is on a hunger strike. To emphasize her plight, she says that were the President to visit her home, all she could offer him is a glass of cold water because she has no gas to heat water for tea or coffee. The President is sympathetic. He assures her he will work with the Mayor to see to it that her problem is solved without bureaucratic delays. The crowd greets his statement with a great burst of applause and the woman sits down, beaming at the good fortune which has come her way.

The President says he will now respond to the girls who answered his questions. He rejects their complaints about insufficient recreational facilities. If they want to change things, they should make demands to the responsible officials. "How old do you think Golda Meir or David Ben Gurion were when they began to change their world?", he asks rhetorically. He deals with Kfar Oranim's poor image which its residents keep perpetuating. He is sad to report this same reaction in other development towns. He tells the girls that Kfar Oranim will gain status in their eyes when they take pride in themselves.

The President has overstayed his time in Kfar Oranim. He has to leave to meet the philanthropists who are waiting at the Junius Hotel. He arrives there and is seated at the head table. A well-known Israeli industrialist appeals for funds to build a swimming pool and sports complex in Kfar Oranim. He says it is unthinkable for the people of Junius to be indifferent to the needs of their less privileged neighbors. He introduces the President who speaks in a similar vein. This is the first time since he became president that he has made such an appeal. He feels that it is unhealthy for an affluent community to ignore the problems of its neighbors.

Pledges are announced. The first speaker will give the equivalent of $55,000. The next gift is for $20,000 and then there is one of $5,000. Several people give $2,000; others pledge $1,000. One donor says she will give $2,000 and that Morris and Stella who are out of the country are prepared to contribute between $80,000 and $100,000. She adds that Morris and Stella expect the pool to bear their name. The pledging continues raggedly. It is obvious that no one was canvassed in advance and that this amateurish effort has had no help from professional fund-raisers. It degenerates into a helter-skelter affair. Finally, someone gets up and says the total pledges are far short of what is needed to start the work. Donations must be doubled but this appeal gets no response. The chairman tries valiantly to end on a high note, saying that while the amount raised is below expectation, he and his friends will persevere until their efforts are successful.

As I leave, I meet the architect who refused to continue work without payment. I ask if he will stay on the project. He replies that in view of what he was paid so far, he should be considered the first contributor to Kfar Oranim's pool.

March 7, 1983 — Kfar Oranim

The Croydon delegation is due next week for its annual budget review. I am on my way to meet Eitan to check the program. We need to review the tasks assigned to various people.

As I drive, I review what I want to take up with the delegation. Last year's visit showed the usefulness of a face-to-face exchange and I look forward to our session. I am better prepared this year after 18 months on the job.

I envisage a wide-ranging interchange including factual information which is in short supply. We are in a period of interregnum as we wait for a new director. Hanoch's resignation took effect two weeks ago. The mood is static, yet restless — a prolonged transition that yields rumor-mongering. There is talk that Kfar Oranim is in a winding-down stage in Project Renewal. I don't know how much credence to give the gossip but it is unsettling. A complication is my plan to be abroad during August and September. If the change is some years off, I could ask someone like Uri to pinch hit for me. However, if what is being bruited about is more immediate, then I must ask the delegation to replace me so that a new person can take over for what may be a different phase. I must deal with these issues while the delegation is here.

I am pleased that the delegation agreed to meet with the professionals, a step that I hope will bring them together in an organized collectivity. The need is becoming clearer each week. Were the group now in existence, the agency heads would not feel so isolated in dealing with the Mayor and the Town Council. The presence of such an ongoing body would have a bracing effect on Uri and Tamar in their encounters with Kfar Oranim's elected officials.

The question of the lathes is on my mind. This costly purchase might have been prevented had there been a coordinating group to provide guidance. Without it, the professionals saw what happened as a personal matter between Aaron and the Mayor. They played no part in Aaron's securing approval to buy the lathes even though they all knew that he was persona non grata with the Mayor.

Mark sees the coordinating group as a self-evident good. He wonders why I waited so long to start it. His letters are cordial and his frankness is rancor-free but he questions what he sees as my undue caution. He wants me to be more aggressive in this and other matters. Getting into a polemic with Mark will complicate our correspondence. When he is here, I hope to explain that aggressiveness is not needed to nudge Yuval and his colleagues, as I have been doing. Nor is Croydon asked to apply a push that Mark may think is lacking here. Coming from a community accustomed to planning and coordinaton, the delegation can exercise a positive influence on Yuval and his colleagues. Expression of sympathetic interest by the delegation and trading ideas on the subject could be an incentive to Kfar Oranim's agency heads.

Mark's use of "aggressiveness", implies a wish for more direct, unequivocal behavior on my part as Croydon's representative. That can only come about if Mark responds clearly to the initiatives about which I have written him. My role was just emerging when the delegation visited last year. It is now more crystallized. My efforts to organize a three-way support system were pursued in a tentative manner. They can be fully activated once Croydon gives me a go-ahead. This requires the delegation spending time in Junius and engaging Junius as a participating host to Croydon visitors. Such involvement, legitimated by Croydon, would enable me to get to the larger Junius community. The importance of the Junius support system goes beyond its potential in economic aid. Junius could become Kfar Oranim's third power center after the Town Council and the Steering

Committee. If the neighborhood activists were bolstered by Junius, they could function from a position of strength in their lobbying activities. The Mayor would have to reckon with such an organization. Now, he can keep the neighborhood activists ineffectual. Tamar works well with them since being freed from the obstacles that Aryeh put in her way. However, to stand up to the Mayor and other decision-makers, she needs influential supporters such as could be provided by Junius.

The essential question is not whether I am aggressive enough but rather whether I can bring to fruition a coalition of Kfar Oranim, Croydon and Junius. Entrusting a task of such scope to a person far from the sponsor is a risk for Croydon, especially if there is uncertainty about adopting my strategy. Perhaps Croydon's original involvement was meant to extend solely to its distant partner and not to Junius. Perhaps, there was no intention of getting deeply into partnership with Kfar Oranim. Inter-community coalition building to raise Kfar Oranim's morale may be more than Croydon wants.

Other elements in my role need clarifying. Is the delegation still cool to the idea of aided self-help coming from Junius as it was last year? What about the growing expectation of activism on my part in dealing with Project Renewal headquarters and in confronting government officials? Does Croydon appreciate my steady advocacy within Kfar Oranim or is it interested only in externally directed pressure?

Mark and I have lots of work to delineate my role. We have to differentiate areas where I can function assertively from those in which lack of authority in the role of liaison-consultant cannot be overcome by aggressiveness. Yet, if I am to judge by last year, we will not have time for a comprehensive review and assessment. If Mark could remain after the delegation leaves, we could handle these questions. This is an ideal to be hoped for.

My ruminations end as I arrive at Eitan's office. We go over the schedule. Everything seems to be in order. To make sure that we are ready for last-minute hitches, we decide to meet once more before the delegation arrives. I am concerned that Leah will conduct the budget reviews instead of Vered. Eitan says that Vered has been assigned elsewhere and will not return to Kfar Oranim. I am sorry since she had a good impact on the sub-committees. Leah is a tough administrator who can hold her own in an adversarial encounter. However, she lacks the traits which make Vered ideally suited for work with the sub-committees. Moreover, Leah does not have Vered's close contact with them. This is an undesirable change but it seems that nothing can be done about it.

I discuss the visit with Tamar. She took over all the neighborhood work after Aryeh withdrew. She has none of his charisma but her quiet dedication is a great asset. I regret that we won't have the excitement that Aryeh generated last year when the delegation confronted the Ministry of Housing over the open sewers. I am eager for Tamar to tell the delegation about her course for neighborhood activists. Disrupted by the Lebanese war, it has not started again. Emphasis on leadership skills, civics and organizational know-how will no doubt impress the delegation as a basis for social action.

Tamar talks about one unanticipated consequence of the Camp David agreement which may have an impact on Kfar Oranim. As a result of the accord, a Sinai settlement was evacuated. Some of its former residents bought homes in Junius, having been richly compensated for leaving the Sinai. These nouveau riche were attracted to the posh villas of Junius even though they have little in common with their upper-class neighbors. The newcomers are kindred in spirit to the residents of Kfar Oranim. Tamar and her indigenous leaders are trying to encourage contacts between these people and Kfar Oranim residents.

As I listen, I can't help projecting into the future. A handful of public-spirited and financially secure individuals could work with Kfar Oranim on economic development. The idea of a chamber of commerce type of structure to push such development has been put on the back burner because of the war in Lebanon. However, mounting concern about the Israeli army being mired in the hills and valleys of Lebanon suggests that this morale-sapping danger will soon end. War re-arranges priorities in Israel. I express to Tamar my hope that we can work with these new Junius residents to revive our economic development efforts. We plan for Tamar to raise this with the delegation since we need to know their reactions to the idea.

March 14, 1983 — Kfar Oranim

Eitan and I give the delegation's schedule a final once-over. He tells me that our plans for the initial meetings are out. Instead of coming here immediately on arrival, the delegation is to have a briefing at the airport. The news is outrageous but not surprising. With travel agencies, airline delays and the Jewish Agency all involved, it is rare that a mission comes through these variegated inputs without last-minute upsets and that knock pre-arranged schedules for a loop. That's why Eitan and I are having today's meeting.

Without Hanoch to offer the briefing he gave last year, I assume the Project Renewal office has whomped up this intervention which takes the time we allotted for sessions at the start of the visit. Eitan just learned about the change. We are bewildered by this bizarre development. The schedule we planned is so full that it will be impossible to squeeze in the pre-empted meetings. This is unfortunate because one was with the agency heads. I counted on this session to initiate the badly needed clearing-house process for exchanging

145

ideas and information. As soon as Hanoch's replacement is available, I will complain about this high-handed interference with the plans we so carefully drew up for the visit.

The change eliminates my preliminary meeting with the delegation. This means I will only have piecemeal parleys between scheduled activities. I decide to prepare a statement for the delegation, listing the topics we need to consider.

March 15, 1983 — Junius

I want to leave my memorandum for the visitors at the hotel but I can't drive because of a bad back. I press my son into service. He reluctantly agrees to take me if I promise that he will be able to get to Tel Aviv in time for an urgent meeting which is vitally important to his career. He stresses that he cannot afford to be late and I assure him that I only need a moment in Junius to hand envelopes to the desk clerk.

At the hotel, I give the clerk the envelopes. I am surprised when he gives me a message to call Mark. My son sees me walking to the house phone and reminds me of his appointment. I assure him that he'll be there in time.

Mark answers the phone and says the delegation has been waiting two hours for this evening's scheduled meetings. My calm voice doesn't reveal my astonishment. Luckily, Mark cannot see my dumbfounded expression. I ask what happened to the delegation's airport briefing. Mark doesn't know what I am talking about. The delegation arrived at the hotel expecting the agency heads and me to be on hand for the meetings on the schedule he received before leaving Croydon. The delegation will be down in the lobby to meet me in a few minutes.

They soon appear and it is plain to see that they are perturbed. I try to explain what happened but they are impatient to get started. They pay no heed to what I am saying and I drop the explanation. It is just as well because my story would only compound the implausibility of what happened. The brand of bedlam known in Hebrew as *balagan* which is produced by bungling bureaucrats strung out at strategic points of touring missions is a staple in the repertoire of Israeli raconteurs. In time, this experience will no doubt become a highlight in my own collection of reminiscences especially when I learn, as I eventually will, which mission was mistakenly picked up at the airport for an unintended briefing. These thoughts come as balm to what is now happening to me.

We move to the same corner of the lobby we occupied last year. Melvin is again the center of the group. But — here, the similarity ends. A year ago, everything was easygoing. Now, we are all tense. Our veneer of poise is a thin raft floating on a sea of uneasiness. The delegation has come from afar to find the painstakingly prepared program bewilderingly awry. I can't blame them for being upset and

146

I have no hope for a fruitful discussion.

My son is standing a short distance away, sending out distress signals. I keep him on hold with a hurried, reassuring glance. He knows that my bad back will make it hard for me to find my own way home but he must get to his important meeting.

Melvin asks what is happening with Kfar Oranim's school system, in keeping with Croydon's having assigned high priority to improving education. I say the introduction of computers has aided in teaching mathematics, English and other subjects. They will see this program in operation and will receive a detailed explanation. The computers are paying off and Croydon's subsidy for this program is a sound investment.

I then do what I must. I inform the group that I have to leave. Melvin does not respond. Instead, he asks about conditions in general with respect to formal education in Kfar Oranim. I say there has been little change. Graduates of Kfar Oranim's elementary schools still have to go to a neighboring town for high school education. A high school in Kfar Oranim would avoid this and pressure the elementary schools to raise their standards. However, the Ministry of Education is not inclined to take the costly step of establishing a high school in Kfar Oranim. I hesitate to go into all the factors that affect Kfar Oranim's school system and Melvin finally says they will let me go. This pointed comment lets me know he is aware of my holding back. His understanding of my reticence is just as valid as the reasons I give myself for it.

March 16, 1983 — Kfar Oranim

We assemble in the Mayor's office where he greets us with great warmth. Leah takes over and launches into a progress report. She emphasizes fiscal matters without the sidelights that featured Hanoch's presentation last year and which captivated the delegation. Recognizing that they can't expect from Leah a wide-ranging overview, the delegation asks straight-forward questions. Within her scope, she has command of the material and the delegation appears to be satisfied.

Leah finishes and we have a coffee break. I talk with each member of the delegation and am agreeably surprised by their cordiality. We go over today's schedule. No reference is made to what happened last night. I am curious as to whether or not they read my memorandum but I do not ask.

We tour the agencies and see visible results of the renovations and building supported by Croydon. These rounds are living progress reports which inspire the visitors. The same vivid testimony is given as we visit the social programs and see children responding to nursery teachers in the day care centers, pupils using the computers and old people meeting in their modest social hall. This clear confirmation of the results produced by Croydon's money may be why there is little quibbling about including in the Project Renewal budget some programs which could be charged to the Town Council budget.

During the day, the delegation sees community representatives and the man in the street as client, patient or student. At the Community Center, the delegation observes people in their natural activities. Some residents take advantage of these opportunities to complain or to advocate for a swimming pool. The visitors listen sympathetically. They are pleased by the progress they see and they are gratified that Project Renewal appears to be a factor in the affairs of the town. Obvious evidence is the covered sewers which the delegation inspects with great pleasure and satisfaction.

The delegation's favorable impression is reinforced by the gala community dinner. The food is a mosaic of culinary ethnicity. Long tables are laden with morsels prepared by women who are skilled in the folk arts of food preparation. Members of the delegation, accompanied by elected officials, neighborhood leaders and community workers, armed with plates and cutlery, move from table to table, each one marked Libya, Morocco, Russia, Rumania and so forth. The women urge the guests to pile their plates higher and higher. They promise the food won't run out; there is plenty more waiting in the kitchen. With ringing invitations to come back for seconds, the guests carry their loaded plates to tables where they sit with residents. Barriers of language are overcome. Linguistic skill is unnecessary to enjoy this gastronomic extravaganza and its accompanying good fellowship. Eventually, the chattering and the eating give way to the obligatory speeches of the local notables and the inevitable entertainment by the Choral Group and the Youth Orchestra.

We finally return to the Junius Hotel and take a breather. That's not entirely accurate because no one seems to be tired. It has been a good day and the delegation is not ready for bed.

Mark uses the opportunity to tell about interviewing candidates selected by Dan to spend part of the summer as counselors in the Croydon Jewish Community Center day camp. He is sure he selected the two best candidates. Dan plainly solved his problem of picking people without antagonizing anyone by passing the buck to Mark. The delegation hears Mark without response. Everyone is mulling over the day's events and lapsing into individual reflections.

After allowing the mood to run its course, I break the silence by mentioning the material I sent concerning the two lathes. I mention that the transaction involved a major expenditure by the youth worker who was feuding with the Mayor and who was headed for dismissal. After much soul-searching, Uri revealed the whole incident to me, feeling that there must be a forthright relationship between Croydon and Kfar Oranim. My comments are received quietly. Mark remarks that this is old history. He questions the use of raking it up now. He voices the consensus of the delegation, judging by the concurring expressions on their faces. It is clear to me that no further discussion of the lathes is warranted.

I am troubled by the lack of interest in this issue but I should not be surprised since I received no response to my written reports. I assumed that the delegation would share my indignation and my feeling that the incident offered a chance to get across some ideas about professional ethics. I am left with the need to figure out my course of action with Kfar Oranim's professionals, despite the delegation's reaction. Synchronizing approaches between two different worlds is a daunting challenge. The pieces of information I sent out have apparently not combined to form an integrated picture of my strategy. Nor is it clear that Croydon can participate in such an issue based on one annual working session. Perhaps, better understanding should have come last year when we were still beginning. Without a meeting of minds, the liaison-consultant role will continue along a cautious path, given an uncertain sponsor in Croydon. I must convey these notions to Mark, no matter how cramped for time we are.

March 17, 1983 — Kfar Oranim

Today's program includes sub-committee meetings to consider budget proposals. First is Formal Education, chaired by Yael, an indigenous leader. She is a remarkable woman with a large family which does not interfere with her outstanding work as a neighborhood activist. She completed the course organized by Tamar and then enrolled as a BA candidate. The school principals are present to provide details about fiscal and pedagogic aspects of their operations.

Yael calls the meeting to order and resists calls to make opening remarks. This is inauspicious since she is not shy. Her not commenting means that she is not up on the work of the Sub-Committee. I received this impression at budget review meetings.

The principals take over with a strident effort to impress the visitors. They dominate the session with learned and not so learned pronouncements that lack focus. It is hard to believe that they furnished information for the budget. They completely ignore this material which sits under their noses. A delegation member asks if special training is given to teachers to enable them to deal with pupils from families considered to be deficient in cultural development. Instead of answering, each principal tries to out-do the others with an oration bemoaning the sorry lot of the educator in a small town and the low status which Israeli society assigns to teachers, especially those who provide education to children from culturally deprived families. Leah valiantly tries to translate these perorations into English. The principals enjoy being translated even though they are perfectly capable of speaking English themselves. They are oblivious to the waste of time.

time.

Yuval, who now handles the cultural enrichment program could answer the question briefly in English but holds back to avoid offending the principals. His replacement is too new to intervene and remains a mute witness to the principals' damaging performance. Eitan catches my message to cut the orations but the reproofs he hisses in Hebrew are ignored. The principals are off on their own misguided direction and cannot be untracked. I am tempted to suggest that Melvin ask the Mayor, Yuval or Eitan to answer the question but that would be a blatant slap at the principals. The last thing needed is four offended principals after the delegation leaves.

Had Vered been present, she would have saved the day by politely shutting off the principals' witless filibustering. Melvin displays considerable patience but finally reaches a breaking point. He throws up his hands and declares enough is enough. He announces that the meeting is over, speaking with determination that precludes any negotiation. Translations are superfluous. What happened is crystal clear to the Kfar Oranim residents who rise from their chairs in disbelief.

Melvin's decision to adjourn the meeting is backed by the rest of the delegation. They support his further decision to shorten the visit since it is apparent from this session that the sub-committees are not prepared. The delegation had come for budget discussions, not long-winded speeches.

News of this move distresses the Mayor, the Town Council and the Steering Committee. Why should the whole town be punished for the stupidity of the principals? They can't believe that the visitors who always show understanding and tolerance should adopt such drastic action. I make no attempt to calm them nor to explain the delegation's decision. Instead, I say we have to learn from what happened. I am willing to sit with them and analyze this unfortunate experience so that we can avoid such a shambles next time. They agree this is necessary but, at the moment, they take little comfort from my words.

Judith from Project Renewal's Jerusalem office appears and, unexpectedly, she is accompanied by Hanoch's successor, Marek. He is still learning the ropes and sensitizing himself to the complexities of his job so that he is not yet ready to take charge. Leah must have alerted Judith to this morning's debacle and Marek came along to put out the smoldering fire that started several hours ago. The delegation exudes general irritation in which the officials from Jerusalem are included for not preparing Kfar Oranim for budget discussions. Marek is palpably blameless and his innocence has a calming effect. He does not try to divert the delegation from its insistence on heading for Jerusalem to complete budget discussions there. The decision to end the visit to Kfar Oranim is irrevocable.

I have no opportunity to exchange views with the delegation. Mark is arranging the move to Jerusalem a day early. I buttonhole him for a moment just before departure time. It is not an appropriate occasion to assess what happened but an evaluation is bound to come. I make the point that the delegation should remember its positive reactions, especially to the progress among the indigenous neighborhood leaders. I hope that this will balance the adverse response to the poor showing of the principals.

Mark has a parting comment. As he has previously written, Croydon would like to see more aggressiveness in the liaison-consultant role. The delegation wants more involvement in community affairs from the emerging cadre of residents who seem ready to assume increased leadership responsibilities. He says I should focus more intensively and more actively on leadership development. He adds that he finds my reports too long and too circumstantial. He asks me to consider his limited time since he has to cope with many other demands. Project Renewal is a small part of his total work load. I tell him there are many things I want to say but I'll have to put them in a letter. At this, we both laugh. I promise to keep it short and we part with a friendly handshake.

March 18, 1983

I write to Mark, alluding to what I consider to be imbalance in the delegation's reaction. Confusion at the outset of the visit evoked less of a reaction than my embarrassment led me to expect. I note that there was evidence as to progress in developing leadership in the neighborhoods. I remind him that the delegation saw this with enthusiasm. What happened at the Sub-Committee on Formal Education was a breakdown resulting from Vered's withdrawal. She prepared the sub-committees for their budget submissions in the past. The time between Hanoch's leaving and the arrival of his successor created a further gap.

As for the liaison-consultant role, I understand the desire to have someone who would be more aggressive. I assert that my orientation is based on gradual change through developing inner community resources. Since I plan to leave soon for an extended trip to Canada, this would be a good time to appoint a new liaison-consultant. I am prepared to stay until a replacement arrives up to the date of my departure.

Mark sends a warm letter of appreciation for my work in establishing the close link between the two communities and asks that I remain until a successor is named. He expresses the hope that we will continue to be friends. I reciprocate his feeling. Mark conveyed a deep commitment to Project Renewal when we first met. I did not then know the extent of his responsibilities at the Croydon Jewish Federation. He cannot help feeling torn between his dedication to Project Renewal and the other Federation tasks which weigh on him.

March 25, 1983 — Kfar Oranim

I have two important personnel matters to discuss with the Mayor. First is the question of Uri's fringe benefits. I am eager to see these payments continue to prevent Uri from leaving. The Mayor and I agree to recommend to the Steering Committee that the expenses be paid out of Project Renewal funds. I tell the Mayor that I wrote to Croydon, advocating this approach and I expect a favorable reply shortly.

The second item is Tamar's status. She received a dismissal notice from the Town Council. I warn the Mayor that there will be chaos if this is permitted to stand. I tell him about the steps being discussed to prevent the Town Council from firing Tamar. The activists and the Neighborhood Council will send a deputation to say that all neighborhood work will come to a halt unless the Steering Committee reinstates her. Project Renewal, Jerusalem is also talking about sending a delegation to demand that Tamar be kept on the job. Other steps are afoot. I mention that Tamar made a fine impression on the Croydon delegation. Croydon will question the wisdom of letting her go without cogent explanation. The Mayor takes what I say to heart. He says he values my advice and he will do what he can to keep Tamar.

April 6, 1983 — Kfar Oranim

Dan, Yuval and I plan for receiving the Croydon Young Leadership Group which will visit next week. The tour will begin at the computer learning center where the visitors can talk with students about using scientific technology rather than a teacher to learn. The guests will then be entertained by the Youth Orchestra and the Choral Group. They will have time to talk with the performers to learn how modern Israeli youth feel about the old Zionist songs and the newer music coming from America and Europe. Folk dancing and a light supper will conclude the visit.

April 13, 1983 — Kfar Oranim

I meet with Meron, Yuval's replacement as head of the school system. We review the mess the principals made of the meeting with the Croydon delegation. He is concerned about this but he is more worried about the education budget freeze which went into effect after the delegation meet representatives of the Ministry of Education. He tells me that no expenditures can be made until the Ministry checks on the Kfar Oranim program. I called the Jersualem Project Renewal office and learned that $50,000 is being taken from the Community Center budget and added to the formal education budget.

This action will create problems in Kfar Oranim but it enables me to assure Meron that all is not lost. I tell him that much can be recouped if the meeting with the Croydon delegation is used as a lesson. Meron asks me to tell him how to do so. I reply that he must become a leader and teacher to the principals. He has a year to develop a well-planned, integrated approach to school needs, ranked and supported with hard data. Last minute scrambling to answer questions must be avoided. The principals need to learn to be thoughtful, prepared planners. I tell Meron that I am ready to help him. He is eager to follow my advice and I recommend he begin by drawing up a list of needs. He is not sure how to go about this and we discuss what he has to do. We agree to meet in two weeks to talk about providing the principals with planning skills.

I see Yuval to pick up where we stopped before the visit of the Croydon delegation. I use the sorry example of the session with the principals to point out that the social welfare professionals would not have come out much better had it not been for the enthusiasm generated by Tamar and her neighborhood workers. The absence of day-to-day planning in Kfar Oranim leads to lack of consensus among the professionals. This quickly communicates itself to the Croydon delegation which is accustomed to a planning approach.

Yuval agrees but says he is not the person to start the planning process. He suggests I try Dan. I demur because Dan has no feel for a planning approach to community problems. However, I agree that Yuval's decision to hold back is wise. He is not a strong figure and he has no clout to back him up. My position is more prestigious than his but I have no executive authority. I cannot say that Croydon will withhold funds unless the Steering Committee becomes seriously involved in social planning. If I took such a step, the Jewish Agency would shoot me down. I tell Yuval that the experience of the principals sets an example of what not to do and highlights the need for systematic planning. I want to exploit the fear generated by freezing of funds by the Ministry of Education.

While we wait for the Croydon Young Leadership mission to arrive, Dan tells me he is angry about the $50,000 cut in the Community Center budget. I try to calm him but I do not tell him that the money was taken from his budget and given to formal education. This would only add fuel to his fire. Fortunately, the visitors arrive, ending our conversation and dispelling his anger, at least for the time being.

The mission is greeted by the Youth Orchestra and their performance is well received. The young musicians are a sure fire success. At the computer center, the group proves too large for an exchange with the pupils. However, the visitors are interested in this innovative approach. This stop sets the pattern for the visit. It is more passive than planned and there is little opportunity for give and take between the visitors and the residents of the town.

After our tour, we return to the Community Center for a rousing performance by the Choral Group. The hour is late and there is no time for discussion nor for folk dancing. Nevertheless, the visit is a huge success and Choral Group members are invited to accompany the visitors to dinner at a nearby restaurant. On the bus, a performer takes over the microphone and teaches the Kfar Oranim song. The mood is very convivial.

Uri and I say good-bye to the visitors. As we walk to our cars, he asks if I heard anything about his request for the Croydon Jewish Federation to meet his travel expenses and pay for his overtime work. I have not had a reply. He asks me to take the matter up with Leah since the Jewish Agency could authorize the payment. The Jewish Agency would be more receptive if Croydon approved. He needs to know since he has a job offer. He prefers to stay in Kfar Oranim because the mess he found when he began has not been completely cleaned up. He would like to leave with a sense of accomplishment. The situation challenges his professional competence but he cannot wait much longer since he cannot support his family without the supplementary pay. He says nothing about my influence on his decision to remain but we both know that it is a factor in his thinking. I assure him I will talk to Leah as soon as I can and I will also press Croydon for an answer.

April 14, 1983

I telephone Leah to discuss Uri's situation. She is unmoved by the possibility of his leaving. She will check into the rules which cover supplementation but she doubts that the Jewish Agency can make the payments. I insist it is done in other communities and I tell her that I am concerned about the Welfare Department's ability to deal with Kfar Oranim's needy families if Uri leaves. She is fixed in her lack of concern. Preserving Tamar's job has priority for her.

I call Uri to tell him of my unsatisfactory chat with Leah. I say that my own future relationship with Kfar Oranim is uncertain. If I can't help maintain high quality service in the Welfare Department by keeping Uri on the job, then I am failing Kfar Oranim. Uri thanks me for my support.

April 18, 1983 — Kfar Oranim

I attend the Independence Day celebration in the former movie theater, now an empty hall that is used occasionally for community events. Ariela heads the judges panel for a song festival with prizes for the best performers. The Mayor reports that she has agreed to pull together all the efforts to provide a swimming pool for the town.

The Choral Group performs and the Mayor announces that the Town Council has voted 25,000 shekels toward its South African trip. Ephraim reports a gift of 10,000 shekels from the Labor Party. The crowd applauds thunderously at this news which now assures enough money for the trip.

April 25, 1983 — Kfar Oranim

Concerned individuals meet to discuss the Ministry of Education's decision to freeze the formal education budget. Ofir, representing the

Inter-Ministerial Committee for Formal Education in Israel, came from Jerusalem to chair the session.

He begins in friendly fashion, saying he wants to hear candid opinions about the town's school system. People speak in a diffuse manner. Judith from Project Renewal, Jerusalem makes critical comments which provoke the local residents. An angry outburst from a principal annoys Ofir. He asserts that Kfar Oranim cannot afford quarrels considering the state of education in the town.

The meeting calms down, and, for the next three hours, opinions are expressed. There is an undertone of vexation at the unfocussed nature of the comments.

Ofir tours the educational facilities. At the computer center, he is told with great pride that the number of computers is to be doubled so that parents can learn skills to help their children. Ofir says there will be no money for this purchase. In his judgment, the room is too small to accommodate more computers. He speaks with authority. I hold my tongue during the tour and the preceding meeting. I shall talk to Meron later. Although he is Director of the school system, he kept quiet and I worry about this failure to speak up. I wonder if he is ready for his job responsibilities.

April 28, 1983 — Kfar Oranim

Ralph's contract was not renewed and there is no one to follow through on the pen-pal program. I ask Yuval to take this on; he helped launch the program originally. He vaguely recalls the program. He agrees to take over but he needs a week's delay because he is busy preparing his budget. We plan to meet in a week to review arrangements for the program.

Ralph's departure left no one to see to the visits by the High School students. I ask Tamar to look after it. With her characteristically cooperative manner, she agrees but she reminds me that her future in Kfar Oranim is up in the air. The Mayor is dragging his feet about her re-appointment. Moreover, he fired the neighborhood workers. She is to see him soon. Unless she gets a written contract, she will leave. Meanwhile, she will follow up with the High School.

I see Uri whose situation remains precarious. The Town Council stopped paying him for travel and overtime work. The Mayor failed to attend a meeting to consider dismissing a receptionist who is excessively absent. Uri is not surprised that the Mayor stayed away. He claims that this is typical. I change the subject to ask Uri if he would consider becoming my successor as liaison-consultant. I can't speak for Croydon but I am ready to recommend him. He expresses interest.

I meet with Shimon, the newly appointed youth worker. I supported his efforts to find an office. He was moving from place to place, unable to put in a full day's work. I talked to the Mayor and an office was finally assigned. Now, Shimon is trying for a telephone. Nothing comes easy in Kfar Oranim.

Despite the impediments, Shimon started on his tasks. He persuaded the army to send a supervisor to work with youth approaching military age and with those already called up. Shimon is dealing with some youngsters who ran away from the army and has convinced six of them to return. An army officer will start indoctrinating these youth into the reasons why Israelis must bear the burden of military service.

Shimon has been asked to organize a workshop for youth workers in the region. I commend him for this and for his good beginning. I say I will write to Croydon about his efforts and let him have Hebrew translations of my reports.

May 3, 1983 — Kfar Oranim

Tamar and I discuss arrangements for the visit of the High School students. It is scheduled for the end of May. Tamar has matters well in hand.

Shmuel, Director of the Junius Golf Club, telephones in distress at the lack of word from Croydon about the tour of golfers. They are scheduled to leave shortly. I tell him that I wrote and telephoned Croydon. We must simply wait for a reply. He says other American Jewish communities are ready to host the golfers. He asked the chairman of the Jewish Agency to pressure Croydon. I promise to let him know as soon as I hear anything but I avoid joining in his frustration.

May 7, 1983 — Kfar Oranim

My wife and I attend a celebration of the Labor Party adult education program. After the entertainment, Ephraim, head of the Labor Party branch, describes the program, saying it provided adult education to 2,500 people this past year. He mentions Project Renewal's contribution of 350,000 shekels and I am warmly acknowledged as Croydon's representative.

The entertainment resumes and Dan asks me to step out to tell me how worried he is about Croydon's silence regarding the golfers' visit. I assure him that I expect to hear from Croydon in the next few days but he remains troubled. I suggest that he write to Croydon if he feels so strongly and he says that he will do so the first thing tomorrow morning.

May 12, 1983 — Kfar Oranim

I meet with the Council of Neighborhood Activists. This group of residents has taken Tamar's course in community leadership. Their main task is to keep the apartment houses and their surroundings in good order. I was invited by Tamar to help them develop guidelines for their work. Sixteen members are present. Ovadiah is also in attendance and he starts the meeting by reporting on activities to make physical improvements in the town. There is general satisfaction with him and with the work that is proceeding under his direction.

Tamar asks me to introduce the subject of a program for the Council of Neighborhood Activists. I briefly indicate my impression that they have a core interest in housing, its improvement and maintenance as well as in physical betterment generally. They should keep emphasizing this central purpose but they should broaden their concerns to other matters which harass the residents. The Mayor represents them in regard to the pool and sports area, for example, but they are citizens who should have the final say. The Mayor is their representative and spokesman, not their "boss". How can they make government officials accountable and responsive without being seen as trouble-makers? They need to extend their purview to delinquency, crime and physical development.

My comments evoke a litany of complaints. Each speaker adds to the long list of woes. They feel hopeless. They have vainly tried to force the hands of the town's officials on a number of issues. They are pawns in the hands of local, regional and national politicians.

One speaker asks how they can move into direct contact with Croydon. Others echo this query, saying such interaction could give them more clout. Several refer to the meeting with the Croydon delegation during its recent visit. They found it to be heartening and supportive. I say they can count on Croydon's being on their side but they must recognize the limitations that inhere in Croydon's location half way around the world. More immediate support might come from Junius, if we approach its residents not as supplicants but as neighbors who should tackle common problems together. The group likes this idea of cooperating with Junius residents as equals.

After an hour of further discussion, I suggest we not let this evening's ideas melt into nothingness. I recommend that three representatives be selected to work with Tamar, Ovadiah and me on refining these thoughts into a clear plan. A draft program should be presented at our next meeting. My recommendation is unanimously adopted.

Afterwards, Tamar and I set a date for the small group to meet. She is pleased with the outcome of the session. I point out that it is only a beginning. Unfortunately, she knows this only too well based on her frustrating and sad experiences. I am encouraged that she is not threatened by my entrance into her work with the neighborhood activists.

May 10, 1983 — Junius

I see Shmuel, Director of the Junius Golf Club, to tell him Croydon is unenthusiastic about the proposed visit of the golfers. He is bitter about this response. He hopes the head of the Jewish Agency, whose support he enlisted, will change the Croydon's leaders' minds.

Kfar Oranim

Tamar says the Mayor has restored the jobs of two of the four neighborhood workers. The third worker must apologize for what the

157

Mayor took as an insolent remark in a recent exchange. She will then be re-hired. The fourth worker is not competent and Tamar decided to let her firing stand. Tamar's own contract has not yet been signed but she expects to be re-appointed because of her firm support among the neighborhood workers and activists. She knows why it is taking longer this year than last since 1983 is an election year with all its heightened tensions and petty politics. I say I hope I can help free her from this annual cat and mouse game since her usefulness is highly circumscribed during these protracted negotiations. Tamar says she is considering other job offers since she too wants to be free of the uncertainties. She is increasingly tired of the bizarre accountability demanded by the Mayor.

I see Uri who tells me he was offered a job as head of the Welfare Department in another town. He must reply by the end of the week. He prefers to avoid a decision until learning if Croydon is willing to hire him to replace me as the liaison-consultant. If he had that job as well as his present one, he would remain. He asks me to cable Croydon requesting an immediate reply. Should he come to Croydon for an interview when he visits the United States in July? I promise to send the cable but I cannot guarantee an answer in time for him to make a decision about the job he has been offered.

May 19, 1983 — Kfar Oranim

Eitan and I review the invitation received by two Kfar Oranim teenagers to spend the summer in Croydon. Eitan wants to know how the trip will be financed. He points out that Project Renewal in Kfar Oranim has no funds for this. I say I expect to hear from Croydon shortly about this matter.

I ask Eitan if there is truth to the rumor that he is leaving Kfar Oranim. He confirms the rumor, saying he wants to get back to the field of education. He plans to leave in August to take a job as principal in another town.

We discuss the 1983-1984 budget which has been approved by Croydon. He saw the approval letter and he thinks he can readily provide Croydon with the requested clarifications. He is more concerned about the rate of exchange which the Jewish Agency uses in determining the actual appropriation to Kfar Oranim. After the Jewish Agency takes its cut for overhead, there is entirely too large a discrepancy between the dollar amount approved by Croydon and the shekel allocation which Kfar Oranim finally receives from the Jewish Agency.

He raises another matter that disturbs him, the Mayor, Dan and others. They resent the procedure of final budget decisions being made by Croydon and Project Renewal. For example, he asks rhetorically, "what right did Project Renewal headquarters have to transfer money from the Community Center budget to formal education? Why wasn't

Kfar Oranim consulted?" I have heard this complaint sharply from Dan. Eitan is loathe to raise the question with Project Renewal officials since he wants to avoid a squabble. He asks me to talk with them about these issues and I agree to do so.

May 20, 1983

I telephone Project Renewal headquarters in Jerusalem but three of the four officials I ask for are away. I talk with a fourth one who says I should wait until the head of Project Renewal returns from a trip abroad to raise my questions. I already asked for an appointment to discuss the considerable dissatisfaction that is growing in Kfar Oranim, especially with Leah, the Regional Office representative. I say that clearing up the question of the difference between dollars and shekels in the allocation is an urgent issue which cannot wait. She transfers my call to another official, Rolf, who is abrupt and gruff. He tells me to talk to Leah. This matter is under her jurisdiction. He has no time to chat with every community that is discontented or wants clarification. Since he is rude and unhelpful, I thank him and hang up.

Rolf calls back a minute later to make amends. He says I did not let him finish and I cut him off. I reply that I hung up but I didn't cut him off. There was nothing else for us to discuss. In a mollifying tone, he says it is improper for him to deal with matters in Leah's baliwick. I say that we have been waiting ten days to get Leah's reply. He warmly repeats that he can't intervene. It's Leah's responsibility. He wants to avoid trouble. This time, we end with less animosity.

I decide not to call Leah because the likelihood is that she will not give me the information I want.

May 24, 1983 - Kfar Oranim

The Sub-Committee on Alienated Youth meets today. While we wait for the members to assemble, Eitan asks for an evaluation of Shimon, the new youth worker. I tell him that Shimon is an earnest person who is too over-anxious to do a good job. He has little background in youth work and is nervous about admitting it lest he be seen as the wrong person for the job. He needs encouragement and supervision. Eitan thanks me and asks that we meet soon for him to get a full evaluation.

A few members of the Sub-Committee, all professionals, straggle in. Besides Eitan and me, only Shimon, Uri, Tamar and Jared are present. Jared is an assistant to Leah in the Regional Office of Project Renewal. He knows a lot about work with youth and he floods the meeting with his expertise, much to the discomfort of Shimon whose report and participation in the discussion bear out what I had told Eitan earlier.

When we finish, Jared and I talk about Shimon's need for

supervision. He will get someone from the Ministry of Labor and Social Affairs to take this responsibility. He will help Shimon focus on the administrative and planning aspects of his task, leaving the direct work with youth to qualified individuals. We agree to work together to help Shimon and Jared assures me he will make the necessary arrangements.

Uri is disappointed by Croydon's decision not to invite him to be interviewed for the liaison-consultant job. There are other plans to fill the position. He has made no decision about the job offer since he has to report soon for military reserve duty, after which he will visit the United States. He will return to Israel at the beginning of August. In effect, he has turned down the job offer. I suggest that, while he is in the United States, he should telephone Mark in the Croydon Jewish Federation. Perhaps, if more time is needed to replace me, Uri can be given an interim appointment. He might use as a reason for his call the question of Croydon volunteer dentists. This is appropriate since most of the patients would be clients of the Welfare Department.

May 30, 1983 - Kfar Oranim

Tamar and I meet to follow up on the session with the Council of Neighborhood Activists. We discuss ways of getting the members to move beyond property maintenance. I predict they will lose interest if they are restricted to this technical concern. This has occurred elsewhere. We recognize that this is no simple task since the Town Council would no doubt prefer to see the activists maintain their narrow stress on property maintenance, thus avoiding any threat.

We consider the possibility of cooperative activity with Junius. The idea of a joint summer camp surfaces. Eight to 10 families with small children have recently bought homes in Junius, using the compensation they received for evacuating their Sinai settlement under the Camp David agreement. We discussed working with them inasmuch as their background is similar to that of many Kfar Oranim residents. I encourage Tamar to urge the activists to make contact with these people. She tells me the Council of Neighborhood Activists has chosen three representatives as decided at the May 12, 1983 meeting. They plan to get in touch with Junius' Committee of Residents.

Tamar is light-hearted today. She learned that Ovadiah will probably move from his physical planning job to become head of Project Renewal when Eitan leaves. Since he knows little about social welfare, he told Tamar that he intends to appoint her as his assistant with responsibility for Project Renewal's social welfare activities. This will free her from dependence on the Town Council for continuity in her position. I listen and inwardly decide to check all this with Eitan.

We attend the meeting of the Steering Committee which starts about twenty minutes late with 22 people present.

First is a request for money to subsidize 34 students chosen to take special courses designed to keep them from falling behind in their school work. The hope is that this will avoid their becoming drop-outs. The request is approved.

The second item evokes more response. It calls for money to train Kfar Oranim youth as lifeguards. With some irony, members ask the location of the pool that warrants such training. Eitan replies that the training will enable Kfar Oranim youth to get jobs elsewhere. The request is approved with the stipulation that Eitan carefully records that the money will be available to all youth who wish to apply.

The third request produces much more discussion. The Community Center wants $564,000 to enlarge its facilities to establish a conservatory in Kfar Oranim. Eitan presents the request in rapid-fire order that takes two minutes. Questions show uneasiness about okaying so big an expenditure quickly. Despite the uneasiness, the request is approved without a vote.

Eitan plunges on, taking the first sign of consensus as approval. The last item is transfer of $50,000 from the Community Center budget to formal education. Bitterness is expressed about this decision having been made by Project Renewal, Jerusalem and Croydon. Supporters of the Community Center are angry while those concerned with formal education speak gingerly to avoid more hostility. It is clear that they strongly favor transferring the funds. Everyone condemns the manner of the transfer. The Mayor says there is no point in opening the issue unless the Croydon representative is ready to nullify the decision. Otherwise, he says, we must look to the future and figure out how to prevent such decision-making from now on. I obviously can't overturn the transfer so I do not respond. Instead, I address the procedural question. We need to review the roles of Croydon, Kfar Oranim and Project Renewal, Jerusalem in decision-making. A meeting for this has been set and the Mayor asked me to attend.

I say the decision should not have been made without Kfar Oranim. Furthermore, it should have been announced by the head of Project Renewal, not by one of his staff. My comments ease the tension but the noise level stays high as several people speak at the same time. No one is angry at Croydon; the issue is seen as lying between Kfar Oranim and Project Renewal, Jerusalem. There is reluctance to express opinions which may sour relationships between Kfar Oranim and Croydon.

June 2, 1983 - Kfar Oranim
I see Shimon in his new office which is neat and orderly. He tells me of his accomplishments since we last met. His report focuses on individual youth. I say he clearly works hard but he must think of himself as administrator, planner and program director rather than as worker with individuals. We need to know the extent of the alienated

youth problem and the categories into which they fall. We also need costs, personnel and program results. Listing specific instances may be used illustratively but, if that is his whole report, it does not enhance his position as head of the total program. I suggest we wait a few weeks before we meet again at which time I will expect a report which gives a picture of the full program. I try not to be critical but Shimon perceives my comments as being negative. Nevertheless, he promises to provide the kind of report I outlined for our next session.

I see the Mayor to get his reaction to a suggestion from Croydon that $35,000 be re-directed in the budget to finance a study of Kfar Oranim's potential for attracting industry. The Mayor is adamantly opposed. The information is already available. He would go along with the idea if Croydon has a volunteer expert to do the research at no cost.

I switch the conversation to the dental clinic and ask about the status of the contract. The Mayor says this is up to Eitan. He doesn't know what is happening — or rather, not happening — about dental services and so I drop the subject.

We talk about the meeting with the new head of Project Renewal. The Mayor indicates that his hand has been strengthened by the recent discussion at the Steering Committee.

I go to see Eitan and ask about the rumor that Ovadiah will replace him. He says it is true but that it will be a provisional appointment for a few trial months. We discuss the dental clinic contract. Eitan plans to conclude arrangements with Kupat Holim. Once he does his work, it will be up to Project Renewal, Jerusalem to follow through. I say I will keep on top of this.

I ask Eitan for his reaction to the study proposed by Croydon. He laughs and brings out a paper which he says has information that he and Vered prepared. Then he shows me a report on the economic potential of Project Renewal communities written by Haifa University. The section on Kfar Oranim comes word for word from the work that he and Vered did. That's why he thinks so little of social science studies. I disagree but I don't want to make an issue of it.

Eitan leaves business to tell me that Dan is running for Mayor in place of Shaul who will not seek re-election. This verifies the information that Dan shared with me a few days ago. At the time, he said he was on the verge of announcing his candidacy especially since Noam urged him to run.

June 9, 1983 — Jerusalem

I see Project Renewal officials to discuss forthcoming visits of two groups from Croydon. They are scheduled for days when Dan will be away and we will have to make do with the limited skills of his assistant.

I talk with Stephen about problems between Kfar Oranim and Project Renewal staff, especially Leah. Her insensitivity irritates the professionals and the officials. We also talk about the Steering Committee. It is failing to fulfill its function as a planning group for two reasons: first, it runs as an executive group for its sub-committees, not as a social planning body; second, neighborhood representatives come to the Committee as aggrieved individuals lodging complaints, not as responsible delegates. I want him to understand these problems before Marek, the new head of Project Renewal, comes for his first formal visit with Kfar Oranim's leaders. I hope the meeting will go beyond a getting-to-know-you ceremony.

June 13, 1984 - Kfar Oranim

I meet with Dorit and Shula, the two teen-agers selected to spend the summer in Croydon. We review arrangements for the trip. I tell them to call if they have questions.

June 14, 1983 - Kfar Oranim

Tamar, Eitan and I sit with a representative of Project Renewal, Jerusalem to discuss the forthcoming visits of two Croydon groups.

Before we start, we must handle a problem of Dorit and Shula who are about to leave for Croydon. An unanticipated cost of $50 for travel tax has been presented to them. Their families cannot meet this expenditure. Eitan calls Project Renewal in Jerusalem and, after a stormy discussion, the matter is settled. The Project Renewal office will arrange payment.

We then assign responsibilities as to who will do what when the Croydon visitors arrive. I cannot be present for one of the visits because of my university responsibilities. The Project Renewal representative offers to come from Jerusalem on that day to make the necessary explanations to the visitors.

After the meeting, Ovadiah tells me he is interviewing a candidate for the youth worker job for the group to work on physical improvements. He is glad that our idea of the youth work project may actually materialize after a year of trying.

June 20, 1983 - Randor

Tamar and I come to the hotel where Shulamit is running a day-long institute on child-rearing for young mothers. The morning session ends and Shulamit comes toward us but is held up as people engage her in conversation. She throws us an occasional glance that says she will be with us just as soon as the group releases her.

As we wait, I think that Shulamith and Tamar would be better off if they could air their differences in the company of their professional colleagues. Such a group could focus on the community implications of their conflicting views about neighborhood activism. I fear that the encounter they are about to have may get caught up in temperamental differences.

Shulamit has a strictly establishment view of the indigenous leaders in Tamar's course who make up the Council of Neighborhood Activists. They are trained at community expense and receive a small stipend from Project Renewal. They carry part-time responsibilities for organizing house committees to oversee property maintenance, caring for lawns and gardens and maintaining proper standards of street sanitation. Shulamit feels the activists have enough to do without getting involved in social action and being dragged into local politics.

Tamar agrees that the activists must carry out the tasks identified by Shulamit. She also agrees with me that limiting them to maintenance work will trivialize their role and kill their enthusiasm. She believes that social action is a legitimate part of their task and she wants them to work on such community needs as a safe beach, a playing field, and an industrial zone for small businesses.

Tamar thinks the activists should link residents, the Town Council and the Steering Committee. I support her views but I wonder if she can hold her own with Shulamit. My role as facilitator is vague. I wondered about this meeting; I will leave soon and there will be no follow-up. Tamar and Shulamit talked with me about each other and I decided to go ahead with this opportunity for them to meet away from Kfar Oranim. I hope there will be clarification of their views on activism and of Shulamit's complaint that Labor members are excluded from Tamar's course. This issue is simple to resolve since it hinges on facts. However, it is explosive.

Shulamit finally ends the conversation that stalled her progress toward us. We begin with idle chatter over a snack. We have about ninety minutes before Shulamit has to return to the afternoon session. I am content to join in the banter and the relaxed feeling among the three of us. I hope it will last but, unfortunately, the pleasant mood evaporates as we get down to brass tacks.

Shulamit repeats what she told me and what Tamar heard through the grapevine. She is calm and she intersperses her criticism with appreciation for Tamar's ability as organizer of the training program. However, she firmly objects to the omission of the Labor group. She says that unless a change is made, she will take action to force different arrangements.

Tamar becomes observably tense. She sharply denies Shulamit's allegations. For someone who fears Shulamit, she shows surprising hostility which she has difficulty controlling. I wonder if my presence frees her to lash out and assert herself so strongly. I understand her frustration. She sees Shulamit as having the best of both worlds with recognition as a leading professional and as a member of Kfar Oranim's power structure. By contrast, Tamar has to pay for identifying with Yehuda who is challenging the power structure. She dare not assert this loyalty openly since she must maintain a rigid professional posture.

The Documentary

She is not serving her best interest as she pours out her anger.

Shulamit remains calm. She reins in her awesome temper. Tamar converts the discussion to an effort to settle private accounts. Her wrath is at the surface while Shulamit's is just below. In all this crackling fury, how does one distinguish the sparks that light up problems which need to be resolved between them? I ask myself again: why did I agree to this meeting? No moderator, neither aggressive intervenor nor nudging gradualist, can hope to rescue them from each other at this one sitting. Can I refuse to become involved because I see no immediate solution to their problem? Isn't the very act of reaching out a good thing in itself? The human service professions have not settled the question as to what is more enduring: the problem solved or the relationships which are established in the course of problem-solving. This meeting reveals the actors in a real life drama on a stage called community. They vary in their motives, their postures and their methods but, because the drama is real, it is never as neat and trim as theorists on community organization and community development would have us believe.

June 2, 1983 - Kfar Oranim

I talk with Tamar about yesterday's meeting. She is still tense and is now uncertain about having the activists move beyond the work of property maintenance. She is bitter about Shulamit and she speaks of her with unconcealed contempt.

We are in the lobby of the Community Center. People keep interrupting. Ovadiah stops by and asks whether or not Tamar has considered his job offer. I take the initiative and urge Tamar to accept. She is in a lonely position and cannot stand up to the antagonism of Shulamit and the Mayor. When Ovadiah takes over from Eitan, she will be protected by a strong personality who is eager to have her work with him.

Although Tamar is not properly prepared for the job's demand for planning skills, I know she was not ready to work with the activists either. The town can't afford to lose a person with her potential and her devotion. With my encouragement, she promises to answer Ovadiah soon. She is inclined to accept since she is fed up with bickering. I point out that, although she won't have much time to work with the activists if she takes the position, she can exert influence on them. We agree to meet again next week to review Shulamit's reaction to the work of the activists with Junius.

The Croydon visitors are late. There are 85 of them. Unfortunately, the Mayor is not here to greet them; he is at a funeral. The Youth Orchestra is also not available because it is away for a special program. Despite these problems, the visit goes well. We tour the agencies and the visitors are delighted to see the heart-warming sight of children at play. They comment that it is good to see their contributions being

165

put to such good use and they want to make cash donations on the spot but I ask them to wait, saying that we can consider this at the end of the visit.

After our rounds, we assemble in the Community Center. I tell the leader of the group of the desire to give money and I make the alternative suggestion that educational material and toys be sent to Kfar Oranim. I say the gifts should be sent in care of Eitan who will insure equitable distribution among the town's child-serving agencies. I discourage cash gifts and suggest instead that they increase their donations to the Federation when they return to Croydon.

Eitan gives a brief message and I translate. The leader of the group speaks in Hebrew which makes a big hit and the session ends on a high note. Before the visitors leave, refreshments are served, adding a friendly and warm touch to the farewell. The visitors are highly gratified with their "twin" community. The distant partnership has become real.

June 27, 1983 - Kfar Oranim

I meet with a university researcher who is gathering data on Kfar Oranim as part of a Project Renewal study. He asks me about the liaison-consultant role. I emphasize my focus on community development. He says that a liaison-consultant he recently interviewed stressed external relationships with the Jewish Agency and the Ministry of Housing as primary tasks. I say our differences may be due to lack of a well-thought out approach to the role of liaison-consultant by the national bodies. I inquire as to when the results of the study will be published but the researcher does not know.

June 28, 1983 - Kfar Oranim

I arrive at the tail end of a visit by another Croydon group, having been delayed by a university commitment. The town tour is still going on and I wait in the Mayor's office. Dan just returned from out-of-town and he is also waiting. He tells me he has definitely decided to run for Mayor. He asks my help in composing a letter to Melvin, the chairman of Croydon's Project Renewal Committee, formally announcing his step. He wants to advise Croydon because he will have to resign as head of the Community Center which receives Project Renewal funds. I agree to help but we need a more convenient time since our visitors now arrive. The group consists of eight leaders of Croydon's Jewish Federation. They express satisfaction. The town is cleaner; there have been improvements in housing and in surroundings of the apartment blocks; agency facilities have been enlarged and bettered. They are also gratified by what they saw of the social programs.

The Mayor makes a presentation to Phillip, a member of the group, who is also United States Chairman of Project Renewal. He was responsible for prodding Croydon into becoming part of Project

Renewal. The Mayor gives Phillip a scroll which is read in Hebrew and then translated.

A discussion with the activists who are present follows. Questions are raised about community needs. The activists' replies demonstrate a circumscribed and narrow outlook. I intervene to explain that they do not deal with general community needs because their work is presently restricted to property maintenance. I introduce Tamar and tell the visitors that she and I are trying to extend the activists' community involvement. I indicate that we are meeting resistance since a broader scope of activity is seen as a threat to the authority of the town's official leaders.

We end the visit in an agency which helps mothers to improve their interaction with their infants. The objective is to assure early acquisition of social skills. After observing the program in action, the visitors are served refreshments.

As we enjoy the hospitality, the visitors ask questions. They get a richer response than they received from the activists. The mothers talk about their backgrounds. They speak perceptively about the problems and rewards of living in Kfar Oranim. The good feeling which prevails is enhanced when the mothers get the visitors to join in a sing-song. The visit ends as the visitors proceed to dinners with host families.

July 8, 1983 - Kfar Oranim

I meet with Dan to compose the letter to Melvin about his intent to resign from the Community Center to run for Mayor. He greets me with the news that the Minister of Interior has appointed an investigating committee to look into the town's affairs. Preliminary findings indicate that the Town Council does not meet acceptable standards. Funds coming into the town are either missing or mismanaged. The investigating committee will report on July 27, 1983. One possibility is a recommendation to appoint a government committee to run the town for four years. This would mean no election next October, as presently scheduled. Dan heaves a sigh of relief. He says this news came before he formally announced his resignation. Now, of course, he will not resign and, as for the future, Dan throws up his hands as if to say, "who can tell?". He says that things may turn out to be quite serious but he touches his mouth to show that his lips are sealed. On this enigmatic note, we part.

I meet with Tamar for further discussion of Shulamit's opposition to broadening the work of the activists. Shulamit belongs to the coalition governing Kfar Oranim and neither she nor the Mayor want political flak from the activists. She insists that they confine their work to property maintenance.

I tell Tamar that while property maintenance is not to be under-rated, it is too restrictive. In my judgement, which Tamar shares, such sharp limitation will irritate the activists and cause them to lose interest. I encourage her to hold firm to her aim of enlarging their scope.

I suggest we convene a meeting of community leaders for me to report on my work. I could deal directly with the emerging conflict between the activists and the leaders by trying to help the leaders understand that they need a wide base of concerned citizens for the good of the town.

I would tell the leaders that the activists need broader purposes to maintain their enthusiasm. I could speak freely since I am an outsider who will be leaving shortly. I cannot be accused of having a conflict of interest. My objective is solely the well-being of Kfar Oranim.

Tamar likes my approach and she says that she will try to set up the meeting.

We discuss the investigating committee. Tamar thinks Yehuda, the Mayor's rival, may have a hand in this development. His interest in municipal affairs is driven by hostility for the present Mayor. Some of Yehuda's supporters are disenchanted with his single-minded pursuit of old quarrels.

Before I leave town, I talk with a few others about the investigating committee. The news is on everyone's mind. One opinion is that Kfar Oranim will be run by an appointed government committee and there will be no municipal elections in 1983. Others do not agree, saying the investigation will blow over and the elections will go forward. There is no consensus.

July 13, 1983 - Kfar Oranim, Junius

Eitan and I discuss the forthcoming visit of 65 Croydon people. There is confusion about their arrival time, each of us having received different information. Eitan calls Jerusalem and gets the final word. This visit is part of a large mission of unmarried individuals who are touring Israel and visiting their "twin" communities. The Jewish Agency will not make special arrangements for the people from Croydon and we draw up plans to receive them.

I go to the Junius Golf Club, hoping to see its Director, Shmuel. His pressure on the Jewish Agency chairman resulted in Croydon's finally agreeing to host the golfers. They just returned from their visit. He is away but the secretary tells me that the trip was "fantastic". The golfers were warmly received and gifts were heaped upon them. They came home laden with golf shoes, golf clubs and other equipment. She shows me pictures taken on the trip, all depicting the golfers in high spirits. She says the golfers will remember this experience as the high point of their lives. I say the trip is a high point in Kfar Oranim too. The Mayor, the Community Center Director and others keep harping on the wonders of the visit.

I return to Kfar Oranim to see Shulamit at her request. She wants me to help Tamar with a problem about the activists. She goes over the same ground we covered when the three of us met. This time, I get a different view of the situation. Shulamit says Tamar is either politically motivated or is being used by Yehuda, the Mayor's antagonist, to create a bloc out of the activists to oppose the present Mayor and back Yehuda to become his successor. Shulamit thinks Tamar is more and more involved with Yehuda's supporters.

She says that Tamar recently changed the eligibility requirements for serving as a neighborhood representative to the Steering Committee. A new prerequisite is graduation from Tamar's course. Shulamit shows me a memorandum stating this change which was adopted by the Neighborhood Council. A majority of the members are graduates of Tamar's course. Shulamit tells me that when the Neighborhood Council took up this proposed change, the opposition was shouted down in a raucous session where chairs were thrown and where the conflict was just a hair's breadth away from violence.

Shulamit says Tamar holds endless meetings where nothing is accomplished. The streets remain dirty and the gardens are neglected. The activists should concentrate on cleanliness; there is much to be done. She regrets that Aryeh is no longer active. He preceded Tamar as the community organizing force and his vision of social change had the aim of making Kfar Oranim a cleaner and better place to live. She reminded me of his clamor concerning the open sewers which led to action by the Croydon delegation and, eventually, by the Ministry of Housing. Shulamit claims that Aryeh was hounded out of public life because the powers-that-be held him in contempt and regarded him as nothing but a loud-mouth.

Her sense of loss about Aryeh's departure is surprising since their exchanges were always charged with fury. I have heard this regret about Aryeh's withdrawal from others who value Tamar but see her as a capable technician rather than as an inspiring leader which, in retrospect, is how they perceive Aryeh. Their opinions when Aryeh was on the scene do not tally with their views today.

I agree with Shulamit that a training requirement as a condition for serving on the Steering Committee is contrary to democratic practice. However, I point out that limiting the activists to property maintenance and seeing efforts to broaden their area of concern as a political threat is contrary to the freedom they need as indigenous leaders. She accepts widening their scope of activity at the neighborhood level but she feels that Tamar wants them in politics and does not separate her political views from her professional tasks. Shulamit asserts that she has a responsibility to protect the interests of her political party. She will see to it that a proper balance is maintained in the Neighborhood Council even if this means a fight with the group that now holds power. I say that Tamar may indeed be a supporter of Yehuda but she is too uncertain and too insecure to know which way to move. She is drifting in her work and she is too scared to act in a forthright professional manner for fear of being accused of throwing her lot in with one side. She knows she is seen as a supporter of Yehuda because her family is openly in his camp but she really wants to get out of the political rat race. I suggest that we might help Tamar focus on her professional role by appointing a committee of the Neighborhood Council with power to formulate its program and to guide Tamar in carrying it out. The tasks of determining the role and program of the Neighborhood Council should not be left solely to Tamar. That function belongs to the Council. I point out that if persons like herself took these matters in hand, Tamar could focus on serving the Council professionally without regard to her political opinions. Shulamit agrees with my approach and we decide to work together to develop a more effective view of citizen action in the Neighborhood Council, thus lifting suspicion from Tamar.

July 18, 1983 - Kfar Oranim

I tell Tamar about my discussion with Shulamit. She says she is ready to try to get things straightened out. The plan we had discussed for a meeting of the community leaders has to be abandoned in view of the investigation of the Town Council. Tamar has still not decided what to do about Ovadiah's job offer. I suspect she hopes that elections will take place after all and that Yehuda will become the Mayor. This is her dearly wished-for solution to her problems.

Tamar thinks that the present Mayor may decide to run if he escapes unscathed from the investigation. Since the group in power has designated Dan as its candidate, this decision by the Mayor would create a three-way race in which the Mayor will take votes away from Dan, insuring Yehuda's election.

I cannot dismiss this speculation. Politics preoccupies all of Kfar Oranim this summer. Problems such as delinquency, improving the schools and attracting industry have all fallen to a lower order of priority.

July 21, 1983 - Kfar Oranim

Yuval and I review the schedule while we wait for the 65 visitors from Croydon. He is uneasy because neither Eitan nor the Mayor are here today. Tamar is in bed with a high fever. To complicate matters further, we cannot visit the dental clinic since a family has "occupied" the premises in protest against their inability to find housing. The Deputy Mayor has been negotiating with them but has failed to dislodge them.

The visitors arrive and are greeted by the Deputy Mayor. Yuval carries the main responsibility for telling the Kfar Oranim story. A representative of Project Renewal, Jerusalem and I add our words of welcome and the group is taken for refreshments before the tour begins.

Our first stop is a day camp where children sing songs of welcome. The visitors mingle with the children and join in the songs. They may be unmarried people but they act like mamas and papas. We drag them away, insisting there is a schedule to follow. On the way to the buses, members of the group spy a soccer game in progress. They run to the field and soon, visitors are kicking the ball with a bunch of Kfar Oranim youngsters. They organize a game; the sun beats down but the players and the spectators are impervious to heat. The game goes on for an hour and ends in a tie. The schedule is in shambles but who cares? A great time is had by all.

The rest of the tour is anti-climactic. Nothing can top the visit with the children in the day camp and the impromptu soccer game. If the visitors were not so tired from these two activities, they might have wondered as we pass the dental clinic about its conversion into a temporary residence. But — no one notices or cares. The visit ends in the Community Center where, despite their weariness, the visitors ask questions which are fielded by Yuval and me. They give us gifts for the children and they leave inspired and exhausted by the experience in their "twin" community. The visit was a huge success in spite of our initial fears about the absence of several key individuals.

July 24, 1983 - Kfar Oranim

My wife and I arrive at the Community Center for the send-off to the Choral Group before the tour to South Africa. The auditorium is filled and the heat is oppressive. They perform in the usual spirited fashion. Having heard them many times, I escape the heat and the crowd by going to the lobby.

I meet Mordecai who is running for Mayor, if the election is held. He is on the same ticket as Dan and people think he will become Deputy Mayor. He tells me the election will be held. The Mayor is an honest man and there will be no theft found. The problem of the town's finances is wholly due to an aged, incompetent comptroller whose antiquated methods jumbled the financial records. He has been fired. A few days ago, Yuval told me the comptroller is being made a scapegoat. He also said he was interviewed by the investigating committee and was surprised by many questions about Dan. Yuval thinks the investigating committee will recommend holding the election if they judge that Dan will make a good Mayor.

Mordecai reiterates his belief that elections will be held. He hopes for more votes than Dan which will surprise everyone. He will wind up as Mayor with Dan as Deputy. I point to the town square and say that as Mayor, he should fix it up to serve as the place for the kind of celebration now taking place in the uncomfortable and crowded auditorium. I tell him I have tried to interest Dan in overhauling the town square without any success. Mordecai smiles knowingly.

The concert is over and the speeches have begun. The crowd starts to leave the auditorium. The Mayor sings the praises of the Choral Group and thanks a number of people for making the trip possible. He points to several Junius residents, including Ariela and Noam who contributed generously to the cost of the airplane tickets. He mentions others who made donations and the affair winds up with loud applause.

Dan runs up to invite my wife and me to a reception for the youngsters and the contributors. We follow him to the reception where everyone is convinced that the Choral Group will be a smash hit in South Africa. I hope so. For all its problems, Kfar Oranim will not be denied its dreams of glory.

July 30, 1983 - Kfar Oranim

As the date for my departure approaches, I meet with the Mayor who is eager to arrange a farewell affair for me. I ask him to wait until Croydon selects my successor so that the new person can be properly introduced at my send-off. I am anxious to do this in the hope that the initial presentation of the next liaison-consultant can be an improvement over the hobbled one I received from Hanoch when I started out.

The Mayor agrees but wants some dates. This proves to be impossible. I have some tasks at the university which I must finish before leaving. This keeps me busy. The Mayor also has a tightly-packed schedule. The investigating committee recommended that the election proceed and, even though he decided not to run, he is heavily engaged in the campaign which is being hotly waged. This is taking up all of his time.

We finally decide to postpone the farewell party until I return from overseas.

October 10, 1983

On my return, I learn that Yehuda has been elected Mayor. He hardly knows me and my successor is now well ensconced in the job so I decide to drop the idea of a farewell party.

CHAPTER FOUR

THE CROYDON PERSPECTIVE

The foregoing documentary records events in Kfar Oranim as seen from the vantage point of the liaison-consultant. To round out the picture, some of these developments will be presented from the Croydon perspective. Also, since Croydon has continued its involvement with Kfar Oranim, we account for what happened since the last entry in the documentary.

No detailed record exists in Croydon to match the thorough chronicle kept by the liaison-consultant. Aside from letters, memos and minutes of meetings, reports by the delegation on its annual visits constitute the most definitive statements of reactions from Croydon.

The April, 1981 visit was the beginning of Croydon's partnership with Kfar Oranim. Reference has been made to that visit and to the recommendations which flowed from it. One of these recommendations led to the employment of the liaison-consultant. By the time of the second visit in April, 1982, he had been on the job for seven months.

At the end of each visit, formal reports were prepared and submitted to the Board of Directors of the Croydon Jewish Federation. Abbreviated versions of the reports follow:

From April 23 to April 29, 1982, the delegation visited Kfar Oranim in order to evaluate the community's progress and use of Project Renewal funds during 1981-1982 and to formulate recommendations for 1982-1983.

Meetings were held with residents and officials of Kfar Oranim, with representatives of the Israeli government and with staff members of Project Renewal.

The general feeling of the delegation is that progress has been made during this first year in terms of resident participation in community affairs and rehabilitation. With the assistance of our liaison-consultant, we reviewed last year's budget items and we are reasonably confident that approved items have either been implemented or are in progressive stages of implementation.

While we were in Kfar Oranim, a Croydon Young Leadership Mission visited the town. Together, we took part in a ribbon-cutting ceremony to open a family health center that was completed this year as a result of Croydon's funding.

173

We were impressed with a town hall type of meeting we attended in which residents were encouraged to voice their concerns. We saw this as a positive sign of community involvement; it demonstrated a great deal of improvement over what we experienced in our 1981 visit.

It was obvious to the delegation that the Israeli government's willingness to focus on the town was hastened by Croydon's "twinning" with Kfar Oranim. This was apparent in the completion of work on renovating an elementary school and the promise to cover the drainage canals in six months.

It is imperative that more opportunities be developed this year for people-to-people affiliation between residents of our two communities. A pen pal program is now under way and more such programs will be needed if we are to strengthen Croydon's ties to Kfar Oranim.

Our "twin" community continues to have a population with low socio-economic status. Large families comprise almost 40% of the population. A little more than 25% of the Town Council budget is spent on welfare assistance. The proportion of marginal youth is one of the highest in the country. Kfar Oranim has neither a local secondary school nor a satisfactory vocational training program. Municipal services depend on out-of-town professionals and are generally of poor quality.

Kfar Oranim cannot expand eastward or westward because it is bound by two highways. The only land for development is in the southern part of the town. Infrastructure is defective. Roads need repair and the drainage canals have to be covered. Sanitation services are inadequate. Filth and refuse create a depressing atmosphere for residents and visitors.

The neglect of physical surroundings may be explained in part by the fact that two-thirds of Kfar Oranim's families rent their apartments instead of owning them in accordance with the prevailing Israeli pattern.

A special problem is posed by the 250 families who come from the Caucasus Mountains of Russia. They are concentrated in one section of the town. These people came to Kfar Oranim seven years ago. They cling to their traditions and to their previous way of life. As a result, they are alienated from the rest of the population. They are ghettoized and their children are segregated in school.

Kfar Oranim enjoys some advantages. Among these are:
1) The town is located in central Israel, close to the sea.
2) There is an active "build-your-own-home" program which might attract new residents and prevent the departure of current residents.
3) Land is available for development of a light industrial center.
4) The Community Center is thriving, active and dynamic; it has the potential of serving as a regional music center.

5) A contract has been signed to establish a regional technological vocational program which may attract professional personnel and improve Kfar Oranim's image.

In spite of problems, which include the bureaucracies of the Israeli government and the Jewish Agency, the delegation continues to believe that Project Renewal offers Croydon and other Diaspora communities an excellent opportunity to be intimately involved with Israel. It helps to rehabilitate Israeli communities and encourages the development of local leadership. We see discernible impacts of our partnership with Kfar Oranim. There are seeds of community organization and indigenous leadership is slowly emerging.

The people of Kfar Oranim are beginning to plan and to set priorities. They are collecting data, delineating their problems and developing a strategy for improving their community. They have identified several over-all aims:
1) Improve the formal educational system, beginning with early childhood.
2) Develop local community organization and leadership.
3) Strengthen the informal education system in the areas of music, sports and club activities.
4) Improve local services by reinforcing professional personnel in health, education and social services.
5) Establish a vocational training program for marginal youth.
6) Integrate the Caucasian immigrants into the general population.
7) Improve the defective physical infrastructure by repairing the roads and covering the drainage ditches.
8) Construct two commercial centers to replace the existing ones which are health hazards and aesthetic nuisances.
9) Build a light industry center to bring together the many small workshops now scattered throughout the town.

The delegation concluded its visit with a final session at Project Renewal, Jerusalem where it met with the Director and members of his staff. We ascertained that $708,692 was spent in Kfar Oranim in 1982-1982 by Project Renewal, using funds contributed by Croydon. This money made it possible to renovate and expand a day care center, dental clinic, family health clinic and the Community Center. Funds were also spent for adult education, leadership training, Community Center activities and family health programs.

Our recommendations are as follows:
1) It is our understanding that the Croydon Jewish Federation has only sent Project Renewal $277,000 for 1981-1982. We understand further that another $146,000 will be remitted shortly for a total of $423,000. Since $708,692 was spent by the Jewish Agency in 1981-1982, we urge that payment of the remaining balance be accelerated.

2) For 1982-1983, we recommend expenditure of $954,380 with the following stipulations:
   a. We retain the condition imposed on our 1981-1982 grant to the effect that future commitments are contingent on progress in 1982-1983, as determined by our delegation with the help of our liaison-consultant.
   b. The allocation of $100,000 for a program to serve alienated youth is to be released only after Croydon has received, reviewed and approved a plan for this purpose.
   c. The allocation of $35,000 to prepare architectural plans for a music conservatory is to be released only when the following conditions have been satisfied:
      i. Completion of all zoning, planning and permits to accomplish construction.
      ii. Receipt of the 1981-1982 and 1982-1983 Community Center budgets, itemizing all expenditures and sources of revenues.
      iii. Written assurances that the Ministry of Education and the Israel Community Centers Corporation will continue to fund the Kfar Oranim Community Center subsequent to Project Renewal.
3) A program costing not more than $10,000 should be established to clean up and beautify the town. There should be an intensive volunteer clean-up campaign to achieve physical cleanliness and to improve civic pride.
4) Priority is to be given to upgrading the educational system and developing a stronger economic base for Kfar Oranim. Croydon's continued involvement with Project Renewal requires commitment by the Israeli government and the Jewish Agency to emphasize formal education and economic development for Kfar Oranim.

These recommendations were all accepted and approved by the Board of the Croydon Jewish Federation.

As indicated in the documentary, the March, 1983 visit was not as well organized as the first two visits. The delegation was disappointed with lack of supporting data in the budget request. There was a feeling that preparation for the visit was faulty and not nearly so comprehensive as in 1982.

Nevertheless, the delegation was pleased with improvements since the 1982 visit and was proud of the accomplishments made possible by Croydon's association with its distant partner. Among the gains noted was a lifting of community morale with feelings of hope for the future. The beautification program was going forward and the town looked cleaner. Construction was underway to improve and expand housing. The drainage ditches were covered.

By contrast, there was no evidence of progress in the two areas considerd by Croydon to warrant highest priority — formal education and economic development. The delegation found a shortage of school teachers and considerable illiteracy among the children. The caliber of education in Kfar Oranim appeared to be low.

Because of reservations about the quality of formal education in Kfar Oranim, the delegation arranged to see the Director-General, Ministry of Education. It was made clear to him that the poor educational system in Kfar Oranim is viewed as a major problem that could impede Croydon's participation in Project Renewal unless steps are taken to upgrade the quality of education in the town. Data were requested to show comparative achievements between Kfar Oranim students and those from similar towns.

As a symbol of its concern with formal education, the delegation decided to recommend that $50,000 be transferred from the music program and be earmarked for formal education activities in the summer months.

In regard to economic development, the delegation urged that a qualified individual be appointed to do a study of the town's labor force and its capacity to attract new industry. Hope was expressed that such an individual could help Kfar Oranim to become aggressive in seeking new industry, trade and business so as to strengthen its economic base.

The delegation was reluctant to approve construction of two tennis courts in Kfar Oranim. Verbal assurances were given that Junius residents were willing to pay 25% of the cost but the delegation insisted on having these assurances in writing. The delegation requested clarification from the Karen Malka Tennis Center as to its readiness to supervise the new facility. Until these two conditions are met, the delegation recommended no funds for tennis courts.

During the visit, Mark and one member of the delegation interviewed ten teen-agers to select two for a summer in Croydon. They are to be part of a camping program where they will be given leadership training. They will also get a taste of American family life by being placed for short periods with host families that have teen-aged children of their own. Two Kfar Oranim youngsters were selected and plans were made for their visit to Croydon.

In sessions with the liaison-consultant, the delegation stressed its expectation that he take a more aggressive role in the affairs of Kfar Oranim. By and large, however, the delegation expressed satisfaction with his work and came away from the visit generally feeling pleasure in the results of Croydon's being "twinned" with Kfar Oranim.

Some Developments Since October, 1983

A new liaison-consultant was appointed and is on the job to the time of this writing. She has pleased some members of the Croydon

177

Project Renewal committee by her aggressiveness. Others have been concerned that she places too much emphasis on getting things done without regard for strengthening the capacity of Kfar Oranim's residents to do for themselves when Croydon's involvement ceases.

In 1986, after five years, the Croydon Federation Board of Directors voted to extend the period of "twinning" for three more years. During the initial five-year period, although the Board had authorized the expenditure of up to $1,000,000 a year for a maximum total of $5,000,000, only $3,200,000 had been spent. It was anticipated that the remaining $1,800,000 would be spent from 1986 to 1989.

Croydon continued to emphasize the importance of paying attention to formal education and economic development. It appeared that a breakthrough had been achieved in 1986 when a contract was signed with an Israeli university school of education to take major responsibility for improving schools in Kfar Oranim. The arrangement had some beneficial effects on the students and teachers but was terminated in 1988, partly because of difficulties with Israeli government bureaucrats. A new contract with an Israeli educational technology institute was signed for 1988-1989. This organization seems to be having some success in improving Kfar Oranim's schools..

Economic development continues to move slowly. A qualified individual was finally hired in accordance with the delegation's recommendation in its 1983 visit. His achievements were minimal in that no new industry was attracted by virtue of his efforts. He identified a number of factories that were willing to re-locate in Kfar Oranim if funds were provided by American investors. This approach yielded no results and he left. In 1988, a promising start was made on an attempt to foster economic development by building a light industrial park in accordance with one of Kfar Oranim's objectives as listed in the report of the delegation's 1983 visit. A Croydon donor pledged $250,000 towards building units for local artisans such as plumbers, electricians and carpenters. By moving from their backyards, they could expand operations and create new jobs.

An election was held in 1983, as reported at the end of the documentary, and Yehuda became the Mayor with Dan as his Deputy. They soon quarreled and Dan resigned to go into business. As the new Mayor, Yehuda stressed cleanliness and he made great progress in beautifying the town. The town square was substantially improved; a new entrance plaza was created; a number of parks were constructed; waste bins were placed all over the town. Visitors now invariably comment on how clean the town is and how much better it appears.

Supporters of Mayor Shaul did not reconcile themselves to Yehuda's accession to power. Shulamit and Ephraim emerged as leaders of the opposition to Yehuda. During the 1988 visit of the Croydon delegation, Ephraim revealed that he had not spoken to Yehuda since his election in 1983. The fierce in-fighting which characterizes politics in a small Israeli town continues to rage.

Tamar, whose family supported Yehuda and who herself was his advocate, took on increasingly important postions in his administration, eventually becoming the Director of the Kfar Oranim school system. In some ways, she represents one of the major achievements of Croydon's involvement with Kfar Oranim. The liaison-consultant nurtured and supported her, helping her to develop the capacity for greater responsibility.

Eitan, the Executive Secretary of Project Renewal, left to become school principal elsewhere and has had no further connection to Kfar Oranim. He was succeeded by a series of individuals, each of whom held the post for only a short time. None demonstrated Eitan's ability to direct and manage Project Renewal in Kfar Oranim.

Uri, the Welfare Department director, also left after no arrangements could be made to reimburse him for his travel expenses and overtime work. Croydon paid these costs directly to him for a time but Project Renewal officials, especially Leah, disapproved of this arrangement and it was discontinued, leading to his resignation.

Yuval, the former Director of the school system, stayed for several years in the position assigned to him by Mayor Shaul. However, he was unhappy with his demotion and with the caliber of the people who succeeded him, considering himself to be their superior. He finally found a job in another town.

In 1989, Dan was elected Mayor of Kfar Oranim. It is too early to tell what this will mean for the town.

The Croydon Project Renewal Committee has remained relatively stable and continues to make annual visits. Melvin's outstanding work as chairman was recognized by the people of Kfar Oranim during the 1987 visit when a street was named for him in a delightful ceremony. One other member of the delegation who made the original visit in 1981 remains active.

Mark left Croydon to move to a larger city where he has an important executive post in its Federation. He looks back on his Project Renewal days as the most satisfying experience he has had in his long career in Jewish communal service.

Residents of Junius are less active as volunteers in the town although Noam and Ariela continue to be interested. Nothing ever came of the idea to involve those who moved to Junius from the Sinai. One Croydon couple settled in Junius and they serve as volunteers in Kfar Oranim. From time to time, they make financial contributions to various causes in the town and, each year, when the Croydon delegation visits, they host a large reception which brings Croydon, Junius and Kfar Oranim residents together.

To this day, the town does not have a swimming pool and no

arrangements have been made for use of the seashore. This remains a sore point with the residents of Kfar Oranim.

The consequences of the "twinning" process are clearly evident in the physical improvements that have been made in Kfar Oranim. Housing is better; day care centers have been renovated and expanded; the dental clinic is functioning; educational facilities have been improved; the town is much cleaner than it was in 1981.

Less observable but nonetheless present are significant steps forward in Kfar Oranim's self-image. Community morale is higher than it was when Croydon first became a partner of Kfar Oranim. This is manifest in what may be the greatest impact that Croydon has had — heightened participation in community affairs by residents of the town. Their capacity for decision-making has been substantially strengthened. It is essential, however, to be constantly alert to the tendency of officials in Jerusalem, both in the government and the Jewish Agency, to revert to the predominant Israeli pattern of highly centralized control. One illustration occurred in 1986 when the delegation discovered that the proposed budget for the coming year had been drawn up by Project Renewal officials in the Regional Office and in Jerusalem. Difficulty had arisen in the composition of the Steering Committee and, instead of straightening this out or finding an alternate way of assuring citizen participation in the budget process, the officials found it simpler to fall back on the traditional method, ignoring the residents and deciding for them. The delegation refused to accept this breach of the participatory process and froze the budget until it could be corrected.

Another illustration took place in 1987 when Marek, Hanoch's successor, came to Croydon with a recommendation for using the funds that had not been expended during the first five years. Excellent as his suggestions may have been, they emerged completely from his office in Jerusalem with no participation by the people of Kfar Oranim. The Croydon Project Renewal Committee refused to consider Marek's recommendation until there was reason to believe that it represented the wishes of Kfar Oranim residents.

It is hoped that the habit of taking part in making decisions about matters which affect them will become so ingrained in Kfar Oranim as to enable its citizens to stand up against Jerusalem bureaucrats without Croydon's intervention.

The association between the distant partners represents a new pattern of relationship between Israel and the Diaspora. Croydon visitors to Israel usually spend time in their "twin" city, Kfar Oranim. They see its residents as their "family" in Israel and they are always made to feel welcome as family members. There is no anonymity in the connection between donor and recipient but there is a sense of healthy partnership which flourishes in face-to-face encounters.

Most Jewish residents of Croydon are Ashkenazim. Their visits to Israel ordinarily bring them into contact with other Ashkenazim. Since the "twinning" with Kfar Oranim, Croydon residents interact with Sephardim who now make up a majority of the Israeli population. This connection with the man-in-the-street fosters greater understanding between Israelis and Diaspora Jews.

The movement begun by the liaison-consultant in 1981 has gained momentum during the ensuing seven years, never in a straight line, but steadily maintaining its forward progress, to the benefit of both communities.

CHAPTER FIVE

CONCLUSION

Having followed the liaison-consultant sequentially over a period of two years, we will now examine some of the interactions analytically in order to learn from the practice of one community worker in one place what implications there may be for community work generally. The material selected for analysis is deemed by the authors to be significant but we offer only one of many possible retrospective views. We aim to encourage readers to take active roles as analysts so that they may arrive at independent evaluations based on their own selection of sequences from the documentary. In the initial part of our concluding chapter, we address the cross-cultural influences on the role of the liaison-consultant.

By the time the liaison-consultant arrived for his first day in Kfar Oranim, he had three differently stated ideas on his role, each of which manifested the culture of those who enunciated these views. The first notion reflected Jewish communal organization in North America. It was conveyed by the Croydon sponsor during the liaison-consultant's meeting with the Croydon Project Renewal Committee on June 23, 1981. A second definition, derived from a different perspective, came a month later on July 23, 1981 during the introduction of the liaison-consultant by a senior executive of Project Renewal, Jerusalem at a meeting of the Kfar Oranim Steering Committee. The third view came at that same meeting from members of the Steering Committee.

Later, there were additional perceptions of the liaison-consultant role, also showing cultural weight. Some were implicit in the attitude and behavior of the definer. For example, the interplay between the liaison-consultant and Eitan, the Executive Secretary of the Steering Committee yielded one view. Another angle was based on the approach to the liaison-consultant by Ariela, the influential volunteer from Junius, Kfar Oranim's affluent neighboring community.

The existence of varying delineations of the liaison-consultant's role is similar to the situation in which people are perceived differently in their private lives because they inevitably occupy multiple statuses. The individual may be regarded one way as a spouse, another as a parent, a third as a friend, a fourth as a job-holder and so on. However, in the public arena, it is essential for the prestige of a practitioner's calling that his professional status remain consistently high as he moves from sector to sector in the community. This result is easily achieved when the profession has established its reputation on a foundation in science which provides a disciplined body of communicable knowledge and technical competence to solve problems. Such professions demand from their practitioners a universalistic approach based on the intrinsic nature of a need and not on who is presenting it. (1) Myths and symbols abound in the classical professions such as medicine which endow the physician with a high measure of ascribed status even before the helping relationship begins. As Everett C. Hughes points out, "A status is never peculiar to the individual; it is historic. The person, in status and in institutional office, is identified with an historic role." (2)

The liaison-consultant did not enter Kfar Oranim decked out in the aura of an age-old symbolism that would have accompanied a new doctor coming to town to open his office. Community work is a comparative late-comer to the family of professions and it has to acquire (if it ever will) the mythological trappings that help endow the practitioner of an ancient calling with a singular mystique. Does this mean that the community worker functions in a role that depends largely on how it appears in the eyes of the beholder? Up to a point, this may well be the case in certain situations, at least at the outset. Murray Ross maintains that during the initial period when the worker seeks to entrench himself in the community, he is called upon to interpret his role "persistently and consistently, in a great variety of situations. It will be only after a considerable period of time, during which the people of the community will attempt to change his role many times, that his role will be understood and accepted — and then only if . . . performed consistently and well." (3)

Indeed, the process of entrenchment faced by a new community worker poses more of a challenge than a new doctor or a new lawyer confronts on entering a fresh local scene. Yet, it would be incorrect to say that the community worker is completely on his own in transforming himself from a total stranger into a community's trusted inner resource. The liaison-consultant did not come upon Kfar Oranim as a doctor automatically casting an image of high status. However, he was not empty-handed. He had delegated authority, furnished by the Croydon Jewish Federation with prestige and power specific to the tasks he was expected to carry out.

Community work relies neither on ancient myths nor on traditional symbolism in attesting to its universality. It has no science-based methodology that protects humans from imminent threats to life. For community workers, legitimation comes largely as an act of explicit attestation from an authoritative source. In other words, a widely recognized sponsor either from the public or voluntary sector certifies the community worker's legitimacy as a helping professional.

This type of legitimation is ideally suited to achieve status for the practitioner in the eyes of the client or beneficiary, whether individual, family, group or community. The credentials brought by the liaison-consultant from the Croydon Jewish Federation were acknowledged by the people of Kfar Oranim who saw themselves as beneficiaries of their distant partner. However, the liaison-consultant's ascribed status was partly repudiated by the senior official of Project Renewal, Jerusalem in his introduction. Similarly, Croydon's sponsorship of the liaison-consultant did not hold the same meaning in Junius as in Kfar Oranim. Thus, legitimation of community workers tends to put their professional status on a sliding scale often depending on whom they relate to in a given situation.

Whether the inconsistency inherent in the practitioner's relationships with public figures throws into question the professionalism of community work is an issue which will be explored later.

Continuing our examination of the phenomenon of unevenness in the liaison-consultant's professional image, we need to remember that the characteristic of role incongruity (4) preceded any interaction with the people who attended the Steering Committee meeting on July 23, 1981. The residents of Kfar Oranim had already extended their unspoken but cordial welcome to the liaison-consultant before they exchanged their first words after the meeting ended. The liaison-consultant had yet to meet the official from Project Renewal, Jerusalem who formally introduced him to the Steering Commitee. The introduction questioned the liaison-consultant's role, as seen by Croydon and simultaneously instructed the Committee to treat the liaison-consultant in accordance with Hanoch's definition of the role and responsibilities. What he had to say on this subject at the Steering Committee meeting was consistent with his general approach to representatives of the overseas communities and stemmed from the culture of the bureaucracy in which he played a leading role.

In the course of gathering information for this study, we learned that when Hanoch first assumed his position in Project Renewal, he clearly stated his implacable opposition to the idea of overseas communities having representatives in their "twin" communities. Subsequently, he relented but refused to give the liaison functionaries any official recognition in Project Renewal. Their uncertain status which issued from this slight shift in attitude was no symptom of personal ambiguity on Hanoch's part. Rather, it was produced by a significant modification in the functioning of the Jewish Agency that had come with the inauguration of Project Renewal.

From its inception in 1929, the Jewish Agency served as direct funding source for social and economic development expenditures in Palestine and after 1948, in Israel. However, in the "twinning" approach, for the first time, overseas communities that gave money had direct contact with beneficiary communities that received it. In this process, the Jewish Agency retreated, at least in part, from the commanding position of dispenser and controller of overseas funds to become a transfer conduit. This was the case - a bit blurred - with Croydon's grants destined for Kfar Oranim.

Aside from Project Renewal, the old arrangement still prevails. The United Jewish Appeal sends lump sums collected by North American Jewish communities in their annual drives to the Jewish Agency in Israel. The money is not tied to any community neither on the giving nor on the receiving side. The Jewish Agency distributes money in accordance with needs and priorities established in Israel without active involvement of the overseas communities where the funds are raised. Some structural changes pay lip service to the idea of overseas donors participating in decisions about use of the money, but, basically, responsibility rests with Jewish Agency bureaucrats, as illustrated by expenditures to absorb and settle recent arrivals from Ethiopia and Russia.

By contrast, in Project Renewal, as illustrated by Kfar Oranim, the decision as to its annual allocation now rests not with the Jewish Agency but with the Croydon Jewish Federation to which Project Renewal, Jerusalem functions mainly in an advisory capacity. Similarly, Project Renewal Jerusalem advises and aids Kfar Oranim, helping the Steering Committee and its sub-committees to conduct reviews of the programs funded by Croydon and to prepare the annual budget for submission to the Croydon Jewish Federation. The shift from the role of virtual funding source to a mediating role between the deprived neighborhoods and towns in Israel and their distant but clearly identifiable overseas benefactors constitutes a precedent-setting departure from the past and a significant reduction in the power and authority of the Jewish Agency.

For the overseas communities, there is a further advantage to the policy of "twinning" and direct allocations as compared to the anonymous lump sum transfers that give the Jewish Agency full authority over the money which is donated. The North American communities are now in a position to require accountability from their beneficiaries in Israel in much the same manner as Jewish federations operate with the local agencies whose budget deficits they cover through annual allocations. Thus, the outreach made possible by the "twinning" process offers a double gain. It creates living bridges and a sense of true partnership in a humanitarian social project and, for the first time, it offers the possibility of dialogue between the communities providing the funds and their Israeli beneficiaries.

For the givers from abroad, especially those residing in North America where unified fund-raising and social planning are integral to organized community living, accountability between giver and receiver is more than an actuarial refinement. It is a cultural imperative. As Lipsky maintains, "Accountability is the link between bureaucracy and democracy. Modern democracy depends on the accountabilty of bureaucracy to carry out declared policy . . " (5) Andron, dealing with the same theme, points out that accountability emerged as a major issue in the 1980's in the philanthropic relationship between Israel and its North American supporters. He goes on to indicate that a society's administrative culture shapes operative principles that may confuse the outsider. (6) Not infrequently, such baffling situations would arise between "twinned" communities which saw themselves from afar as partners sharing the same faith and the same historic fate but which, paradoxically, proclaimed their age-old mutuality in different languages and from different cultural perspectives. This confusion was particularly evident in dealing with the question of Kfar Oranim's accountability and the liaison-consultant's role in monitoring it as viewed differently by Croydon and by Project Renewal, Jerusalem.

During its first two years (1978-1980), Project Renewal was dominated by the Israeli government. The ministries of Housing, Labor and Social Affairs and later, Education and Health, functioned on the basis of what was defined as a conjoint arrangement. They carried on their respective activities in the localities with general guidelines set by the Social Policy Team. This Team was responsible to the Deputy Prime Minister who appointed Marcus, a political scientist, to head its work. Two important decisions which were to have a lasting effect on Project Renewal came soon after the Social Policy Team was established. The first was aimed at extending the Ministry of Housing's approach to urban renewal from its traditional preoccupation with housing to include the social dimension of rehailitation. This brought under its purview such urban problems as care of the aged, delinquency and community morale. The second policy decision of the Social Policy Team had as its goal the transformation of local residents from passive recipients of rehabilitation efforts into participants actively involved in the renewal and development of their own communities.

The moving spirit behind these two important decisions was Marcus. His American background was undoubtedly a factor in shaping his approach to urban renewal. He envisioned Project Renewal as adopting a "fusion of community development with more formal democracy". This idea eventually found expression as an operating reality in the form of the local steering committees. (7) Moreover, his perception of urban renewal as a process incorporating both physical and social planning was adopted as a key principle in Project Renewal.

Members of local steering committees had grown up with a view of democracy as having to do with their freedom, once in four years, to seat and unseat national parties vying for their votes. They had little or no experience in the realm of participatory democracy which they were called on to practice, to legitimate and to encourage in their communities.(8) Ironically, Israel, the country which pioneered in community participation at the broadest base through the collectives (kibbutzim) and the cooperatives (moshavim) failed to perpetuate this tradition in Project Renewal. This approach had to be re-interpreted and re-introduced on the basis of community development in Third World countries where participation was used to energize local populations in remote villages. Community participation was reaffirmed in the industrialized countries in the 1950's when they began to adapt community development to the problems of rural and urban poverty within their own borders. This experience was brought to Israel by the distant partners from North America.

If Israel was a generation late in discovering community development, it is due, in large measure, to the fact that local political and economic initiative is heavily circumscribed. The passivity of people living in an isolated village of an impoverished Third World country rests on the scarcity of means. By contrast, the deadening of initiative in Israeli towns may well derive from a surfeit of resources coming in from the outside.

Ernest Stock vividly and perceptively described this situation in a 1966 article. The excerpt cited here bears directly on the problem of centralization in Israel in the 1980's. "Just as there is a physical plan for buildings and for the infrastructure of public utilities, so there exists an institutional blueprint . . . common to all of the towns, come ready made from central repositories. A local council (municipal government) is appointed by the Interior Ministry, with party representatives serving . . . according to . . . their presumed relative strength in the embryo community. A labor council is established by the Histadrut to represent . . . trade unionism in the town's economy. Kupat Holim opens the first clinics . . . The religious authorities see to the establishment of a religious council and a local rabbinate. The Jewish Agency offers newcomers their first contact with officialdom . . . for initial sustenance. Amidar. . . opens an office to administer public housing . . . The Labor Ministry's employment exchange is a key agency from the start; no less important is the welfare bureau (Lishka) which, though administratively a part of the municipality, depends for policy guidance on the Welfare Ministry." (9)

With Project Renewal facing such overarching centralization bred so firmly into Israeli culture, Marcus' ideas could be expected to be slow to bear fruit. Indeed, local steering committees came into existence only toward the end of 1979.

Further resistance to participatory democracy was expressed during the first two years of Project Renewal when it was mainly concerned with physical renewal — restoring gardens, renovating decrepit apartment houses, repairing broken sidewalks and the like. Contractors who brought artisans into the neighborhoods to carry out these improvements were bewildered and frustrated by the passive and, at times, sullen responses of the residents. The contractors would ask the community workers why there was such indifference, often tinged with hostility. The workers would say that many residents had other priorities. Some wanted their apartments enlarged instead of the outside walls painted. Others wished to see a decent school building — a facility which did not exist in many neighborhoods. Often, people felt it was more important to improve the sewage system rather than to repair the sidewalks. Community workers would suggest that residents of the areas being improved should be consulted. "What!" the outraged contractors howled, "go chase around to meetings? Go argue with people who don't know what they're talking about?" They would demand answers to more questions. Do the community workers and the residents care that the contractors had to sweat blood to get the building trades to show up according to schedule? Do they realize the penalties for failing to finish the job on time — for reasons over which the contractors have no control? They were bitter about the contradictory whims which often faced them. On one hand, they were expected to engage in time-consuming consultations with residents. On the other hand, they were penalized if they didn't complete the job within stipulated deadlines.

The community workers took the brunt of the discontent that prevailed among the contractors and also among the managerial personnel who worked within this comprehensive effort. These individuals felt that the community workers might have been more forthcoming in trying to elicit a nod of appreciation from the residents. They expected more cooperation from community workers who were bringing the blessings of Project Renewal to these deprived people. Managerial functionaries tended to respond with uneasiness to the community workers. They feared that if the community workers' notions about citizen participation were not kept in check, then the kind of billowing turbulence that took place in North America in the 1960's would be brought to Israel. Thus, the high degree of centralization which characterized the relationship between officialdom and local communities was perceived by contractors, managers and experts as a social good which provided a stability that had to be maintained.

This outlook took a pounding in 1971 when the Israeli version of the Black Panthers emerged in the slums of Tel Aviv and Jerusalem to challenge the establishment. However, the fear that Israel was in for an era of confrontation similar to that which had been generated in the United States by the Black Panthers was short-lived. The Yom

Kippur War came along in 1973. As has always been true in Israel, the first announcement of a general mobilization puts domestic problems on the shelf.

Widespread militant activism did not become a real issue again. However, its memory lingered into the late 1970's with enough impact to awaken worries that community workers could conceivably touch off the kind of militancy which the society tasted briefly in 1971-1972. Transferring anxiety from the Black Panthers in the slums of Jerusalem and Tel Aviv to the community workers only served to prove how faulty memories can be. In actual fact, those community workers in particular and social workers generally played a minor role in the spell of public confrontation that came in 1971-1972. (10)

During the first two years of its existence, Project Renewal had little impact on the tradition of centralization which held sway in Israel, especially between government officials in Jerusalem and local municipalities. Mayors of development towns and other small localities received as much as 90% of their budgets from the Ministry of Interior. They came to Jerusalem, hat in hand, to negotiate with the Ministry on behalf of their towns. By and large, the ingrained practice and policy of centralization went unchallenged. It was accepted as inevitable by most people. Israelis had grown accustomed to having the central government amass immense emergency powers in the face of threatened and actual wars. They accepted enormously high taxes as absolutely essential for defense and security. Although such powers are supposedly temporary, they are rarely surrendered in peaceful periods. For example, the two world wars concentrated tremendous power in the federal governments of the United States and Canada. The increase in the flow of power to Washington and Ottawa has, to a great degree, been irreversible. Similarly, the unceasing state of belligerence by its Arab neighbors has been the reason for persistent centralization by the Israeli government. Its high salience as a rallying force in Israeli society has been accepted as one of the inexorable conditions of the country's existence.

The entrenched public attitude in favor of centralization was not conducive to community participation. So long as the emphasis of Project Renewal was on physical improvments, there were things to be done and achievements to be recorded regardless of the attitudes among local residents. Moreover, there were statistics to prove forward movement. Within the first year of operation, Project Renewal made demonstrable physical improvements in 65 neighborhoods and towns. (11) However, when interest in the social aspects of renewal began to burgeon, the need for active local involvement became self-evident. A move in this direction was bound to come as the participation of overseas "twinned" communities increased. The high value placed by North American Jewry on community participation had an inevitable impact.

Several factors combined to create a thrust for change as Project Renewal headed into its third year in 1980. The Ministry of Labor and Social Affairs, unlike the other arms of government, favored community development approaches that stressed community participation. In response to the first signs of interest in neighborhood activism, as it is usually referred to in Israel, the Ministry opened a school for 29 students who had been identified in their localities as potential community leaders. This took place in 1980. By 1985, there were 75 such schools which sent 1,700 trained graduates back to their communities. Three institutes for social education and three universities had been recruited to guide in planning curricula and training of instructors for this form of adult education. (12)

Also in 1980, partly to accommodate the expanding interest of overseas communities in Project Renewal, the Jewish Agency created a Renewal Department to replace its existing administrative apparatus for dealing with Project Renewal. A leading role in this greatly enlarged operation was assigned to Hanoch who had joined the staff of Project Renewal in October, 1979. Until the establishment of the Jewish Agency Renewal Department, the Israeli government held center stage in urban renewal generally and in Project Renewal in particular. The Ministry of Housing was the sole repository of whatever urban renewal efforts preceded Project Renewal. In fact, when Project Renewal was launched, the Ministry went to its own archives to retrieve the Report of the Authority for Construction and Clearance of Urban Areas, established in 1965. Although an impressive program had been drawn up by the Authority, only a few plans were implemented.

These desultory dabblings had little in common with the vast scope of Project Renewal. However, data produced by the Authority's study provided a fund of knowledge on which Project Renewal was forced to rely since it was ushered into being without any preliminary research of its own.(13) The ready-made information base of the 1965 report helped shape the policy decisions which set the stage for leadership by the Ministry of Housing in the first years of Project Renewal. Reinforcing the Ministry's central role, the Social Policy Team, headed by Marcus, made contact with physical and social planners, public figures, social scientists, and members of the helping professions. Periodically, the Social Policy Team invited this elite constituency of specialists to deliberate over progress reports and papers delivered by recognized experts. This enhanced the prestige of Project Renewal and solidified the pivotal role of the Ministry of Housing.

When the Jewish Agency created its Renewal Department in 1980, a perceptible change took place. The emphasis on cultivating a supportive group of Israelis begun by the Social Policy Team gave way to concentrating on the overseas communities. There were cogent reasons for this development. Most important was the urgent necessity of maintaining a flow of philanthropic gifts from overseas. The Israeli government was regularly providing its share of Project Renewal funds out of tax revenues but overseas contributors had to be prodded to make their donations year after year. Among the sustained promotional techniques was the stress placed on the "twinning" process as an historic opportunity for communities geographically distant, yet sharing the same heritage, to become partners and to meet face to face. The indefatigable Hanoch spanned the distances and proved to be an effective match-maker in "twinning" donor and beneficiary communities. Contributions increased as did the frequency of visits by the overseas communities to their partners in Israel. By 1982, the investment in Project Renewal which now embraced 82 neighborhoods and towns had more than trebled.

The new emphasis served the interest of the Croydon Jewish Federation in the search for accountability from Kfar Oranim. It also was invaluable for the Renewal Department in Jerusalem as a means of circumventing the obstacle course that decisions had to confront in the Jewish Agency bureaucracy regarding the tiniest expenditure to be made in a given locality. One informant interviewed by the liaison-consultant pointed out that, previously, every single item in every program had to make its long, excruciating journey from one committee to another and from one official to the next one higher up in the hierarchy. This meant, for example, that appointing an instructor to teach folk-dancing on a part-time basis might take months before final approval was ultimately extracted. These inordinate delays could now be avoided by the annual meeting of the Croydon delegation and the Kfar Oranim Steering Committee. Together, they would examine line by line the proposed budget for next year and they would review Project Renewal activities during the previous year. The Croydon delegation's approach was the same as that used by Croydon's Jewish Federation in dealing with its local beneficiary agencies. Croydon could ensure the flow of funds to its distant "twin" in Israel. Approved programs could proceed with minimal delay. There would be no need to spend an eternity waiting for decision after decision, trailing item after item as each subject made its way at snail's pace from Jerusalem to Kfar Oranim.

Some overseas communities do not send representatives to conduct annual budget reviews with their partners in Israel but simply make occasional visits. This is relatively rare but when it occurs, the Jewish Agency is quick to fall back on its traditional pattern of serving as the virtual provider of funds. The vast majority of overseas communities do sit with their Israeli partners to review annual budgets. Except for an occasional delay in transferring funds, this approach effectively opens the door to prompt implementation of Project Renewal activities in Kfar Oranim as approved by Croydon. The bureaucratic labyrinths and pitfalls which plagued the relationship between Kfar Oranim and the Ministry of Housing were in stark contrast to the promptness of Project Renewal, Jerusalem in carrying out commitments made by Croydon to the residents of Kfar Oranim.

Hanoch was not above playing a pseudo-facilitating role in which the Steering Committee was encouraged to pour out a litany of woes regarding delays by the Ministry of Housing in completing the physical improvements it had obligated itself to carry out. (April 18, 1982) Other than providing a release for pent-up feelings, there was little that Hanoch could do to propel the Ministry into action. He was no doubt trying to create an invidious distinction between the Renewal Department's sensitivity to people's needs as contrasted to the indifference of the Ministry of Housing. While he showed great resourcefulness in spearheading the move to annual budget reviews, he found it almost impossible to make a dent in the cumbersome administrative quagmire within his parent organization, the Jewish Agency. He was much less likely to prevail in getting the Ministry of Housing to speed up its provision of services to Kfar Oranim.

The measure of authority gained by Croydon through the annual budget reviews was apt to be seen by the Ministry of Housing as an outside intrusion into Israel's internal affairs. Marcus made himself clear on this when he and the liaison-consultant drove home from Kfar Oranim on April 11, 1982. He was an advocate of citizen participation provided, it seemed, that it was limited to citizens of Israel. This expressed an attitude in 1982 which erupted forcefully in 1988 when the Israelis objected to criticism by some American Jews regarding the handling of Palestinian rock throwers.

Centralization of power remained firmly fixed in the public sector. In the voluntary sector, exemplified by the Jewish Agency, there was some evidence of change. This came about as the Jewish Agency galvanized support for Project Renewal from overseas communities. The price paid by the Jewish Agency was retreat from its role as virtual benefactor. Instead, it became a mediator between the two communities which it had brought into direct, visible relationship with each other. This shift required a reduction in centralized domination by the Jewish Agency, a power which it relinquished with great reluctance and only in part.

The overseas communities, having achieved substantial control over their allocations to their distant partners, sought to broaden their autonomy still further by trying to reduce the mediating role to which the Jewish Agency had been relegated. One expression of this effort was the demand for the right to appoint a liaison-consultant who would be solely accountable to the overseas community, who would be paid directly by that community and who would serve as a living link to the locality being rehabilitated. While this demand was acceded to, Hanoch had no intention of allotting to the liaison functionary any authority or any share of the Renewal Department's mediating role between the Israeli communities and their overseas benefactors. In his eyes, to do so would weaken the link between Project Renewal and the sponsoring communities. The Croydon Project Renewal Committee saw the situation differently. It perceived its liaison-consultant as playing a mediating role in the day-to-day contact with Kfar Oranim, especially in fiscal matters, the area that Hanoch was determined to control.

Croydon's attitude was based on the social planning orientation which its representatives brought to negotiations with Kfar Oranim and with Project Renewal, Jerusalem. The Croydon Jewish Federation is part of a uniquely American pattern in community organization, pioneered by the American Jewish community. From early days, this initiative has been the precursor of a development which has produced thousands of planning councils and united funds in most North American communities. (14) This tradition does not extend to Israel. While the community planning and organizing approach to philanthropy with accountability as its paramount assumption has been taken for granted in North America for the better part of a century, it is not a feature of the Israeli scene. Ralph Kramer, in a study of Israeli voluntary agencies, found that they are "highly autonomous with relatively low accountability and an absence of structures for inter-agency planning or joint fund-raising. They were governed by a small number of self-perpetuating board members, typical of 'minority rule' in voluntary associations and with little participation of their clientele." (15)

Project Renewal, Jerusalem was not bound by assumptions based on the point of view which conditioned Croydon's representatives. The differing mind sets of these two interacting parties shaped the liaison role which was meant to enhance the "twinning" process. Tactics and strategies adopted by the liaison functionaries representing 48 different overseas communities were also significantly influenced by variations in attitudes toward community organization and social planning. The interventions of Croydon's liaison-consultant exemplify a community worker's attempt to test consciously and deliberately a professional helping role that was conditioned by these predominant differences which were clearly a function of cross-cultural diversity.

The Liaison-Consultant's Role and Its Components

We will now consider the components of the liaison-consultant's role. These should be seen in light of the fact that Project Renewal, Jerusalem had selective interest in the work of the liaison-consultant in Kfar Oranim, limited to a few components of his role. Similarly, Croydon was not equally concerned with every aspect of the liaison-consultant's daily pursuits. Fluctuations in response were due to the varying weight that Croydon and Project Renewal, Jerusalem gave to the different activities of the liaison-consultant. An examination of the elements comprising the liaison role will be helpful in understanding the diversified reactions of Croydon and Project Renewal, Jerusalem.

In a study of the "twinning" process as it affected six localities in Israel and their distant partners overseas, Daniel Elazar and his colleagues identified five distinct characteristics that are integral to the role of the liaison functionary. These are described as: communicator, linker, troubleshooter, initiator and delegate.(16) The following portrayals are drawn not only from the Elazar study but also from information received by the liaison-consultant in interviews with other liaison functionaries in various Project Renewal neighborhoods as well as from his own experience.

1. **Communicator.** In this role, the liaison functionary transmits information but also processes it to clarify, interpret and acquaint the distant sponsor with the intricacies of Israeli culture. This communicating role provides an opportunity for the liaison functionary to help the overseas partner to learn more about the Israelis involved in Project Renewal who must be considered in their support of the program. Although styles of communication differ, in the great majority of cases, the content transmitted is voluminous and continuous.

2. **Linker.** This role calls for developing the liaison idea into a method especially suited to the inter-community outreach known as "twinning". Among other things, this means encouraging and planning for the involvement of volunteers from the overseas community; recruiting, where appropriate, the active support of the overseas partner in lobbbying and pressuring government ministries to secure better or more prompt provision of services to the "twin" community; participating with Project Renewal, Jerusalem in planning for and receiving overseas groups visiting their "twin" community. These linking encounters commence with people from distant parts of the world, speaking different languages, subject to different cultural influences, being brought together as strangers. In the course of a visit, lasting a few hours, they become kindred spirits in a relationship that is activated by an awakened sense of their common heritage. During the annual budget reviews, the liaison functionary performs the duties of a staff executive to the visiting delegation. This linking function is seen by many liaison workers as the heart of the liaison process.

3. **Troubleshooter.** This role entails advocacy as well as an ability to be located at strategic junctures in approved programs which require

external pressure in order to get carried out. The troubleshooter often steps in to ward off an emergency. Sometimes, it may be a matter of crisis intervention after the emergency has occurred. At other times, the troubleshooter is prompted to act by inherent traits of personality. When temperament becomes an excessive motivating factor for action, the troubleshooter inevitably becomes the target of the trouble.

4. **Initiator.** Acting in this role requires the liaison functionary to command the necessary expertise to conceive and launch programs. This capacity is not uniformly valued in different sectors of the community. The proposed projects do not always derive from a broad-based consensus but may rather represent the initiator's own convictions regarding community needs. There have been instances of programs starting with considerable enthusiasm at the outset but which later came to haunt the initiator. The ability to stir up a flurry of beginning support was not undergirded by the capacity for long-range planning so essential to sustain the interest evoked at the inception of the project.

5. **Delegate.** Perhaps the most problem-laden aspect of the liaison functionary's role is that of delegate. Generally, this component is not subjected to thorough negotiation between Project Renewal, Jerusalem and the overseas communities, resulting in what amounts to a jurisdictional dispute. This is almost certain to take place since Project Renewal, Jerusalem sees itself as authorized to maintain a direct relationship with the overseas communities, a responsibility not to be usurped by an outside liaison functionary. However, this attitude runs counter to the liaison's conviction that the course of events can be influenced, based on his sense of accountability to the overseas sponsor. Another sustaining element is the unchallenged evaluative stance which the liaison functionary is able to maintain in the flow of information provided to the sponsor. Recourse to such independent contact with the community abroad through writing or by telephone*, whenever the need arises, is the principal ingredient in the liaison functionary's sense of authority. It is far more important than empowerment as a delegate which is often like a signal that loses strength in the course of being transmitted from a great distance.

These five components of the liaison functionary's job presuppose seasoned practitioners who have the skill to carry out the full range of tasks that comprise the work role. In the early stages of the assignment, all community workers inevitably go through a stage of trial and error. Intervention and orientation are intertwined and initiatives are tentative until sufficient experience has been acquired to handle the role with full authority. This initial period of venturing into practice while still learning the job may be described as a reconnaissance phase.

The telephone was rarely used between Croydon and Kfar Oranim

Subsequent steps in the development of a practice methodology are posited on assuming that a stable work setting exists which facilitates the progress of the new practitioner, moving from a point of entry to the more complex levels of the role. Such an ordered process of settling into the job would include periodic consultation or supervision in the case of the novice. In addition, there would be available reading material to enhance the worker's self-development. This is the procedure followed by North American social planning councils or their equivalent. These conditions do not apply to the liaison functionaries who represent overseas communities in Project Renewal. They are a long way from achieving the prerequisites of community work that have been institutionalized many years ago in North America.

The idea of overseas communities appointing their representatives in Project Renewal came from Daniel Elazar, head of the Jerusalem Center for Public Affairs. In a 1979 report by the Center, he stated, "many Americans feel the Jewish Agency by itself is an insufficient diaspora presence and want relationships developed which not only can involve twinned communities in some on-going non-superficial way, but also provide some independent mechanism which can monitor and evaluate progress and process in a manner which helps all parties involved in Project Renewal." (17) Later that year and early in 1980, the Jewish community of England, as well as of three American cities, followed Elazar's suggestion and appointed liaison functionaries.

In 1981, when the Croydon Jewish Federation decided to appoint its own representative in Kfar Oranim, the job was still very much of a probing venture without a structure, without definition and without any conceptualization of the role. The prospective liaison-consultant, coming to Croydon to be interviewed for the job, pondered the pioneering nature of the assignment that was in the offing. He had just completed a year's sabbatical from his Israeli university and was about to return home when Croydon invited him to visit his prospective sponsor.

At the meeting in Croydon, the desire for an "independent mechanism which can monitor and evaluate progress and process" was echoed during the brief formalities of introduction. This was repeated in the "getting-to-know-you" aftermath when the liaison-consultant, no longer prospective but virtually appointed pending some administrative procedures, was guided by an academic colleague who had brought him and Croydon together. As they moved among the people standing about the room, Croydon committee members voiced their concern about Kfar Oranim's low community morale. They had either been told about this or learned it first-hand in the course of their visits to the Israeli town, now officially their "twin". They wondered what could be done about the high delinquency rate, the depressed economic situation and the paucity of job opportunities which combined to make more people leave Kfar Oranim than to settle there.

These thoughts were not being aired just for the purpose of making small talk. It was evident that the Croydon committee members were voicing aims which they hoped to achieve with the aid of the liaison-consultant. He was not pressed to lay out his formula for dealing with these matters thanks to a prevailing spirit of implicit understanding that it was far too early for solid professional judgements. But — it was not too early to think professionally. The liaison-consultant's preliminary reconnaissance phase was at hand. What was said in Croydon gave rise to the first tentative thoughts on principles of intervention. The scatter of opinions, suggestions and comments which came from the Croydon committee members fell into three categories:

First, there was the concern about Kfar Oranim's well-being as a community. This was uppermost in the minds of some individuals and emerged as a major theme. A reading of the demographic material about Kfar Oranim produced realization that what was being said in Croydon was good for what ailed Kfar Oranim. Still, its residents could not be expected to strive collectively to reach goals identified and supplied by a community thousands of miles away. A change for the better in Kfar Oranim's fortunes would depend on raising the morale of its residents and helping them to cultivate more positive attitudes to their town. To increase confidence in their community called for improving the town's economic outlook and for creating institutions that would enrich its social life. For the time being, these were provisional guidelines until the liaison-consultant became actually involved with the residents of Kfar Oranim. Before that contact, the liaison-consultant's familiarity with depressed communities in Israel suggested to him that a process of change in the town called for a helping relationship that emphasized inner growth and development. This could be a slow, even painful, process. Moreover, it could not be rushed by external proddings geared to the expectations of Croydon. A crucial factor was Kfar Oranim's receptivity to change and this had yet to be determined by the liaison-consultant although Croydon's delegation which visited Israel in April, 1981 believed that such readiness was present. Even at this very preliminary stage, it was clear to the liaison-consultant that the target of the relationship was the town in Israel, not the sponsor in Croydon.

A second theme that emerged in the conversations between the liaison-consultant and the Croydon committee members was the nature of the inter-community contacts made possible by the "twinning" process. In North America, community workers in settlement houses and community centers have tended to keep their affluent sponsors and deprived populations apart. Going back to the turn of the century, their standing complaint has been that rich board members seek to exert a paternalistic influence over the disadvantaged. (18) By contrast, overseas visitors arriving in Israel to dedicate a community center or other facility which they have financed or to attend a budget review are always enthusiastically received by their beneficiaries. The bogey of paternalism never haunts these get-togethers. On the contrary, these periodic interactions are invariably warm, festive occasions. Rather than eschewing them as community workers in America tend to do, the liaison-consultant felt that face-to-face contacts should be encouraged. This would position him as fostering a linking relationship between the two communities and would help them to reach out to each other as partners. The onus for making this direct contact possible would fall on Croydon since its residents possessed the means to travel. Visiting missions to Israel create ad hoc contacts which, as a rule, last for only a few hours. Beyond that, the overseas partners differ in the direct connections they establish with their Israeli "twins". It remained to be seen what kind of relationship Croydon would set up and whether exchange visits between youth groups, volunteers, missions and annual budget reviews were to be instituted.

The third theme was the monitoring role of the liaison-consultant and this brought an undertone of determination into the discussion. Mark, the senior staff member of the Croydon Jewish Federation assigned to Project Renewal, and one or two others called for more accountability for the funds they were providing to Kfar Oranim. Mark stressed the need for information as to what was transpiring day to day at the Israeli end. As monitor, the liaison-consultant was solely responsible to Croydon and was expected to provide a steady flow of observations. In this aspect of his role, the liaison-consultant was seen as bringing Croydon greater mastery over its participation in Project Renewal. In effect, the liaison-consultant was being told that ongoing accountability to Croydon was to be one of the major components of his work in Kfar Oranim. He assumed that his monitoring task carried the same weight as the other aspects of his role which, taken together, went to determine his status as Croydon's representative in Israel. Some of Croydon's expectations were related to its earlier reluctance to become involved in Project Renewal which led to its independent decision to employ a liaison-consultant without even knowing about Elazar's suggestion that this be done.

In order to carry out the various components of his role, the liaison-consultant would need to move beyond the borders of Kfar Oranim. He would have to extend his contacts to include government officials in Jerusalem and regional offices as well as staff of other public bodies involved in Project Renewal, either directly or indirectly. Such contacts were essential since the services that made renewal activities possible in Kfar Oranim came from many of external sources. However, monitoring would not be an important part of this role component.

These relationships would be geared primarily to gathering information as part of the communicator function. They would also probably be useful in testing possibilities for lobbying to secure cooperation for various projects. One example was the contact that was established with the government housing corporation in the effort to develop a youth cooperative for contracting maintenance services to physical renewal projects.

Basic to the monitoring function is the quest of the overseas communities for fiscal accountability with regard to money they give to their "twinned" communities in Israel. Croydon's surveillance would not apply to tax funds allocated by the Ministry of Housing and other public entities. The Israeli government is the sole auditing and controlling authority for these internal expenditures which go directly to Project Renewal neighborhoods and towns. Croydon's funds are philanthropic and so the fiscal relationship is not with the government but with the Jewish Agency and its Project Renewal department. By the rules of this arrangement, Project Renewal neighborhoods and towns are not the direct recipients of the funds which come from their distant partners. The funds are routed to each location, Kfar Oranim included, via Project Renewal, Jerusalem. Because of this state of affairs, Croydon was eager to have the liaison-consultant begin his monitoring function at the level of Project Renewal, Jerusalem, a completely unrealistic expectation given the prevailing attitudes in Israel.

In 1980, the Renewal Unit of the Jewish Agency acquired the status of a full-fledged department, an important move upward in the bureaucratic hierarchy. In the ensuing year, the new Renewal Department achieved a dominant position as the national body guiding Project Renewal neighborhoods and towns. It exerted a commanding influence over the liaison functionaries who represented the overseas communities and who continued to go about their work as disembodied solo practitioners left to their own devices with no recourse to any organized reference group in Israel.

This highly individualized and isolated way of operating underwent a slight change in 1981 when the community representatives gained an unofficial resource in the form of the Jerusalem Center for Public Affairs. The Center's offer to organize monthly meetings of the liaison functionaries provided their first opportunity to compare notes and to discuss problems in their daily work. Following up on this initiative, the Center became interested in the responsibilities carried by these workers. In time, this interest produced some helpful information of a general nature which threw light on the roles and problems of the liaison functionaries as they tried to enhance the "twinning" process between distant partners.

After the June 23, 1981 meeting in Croydon and his subsequent appointment as Croydon's representative, the liaison-consultant returned to Israel but held off traveling to Kfar Oranim or to Project Renewal, Jerusalem. Before he left Croydon, the liaison-consultant had been informed by Mark that he wished to be present when the liaison-consultant made his first visit to Croydon's "twin" community. Mark said that he and his wife would soon visit Israel. This would give him the opportunity to join the liaison-consultant when he initiated his association with Kfar Oranim. His sponsor's participation in introducing him was welcomed by the liaison-consultant.

As they drove to the first meeting in Kfar Oranim, Mark mentioned that Hanoch had stated both in conversation and in writing that he was ready to recommend a suitable candidate as liaison-consultant for Kfar Oranim. Mark took some pains to point out that Croydon had not picked up Hanoch's suggestion, preferring to make its own appointment. He mentioned this on the initial meeting in Croydon. The impression Mark gave on both occasions when he referred to this matter was that he was rather pleased about Croydon's asserting itself without being deterred by Hanoch's disappointment nor perhaps by his displeasure.

Hanoch's offer to recommend a candidate for the job of liaison-consultant was touched on twice by Mark, once in Croydon and once en route to Kfar Oranim. During that drive, Mark also told the liaison-consultant that Hanoch would be introducing him to the Steering Committee. For Mark, this was the obvious thing to do since he did not speak Hebrew and, therefore, could not make the introduction himself. The liaison-consultant raised no question about this arrangement. He accepted it as a detail that Mark had worked out without thinking about it one way or another. However, the show of Croydon's independence in selecting the liaison-consultant was another matter. Not only was it mentioned twice but it was conveyed with implicit avowal of satisfaction on both occasions. It was clearly meant to be a message of some significance. The liaison-consultant was not yet in a position to judge just how important this message was. His limited acquaintance with Project Renewal was gained in the first two years of the program before Hanoch came to prominence. There had been no previous occasion for him to meet Hanoch.

Mark did not pursue the question of Hanoch's effort to help pick the liaison-consultant. Perhaps he dropped the subject in order to move on to other matters. Whatever prompted Mark to leave the issue, the liaison-consultant decided to let it rest. He was preoccupied with his own thoughts about the three approaches to community work in Kfar Oranim that had crystallized in his mind after the meeting in Croydon. The three themes (as he had originally perceived them) were now taking on the nature of scenarios projecting him into the meeting which was about to take place.

The Steering Committee would be hosting Mark, his wife and the liaison-consultant. As local authority for Project Renewal, the Steering Committee is the focal point for help flowing into the community from the government and Croydon. The liaison-consultant hoped the visitors would be welcomed by the Steering Committee speaking for a community that saw itself as a full-fledged partner in Project Renewal. From what he had heard thus far, he was concerned that the Steering Committee might greet them exuding a defensive-apologetic client community syndrome. Croydon's stated objective was to use their assistance for aided self-help and strengthening inner resources in Kfar Oranim. Some of these inner resources would become visible as urban renewal took hold in the houses and streets of Kfar Oranim. Other inner resources would, hopefully, be seen in the enhanced moral fibre of the town's residents and in increased confidence in their community. These are preconditions for social and economic improvements. They are the goals of growth and development characterized by heightened community morale.

The presence of Mark and his wife will symbolize Croydon's reaching out to establish direct contact with its "twin" community. Whether the joint undertaking in renewal can become the nexus between two distant partners bent on moving beyond the philanthropic relationship to a dynamic link based on their mutual sense of a shared fate or whether it simply remains an aspiration that hovers beyond reach will depend on overcoming the barriers standing in the way of this goal. The first barrier is the great distance that separates the two communities. The second is the high cost of travel to overcome this barrier — a cost which makes the trip a one-way proposition from Croydon to Kfar Oranim. There are deep differences in culture, tradition and language which constitute potent barriers to overcome whenever there are face-to-face encounters between the two communities. While all these are formidable obstacles, experience has shown that they do not deter Israelis and their overseas visitors from savoring a genuine sense of solidarity arising from the basic values which bring them together. To enhance the partnership would mean capitalizing on the feelings of a shared heritage by careful planning and thorough liaison work.

The simultaneous presence of Mark and Hanoch in Kfar Oranim would emphasize the inter-organizational relationship between the Croydon Jewish Federation and Project Renewal, Jerusalem. Linking and mediating tasks in this aspect of the liaison-consultant's role will call for deep understanding of the social, political and cultural dynamics that shape these two organizations. Feelings of common heritage and ethnic kinship go only so far in the realm of organizational vested interests which are at stake in this interaction. The liaison-consultant assumed that this aspect of his role would rely largely on community organization principles rather than community development which is more applicable to his work in Kfar Oranim. This was as much of a preconceived notion as the liaison-consultant would allow himself at this point. (19)

For the rest, he would not have to wait long to see. His ruminations ended as the car entered Kfar Oranim. The liaison-consultant was bringing with him a few ideas gleaned from the meeting in Croydon and from his knowledge of community organization and community development. He had rendered these ideas more concrete by converting them into scenarios of sorts on the way to Kfar Oranim for the first encounter. These probes were primarily for the purpose of posing questions to himself. If they failed to hold for the reality he was about to face, they could easily be set aside since questions were easier to shed than preconceived ideas. The liaison-consultant was not coming to Kfar Oranim with a clean slate nor was he coming with his mind already made up. He was coming with some tentative notions and with extensive professional experience. He expected his work in Kfar Oranim to expand his learning about community work and about the interaction of two cultures exemplified by the distant partners Croydon and Kfar Oranim.

The Move From Contemplating to Implementing the Work Role

Kfar Oranim seemed more like a village than a town. It is a typical Israeli small municipality. The place held no first impression surprises for the liaison-consultant. He parked in front of a large square which obviously served as the town plaza. The liaison-consultant, Mark and his wife hurried out of the car. They were a few minutes late because they had taken a wrong turn after leaving the main highway.

Listening to the introduction that Hanoch was giving, the liaison-consultant felt an uneasiness which only became clear to him later when he pondered the reason for his reaction. Using the ideas expressed at the June 23, 1981 meeting in Croydon, he was able to begin thinking in a rudimentary way about role structure. On the basis of his general knowledge about the principles of community work, he identified the differential interests of the three partners in Kfar Oranim's Project Renewal program. The nature of the interrelationships that were bound to evolve preoccupied the liaison-consultant as well. Also, while awaiting Mark's arrival, he had spent a good deal of time thinking about various orientations that might be utilized in working with the three partners. The liaison-consultant attached labels to these orientations: community development, inter-community liaison and community organization.

What he lacked was acquaintance with any Kfar Oranim residents or with anyone in Project Renewal headquarters. Not having met any of the people with whom he would be dealing on the Israeli scene, his ponderings during what was termed the reconnaissance phase produced static models of practice. Paradoxically, the Project Renewal partners in far off Croydon were flesh and blood people while those in Israel were still abstractions. Hanoch's introduction instantly actualized the the human element which had not yet been encountered. His statement lifted the liaison-consultant out of the contemplative stage into dynamic involvement with reality.

Ready or not, he had to decide what to do about the interpretation of the liaison-consultant role that Hanoch was giving to the Steering Committee. Taking issue with him meant bringing Mark into the dispute. As the representative of the liaison-consultant's sponsor, Mark would have been forced to challenge Hanoch's assertion. Had he understood Hebrew, the language used by Hanoch, Mark would have had to decide whether or not to differ with Hanoch in front of the Steering Committee. Under the circumstances, responsibility for deciding fell to the liaison-consultant who had to reckon with several considerations, one of which was the necessity for back and forth translations to keep Mark and members of the Steering Committee abreast of the dialogue. The Committee, as the authority for Project Renewal in Kfar Oranim, was not necessarily bound by Hanoch's views of the liaison-consultant role. Its members listened with deference but betrayed no inkling of their feelings. Whatever their opinions, they were no doubt anxious to retain the good will of a man who wielded Hanoch's power. Their new liaison-consultant would have to think carefully before putting them into the middle of what could be a thankless situation.

If Hanoch's definition were challenged, this would start off all three partners to Project Renewal in Kfar Oranim on a contentious note. In all likelihood, it would also lock the liaison-consultant into a state of friction with an influential Project Renewal official. The additional problem of managing the dialogue while simultaneously serving as translator was especially vexing to the liaison-consultant.

The situation presented a clear case of discretion being the better part of valor. This sensible approach is apt to be chosen by any reasonably cautious individual caught in these circumstances. What, therefore, characterized the decision not to intervene as a professional one? Taken by itself, the liaison-consultant's reaction could have been reached simply by using common sense. His surprise at the unexpected turn of events was not conducive to an elaborate conceptual process.

During his career, the liaison-consultant had been introduced many times and he thought he knew what to expect from Hanoch who was standing in for Mark because of the language problem. He anticipated a play-back of facts culled from the biographical sketch that the liaison-consultant had sent to Mark. As it turned out, Hanoch was no stand-in for Mark.

The surprise created by Hanoch's introduction had an impact on the liaison-consultant's "professional self". The "professional self" is a frail concept which rests uneasily on the age-old undivided self asserting itself in full pristine force. Western man, predisposed to division of labor before it became a socio-economic precept, has partitioned his psyche to accommodate himself to the specialized interests he must master. Thus, we have Economic Man, Political Man, Scientific Man, Professional Man and so forth. On one plane, these are conceptual "selves". On another plane, they are real in that they enable the individual to play roles to the extent that there has been internalization of the knowledge, values, training and skill needed for these superimposed "selves".

In the human services, Professional Man must be alert to his conceptualized professional self since it is the locus of the "repertoire of interventive acts" which the worker brings to bear in the helping process.(20) Another way of putting it, is that intervention, in the professional sense, relies on the practitioner's ability to use self-awareness and insight to arrest the constant tendency to drift back to the age-old undivided self with its involuntary reaction to surprise, its defensiveness and its hunger for recognition. For professional community workers, "arresting the drift" is essentially an ethical proposition to which they are bound. Indeed, it is one of the chief distinguishing features between professional community workers and their lay sponsors or other public figures who strive for the community's well-being.

Lay leaders and public figures function within the constraints of the morals which guide society as a whole. The community worker is additionally guided by self-discipline derived from a code of professional values and ethics. This difference between the two groups does not make one better or more virtuous. The professional worker and the lay person form a collaborative effort with different points of entry into the process of decision making. Their partnership entails different roles, different capacities and distinctive values. In combination, they produce the necessary balance of spontaneity and studied approaches, of committed partisanship and objective intervention — all of which are required for the well-functioning community.

The liaison-consultant expected the introduction to be purely ceremonial but Hanoch used the opportunity for other purposes. One of his aims was to let the liaison-consultant know that Mark and the Croydon group were not the only ones who had a say over the liaison-consultant role. In deciding not to challenge Hanoch, the liaison-consultant recognized that his contemplations about the Kfar Oranim assignment were at an end. Although his official starting day was a few weeks off, the liaison-consultant was confronted with an immediate situation that gave rise to a feeling of concern. He made a conscious decision not to speak out, using his professional self to reach this judgement. Taking a stand, as has been noted, meant forcing Mark and the Kfar Oranim residents to become involved in a quarrel for which they were not equipped. Conflict, according to Georg Simmel, calls for allies.(21). Mark and the Steering Committee, symbolizing the "twin" communities, were the only possible allies. However, their association was in the beginning stage, much too nascent to form a coalition of the type needed to throw its weight behind the difference with Project Renewal, Jerusalem that was shaping up. Did this beginning association have the potential to form a coalition at a later stage? Perhaps, it was this half-formed question that caused the liaison-consultant to be concerned. His passivity was a one time response but Hanoch's view was not. True. But, is this how the liaison-consultant had gone about arriving at his position at the time it was crystallized? Were there really articulate thought formations about nascent coalitions with a footnote crediting Simmel, to boot?

The seasoned practitioner lives with the unanswered question and usually abandons it. However, it often remains uppermost in the minds of workers new to the field. Learners, struggling to integrate the conceptual and the practical in community work, are as much interested in the method of arriving at a decision as in the content of the decision itself. Hence, is the practitioner's intervention consciously nourished by conceptualizing throughout the process or are theoretical principles only elaborated after the event to shed light on what the worker struggled with intuitively?

Obviously, examination of this particular event is such an ex post facto elaboration. Even if a video tape of the proceedings at the Steering Committee were available, an elaboration would still be needed. The truth is that much of the work performed by community workers does not stamp them as palpably different from the people to whom they relate professionally. Were, say, a doctor in the Mayor's office to discuss a public health problem or an architect to deal with new housing, their salience as experts would be a foregone conclusion. By contrast, in the field of community organization and development, "the repertoire of interventive acts" is all too often barely visible. The chronic, if somewhat latent quest by community workers for a more salient professional self is complicated by the ambiguity of their public status. They are members of a profession which may be seen as a science-based art.(22) Generally, however, they prefer to be viewed as identified with the social sciences rather than with a helping art. Yet, their diagnoses as prerequisites to action and their deliberative involvement in helping relationships are characteristic of formulations and activities which constitute a blend closer to art than to science.

To be sure, there are research findings, concepts and principles but they do not come as formulas which yield precise rules of application. In community work, research and theory inform the practitioner's thinking and actions. Similarly, timing, pace and sensitivity to people are not pointers that can be lifted for ready use out of manuals. These are internalized capabilities cultivated in the controlled use of self. There is no specific educational or training regimen for gaining the leadership touch through which the worker imparts high morale and a sense of purpose in the helping relationship. Superior quality of practice comes at some point in the worker's professional maturation. Trial and error are inevitable parts of learning by doing although there can be helpful guidance by a field teacher or a supervisor gifted in the arts of training and coaching the learner. Beyond the acquired capabilities, there are inherent factors such as creativity, intuition and imaginative conjecture. These endowments cannot be drilled in by outside instruction. Some may be enhanced by a teacher who is attuned to the inherent gifts of the learner. These natural flairs are often discounted by those practitioners in the human services who strive for degrees of exactitude more characteristic of the sciences. Yet, some scientists themselves recognize that these unexplained powers may be harnessed to good advantage. For example, Peter Medawar writes, "The form of intuition which, unless we are to abandon the word altogether, might as well be called **inductive:** thinking up or hitting on a hypothesis from . . . whatever we may wish to explain. This is the generative act in scientific discovery . . . 'Creativity' is a vague word, but it is just in such a context as this that we should choose to use it . . . The analysis of creativity in all its forms is beyond the competence of any one discipline. It requires a consortium of the talents: psychologists, biologists, philosophers, computer scientists, artists and poets will have their say. It cannot be learned but it certainly can be encouraged and abetted."(23) The learned and the natural aptitudes cannot be shredded apart to analyze the influence of each on a decision or an action.

The liaison-consultant did not think of Simmel or any other authority at the time he decided not to challenge Hanoch. He was aware of a momentary flash of rising resentment that he knew could rush him into a precipitous response if it were not kept in check. From there on, a reasoned approach replaced instinct although the liaison-consultant was not thinking about tracing the rational move that followed to any particular source. Later, when the situation was reviewed and evaluated, the principle enunciated by Simmel entered the picture to provide insight of a more generalized, conceptual nature which could be applied in the future, with the source, conceivably, to be forgotten in the course of time. It should be pointed out, however, that a principle, including the propounder's name, may flash across the mind and come to the aid of a worker responding spontaneously to a given situation. During their professional development, workers acquire not only informing principles from various thinkers but also what might be called sustaining insights which they rely on and which they retrieve over and over again to shed light on certain types of problems.

More common are concepts and principles that have entered the worker's consciousness, detached from their origins. They are so deeply ingrained that, when the practitioner intervenes, the acquired and the intuitive attributes are barely distinguishable from each other. This makes it all the more difficult to answer clearly the neophyte's query about relative effects of the meditated and the instinctive; both are integral to solving problems in community work.

The situation is analogous to that of the doctor making a diagnosis. How many experienced physicians would remember while examining a patient which of the judgments they were forming or the skillful investigations they were executing or the connections they were creating were learned from an instructor and which were self-taught in the process of their becoming qualified practitioners? The same is true for the more prosaic arts of driving or swimming. There is no telling apart acquired and inherent skills entailed in the learning process. Indeed, making conscious efforts to do so might well interfere with the spontaneity that lends effectiveness to the helping arts.

What can be brought to bear is a general orientation to a practice role that constantly moves between action and the thinking behind it. Perlman and Gurin developed an analyst-interactionist continuum for submitting the range of inputs in decision making to disciplined scrutiny.(24) Their formulation can be deployed productively to reduce the tendency toward undirected behavior and can help to develop balance in the practice role between expertise and leadership capacities. Problem solving requires consideration of specific information, knowledge about general trends and familiarity with new developments. The community worker is often a resource to provide these data. But information and knowledge do not relieve the decision makers of the need to form opinions, to exercise judgement and to accommodate themselves to group consensus. In committee deliberations, the community worker may have to shift from being a resource person supplying information to a catalyst who exercises leadership. The community worker's learning may be thought of as socialization to a work role which bespeaks adjustment to certain external demands of the vocational culture. But, from the dualistic perspective of acquired and inherent characteristics, there may also be an element of temperament which predisposes the individual to resist "the temptation of a rushed verdict and premature action."(25)

The analyst-interactionist model originated in the federated fund raising and central planning movements which took root in North

America at the turn of the century. As a concept, the model is applicable to the roles of community representatives in Project Renewal. It provided anchorage for the liaison-consultant's decision to avoid an encounter with Hanoch. Thus, the atmosphere, free of confrontation, offered an opportunity for the liaison-consultant to take detailed note of what was transpiring.

No doubt, Hanoch violated Mark's intent to bring a touch of cordiality to the first meeting between the new liaison-consultant and the Kfar Oranim Steering Committee. However, to focus on the question of civility would have personalized the issue and diverted attention from Hanoch's stance which was motivated by vested interest. His remarks were of some use to the liaison-consultant since they brought a new outlook to the question of accountability, quite different from that which had been conveyed by the Croydon Project Renewal Committee. Hanoch repudiated the notion that the monitoring role was one of the responsibilities to be carried by the liaison-consultant. Hanoch had no intention of accepting Croydon's representative as a delegate. He was issuing a directive to the Steering Committee which called for the liaison-consultant to be treated as just another Project Renewal staff person. The status of delegate would have to be won over Hanoch's objections. How was he to be over-ruled? Should the liaison-consultant persevere until Hanoch accepted his status as defined by Croydon? Should there be a process of mediation between Croydon and Project Renewal, Jerusalem to pave the way for accommodating the liaison-consultant's delegate status? Had such negotiations been initiated?

The liaison-consultant had a strong hunch that no steps had been taken to test the two conflicting views. Where did one begin to look for an answer that would confirm or reject this hunch? It would have been easier to start with Mark, the proponent of the demand for accountability based on the monitoring role but Mark was here today and gone tomorrow. Given the reality of the situation, the starting point had to be with the opponent of the idea who would remain on the scene to press for his point of view. Accordingly, the liaison-consultant took the initiative and called Hanoch's secretary for an appointment.

The conflict, actual or potential, had long since been resolved in North America. At one time, the federated funds and central planning councils had struggled with the social agencies over accountability. The issue had been resolved in favor of the federated funds and central planning councils. Eligibility for funding and for participation in social planning was conditioned on accountability to the funding and central planning bodies. That occurred many decades ago. Today, monitoring and reporting permeate the social planning process in North America.(26)

209

In Israel, the community representatives may have plans in mind but proper planning conditions with institutionalized channels of communication do not exist as they do in North America. Hanoch was surely conversant with the North American pattern but saw it as having little or no applicability to Israel. Besides, Project Renewal, Jerusalem was not to be confused with an American social agency with accountability to the central funding source. It was much more akin to the central funding organization itself with a well-developed sense of its sovereignty on the Israeli scene.

As the liaison-consultant suspected, the opposing views as to accountability held by Croydon and Project Renewal, Jerusalem had not been broached. This resulted not so much from fear of joining the issue but rather from the widely shared concern for the success of Project Renewal that kept all differences highly contained. Lay leaders, professionals, managers, service personnel and the liaison functionaries all subscribed to the prevailing value of explicitly minimizing differences. Among the liaison functionaries, this point of view emerged clearly during the interviews when the question was asked: What do you consider to be the most important skill and aptitude of the community representative? Almost invariably, the response was that the most effective community representatives possessed a spark that enlivened the partnership between the "twinned" communities, were ingenious enough to get results by knocking on the right doors and had the ability to energize the people in the communities to press their claims. But all these skills had to deployed without raising the roof or creating turbulence that could endanger the benefits of Project Renewal.

This pervasive commitment to the status quo was not conducive to change, even the kind Croydon was seeking in the task of its liaison-consultant. The truth of this observation became clear in the first minutes of the liaison-consultant's meeting with Hanoch in his office. Hanoch maintained the unyielding posture of aloofness that he had adopted three weeks earlier in Kfar Oranim. The liaison-consultant's diplomatically worded request for orientation on fiscal affairs was given short shrift.

Hanoch showed no personal animus toward the liaison-consultant. When his irritation with public officials in Kfar Oranim erupted, he took care not to involve the liaison-consultant in the dour mood he cast over his two assistants who were at the meeting. He treated the liaison-consultant as a subordinate and as an outsider who was not on his staff and he betrayed no expression nor gesture that could be interpreted as a move to sociability. Whether it is conflict or harmony, socialization is essential (27) but Hanoch made it clear by the distance he maintained that there was no likelihood of any association with the liaison-consultant.

After the session in Hanoch's office, the liaison-consultant wrote to tell Mark that he saw little prospect of assuming the monitoring role. This would require the liaison-consultant to sit with the staff of Project Renewal at the outset of the budget process when preliminary recommendations are developed for Croydon to consider. This material is the basis for reviews by the Croydon delegation which comes to Kfar Oranim each year to examine progress during the past year and to consider proposed expenditures for the ensuing year. The delegation brings this recommended budget back to Croydon for final decision by the Board of Directors of the Croydon Jewish Federation.

It was natural for Croydon to expect its representative to be in on the first step of the budget process. The concept of accountability required such participation. But it was not to be; in the eyes of Hanoch, it was contraindicated. Moreover, he had power to impose his will. Shortly after being apprised of the impasse, Mark wrote to Hanoch in an effort to change his mind. On October 16, 1981, Hanoch replied to Mark as follows: "Your decision not to approve changes in some budget items before you have consulted with your Liaison-Consultant is regrettable. We have agreed that the appointment of a consultant does in no way disrupt the direct contact and communication between us. The need to have our requests reviewed and approved by the consultant, before we can receive your approval, is to some extent an expression of non-confidence in the Renewal Department and its staff. We would therefore very much appreciate it if this process is reversed by you and acted upon accordingly."

Hanoch's stance became clearer to the liaison-consultant later when he came into possession of a letter sent to Mark by Hanoch on July 7, 1981. At that time, Croydon and the liaison-consultant were reaching agreement as to the assignment in Kfar Oranim. In part, this letter read: "To the subject of your appointing a liaison-consultant in Kfar Oranim as mentioned before, we shall be grateful if this person will be a professional who can assist the Project Renewal staff in Kfar Oranim in one or more aspects of the Project. If agreeable, we can assist in recruitment of such a person. The decision as to the appointment will, of course, be made by you."

The request that a "professional" be appointed is anomalous since no criteria exist to this day which establish the professional nature of the community representative's role. More interesting is the open assertion by Hanoch that he expected the Croydon appointee to serve as an assistant to his Project Renewal staff. Especially revealing, is the offer to recruit someone for the job. Croydon's decision to act on its own and to ignore Hanoch's offer undoubtedly influenced his attitude toward the liaison-consultant who was selected by Croydon without his participation.

By the time the liaison-consultant saw Hanoch's October 18, 1981 letter, taking issue with the liaison-consultant's intervention in the budget process, the liaison-consultant had begun structuring his role to take into account Hanoch's firm position. In time, the liaison-consultant would have to interpret his approach to his Croydon sponsors.

The Liaison Consultant Role and Its Diversity of Relationships

I The Renewal Department

Relationships in the professional sense are deemed to be strategic by Torcyzner (28) in that they offer planned ways of achieving objectives pursued by individuals and groups. He identifies five variables in the arena of strategic relationships: power, issue, priority, time and legitimacy. Depending on the interplay of these variables, the relationship between the interacting parties may be cooperative or antagonistic with each party behaving in ways that may stress concord or discord and where differences are minimal or maximal.

An important characteristic of strategic relationships is the basis they provide for predicting how each party will respond to its counterpart in a given situation. Torcyzner, using the findings of various social scientists, posits three hypothetical strategies: collaboration, conflict and negotiation. In all three, power looms as a prominent variable in the exchange between the interacting parties. The liaison-consultant considered his options following his meeting with Hanoch on September 16, 1981 and recognized that power was, first and foremost, the crucial variable in determining whether or not a strategic relationship might develop between him and Hanoch.

The capacity to foster the relationship, whether reciprocal or resistant, collaborative or confictful, in Torcyzner's terms, lay with the Croydon Federation. Hanoch's two letters made it clear that he was not going to permit interference with the direct contact between the Renewal Department and the Croydon Federation. He refused to recognize the delegate status which Croydon had conferred on its representative for the purpose of carrying out the monitoring function deemed so essential by Croydon. Consequently, in the absence of a strategic relationship, to use Torcyzner's terminology again, there was no option for the liaison-consultant other than to persevere in an attempt to narrow the distance which Hanoch had fixed on first meeting the liaison-consultant in Kfar Oranim on July 23, 1981.

For a time, the liaison-consultant vainly tried to pursue this approach through third parties. On occasional visits to the Renewal Department, he met with Stephen whose chief responsibility was handling matters related to overseas communities. When they discussed the liaison role, Stephen would lend a patient but deaf ear. He conveyed the unmistakable impression that this was a closed subject. An impromptu emissary came to the fore when the professional head of an American Jewish national organization was in Israel to attend a conference at the Jewish Agency. During a chance meeting, the visitor and the liaison-consultant recalled a curriculum they had developed for use by the Jewish Agency in training fundraisers for overseas communities. The visitor felt their past collaboration on community work training would be of interest to the Renewal Department and he promised to discuss it with Hanoch but Hanoch never followed up with the liaison-consultant on this intercession.

The liaison-consultant's readiness to turn to a third party who might intercede with Hanoch seems similar to a politicized tactic to achieve a working relationship with a high-powered official. The tactic may be viewed in light of Lord Acton's famous indictment about the corrupting effect of power. It may also be viewed from a contrasting orientation to power as being neither good nor bad but rather inherent in the human condition with potential for good or evil depending on the motivations and aims of the individual or group using power to bring about change. Thus, "since the time of Max Weber, who was one of the first to formulate a more pluralistic matter of-fact analysis, social scientists have been developing a more promising approach to this difficult subject" (of power). (29)

In keeping with this outlook, social workers began to rebalance the relationship between poor and rich when Octavia Hill, one of the first social workers, called for privacy of the poor in 18th century England.(30) Succeeding generations of social workers progressively emphasized the capacity of those in need to manage their own lives in accordance with an enhanced self-image that brought them from pauper to the comparatively independent status of client.

In altering the balance between the disadvantaged and the privileged, social workers eliminated untrained do-gooders from a direct connection to people in need, achieving a client-worker relationship in which the worker gained dominance or mastery over the helping role. This evolutionary process was a strategy which entailed shifts in power. The helping function was transformed from what had largely been religiously endowed charity to a secularized human service profession which continued to evolve as the welfare state emerged. This unfolding change is inherently political and the practice method remains political as well. In the view of Plant (31), it is unavoidably so, regardless of whether the social worker's intervention is conditioned by belief in adjustment to the existing environment, by visions of reform or by the conviction that change is needed to alter a fundamentally unjust society.

In the 1960's, the struggle against poverty in the United States concentrated on changing the community and society. Partisan activism called for an avowed "political tactician". (32) Protracted polemics arose among social workers. Many questioned the validity of a politically charged partisan role. Paradoxically, practitioners of the more established social work methods overlooked, in the heat of the debate, the fact that their accepted strategies of working with individuals and groups had come as a result of a thrust which was political in nature. Moreover, their methods were not free of assumptions which remained intrinsically political. Needless to say, the real politics of community work included the liaison-consultant's tactic of seeking to reach Hanoch through intermediaries. This was done to rule out action based purely on the intuition that there would be no possibility to pursue monitoring at the level of Project Renewal, Jerusalem.

II Kfar Oranim

When these efforts to reach Hanoch yielded no results, the liaison-consultant took steps to institute the monitoring function on a lower plane in Kfar Oranim. He held regular meetings with Vered and Eitan to compare the budget estimates they received from Jerusalem with the figures submitted by the Renewal Department to Croydon and then relayed by Croydon to the liaison-consultant. Furthermore, the sub-committee meetings, where the first estimates for arriving at annual budgets emerged from the presentations made by Kfar Oranim agencies, provided insight into the town's Project Renewal activities from the ground up.

These insights gathered reality for the building programs when Eitan took the liaison-consultant on visits to the day care centers undergoing enlargement, the new dental clinic under construction and the apartment blocks being made attractive. Eitan conducted an ongoing check on the prices of building materials, installations and equipment against the figures of the contractors and construction supervisors. He insisted that structural errors be corrected and that schedules be adhered to, making sure that Croydon's money was well spent. With the liaison-consultant as an audience, Eitan's monitoring acquired a sharp edge that kept architects, supervisors and contractors on their toes. Undoubtedly, somewhere in the back of his mind, Eitan harbored the expectation that his tough stance would find its way into the liaison-consultant's reports to Croydon.

Eitan's performance as Executive Secretary of the Steering Committee was a study in role ambiguity. Although he was paid by the Ministry of Housing, he held himself primarily accountable to the Renewal Department of the Jewish Agency. His contacts in Jerusalem were more with the Renewal Department than with the Ministry of Housing. He was unsparing in his cooperation on all matters that aided the liaison-consultant in advancing Croydon's concern for the people of Kfar Oranim. He was very energetic in a pell mell sort of way but never roughshod. In dealing with the liaison-consultant, he was invariably formal and proper. If, on rare occasions, he had to choose between contradicting positions of the liaison-consultant and a staff member of Project Renewal, he would try to escape from the burden of having to choose. When there was no way out, he would do the bidding of Project Renewal, Jerusalem. Eitan knew where the power lay.

The liaison-consultant's role as link between Croydon and Kfar Oranim was not tied to power in the eyes Of Kfar Oranim residents. For them, it was rooted in a more individualized standing connected to prestige. This personalized status was in harmony with the implicit agreement that the liaison-consultant did not intervene in the inner affairs of the local institutional structure. However, accepted policies and implicit agreements do not always apply with equal clarity to all situations. An example is the time (January 24, 1983) that Leah and Dan came to Eitan's office and asked for a confidential meeting regarding some urgent problem that had suddenly surfaced. The liaison-consultant was in the office to participate in interviewing a candidate for the youth work position that had been vacated when Aaron was dismissed by the Mayor. The liaison-consultant had been asked to take part in order to help reach a decision as to the candidate's suitability. Instead of holding the scheduled meeting, Leah and Dan made their unexpected request for the confidential meeting with Eitan and without the liaison-consultant. Dan seemed ill at ease and embarrassed while Leah bore down on Eitan with a determined gaze. For his part, Eitan kept transferring his uncertain look from one person to the next as if he could not decide what to do. The liaison-consultant could not help wondering about the lack of sophistication being demonstrated by Kfar Oranim's senior professionals in coping with an unforeseen situation. Instead of Leah or Dan explaining the need for confidentiality, there was a childish mood of conspiracy in the air as of people about to share some deep, dark secrets. Eitan, despite his evident discomfort, did the predictable thing; he went off to an adjoining office with Leah and Dan. After all, Leah represented Project Renewal, Jerusalem and it was important to placate her even at the expense of leaving the liaison-consultant to cool his heels, to say nothing about the discourtesy to the candidate. The next time the liaison-consultant met with Eitan, he made a point of voicing his irritation, not on the grounds that Eitan had yielded to Leah and Dan, but rather on the lack of discipline about keeping appointments, something that took place all too frequently in Kfar Oranim.

The incident is worth examining since it bears on a practice principle in community work. Did Eitan's exit with Leah and Dan, leaving the liaison-consultant alone in the empty office, diminish the prestige of Croydon's representative in Kfar Oranim? This is not a matter of injured pride although that cannot be totally dismissed. The focus, however, is rather on prestige as an endowment of central importance to the public responsibility which the community worker is called on to fulfill. A practice role rooted in individualized prestige lacks the objective power determined by the practitioner's identification with authority in an organizational hierarchy such as Leah carried in Project Renewal and Dan, to a lesser extent, in Kfar Oranim.(33) Where the practice role is rooted in such authority, the worker has flexibility in risking prestige since there is another source of backing to his status which is linked to specific power, characterized by the term, authority. However, where the role is founded solely on prestige, derived partly from the practitioner's involvement in academia and partly endowed by his Croydon sponsor although not manifest in any clear organizational structure, risking his prestige meant, in effect, that he was putting on the line the only support that undergirded his role. Why did the liaison-consultant take no steps to protect his prestige? Why did he not demand an explanation for this abrupt change in plans at the very last moment? Why did he leave the matter to be taken up with Eitan a week later rather than raising it as the three of them made their way out of the office? Was such passivity not tantamount to a loss of nerve in the situation?

Different interpretations and judgements are possible. The liaison-consultant saw himself as having been invited to serve as an advisor to the three executives. The applicant had not yet appeared so that there could be no demand for proceeding with the interview. The liaison-consultant had no way of knowing the urgency of the unanticipated problem. Responding to it as an emergency that took precedence over the scheduled meeting might have been fully justified. There were other unexplained aspects of the event. If the applicant did not arrive, only Eitan could have disinvited him since the salary for the position was under Eitan's control and the meeting was convened at his initiative. Postponing the meeting in itself could not have affected the liaison-consultant's standing. Was it the graceless way in which it was done that might have had an impact on the liaison-consultant's prestige?

The same question might be asked about these same three people keeping secret the dismissed worker's purchase of lathes. They may have resorted to the conspiratorial folk habit of seeing covert information as a secret to be shared with trusted friends rather than as sensitive material to be kept from or exchanged with others in accordance with objective criteria of confidentiality as an aspect of professional practice. According to Johnson, a professor who helped to conceptualize community organization practice in the 1940's and

Conclusion

1950's, the community worker must be skilled in distinguishing between primary relations appropriate to kinship or friendship groups and secondary relations between groups functionally related to the purposes and aims of organizations, communities and constituencies within the larger society. (34)

This principle, enunciated thirty years ago, is still relevant in societies where the civic culture with its emphasis on secondary relations is in an early stage of development. There are at least two ways of looking at the awkward incident in which the liaison-consultant was caught: a) Eitan, Leah and Dan did not withdraw as spontaneously as it appeared, in which case the issue was an ethical one; b) the incident arose because they functioned as a primary friendship group rather than as three professional workers dealing with a problem, in which case the issue was one of lack of sophistication. The liaison-consultant's response was based on the second interpretation.

III The Mayor

Croydon's representative pursued his liaison activities without interference from Project Renewal, Jerusalem or its regional office. However, the limits set by Project Renewal, Jerusalem in terms of accountability meant that his monitoring function did not extend beyond the Steering Committee and its sub-committees. This arrangement denied the liaison-consultant access to the Trustees of Educational Institutions and Cultural Organizations Committee. In fiscal matters, the Trustees Committee was important since it was the first recipient of Croydon funds sent by the Renewal Department to Kfar Oranim. The Town Council received government funds from the ministries to run the municipality but the Trustees Committee was the repository of philanthropic money designated for the Community Center prior to the inception of Project Renewal. When Project Renewal began in Kfar Oranim, the Renewal Department decided to direct the money from Croydon to the Trustees Committee as well. This fiscal arrangement deprived the Steering Committee of primacy in all matters pertaining to Project Renewal in Kfar Oranim.

Dan, the director of the Community Center, shared many secrets with the liaison-consultant about his political aspirations and, on rare occasions, he mentioned the Trustees Committee where he was an important figure. He was proud of his ploy by which Aryeh's meager remuneration was taken over by the Trustees Committee when the Town Council dropped this neighborhood activist from its payroll. Dan's successful intervention prevented one of Aryeh's town-rocking outbursts. Dan's suggestion was made at a meeting with the Mayor, Eitan and the liaison-consultant. For the most part, however, he avoided discussing the Trustees Committee with the liaison-consultant. Like

217

Eitan, he did not relish the thought of conversations with Croydon's representative that might conceivably complicate life with the Renewal Department.

The Mayor's office kept informing the liaison-consultant about the Trustees Committee, largely because the Deputy Mayor wanted the liaison-consultant's support in his battle with Aryeh for the Chairmanship of the Committee. The Mayor understood the power of the Renewal Department but he was not beholden to Leah in the same way as Eitan and Dan were. He was secure enough to act independently had the liaison-consultant decided to ask him for an invitation to the meetings of the Trustees Committee. Whether the Mayor would have agreed over Hanoch's probable objections was something the liaison-consultant could not predict. In any case, it did not matter. The liaison-consultant decided not to ask the Mayor to get him invited to the Trustees Committee's meetings even though he was dissatisfied with the information that reached him about the work. Much of it had to do with political wrangling. It was more important for the liaison-consultant to know how the Trustees justified taking over Aryeh's salary from the Town Council to prevent a community hassle.

The Trustees Committee was another matter for negotiation by Croydon directly with Hanoch and had to be added to the agenda of items to be discussed with Mark and the delegation during its next visit to Kfar Oranim. Handling this matter with the Mayor would have meant shifting the very correct community-oriented relationship which the liaison-consultant had succeeded in establishing and maintaining with him to one of greater intimacy with a primary type of interaction. The Mayor ventured in that direction on May 11, 1982 when he indicated that he had decided not to dismiss Yuval as a favor to the liaison-consultant.

Johnson has identified the need for a community worker to separate primary relationships more applicable to kinship and friendship groups from secondary relationships appropriate to transactions on a community plane.(35) The insight provided by Johnson had a direct influence on the liaison-consultant's decision not to ask the Mayor's intervention regarding the Trustees Committee's meetings.

Another principle which has received insufficient attention in community work also applies. This holds that the worker must be constantly alert to the difference between problem solving rooted in adversarial party politics and decision making strategies based on social welfare planning. Workers who view their aims from the vantage point of conflicting political doctrines are committed to keeping alive the struggle surrounding differences until one or the other of the contending parties triumphs; to the victor belongs the right to direct the change. It is the nature of political activism to stress conflict from beginning to end in the problem solving process. By contrast, social welfare planning is issue oriented. Need, rather than pre-determined doctrine, determines the strategy. Social planning, concerned with identified need, tends to minimize political differences between participants involved in decision making.

This tendency may be a key aspect of the arena of community decision making which Bolan refers to as the "culture" of planning.(36) Social planning appears on the scene at a stage when the society is no longer a simple solidarity in which control of its affairs is centralized in a single core. The social terrain has become sufficiently diversified and monolithic political thinking has become secularized, allowing several problem solving approaches to co-exist. Israeli society has acquired such social diversity but is so small that its size "leaves little room for any intermediate authority, whether of upper-tier local government or decentralized central government."(37) Thus, in addition to other factors, a geographic element makes for a complex society with an all pervasive organizational structure at the center. Lack of pluralism in decision making may help to explain why politics is so consuming a passion in Israeli society. Accordingly, if the Mayor played the political game to the hilt. it was not due to any personality quirk. Nor did it signify any special characteristic about the community he headed. In Israel, partisan politics is the norm.

In all likelihood, the Mayor would perceive his intervention to facilitate the liaison-consultant's attendance at meetings of the Trustees Committee as a political favor rather than as a personalized chummy sort of amenity. In any case, the liaison-consultant had to steer clear of either involvement because he was taking a stand on the issue of job stability for the community workers which they were viewing as a crisis. He made his position known to the Mayor at every opportunity because, as the elected head of the municipality, he was mainly responsible for the situation, including the low morale among the community workers.

When members of the Croydon Project Renewal Ccmmittee voiced concern about the depressed spirit of Kfar Oranim, the liaison-consultant had no idea that his first point of entry into this problem would be by way of community functionaries. So long as this group of workers remained a political football, it was pointless to talk about citizen participation. Until the people in the neighborhoods were organized to prevent a land grab in the area set aside for small enterprises owned by artisans, their attempts to conduct social action would come to naught. (March, 1982) So long as the Mayor felt threatened when the community workers helped neighborhood residents to make an impact on their elected representatives, community morale remained an abstract subject, to be raised during annual visits of the Croydon delegation.

While the Mayor was at the core of the problem, two other aspects had to be considered: a) Aryeh's determination to use the position of part-time, paid employee as a stepping stone to the political career which he cherished but which had an unsettling effect on the community and b) a hiring policy that explicitly favored local residents but which was seen by some skeptics as a veiled attempt to introduce nepotism as well as political and ethnic factors in selecting candidates for community work positions.

The liaison-consultant's dealings with the Mayor were conducted in circumstances that differed markedly from those surrounding his relationship with the Renewal Department. Like Hanoch, the Mayor was also an authority figure. But unlike Hanoch, the Mayor was in no position to invoke his power to deny a relationship with the liaison-consultant whose presence symbolized Kfar Oranim's benefactor and distant partner. At the same time, the Mayor knew that the liaison-consultant had no authority to impose any course of action on any individual or organization in Kfar Oranim nor to take steps to withhold Croydon's funds. Moreover, in his dialogues with the Mayor, the liaison-consultant was endowed with a prestige that carried a high measure of influence, if not actual power-laden authority. Hence, it was possible to establish something akin to the traditional worker-client relationship.

IV Kfar Oranim's Community Workers

The main target of the Mayor's suspicion and hostility among the community workers was Tamar, the young woman who was in charge of the training course for neighborhood activists. It was no secret in Kfar Oranim that her family sided with the Mayor's sworn enemy, Yehuda, in a feud that persisted for years. Tamar claimed neutrality in the affair, maintaining that she was the victim of guilt by association. This vendetta never came up in the discussions between the Mayor and the liaison-consultant about community work and community workers in Kfar Oranim. The Mayor focused on the quality of services the town received. In response, the liaison-consultant pointed out that smaller localities everywhere are at a disadvantage in trying to attract accomplished professionals. Instead of competing in vain with large and middle-sized urban centers, Kfar Oranim should invest in supervision and staff development. In discussing promising workers who merited such investment, the liaison-consultant always ranked Tamar very high. Reference was never made to her views regarding the battle between the Mayor and Yehuda. The Mayor knew that Tamar was too intimidated by him to become involved in petty conspiracies behind his back, as Aaron, the youth worker, had foolishly done. The dismissal notices which the Mayor sent to Tamar were dictated, he would say, by stringent budget considerations. The Mayor had come to know that the liaison-consultant's cautionary intervention about these dismissals was governed by his concern with their effect on staff morale. At such times, the liaison-consultant relied on his good working rapport with the Mayor and freely presented his opposition to the dismissals. (March 25, 1983)

The liaison-consultant's relationship with Aryeh was also based on the client worker orientation. Aryeh knew that the liaison-consultant did not agree with his attempt to use his part-time job in the neighborhoods as a beachhead for his political career. However, he saw the liaison-consultant as an outsider who was free of the scorn and hostility that his aspiration for leadership had earned him in every sector, including most of the professionals in both Kfar Oranim and the Renewal Department. Aryeh was adamantly opposed to the liaison-consultant's counsel that he withdraw from his poorly paid work in the neighborhoods and pursue his goal in a more realistic and less painful way for himself and for the community as well. In the end, Aryeh did withdraw from public life. Whether this was due to family circumstances or whether the discussions with the liaison-consultant had an effect on his action is difficult to judge. Aryeh never appeared again during the remainder of the liaison-consultant's work in Kfar Oranim to provide a clue as to what led him to his decision.

As for the hiring policy, it produced two replacements in senior positions, both local individuals and both woefully unequipped to assume their responsibilities. For example, Meron, who replaced Yuval in the school system, was totally unequal to the challenge when the principals performed so disastrously during their meeting with the Croydon delegation on March 17, 1983. Yuval, with his English-speaking ability and his poise, would undoubtedly have stepped into the breach to move things along in a manner that was completely beyond the tongue-tied novice who replaced him.

The liaison-consultant did not make an issue over the hiring policy that favored local residents. It was getting close to the time for municipal elections and the important thing was to reach election day with as few dismissal notices as possible being sent to community workers, especially Tamar. There were two points of view about the impending election. Some people were of the opinion that no election would take place because the Town Council had proved itself so inept that the central government would appoint a committee to administer Kfar Oranim. Others predicted that the investigation would clear the Town Council of any wrong doing and go no further than to recommend technical improvements. This group felt that the Town Council's mismangement would turn out to be insufficient to prevent the election. Either way, the Mayor would not be running, according to Dan who had set his cap for the job. This meant that the feud between the

Mayor and Yehuda would be of no further consequence and that greater stability might lie ahead for the community workers. Meanwhile, it was not a matter of just muddling through but rather of hoping and moving doggedly either to the date of the election or to the government-appointed committee, whichever came first.

V Junius: The Three Volunteers

Community development shifted from self help to aided self help with the United Nations avowal that "community development is a process designed to create conditions of economic and social progress for the whole community with its active participation."(38) As militant activism took over in the 1960's, community development without external economic resources was criticized as a futile exercise in community therapy conducted by isolated workers in remote villages facing the ravages of grinding poverty in the Third World.

The aided self-help approach is applicable to Kfar Oranim even though it is centrally located in Israel and not in the remote hinterland of a Third World country. With the affluent community of Junius as a neighbor, Kfar Oranim is more fortunate than any Third World village since it has a resource within walking distance to help in the struggle to help itself. Unlike Croydon, Junius was no distant partner. It would not have to reach out across land and sea to join Kfar Oranim in establishing a chamber of commerce type body to promote the town as a desirable location for industrial enterprises that could increase the number and quality of jobs in the area. Aided self help did not require more money from Croydon. It meant linking the town with centers of commerce and trade in Israel, an activity in which the influential residents of Junius could readily play a vital role. However, encouragement and initiative in the beginning stages would have to come from Croydon.

The notion was too visionary to be a formal project. Other than the three volunteers who were not business people, the liaison-consultant knew no influential Junius residents who could consider the idea. Tamar's neighborhood council still had a long road ahead of it before it could represent Kfar Oranim in a three-way organization with Junius and Croydon. Nevertheless, the idea would not go away. It brought tangibility to the concept of aided self help by means of which Kfar Oranim might lift itself by its own bootstraps.

Translating the idea into reality meant recruiting an affluent Israeli community that had nothing to do with Project Renewal. Indeed, Israel's entire newly emerged middle class is not involved in Project Renewal. By contrast, in the English speaking world which has greatly influenced Israel in its evolution as a welfare society, the middle classes moved toward social welfarism by organizing voluntarily to tackle the problem of widespread need. In Israel, the affluent partner voluntarily organized to battle poverty resides in communities throughout the world, proffering philanthropy from a great distance to the underprivileged of Israel. Now, through the "twinning" process, Project Renewal has made it possible for the overseas partner to become a direct participant in Israel's struggle to meet human needs. What does that do to Israel's newly emerged privileged class? What does it imply for relations between rich and poor in Israel?

The issue has implications which go beyond philanthropy and social welfare. It touches the core of the common heritage which the distant partners avow. If "twinning" means bringing Israeli and overseas communities together based on a heritage shared by all members of the two groups, the encounter could not be limited to the affluent of one community and the poor of another. The partnership would have to include a greater range of people in both communities.

Could a three-way support system involving Kfar Oranim, Junius and Croydon serve as an experimental venture that went beyond the existing linkage between affluent individuals in the Diaspora and members of the Israeli lower class? Direct action to get such a project started on a pilot basis was out of the question in the short range. But there was no harm in initiating contact between Croydon and Junius. Should an opportunity arise to discuss the creation of a chamber of commerce, the conditions would have been created for them to sit together to consider the idea. At any rate, the three Junius volunteers were asking the liaison-consultant to arrange an appointment with the Croydon delegation. Ariela, acting as Kfar Oranim's champion, would be asking the delegation to support the Youth Orchestra's visit to the United States and Dalia would be seeking approval for building a tennis facility.

The liaison-consultant complied with the request of the Junius volunteers. He dared to hope that this session might conceivably turn out to be the first step leading to a three-way support system. (April 24, 1982) Alas! It was anything but the hoped for first step. The members of the delegation were more tactful than hopeful about the chances of the two proposals being approved. The recommendations for the visit of the Youth Orchestra and the tennis facility would need to be examined along with other proposals for the coming year. The members of the delegation made it clear that they could not say in advance what the Croydon Federation would decide.

The evening began pleasantly but the Junius volunteers were soon sobered by what they heard. They reacted as though they had received a verdict and not an opinion. After a polite interval, they departed, leaving an undisguised feeling of disappointment behind. A similar mood warned the liaison-consultant that the chamber of commerce idea could not be rushed. Contrary to his expectation, no cooperative spirit developed to prepare for the long-range goal he had in mind. It was just as well. Aided self help would have to begin with Kfar Oranim itself, not with its neighbor and not with its distant partner. There were no alternatives to the slow, step-by-step process of building a strong neighborhood council in Kfar Oranim that would, in time, be able to take the three-way support system in hand. Meanwhile, the chamber of commerce would have to remain a visionary idea.

Nearly six weeks had passed since the delegation's visit, but Ariela, the leader of the Junius volunteers, was still piqued at the liaison-consultant (June 3, 1982). Repairing the relationship with the other two volunteers would take much less effort since they were not so personally affected by the delegation's cool response to the two proposals. On the other hand, Ariela was, in any event, suspicious of organizational activities with poor people other than direct work with those in need. Her altruism was an aspect of her temperament. The liaison-consultant would have to consider giving up the effort to win her interest in community development or community organization lest it harm his relationship with her, a relationship which was on shaky ground.

Displeasure with the liaison-consultant for the meeting with the Croydon delegation changed the relationship between him, Ariela and the other two volunteers. Modification in the role structure which they brought about symbolized the chasm between Kfar Oranim and Junius. Kfar Oranim residents, starting with the Mayor, constantly asked the liaison-consultant to forward requests to their overseas benefactor. These were mostly screened out by the liaison-consultant as not in the scope of Project Renewal. Many requests that were forwarded, such as the tennis project and the Youth Orchestra trip, were rejected by Croydon. Ariela did not hesitate to express her hurt feelings about Croydon's refusal to fund the Youth Orchestra trip. The conductor, the Mayor, Dan, the parents, members of the Orchestra and others had the same feelings of disappointment but kept their reaction to themselves. Knowing that they lack power to change the nature of their relationship with the worker, clients often lower their expectations without being told to do so. Just how much of this attitude was at work in the sound rapport between the Mayor and the liaison-consultant is a matter for conjecture.

Change in the relationship between the Junius volunteers and the liaison-consultant was demonstrated in the telephone conversation with Dalia on June 3, 1982. She was no longer inclined to rely on the liaison-consultant as a lever to influence Croydon in favor of the tennis project. In fact, she made the project a secret that she did not wish to share with the liaison-consultant. However, she wanted to keep working with him on jobs for Kfar Oranim's youth. Adah, the third volunteer, also retained this interest. This was good news to the liaison-consultant. Perhaps the support system idea was still alive despite the failure of the meeting with the Croydon delegation. Ideas and plans never stood still. Events and incidents shifted them in and out of focus, moving them in and out of reach. How authentic was Dalia's interest in job opportunities for Kfar Oranim's young people? To a large extent, that depended on the follow-up with her two neighbors. Were they really serious about mounting a business venture in Kfar Oranim? Unfortunately, Dalia's interest was never tested. On June 5, 1982, two days after the telephone conversation between the liaison-consultant and Dalia, the war in Lebanon started. Wars, terrorism, strikes and military reserve duty are great disrupters of life in Israel. They come along regularly, causing the most carefully laid plans to topple.

The Liaison-Consultant and Croydon

While many Croydon groups visited Kfar Oranim, it was the delegation which came annually to review the Project Renewal program and budget proposals that objectified his sponsor in the eyes of the liaison-consultant. As soon as the delegation arrived, it would get caught up in a hectic round of meetings with the local people. A festive mood followed the delegation around the town as it met with the Steering Committee and its sub-committees, toured the agencies, sat down with the residents to a welcoming feast of Middle East delicacies or visited host families for home hospitality. The liaison-consultant looked forward to the visits although he only managed to cover a fraction of the items on his agenda.

Continuing contact was maintained with Mark, the senior Croydon Federation official with whom the liaison-consultant kept regularly in touch. He proved to be a highly skilled colleague who was anxious to see his community's involvement in Project Renewal flourish. He was eager for progress in Kfar Oranim. Mark was considerate but candid in his approach to the liaison-consultant. They worked closely as two correspondents far removed from each other who could count on only one face-to-face meeting a year. There was a steady stream of letters and reports dealing with developments, personalities, trends and politics. Occasionally, there would be a telephone conversation. From time to time, Mark was moved to notify the liaison-consultant that the sheer volume of their correspondence was a problem for him since he had other duties besides Project Renewal.

Abundant communication did not bridge some of the differences in outlook. For example, Croydon had agreed to support Project Renewal in Kfar Oranim for five years, the first of which had been completed when the liaison-consultant came on the scene. This stipulation had been arrived at between the Croydon Federation and

Project Renewal, Jerusalem. Physical renewal could probably be accomplished in the four remaining years but there was no way for social and economic renewal to be achieved within the specified time limit. Members of the Croydon Project Renewal Committee voiced their aims and concerns for their distant partner from a here-and-now perspective, knowing that their involvement had time constraints. However, given the reality of Kfar Oranim's situation, the liaison-consultant realized that prospects for change had to be considered in a different time frame. Thus, from the very outset, the liaison role conflicted with the community development role which recognized the need for a long range process.

During the first visit of the Croydon delegation, the liaison-consultant raised the idea of community development as an approach to his role. One delegation member saw the validity of that approach but the other members responded with baffling silence. What did their reserved attitude mean? Were they fearful of becoming entangled in an effort that went far beyond the budget they had come to review?

Hoping for a longer time perspective, the liaison-consultant investigated other possibilities. He explored tying Kfar Oranim with kibbutz industries with venture capital which wanted to locate within or near economically deprived towns. He also looked at government resources for long range economic development that would not call on Croydon to exceed its annual financial commitment. The three-way support system he envisioned also needed a long time and did not necessarily hinge on money. It required a community organization approach that could not be hastened if good, solid relations were to be developed among the leaders of Croydon, Junius and Kfar Oranim. The goal of this joint organization was not envisaged as immediate funding for business ventures but rather as creating links that would bring Kfar Oranim closer to the mainstream of commerce and industry, putting the town into a more favorable position as a site for small industrial enterprises. The idea was not new. It was an adaptation of a well-known approach familiar to American urban leaders whereby resources are mobilized to aid a problem neighborhood or town to improve its economic situation.

These efforts all involved a period of time that would go beyond Croydon's remaining four-year commitment. Therefore, the liaison-consultant was working with two partners who saw the "twinning" process from different time perspectives. His sponsor, Croydon, was interested in immediate change; Kfar Oranim would have to persevere in the face of challenges with long range solutions in the far off future.

The quest for accountability from the Renewal Department and the need for coordination among agencies in Kfar Oranim were further examples of dissimilar responses to the same reality. In each case, the problem was not time, distance nor money but rather contrasting interpretations. Croydon leaders have undergone direct negotiations with Israel's obdurate officialdom that have led to commonly shared exasperations. There are bandied about yarns of harassing experiences that befell many entrepreneurs who, out of altruism or self-interest, tried to start businesses in Israel but who fell afoul of a daunting bureaucracy. This backlog of vexations has, over the years, produced an inexhaustible fund of anecdotes to enliven a social evening, a community meeting or a passing conversation over coffee. These experiences and these irascibly funny stories carry an unvarying caveat: the only way to prevail over a callous public servant is to come to the encounter with an intimidating, hard-nosed insistent self that will not be deterred by the offending bureaucrat's indifference, rudeness, negativism or perversity.

The cogency of this standing message was demonstrated when the table-thumping militancy of the delegation produced results for Kfar Oranim in its confrontation with Ministry of Housing officials over their snail's pace in covering the town's open sewers (April 25, 1982). True, the foot-dragging continued for a time after the delegation left but the threat of it coming back to haunt the Ministry had a salutary effect. The sewers were eventually covered and, therefore, it was natural for Croydon to take a similar view of the liaison-consultant's difficulty in assuming the monitoring role. Both that issue and the one of bringing Kfar Oranim's professionals together for a semblance of a coordinating process were seen by Croydon as calling for an assertive approach on the part of the liaison-consultant. The issues were perceived as everyday examples of dawdling by mulish and ornery public servants.

The liaison-consultant held a different view. He did not see Hanoch as simply taking a stubborn bureaucratic stand on the issue of monitoring. The liaison-consultant understood that Hanoch was dealing with a challenge to his organization on the question of accountability. The Renewal Department was directly represented by Hanoch as a leading official of high authority. In contrast, the liaison-consultant, mounting the challenge on behalf of Croydon, was virtually unempowered to handle the task.

The same lack of power applied to bringing about some coordinating mechanism among Kfar Oranim's agencies. While indifference and inertia were elements in the response of the professionals, basically, they did not see the liaison-consultant as carrying the role of community coordinator. Here again, the liaison-consultant understood their response and was convinced that patient persuasion rather than vigorous table-pounding would achieve the goal he shared with Croydon.

How does the worker deal with different perceptions of reality? This intrinsic factor in community work is often taken for granted even though its presence may be crucial in a specific situation. Social reality may, like Kierkegaard's view of truth, be subjectively arrived at through one's own reflections and not acquired as a finished product from someone else. (39) When the community worker is caught in differences that are tied to distinctive locations, cultures, traditions and time-bound outlooks, there is an abiding sense of pull in different directions that leads to efforts to heed one partner at one time and the other partner at at another time. Thus, the process in Israel was frequently geared to the timing of the sponsoring community in Croydon.

This tendency was particularly evident in the budgeting sessions of the Kfar Oranim sub-committees which had to submit their projected needs for the coming year to annual reviews by the Steering Committee and the Croydon delegation. Sub-committee meetings were dominated by a few people who were adept at following Vered's explanations of the budget items while the rest maintained an embarrassed silence lest they reveal their ignorance. Although limited, this experience marked a real step forward in community participation, thanks to Vered's capable instruction. Her input would have been more effective had she been given the opportunity to work with volunteers who could undertake the slow, elementary task of bringing the inexperienced members of the sub-committees up to the level needed for reviewing the budgets. Vered could not do this since she was responsible for similar work in other Project Renewal communities and her time in Kfar Oranim was restricted. Then, of course, there was the impending arrival of the Croydon delegation. Nothing could be permitted to interfere with this looming annual deadline. Predictably, the most vocal participants at the sessions with the delegation were those who had dominated the sub-committee meetings. Vered enhanced the proceedings by injecting well-timed explanations of the more complex items thus seeing to it that the discussions maintained their tempo. There was an aura of grass roots involvement which somehow included the unskilled silent listeners as well as the vocal participants.

The other discordant element of different experiences at the root of dissimilar comprehensions of the same reality tends to be lessened when the differing views are negotiated directly. It is possible for two sides to consider their separate experiences and, by comparing notes, to reach a mutual understanding or even consensus, if the negotiation of differences is done face-to-face. Thus, instead of explaining and exhorting from afar, the liaison-consultant sought to create a situation in which he and the delegation could do something together about Kfar Oranim's problem in achieving coordination among its community services.

In his frank and tolerant manner, Mark replied to the liaison-consultant's letters on this matter by urging the liaison-consultant not to wait for the delegation to push for an exchange of information in Kfar Oranim. He should take the initiative and do it on his own. There were no polemics over this issue. The liaison-consultant wanted the delegation to talk with professionals about the importance of planning in community work. Mark agreed to schedule this session during the visit but it was clear that he believed the liaison-consultant should go it alone. The liaison-consultant hoped for a session in which the two communities would enter into a dialogue. Croydon, accustomed to conducting its affairs on the basis of planning and coordination, would interpret to its partner the importance of this approach in avoiding the chaos that develops when agencies without an institutionalized means of consulting each other drift into working at cross-purposes. To prevent this exchange from deteriorating into a mere talk fest, the issue of coordination would be tied to the question of accountability or its lack as exemplified by Aaron, the youth worker, who purchased two expensive lathes even though he knew his future in Kfar Oranim was short lived. The discussion would also include the position taken by Kfar Oranim's workers in this matter. This was not being suddenly sprung on them since they helped the liaison-consultant to gather the facts about this incident and they knew that these facts were reported to Croydon.

In effect, the liaison-consultant had taken a step that shifted his monitoring function from the national plane of Project Renewal, Jerusalem where he was not recognized to the local level of Kfar Oranim where he could exercise the monitoring role with far less trouble. Croydon did not react one way or another to his initiative. Nevertheless, in the opinion of the liaison-consultant, the incident of the lathes demonstrated how accountability could be pursued even though the matter was revealed at the local level. His discovery of what occurred gave rise to much uneasiness among the workers who kept the purchase a secret. Eitan was especially worried as demonstrated by his over-eager, hop-to-it readiness to cooperate in putting the pieces of this episode together.

The incident was a vivid illustration of accountability gone astray due to the type of community incoherence that often comes with off-the-cuff problem solving. There were many other examples showing how lack of coordination worked against the best interests of Kfar Oranim. These included:

a) the repeated attempts to start a youth cooperative which came to naught because the different interests could not produce a central structure to take the project in hand.

b) the wealthy resident of Junius who tried to endow Kfar Oranim with a swimming pool but who was hopelessly frustrated because he could not meet the same people twice to pursue his proposal.

c) the phalanx of officials coming from various national government ministries to supervise local personnel without any Kfar Oranim organization to check on the effect this plethora of supervisors had on the quality of service in the town.

d) the ineffectiveness of the President's poorly improvised gathering which summoned Junius' economic elite to contribute money for a sports complex and swimming pool in Kfar Oranim.

There were other examples and the liaison-consultant might have selected any one to show a breakdown due to lack of planning or to hasty and ill-conceived last minute arrangements. The lathes incident was chosen because Croydon gave financial support for the disadvantaged youth program and had a right to expect accountability. Equally important, it would highlight the ethical obligation of the professional workers to be concerned about the community's well-being beyond the confines of their agency interests. If the leadership group representing Croydon established the principle of planning and coordination in connection with an episode that deeply involved a number of Kfar Oranim workers, it was bound to be far more telling than an individual effort at interpretation attempted by the liaison-consultant, no matter how skillfully it was done.

In a brief nightcap session at the hotel with the delegation, the liaison-consultant referred to the lathes but did not get very far. The delegation viewed the purchase as part of a past that was best left unraked (March 16, 1983). The liaison-consultant was tempted to argue against the position taken by the delegation but to what purpose? The opportunity to meet with the professionals had gone awry and the chance to re-schedule the session was slipping by with every passing hour. In any event, because of breakdowns on this trip, the liaison-consultant was not on the secure ground needed to press ahead with a proposal that would tax the time of the delegation, already under pressure from an overcrowded agenda. The opportunity that came to the liaison-consultant but once a year was as good as lost. He would have to bide his time for another twelve months to arrange the type of encounter he had planned for this occasion.

But, first, there was an interval of restorative work to be done through the mails on the rapport which was dented by the string of mishaps that began when the delegation arrived at the hotel. This was the liaison-consultant's view. Mark and members of the delegation probably had other thoughts. Who could blame them? It was time to think about a successor to continue the work begun by the liaison-consultant.

He continued the assignment for four more months during which Mark and he exchanged letters in which they dealt with the type of person who should be considered for the job of liaison-consultant. The present incumbent had placed a good deal of emphasis on inner development and aided self-help strategies which took advantage of immediate opportunities but which conditioned the liaison-consultant

230

to weigh them against future prospects. De-emphasizing the long range might give the replacement a freer hand to cope with ad hoc contingencies and with issues of the day as they impinge on the immediate interests of the Croydon Federation. The liaison-consultant made his thoughts known to Mark regarding the direction a new appointee might take.

The Liaison Role: Its Potential

The liaison-consultant or community representative is a prototype of the *luftmensch* since his role is not grounded in an organizational base of the community's institutional structure. Except for unofficial cooperation from the Jerusalem Center for Public Affairs, the workers have no reference body of their own in Israel. As Hoffman has noted, they have "developed active roles for themselves." (40). In every case, there is an identifiable overseas sponsor but the practice role is not fully legitimated to accomplish its diverse tasks.

Despite disparity between sponsorship and legitimation in the role, Elazar and King concluded their assessment of the work done by these workers with the following observation: "The community representative is a vital element in the forging of a true partnership between Israel, the distressed neighborhood and the Diaspora community. The presence and involvement of a community representative has facilitated deeper and more meaningful ties between the twinned community and the Israeli neighborhood while also serving as a useful vehicle for promoting implementation of the program." (41)

To examine the potential of the liaison role when Project Renewal may be winding down might seem pointless. However, it is widely held that this is not simply a one-time undertaking entering its final stage but rather that it is a process which will continue in some form. Moreover, there is, of course, the applicability of understanding this role and its potential in aided self-help programs elsewhere.

In 1988, the Jewish Agency announced that Project Renewal will be continued and expanded. Just how the new form will retain those elements which have given it enduring impact is not clear. One such element which stands out is the community-to-community relationship made possible by the "twinning" concept. Another is the emphasis on participatory democracy in the lives of local residents in Project Renewal towns and neighborhoods through their sharing in community decision making. Some observers believe that this second element may be the start of a trend toward decentralization in Israeli governmental arrangements. Eliezer Jaffe makes the point that "Project Renewal has . . . instilled a greater readiness among Israel's national and political bodies to increase citizens' involvement in local affairs. The influence of Diaspora Jews in this direction has been major . . . The challenge (in the post-Project Renewal era) will be to find joint projects that will once again spark the interest of Israelis and Diaspora communities and groups that are looking for the intense personal involvement that was offered to and demanded of them by Project Renewal." (42)

Project Renewal vividly testifies to the missing human touch in the abstract transaction symbolized by giving through the United Jewish Appeal. The intense personal connection in Project Renewal stands in direct contrast and included many people. In 1983, residents of Project Renewal communities in Israel were 15% of the total population.(43) Also, Project Renewal meant a very large investment for a small country. By March 31, 1989, almost $1 billion had been spent. Approximately $620 million came from the State of Israel and $309.6 million came from world Jewry.

Intense personal involvement by overseas delegations inevitably aroused curiosity about Project Renewal among residents of the Israeli towns and neighborhoods. This individualized interest is completely dormant under the system of lump sum remittances from local federations to the national office of the United Jewish Appeal in New York to the United Israel Appeal and, finally, to the Jewish Agency in Jerusalem. Understandably, the direct concern of local federations awakened a demand for accountability similar to what they require of the beneficiary agencies in their own communities.

Reinvigorated altruism among communities abroad is a valuable asset which planners should not lose in the next phase of community rehabilitation following Project Renewal. Israeli officials responsible for the program will continue to face pressure for accountability from communities in the Diaspora. It can be hypothesized that, given the perpetuation of community-to-community outreach, liaison personnel will play an important role in the post-Project Renewal era.

The question remains as to whether or not the community representatives can realize their full potential under the present system. The answer is that the current role structure is too restrictive in scope because it is basically individualistic and non-institutionalized. Moreover, it is enforced individualism. As things now stand, the liaison-consultant must tread cautiously on the far edges of the Renewal Department's jealously guarded hegemony over Project Renewal, in order to create a modicum of social space to do the job. The distant partner is helpless in staking out the liaison-consultant's area of autonomy. The sponsor is helpless in other ways as well because its five-year time span often bears little or no relationship to problems requiring long-range solutions. The difficulty does not lie alone in the different time perspectives between the distant partners. Confusion is created when intervention of a purely ad hoc nature is taken for problem solving of an enduring nature as was the case in the illusion

Conclusion

of community participation in the Kfar Oranim sub-committee budget reviews.

The time for changing the community representative's role structure in Project Renewal may be past. However, there is a long-standing principle in community organization which affirms that every new community problem or undertaking means identifying anew the community affected. In other words, the post-Project Renewal phase may bring a new configuration of community which could have a marked effect on the structure of the liaison-consultant role.

Why change? There is general agreement that Project Renewal has had a positive impact. Logic dictates that most of the concepts developed in Project Renewal should be retained in any plan that succeeds it. There are still as many as 200 Israeli communities that need rehabilitation. Why not proceed with them under the present arrangement?

Emphasis on the absorption of Russian immigrants renders it unlikely that Project Renewal, as presently constituted, will be extended. Nevertheless, summing up is essential to savor the taste of achievement and to take stock of lessons to be learned. The success of Project Renewal may come at a considerable price, Jaffe maintains, "Among the project's shortcomings is the unfortunate opportunity it gave Israel's government to put off the formulation and implementation of a national social welfare policy regarding the 200 or so neighborhoods not included in the project."(44) The glamor of Project Renewal may have distracted attention from the distress of places not fortunate enough to be included in the program.

Other costs may come with the benefits. The selective nature of the "twinning" process that pairs affluent Diaspora communities with disadvantaged populations in Israel may have serious consequences heretofore unnoticed. The situation in Israel is quite different in the Project Renewal years from what it was after the War of Independence. At that time, 600,000 Israeli Jews had no choice; they had to call on the Diaspora for money to help settle the refugees who soon outnumbered the host population. Thirty years later, the call to communities abroad to join Israel in a program of social and physical renewal was made under different conditions. In 1948, both the host and incoming populations were in straitened circumstances. By 1978, an indigenous Israeli middle class had arisen but it was excluded from Prime Minister Begin's appeal for philanthropic aid to the distressed communities.

The emergence of the Israeli middle class is very recent, having begun after the Six Day War in 1967. This sector of the population does not have the wealth of a long established economic elite and, like all Israelis, it is subject to very heavy taxes. Nevertheless, it represents a group of Israelis who are in a financial position to help but who were left out of Project Renewal. For an entire decade, the Israeli middle class remained on the sidelines while the government fought against widespread want in Israel by seeking voluntary aid from overseas Jews. At this point in Israel's development, the new middle class should be brought into the partnership between the government of Israel and Jewish communities of the Diaspora. Israeli society has never been so polarized and so driven by ethnic, political and religious differences as it is today. If the indigenous middle and lower classes were brought together in the struggle against want, a new opportunity for collaborative action would open and could help to create the harmonious inter-group relations which are so urgently needed in Israel at this time.

In addition, the Israeli middle class has much to gain from a relationship with the overseas Jewish communities. The middle classes of Great Britain, Canada and the United States have a tradition of exchanging knowledge, experience and information in the struggle against poverty. This process of interchange has produced similar institutions such as adult education, community centers, settlement houses, the social work profession, federated fund raising and social planning all of which are now deeply entrenched in those countries.

Israel has also benefited from this tradition of sharing information among the older welfare states. However, Israel has failed to adapt successfully the social planning culture of the other societies. The difficulties that the liaison-consultant had in getting a semblance of coordination started in Kfar Oranim is characteristic of the society as a whole. A further example of this state of affairs is the manner in which national voluntary organizations in Israel conduct their annual drives for funds. Each organization makes its separate appeal by sending school children to knock on doors. The youngsters come away with pittances. An adult volunteer, trained to solicit prospective contributors would inspire far greater confidence and raise much more money. Better still, wasteful duplication in juvenile fund-raising could be replaced by one federated campaign to be conducted annually. All sectors of the society could be reached by a large body of trained volunteer canvassers, informing the public about the valuable work of these organizations. Experience has shown that a knowledgeable citizenry, relieved from repeated approached for donations, is more willing to listen and to give more generously.

Experience has also shown that the most effective way to spread the message of benefits derived from unified campaigns for support of voluntary health and welfare services is by having a large group of influential community leaders at the helm of such efforts. This approach means that if a well-off community such as Junius is ever to play a role in helping Kfar Oranim to help itself, this cannot come about through a handful of volunteers visiting daily to offer their personal largesse to their favorite charities. It will take concerted, well-organized community action. Other affluent Israeli towns which abut poor ones face the same situation. The community-to-community approach, pioneered by Project Renewal, need not be limited to "twinning" overseas communities with Israeli communities. It can be applied to relationships among Israeli communities as well.

This strategy of change would have much to gain if the Project Renewal leadership were to emulate the tradition of passing on knowledge and experience from one country to the next. The United States learned from Great Britain and Canada learned from both. No doubt, Jewish leaders in these three countries would have much to contribute to Israelis in the art of social policy. Over the years, Israel has developed a large number of volunteers who render valuable services to the aged, the handicapped and other needy people. These voiunteers can provide a base for home grown leadership in social policy if they were helped to understand needs and priorities, to become social planners and to acquire the vision to engage in social change. While the task of creating a just society is a government responsibility beyond the capacity of volunteers no matter how committed or generous they may be, an involved citizenry can be a priceless asset to the government.

The underlying assumption of this scenario is that a major need in the phase to follow Project Renewal is a period of intensive planning based on study, assessment and reorganization. More than fifty years ago, the social theorist, Karl Mannheim, proclaimed that "freedom can only exist when it is secured by planning."(45) The interest in planning expressed here is less rhapsodic and more pragmatic. Evidence abounds to indicate that Project Renewal was propelled into existence far more by improvisation than by a deliberate approach to planned change. Vivid testimony to this state of affairs is provided by Irving Bernstein, among others. He was the Executive Vice Chairman of the United Jewish Appeal in the United States with experience in Project Renewal from its very inception. Bernstein wrote in the Jerusalem Post, "Project Renewal was born in controversy, raised in confusion . . . and kept alive only through the dedication and zeal of a very few people . . . it was learning by trial and error due to lack of preparation . . . which resulted in: twinning of incompatible communities and neighborhoods due to inadequate research and planning; limitation of Project Renewal to five years in order to overcome community resistance . . ." (46)

The liaison function, like so many other aspects of Project Renewal was hardly the end result of a considered approach. The plan advocated here requires many needed changes in the liaison role. There needs to be a shift from the present arrangement which dooms the liaison workers to being individualistic functionaries lacking in authority because they have no institutional base. It is impossible for these solo practitioners to stake out their autonomy when the Renewal Department sets highly restricted boundaries for them. Nor can these workers develop the scope of their role beyond the components identified by Elazar and his collaborators (47) without major change. An overseas community acting by itself cannot correct the situation. Change will come when the overseas communities join forces to insist on new arrangements. They need to establish a satellite agency that is empowered to deal with policy matters, consultation to liaison persons, jurisdictional disputes and similar matters. These issues should not come to the liaison workers until they have been resolved at a higher level. Offices representing Diaspora organizations which are already in Israel are usually one-person operations not equipped to deal with such mediating tasks as jurisdictional disputes, for example. The type of agency proposed here could act on behalf of all "twinned" communities abroad and would give them a presence in Israel that would enable them to participate in planning related to overseas philanthropy.

Accountability exemplifies the kind of concern which should concern all overseas communities. Nor is the issue of accountability limited to Project Renewal. It should be seen in the context of all the aid given to Israel by Jewish communities abroad. Over the past 25 years, this has amounted to $30 billion.(48) This enormous burden has no precedent in voluntary giving on so vast a scale over so long a time. It requires accountability which is increasingly demanded. Advocates of social change such as proposed here are often accused of being utopians or visionaries without any sense of realism. These attitudes are intensified by those who want to maintain the status quo, especially when jobs and vast sums of money are at stake. They would undoubtedly be concerned by the suggestion that Israel's middle class be brought into the picture and they might argue that this might send an unintended message to Jewish communities abroad: ease up on your vigorous labors to raise money for Israel; home grown affluence is being recruited to take up the struggle against need. The risk of this response is not to be ignored since, at its present stage of development, Israel's middle class can provide only a minute fraction of the sums that now come from abroad. However, the risk already exists. Overseas donors inevitably observe the rise of the nouveau riche in Israel. They do not have to visit Israel to see this phenomenon. A noticeable proportion of the Israeli population is frequently out of the country on seasonal travel junkets and holiday making. The Israeli vacationer has a well-heeled image on the international scene. Simultaneously, Project Renewal has effectively given visibility to need and distress in Israel.

These contradictory messages suggest that Diaspora Jewry should keep responding to need in an altruistic spirit but that Israel's middle class cannot remain untouched. History shows that the first wealth producing generation in Western nations is notoriously self-centered. Mass voluntary struggle against poverty in England and America did not come until the children and grandchildren of the tycoons and robber barons achieved ascendancy. The change visualized here would shortcut the hard nosed egocentrism of these pioneer nouveau riche by bringing them into partnership with the "twin" communities abroad. The injection of a massive dose of altruism into this early stage of Israeli middle class development is required.

Leaping to the conclusion that overseas donors are just waiting to step aside as soon as Israel's middle class enters the picture is an implicit denigration of their concern for Israel — a concern which runs far deeper than the prospect of receiving more honorifics. What appealed to them was the opportunity to reach out directly on a community-to-community basis. Similarly, the challenge of working with affluent Israelis to create a voluntaristic constituency for the war on poverty could serve as an important new incentive for the continued involvement of Diaspora Jews in Israeli community renewal.

To move in the direction contemplated here means introducing into Israelis society community planning, community organization and community development as permanent features. These approaches require a different time perspective from the short-range view generally held by the Jewish Agency. For example, Project Renewal was originally seen as lasting only five years. This inadequate period has already been extended and aspects of Project Renewal are becoming a permanent part of the Jewish Agency's procedures.

The long range implications of community renewal must be comfronted. A satellite agency could accomplish this task without reference to the length of time that an overseas community sees itself as being coupled with its distant partner. The liaison role would be augmented by additional components to give it the scope needed for organizing and planning. Liaison personnel would be charged with developing Israeli policy leaders to achieve participatory democracy for all social classes in the Israeli society.

Project Renewal as a Strategy of Change in the Tradition of the Welfare State

Carmon claims that the change brought about by Project Renewal is not radical. It "is basically and essentially another attempt of the welfare state of Israel to deal with 'the social' problem of disparities bewteen the 'haves' and the have-nots This disparity coincides partially with that between citizens of European and American origin and those of Asian and African origin; as such it has far-reaching social and political significance."(49) Why the implication that far-reaching social and political change is less fundamental than radical change? The difference may be more apparent than real. The pain and disruption that militant activists often create with their efforts to bring about social change tends to give these efforts and their results a sham aura of depth. Conversely, changes introduced by the gradualists are apt to be taken for granted because of the stereotype which holds that incrementalism amounts to superficial change.

The protection afforded to the citizen today contrasts sharply with the exposure to hardships and uncertainties that were characteristic of an earlier day. Accordingly, reforms introduced by the welfare state do indeed equate with basic change. In Israel, the welfare society was not established to rescue its working class from the rigors of rampaging laissez faire capitalism as in the West. The founding fathers created an egalitarian society based on an utopian socialist vision. When the State of Israel came into existence in 1948, social and economic class differences were among the smallest in the Western world. Most of the population shared the same modest circumstances. They sought aid from Diaspora Jewry not because they had created an unjust society which victimized poor people but rather to help rescue Jewish refugees from the Displaced Persons camps of Europe and from hostile Arab countries. Aid from abroad was a form of crisis intervention. It asserted the traditional survivalist imperative which bade Jewish communities living in safety to come to the aid of their brethren in perilous circumstances.

It is assuredly true that the immediate effect of Project Renewal is a narrowing of the social and economic gaps in Israel. However, from a historical perspective, it is clear that the condition of social and economic inequality in the 1970's and 1980's was not a pervasive problem in Israel a generation earlier.

Prime Minister Begin's call for world Jewry to share in Project Renewal invoked the same survivalist imperative that existed in the years of mass immigration. It was as though in 1977, the problem also stemmed completely from outside forces at work on the society. Yet, the prevalence of inequality had been exposed with unremitting fury by the same Menachem Begin who attributed this inner moral decline to the Labor government which he unseated. A passionate revulsion for the Labor Party, symbol of the Ashkenazi establishment, dominated the whole being of an individual like Aryeh, the would-be leader of Kfar Oranim's neighborhood residents. This response was very much in tune with the feelings of the Sephardim in the town and, indeed, of Sephardim throughout the country.

Since the ethnic divisions between Ashkenazim and Sephardim run so deep, it may be just as well that Israel's middle class, predominantly Ashkenazi, was not brought into Project Renewal. The Sephardim directed much anger against the urban Ashkenazim who made significant economic progress after the Six Day War while their own status went relatively unchanged. Ironically, they also poured out rage against the Socialist kibbutzim, also predominantly Ashkenazi. This reaction arose because some Sephardim were employed by their neighboring kibbutzim and they regarded the members of these settlements as a snobbish elite of Ashkenazi bosses. To bring these groups into contact with the needy in a benefactor-to-beneficiary relationship would only have aggravated an already tense situation. However, the Project Renewal experience in Kfar Oranim and elsewhere shows that the presence of overseas participants can have a positive effect on inter-ethnic relationships.

The exclusion of the Israeli middle class and the inclusion of overseas Jews in Project Renewal was not the result of a deliberately planned policy. Thoughtful consideration might have foreseen the strange scene in which missions from abroad land in Israel to visit their "twin" neighborhoods while plane loads of Israelis take off, some for vacations and others bent on emigrating. Still others, including many kibbutz youth, are outbound in order to satisfy a wanderlust which will carry them to many parts of the world and keep them away from home for a year or two and maybe more.

Growing negativism toward the kibbutzim as simultaneous symbols of socialism and elitism in the eyes of different antagonists may have influenced some kibbutz youth to drop out for extended periods from the collectives that have given Israel an image as the builder of an unique communal way of life. The decision to leave the kibbutz either permanently or temporarily may be part of an emerging trend among people who find in the hedonism they now can afford an escape from the strident disunity that currently plagues the country. Are these just passing moments in the public mood or do they mark a widening of the gap between rich and poor in Israel?

These questions and similar ones warrant probing through research in order to provide an informed basis for including the better-off members of Israeli society in Project Renewal or in some successor program. Such study would undoubtedly reveal a good deal of self-interest but it would also show the balancing sources of altruism and concern for social justice among the middle class which can make it a potent part of the country's struggle against poverty.

Inclusion of Israel's middle class in these efforts does not mean that the overseas communities can withdraw. The aim of the new approach would not be to replace those already involved but rather to broaden their ranks by obtaining cooperation from Israelis. Continuing to overlook the indigenous sources of altruism could, in time, exact a price in human capital that would not be compensated by gains in donations from abroad. Overseas Jewish leaders are uniquely qualified to cultivate a harmonious relationship among social classes in Israel. They bear none of the symbols of imperialism which the Israelis once associated with the British.

Kfar Oranim offers compelling evidence that its people did not feel the sense of disadvantage with Croydon visitors that it had with the Israeli affluent class. The latter were "people of the villas", as Kfar Oranim residents mockingly referred to their neighbors in Junius. In conversations with the liaison-consultant, the people of Kfar Oranim made clear their resentment at being the source of supply for domestic help in the elaborate homes of their wealthy neighbors. The Junius-Kfar Oranim situation is typical of Gold Coast-Slum relationships in other parts of Israel. Joint endeavor must be based on a cooperative relationship. Jewish leaders from the Diaspora are potentially a valuable conciliating element between residents of adjoining Israeli communities that have large differences in social and economic class.

Project Renewal has given Israel ten years of valuable experience in operating a program that combines government and voluntary resources in a collaborative effort to raise living standards. This experience offers planners in Israel the basis for such an undertaking in the future. It also can be profitably studied by planners in any part of the world concerned with foreign assistance. Project Renewal is the outgrowth of two grand strategies for self-development pioneered by the welfare societies of the West. The first was a voluntary effort mounted by the affluent sectors of the English-speaking world. The second consisted of government efforts to confront the problems of mass poverty.

Voluntary efforts were promulgated by the settlement movement, the Charity Organization Society and the Fabians in 19th century England. Their ideas were promptly taken up in the United States, Canada, Australia and New Zealand and were adapted to the conditions of those countries. Common culture and common language made it possible for visiting emissaries to bring information about innovative approaches to humanized methods of dealing with poor people. As these new ideas became diffused, what began as "scientific charity" evolved into the 20th century welfare states which no longer depend on the voluntary generosity of philanthropists in favor of using public funds to deal with problems of poverty. Between 1929 and 1975, the constant dollar expenditure by government sponsored welfare agencies in the United States grew from $12 billion to $286 billion.(50) This movement from the voluntary sector to government has not gone unchallenged. A theme that has gained prominence among social critics who comment on the 1980's is "the welfare state in crisis".(51)

Israel is a latecomer to the development of increased reliance on the public sector for fighting poverty. However, it is rapidly making up for lost time. Since the 1950's, the North American impact on social welfare in Israel has been potent. The Joint Distribution Committee in Israel, an offshoot of the American Jewish Joint Distribution Committee, has left its mark on care of the aged, social work education, community centers and rehabilitation of handicapped people. Experts have brought knowledge and expertise to Israeli schools of social work, raising standards of teaching and research.(52) These gains have provided valuable resources to Project Renewal in advancing community rehabilitation and community development.

While Israel is a fairly recent arrival among the welfare states, world Jewry has been a pioneering force in overseas aid. The tradition of aid from one Jewish community to another goes back to ancient times when Jews outside of Palestine contributed to the building of the Second Temple. In the modern era, organized programs designed to help Jews facing hardship in various parts of the world began in 1860 with the establishment of Alliance Israelite in Paris. In 1914, the American Jewish Joint Distribution Committee began to function. It has assumed a dominant role in rescuing and resettling Jewish survivors of persecution and in helping to rebuild Jewish communities destroyed by wars. Other agencies which started in the late 19th century are dedicated to more specific goals. For example, ORT sponsors trade schools in many lands, including Israel. Hebrew Immigrant Aid Society (HIAS) provides provides short-term assistance to newcomers in the United States, Canada and other countries. The mainstay of these world-wide aid programs is the United Jewish Appeal in North America and its counterpart in other places.

Outreach to distressed communities is mainly concerned with conserving organized Jewish communal life. In Israel, the goal of such assistance is growth and development more in keeping with the international aid offered by the West to the new nations created after World War II. The Jewish Agency serves as the bridge between Israel and overseas donors. It may be considered a trans-national corporation of diversified social and economic interests, similar to the kind mentioned in the Report of the Independent Commission on International Development. (53)

Attempts to deal with domestic poverty in Great Britain, the United States and Canada began as large scale voluntary efforts and were then taken over by the governments of those countries. In the 20th century, they increasingly relied on their gross national product in the struggle against want. After World War II, the Western countries sent aid on a global scale to the nations newly released from colonialism. Initially, some funds came from international foundations. As the United Nations became more active, there was a shift in emphasis from aid to social and economic development. This outlook led to decreased dependence on foundation grants in favor of reliance on government support provided by the industrially developed nations.

There has been a call for increasing assistance from the industrialized countries to 1% of their gross national product by the year 2000.(54) It is recognized that foundation grants and voluntary contributions will continue to form part of humanitarian aid.

A combination of public and voluntary support is evident in Project Renewal. Prime Minister Begin initially envisioned a partnership between the State of Israel using public funds and world Jewry using funds voluntarily contributed. The goal of rehabilitating distressed communities could not be reached by the government alone since it bears an extraordinarily heavy burden for national defense. At the same time, both the voluntary sector and governments in the West face skyrocketing costs for their domestic welfare programs. Project Renewal has therefore had to take into account the financial burdens and limitations faced by the State of Israel and by Jewish communities abroad. These considerations may have been at the root of the delegation's silence which baffled the liaison-consultant when he talked to its members about community development as the needed approach for releasing Kfar Oranim from its woes. As emissaries charged with maintaining realism in regards to the demands on Croydon for financial support, they were less sanguine than the liaison-consultant about containing the costs of development within the limits of their prescribed annual budgets.

Project Renewal has made it possible for those who raise the money to make final decisions about its use. The overseas partners are at an early stage in seeking accountability but the whole field of international aid is no further ahead. The Independent Commission on International Development, which was previously cited, advocates establishing an independent system of monitoring and evaluation since "present channels of coordination . . . are not working as efficiently as is necessary. The Commission recommends that the United Nations vigorously pursue better coordination of budgets, programmes and personnel policies".(55)

A distinct feature introduced into Project Renewal by the overseas partners which can be attributed directly to community development concepts is local participation in decision making. It has taken the form of community steering committees and their sub-committees as well as energetic neighborhood activism. Elements of community organization, community development and urban neighborhood development are embodied in the liaison role as carried out by the community representatives who practice a type of community work. The role has turned to be problematic in practice because of the inherent contradictions that have dogged it from the time it was first conceived as a community development method in the Third World.

Bugnicourt notes, "during the 1950's, the community development movement assumed the presence of internally harmonious local communities with sufficient autonomy to be able to act collectively in pursuit of their own interests, with a certain amount of technical and material aid and guidance from outside . . ."(56) It was a time when social theorists saw themselves as joining with planners to pursue development strategies geared to "the communities as the seeds of a new society". However, several forces have combined to thwart such optimistic expectations. These include the exponential growth of advanced technology, especially in the area of mass communication, uncontrolled urbanization and the regulatory aspects of services provided on a national basis. These forces have disrupted traditional community patterns which emphasize stability and the enrichment of local organized life rather than geographically unconfined individualistic career goals. Bugnicourt asserts that the aims of community development are frequently hampered by the community workers themselves because the participatory approaches devised by the local residents have to be filtered through the ideas of experts on what constitutes good community participation.(58)

During the latter years of the 19th century, social workers dealing with poverty thought they had discovered the secret to self determination by creating a zone of autonomy for those needing help by keeping them away from lay people who were untrained in the art of helping. In the middle of the 20th century, community development workers thought they could assure maximum participation within deprived areas by isolating themselves and their communities from sponsors of aid programs. However, the community development workers could not separate themselves from the values of careerism. They became the carriers of that from which they sought to protect their charges. Inevitably, the practice role that the liaison-consultant carried in Kfar Oranim was marked by these inherent flaws that have been built into it.

The Ambiguity of Power in Community Work

The phenomenon of power continues to plague the human service professions as an unresolved problem. This self-perpetuating dilemma is due to power's disreputable image despite its ubiquitous presence in human relations. According to Hobbes, the very use of power implies misuse, beginning with early man who, driven by selfish interest, lived a short, brutish life by the power of his will forced on others.(59) Individualized warfare receded when the struggle for survival became a collective concern that was placed in the hands of the ruling head thus enabling the prehistoric founders of human society to arrive at a way of living together. In the dawning of socialization, as posited by Hobbes, we detect no essential alteration in the nature of power as an individual possession and as a delegated force assigned to the ruler. As this human force changed, it may have acquired a new ambiance but it was not accompanied by any ennobling quality as it moved from the private space of the cave to the public arena of the horde.

This is confirmed by the recorded behavior of those wielding society's delegated powers: rulers, military men, monarchs, dictators, religious leaders and other despots who plotted, schemed and tortured to aggrandize the power which was assigned to them by their followers. The chronicle of their demeanor has come down from the Biblical period, from ancient Greek and Roman times, recounting the unabated abuse of power throughout history. Philosophers, historians, social scientists and artists have heaped opprobrium on power as synonymous with oppression. Our own era will be remembered as the epoch of Hitler and Stalin who victimized countless millions with their evil power.

The 20th Century will also be remembered for Roosevelt and Churchill but we do not speak of them as benefitting countless millions with their good power. Indeed, the phrase, "good power" in juxtaposition to "evil power" sounds clumsy, almost absurd. Why is that so? Because the accepted link between evil and power lends itself to handy use as a common expression. By contrast, implicit symbolism of power as a good has evolved to provide a basis for idiomatic use. Why the lack of symmetry in the description of power as evil and power as good? (60) Probably because power is generally perceived as a necessary evil at best — not to be trusted even in the hands of good leaders deploying power to good ends.

If this is the case, if power is a necessary evil at best, then, morally speaking, it is not something to be desired. This outlook is rife among human service professionals who ceaselessly agonize over power as an element inherent in their practice roles. Paradoxically, powerlessness in clients who are unable to cope with their problems, is seen as helplessness, often attributed to a grasping society which victimizes those who cannot cope with the harshness of the competitive world. One of the principal approaches to restoring the client, whether individual, group or community, to effective functioning is referred to as "empowerment". In light of the immorality so frequently attached to power, one cannot help wondering whether empowerment marks the emergence of a benign phenomenon or whether empowerment is a necessary evil which clients need to rejoin the human rat race.

These contradictory attitudes toward power illustrate the inconsistencies and ironies which were built into the daily practice of community workers as they pursued their responsibilities. They were present in different guises as the scene shifted from one focal point to another in the liaison-consultant's activity in Project Renewal and they were most vivid in his relationships with Project Renewal,

Jerusalem.

The liaison-consultant, confronted with Hanoch's repudiation of his monitoring function, was acutely aware of his helplessness. Hanoch, with his rigid politicized view of power, was not about to change his outlook. This created for the liaison-consultant a predicament similar to that of the powerless client. He saw empowerment as morally justified and totally desirable to bring a hard-nosed official around to a more reasonable view of Croydon's request for accountability. The liaison-consultant's role, as structured, bore testimony to the need for power to make things happen.

By contrast, his relationship with Kfar Oranim, based on his ascribed clout, referred to earlier as prestige, was seen by the liaison-consultant as a phenomenon not so devoutly desired. His discomfort at having ready-made authority at his disposal went hand in hand with the awareness that it was part of the legitimating mandate he needed for acceptance in Kfar Oranim. To get around "showing the flag" or flaunting his mandate, the liaison-consultant tried to avoid use of his authority as much as possible.

He expected the Steering Committee to balk at the liaison-consultant's monitoring function which pervaded his role in Kfar Oranim. However, the Committee members did not see it as a coercive imposition by Croydon. They saw accountability as cutting both ways in serving Kfar Oranim's partnership with its "twinned" community. When a payment from Croydon was overdue, Eitan, the Mayor and others prodded the liaison-consultant to wire or telephone for immediate remittance of the allocated funds. Similarly, the neighborhood activists clamored for the support of Kfar Oranim's distant partner, demanding that the liaison consultant secure a written statement from Croydon backing them in their struggle for greater recognition by the Town Council. They wanted Croydon to make good on its avowed support for grass roots involvement.

Since Kfar Oranim was not a helpless client in the relationship with Croydon, what was the source of the asymmetry that assured role mastery for the liaison-consultant in his dealings with the local leadership? The source would have been difficult to locate in specific acts or incidents. It was primarily a quality which permeated the relationship. There was rarely a need to articulate this implicit understanding or to make it explicit. The liaison-consultant was constantly aware of the contrasting situation which prevailed in his relationships with Project Renewal, Jerusalem, with Ariela, the Junius volunteer, and with Shaul, the Mayor of Kfar Oranim. Ariela could break the relationship with the liaison-consultant when she was displeased but the Mayor did not resort to such action no matter how disappointed he was with the town's distant partner. He controlled his reaction even though he was bitter, for example, about the denial of his request for additional funds to bail him out of the deficit his sanitation department incurred in trying to meet Croydon's demand for cleaner streets.

This reaction was at marked variance from the liaison-consultant's previous experience.(61). His earlier dealings with government officials and agency heads were characterized by relationships of parity. Concepts and principles of practice theory offered few clues to overcome this problem of structured disparity. However, social science is not the only source open to practitioners searching for illuminating insights into problems that arise in the course of their work. To come to grips with this particular situation, the liaison-consultant changed perspectives from a social science vantage point to an existential outlook which saw the dialogue in Kfar Oranim as between parties locked into differing status positions that neither could alter. It then became a challenge for the liaison-consultant to reach out from the confines of his status to the Kfar Oranim leadership which was in a client-like situation. This principle may seem abstract but it is not difficult to achieve in reality. At the first meeting in Kfar Oranim, Hanoch set up a formal relationship with the liaison-consultant while the Steering Committee created different links with just a few unspoken gestures.

This does not mean that the power factor was eliminated. Eitan always took account of it in his bustling role as executive secretary of the Steering Committee, whether he was relaying gossip that came straight from the horse's mouth or playing petty politics to gain something or give something away. Power figured in all meetings with the Mayor although it was possible to move beyond it to establish a relationship in some depth with him. With Yuval, Tamar, Uri, Aryeh and other local workers, the liaison-consultant developed a relationship of trust which aided them in their struggles with local and national officials and helped to maintain stability in the services provided by Kfar Oranim's social agencies.

Playing the Role and Acting the Role

The introduction of advocacy in the 1960's (62) elevated personality to a more commanding position than had been true earlier when the enabling tradition held unchallenged sway. Enablers who lay stress on mediation as a technique to facilitate problem solving maintain a low profile no matter how important they may be to decision makers. Neutrality and objectivity are stressed to insure an even tone of expertise and to play the role of impartial practitioners who will not rock the boat as it navigates toward a choice of action.

Advocacy as a method of intervention was well suited to the turbulence of the 1960's. It involved confrontation between the lower class and the affluent, escalating the threat of dire consequences until conditions were met and the menace diffused. Another type of activism came from militants who were frequently economically privileged youth. Their disruptive tactics (63) were not class-based. They were counter-cultural confrontations that took the form of social action turned into social antics or absurd theatrics which used fierce ridicule and lampooning derision to undermine the entire structure of authority, embracing child and parent, student and teacher, employee and employer.

Advocacy failed to bring about a basic change in the human condition. When its novelty wore off, advocacy was scaled down to its true potential, dislodged at a later stage from its politicized rationale and moored increasingly to a model derived from law.(64). In due course, advocacy was accepted by the helping professions as another approach alongside of enabling. In community work, advocacy offered the practitioner the option of a factional role in contradistinction to the neutral, non-partisan enabler. It also revealed a new side to practice, calling for a more visible, more spirited partisan worker committed to the needs of a particular client or group in community affairs. The introduction of advocacy led to a sharp and protracted debate on the propriety of bringing militance and activism into the helping professions. The focus of the argument was ethics. Polemics obscured another, less salient though no less important question regarding the ingrained passivity implicit in the enabler role which had become entrenched through education and hallowed as a moral good. Advocacy demanded assertiveness and bold intervention for which many a veteran lacked the temperament.

In its initial phase, advocacy tended to be championed by younger workers who were not shackled to the establishment nor to deeply internalized passivity. The new breed of practitioners felt freer to adopt a posture of confrontation on behalf of their clients. In time, the novelty of the advocate's style, with its calculated aggressiveness, wore off and advocacy became a method taken for granted by community workers just as it has been by lawyers.

Individualistic Acting Out versus Social Activism

Enabling and advocacy have different histories shaped by the societies which produced them. Nineteenth century England sought limited change to relieve suffering of the pauperized masses but without the violence and blood-letting which revolutions, especially the French Revolution, brought to Europe. Preference was given to the enabling functionary, pioneered by the Charity Organization Society and the Fabians. Class harmony was favored over class conflict. In the United States of the 1960's, civil rights for Blacks, empowerment of the poor,

247

women's liberation and the anti-Vietnam war struggle all sought a place in the mainstream, "a piece of the action", as the popular saying went. In the final analysis, this aim was at odds with revolutionary change. Disruption rooted in populism was designed to achieve specific changes; it was not a Marxist class war designed to overthrow the power structure and its governing regime. In the social welfare sector of the 1960's, the advocate functioned to secure reform through militant activism in the interest of the disadvantaged.

The enabling and advocacy approaches came to Israel detached from the social and historical roots that fed them in the United States and England. On the Israeli scene, enabling and advocacy are perceived by students and teachers alike as practice skills to be learned in the course of educational preparation. In North America, the advocacy approach fostered a complex of alternate agencies such as church basement and storefront operations which provided the activists with their "natural habitat". Thus, the advocates playing a more forceful role were not simply acting out or behaving temperamentally. Their intervention was determined by groups and agencies which assumed direct responsibilities in pressuring for change. In Israel, the prevalence of government centralization was a barrier to establishing agencies that were alternate, let alone counter, to the establishment.

This is true even though community workers in the early phase of Project Renewal who suggested citizen participation were regarded as advocates of disruption by the planners and building contractors who were under pressure to finish their work by stipulated deadlines. Adding citizen involvement to their troubles was dismissed as needless humbug by the harassed planners and builders. The community workers, far from stirring up trouble, were simply voicing the mood of residents in the depressed areas. The planners and builders turned a deaf ear to the community workers and pressed ahead with physical aspects of Project Renewal only delaying the day when they would have to come to terms with the need to involve the residents of the places undergoing rehabilitation.

When protest is not accommodated at the community level, it goes underground in totalitarian societies. In a democracy such as Israel, it may become individualized. Thus, acting out has become a kind of do-it-yourself militance often used by people bringing their needs to social welfare agencies.(65) This led the Welfare Department in Kfar Oranim to station a guard at the entrance to protect the staff from violence threatened by enraged clients. However few the results gained by tantrum may be, it is always a perilous exercise precisely because it is individualistic and lacks the built-in constraints of responsible community legitimation.

Now and then, the Steering Committee resorted to a form of simulated militance which, in essence, was acting out, to remind visiting functionaries that they had ventured into the client's turf. For example, when the head of the local Labor Party branch was piqued by a remark made by Leah of the Project Renewal regional office, he hurled a rejoinder at her which touched off a deafening uproar. Leah remained in full possession of herself, retaining her poise throughout the outpouring of hostility. She was in Kfar Oranim and the spontaneous eruption had to be borne on the home turf of the Steering Committee. But this show of temper gained nothing. She knew that if a major issue arose, the Steering Committee could not tackle it without the intervention of the regional office — her turf.

The Study as Watching Brief on the Behavioral Aspect of Intervention

The liaison-consultant's ongoing self-evaluation proceeded not so much as a review of how he had behaved but as a watching brief he kept in the act of behaving. The opportunity for such scrutiny was a motivation which led the liaison-consultant to accept the Kfar Oranim assignment. As a consequence, self-analysis moving in tandem with intervention was integral to the entire process. There was constant self-questioning prior to such events as a meeting with the Mayor, with the Junius volunteers or with Leah. The self-questioning proceeded as much as possible while the event was in progress and immediately on its conclusion. This differs from spontaneous internal deliberating which occurs as one meets and chats with people. The distinction may be gleaned from the type of question the liaison-consultant would put to himself: what guiding principles did he bring to the encounter? In what way did these principles determine his behavior? Were goals the basic determinant or did psychological predisposition play the decisive role? Such questions made for ordered rather than random introspection.

The goals at stake were present in virtually every encounter along with psychological knowledge and skill factors. However, the primary factor in determining outcome was the role structure. Thus, when the liaison-consultant was meeting with the Mayor about the problem of sanitation or about the discord which plagued his relationship with many workers, the liaison-consultant was functioning as advocate on behalf of the local workers and, in a sense, also as advocate for Kfar Oranim's distant partner. The Mayor had to deal with these issues not necessarily on their merit, as far as he was concerned, but because the liaison-consultant kept them high on the agenda. Ignoring them meant that the Mayor would run the risk of incurring Croydon's displeasure. Often, he tried to turn the role around by asking the liaison-consultant to be his advocate. Mayor Shaul wanted his request for additional funds forwarded to Croydon and he pressured the liaison-consultant to plead his case with Croydon by pointing out that its request for clean streets had put the sanitation department into deficit. The Mayor produced no figures and the liaison-consultant could not ask him to reveal budgetary information for which he was accountable to the Ministry of Interior. This meant that the Mayor was asking the liaison-consultant to act as his advocate without providing a factual basis for playing this role. The liaison-consultant could not intercede on the Mayor's behalf.

The liaison-consultant role varied structurally since it was not always pegged to an asymmetric relationship. In dealing with Aryeh, the Mayor saw the liaison-consultant as a sympathetic intermediary, ready, as he perceived it, to try to bring this uncontrolled neighborhood activist to his senses, thus calming the explosive mood which his acting out created at Steering Committee meetings. For the Mayor, this had high priority since he often felt overwhelmed and helpless when Aryeh's volatile temper took flight.

With Croydon, the abiding question was how to establish a deeper working association. The challenge was ever present although it often felt like an evasive paper chase. The liaison-consultant's mediating between Aryeh and the Mayor or making representations on behalf of the professional workers were seen as local matters in which Croydon should not become involved. Activities such as sanitation or setting up a pen pal club between the young people of Croydon and Kfar Oranim were perceived as appropriate to the liaison-consultant role. To deal by letter with these activities and the different priority attached to them by each partner would have substantially increased the flow of letters which already demanded too much of Mark's time. Written explanations for a course of action and its urgency lacked the dynamic which comes through in face-to-face give and take in which urgency and explanations are fused into one.

Letters and memos did not allow the liaison-consultant to play the role of advocate which he needed in a prodding relationship with his own sponsor. Providing information is one thing; convincing the sponsor of the necessity for a certain course of action is another. What is required is a relationship of trust cultivated through personalized rapport between worker and sponsor, no less than between worker and client. Conceivably, a satellite organization serving all the overseas communities in Project Renewal could help to build a relationship of mutual confidence beween the sponsoring community and its representative, separated from each other by a great distance.

In relation to Project Renewal, Jerusalem, the role of the liaison-consultant remained unvarying, as we have seen. In other situations, changes were wrought by time. In the case of Dalia, the Junius volunteer, for example, they began with her expecting the liaison-consultant to help her bring a tennis center to Kfar Oranim. When that expectation became unrealistic, the role was reversed. Dalia became the one with the potential to aid the liaison-consultant in gaining access to the business people in Junius.

The liaison-consultant tried to keep the differing role structures and the different types of role play which they entailed compartmentalized as much as possible. He hoped to minimize the spill-over of negative effects from the Project Renewal, Jerusalem situation to Kfar Oranim. But that was not always possible. Sometimes, the liaison-consultant's different worlds came into contact with each other. As previously described, one such occasion came out of the blue when Leah flounced into Eitan's office with Dan in tow, and demanded an emergency meeting in place of the scheduled interview with a candidate for the youth work job.

Because of the childish secrecy and general immaturity which was displayed, the liaison-consultant put no obstacles in Eitan's way by insisting that he keep to the original meeting. Hasty thought was given to the consequences of such a decision on his status in the working relationship with Eitan. There were two other considerations, one, ethical and one, tactical, which merit exploration.

Putting pressure on Eitan was the easiest way out of the dilemma. It also offered the liaison-consultant a chance to remind Eitan of his obligation to Croydon. But, that would be "showing the flag", a bullying strategem which the liaison-consultant was determined to avoid in his relations with the people of Kfar Oranim. However, not all was noble in the liaison-consultant's reckoning with this passing bit of gamesmanship. Since it was Leah who created the crisis for Eitan, it would have been appropriate for the liaison-consultant to ask that she desist from disrupting Eitan's schedule. However, she was not going to be bested in a confrontation with the liaison-consultant inasmuch as she took her cue from Hanoch in defining the relationship. Eitan's course of action was predictable in view of his dependence on Project Renewal, Jerusalem and its regional office as he pursued his day-to-day responsibilities. By not putting Eitan to the test openly, the liaison-consultant earned his gratitude, as borne out by his apologies and penitential attitude for the next several days. Loss of face was contained and damage to the liaison-consultant's standing in Kfar Oranim was minimized. Dan, who was taking careful note of what was transpiring in Eitan's office, could be counted on to report the incident in full the next time he exchanged gossip with the Mayor. He would not be able to report the liaison-consultant's capitulation in an outright test of wills with Leah.

Discussing status and role conceptually is an academic exercise inevitably more elegant than is the guarding of status and prestige in its self-serving practicalities. The politics of role playing are deeply implanted in the player's personality and, in the full range of the game, embrace family, friendship group, organization, community and, ultimately, society. Only a hermit who forfeits human relationships can dispense with the game on ethical, spiritual, aesthetic grounds, or for any other reason which may suit the purpose of a determined recluse.

The Concluding Phase of the Liaison Role

The liaison-consultant's decision to place his role in other hands came partly because his status had visibly eroded in the eyes of Kfar Oranim's professionals, especially Eitan. This development began with the liaison-consultant's demand for accountability from Eitan in connection with the hare-brained use of funds to purchase two costly lathes. This was one demand which secured his ready cooperation, along with that of Project Renewal Jerusalem and its regional office, all abetted by worried anticipation stimulated by the report to Croydon which was made by the liaison-consultant. Others in Kfar Oranim with varying degrees of involvement in the purchase were also concerned. Everyone anticipated with some anxiety a demand for accountability by Croydon's delegation during its next visit. Much to Eitan's relief, no such demand was made. The implication of this non-event was not lost on him. It deeply affected his working relationship with the liaison-consultant who was responsible for building toward a moment of truth that never came.

What was so significant about this incident as to influence the liaison-consultant's decision to terminate his work in Kfar Oranim? It was one of several factors which converged about 20 months after the liaison-consultant began his assignment. Perhaps, this much time was needed for the role to crystallize and for the factors to come together in a pattern which allowed the liaison-consultant to weigh the separate insights gleaned with respect to the overall situation. Allowing the irresponsible purchase of the lathes to pass off as another "local" matter without insisting on on accountability when the liaison-consultant had worked so hard to prepare Kfar Oranim's professionals for this demand, trivialized the crisis which he had built up. This threatened the viability of the working relationship with Eitan. The incident vividly highlights the disparity between the flesh and blood relationship which existed in the liaison-consultant's association with Kfar Oranim and his contact with Croydon which relied on correspondence.

Another factor in the decision to leave was the limitation of the liaison-consultant role to immediate tasks surrounding the grant and the Project Renewal programs. The potential import of the role as an inter-cultural linking agent was not realized principally because of externally imposed constraints. As things stood, the role was subject to an excessive number of circumscriptions which prevented intervention in the depth required for such complex tasks as raising community morale, for example.

That insight became apparent to the liaison-consultant early on. Given the problem of contending with an absentee sponsor and being under the heavy domination of a proximate power structure, the tenuous contact which the liaison-consultant pursued as a virtual loner with the three Junius volunteers was a quixotic search for a support system to help Kfar Oranim stand on its own feet. This may be true, but the community worker must be prepared to battle the inner skeptic, the assailing moments of cynicism and and the messages of doubt coming from intuition while carrying out a task in which failure is almost certain. In this case, the naiveté was not the liaison-consultant's nor, for that matter was it Croydon's. An illusion coursed through most, if not all, of the overseas Project Renewal communities which escalated hope into belief and, then, into the expectation that utopian aims would be realized throuqh Project Renewal. Accordingly, Croydon hoped, believed and expected that Kfar Oranim's morale would improve by means of the supportive relationship with its distant partner.

The liaison-consultant probed this objective and worked for its achievement. However, as the documentary shows, it is possible to send financial support over a distance but inter-community support to raise morale requires outreach at close range. The liaison-consultant's efforts lacked the scope to move Kfar Oranim and Junius toward the desired goal of a support system. This was clear from the outset but the activity fulfilled a useful purpose by rendering insight and understanding. It revealed the illusionary nature of the expectation that the liaison-consultant could raise the morale of a depressed community on the basis of his role as it was structured. Under the best of circumstances, this goal was not attainable without involving the indigenous middle class. This requisite had been overlooked by the fund-raisers whose primary interest was in using morale-building as a slogan to maximize financial contributions by the overseas communities to Project Renewal. What is being recommended here is a social planning view of morale-building with enlargement of the "twinning" process to include the newly emerged affluent people of Israel. This would harness a great reserve of untapped energy for renewal tied to a strategy of social change rather than exclusively to the contingencies of philanthropy.

Was the study an explicit part of the assignment? No, it was not requested by Croydon. This question has an ethical connotation which warrants consideration. Does the practitioner have the right to launch into a study for which the sponsor has not asked? Had it cut into the working time of the liaison-consultant, the venture would have called for prior clearance by the sponsor. Since this was a self-study, no approval was necessary. It was an exercise in disciplined introspection regarding the worker's intervention in which the conceptualizing, the planning, the behavior and the written materials were continually subject to evaluation during the full period of the assignment. The study was an intensified aspect of practice in which the worker engages on the job, in any event. Moreover, there is an explicit ethic and obligation which enjoins the professional practitioner to make available, where possible, concepts and information based on specific experience for the enrichment of practice generally. In a professional sense, the study was therefore an integral part of the assignment.

The time element is not the only factor to be considered. Even if the effort in self-analysis did not take time which belonged to the work in Kfar Oranim, is it possible that it affected the nature of the role? Might it be that the preoccupation with self-analyzing and introspecting exerted a pacifying influence on the liaison-consultant's intervention? Did it contribute to a self-limiting involvement which reduced the liaison-consultant's ability to respond effectively to Croydon's request for more aggressiveness? These questions will be left for the reader to ponder except that the very fact of raising them indicates the liaison-consultant's awareness of the problem.

In the judgement of the liaison-consultant, Kfar Oranim was not ready for an assertive advocate. The minimal back-up for advocacy was lacking as evidenced by the helplessness which pervaded the negotiations that the leaders of Kfar Oranim conducted with outside authorities to provide the residents with a beach, to secure industrial space for workshops and small businesses or to replace the open culverts with an underground drainage system. With respect to the culverts, not until the Croydon delegation pressured the Ministry of Housing was there any progress made in getting the open culverts covered.

Without a power source to draw upon from the neighborhoods, from the Town Council or from the Steering Committee, advocacy would be initiated from a position of weakness and amount to hardly more than personalized acting out, a phenomenon all too familiar in Israel as a tantrum symbolizing the activists' powerlessness. Hence the need for a preliminary period of building local groups such as the one which Tamar had begun to organize with the aim of securing a broad base of support for community participation and citizen action to attain goals which Kfar Oranim had yet to reach. This process of maturation can sometimes be foreshortened by an unanticipated development.

Hanoch's resignation was such an unexpected turn of events. His leaving was coupled with the impending municipal elections or the special committee appointed by the Ministry of Interior to run Kfar

Oranim. Either way, it meant that the existing power structure was about to give way to a different combination of leaders in Project Renewal and in Kfar Oranim. The new people would find liaison-consultants to be an entrenched feature of Project Renewal. It was a propitious time to put the liaison-consultant role in new hands.

The Liaison-Consultant as Harbinger of Change

Social change may promise betterment but there is always the dread of going through the unknown to get to the good life dangling at the end of the promise. Community workers want to be regarded as agents of change. Yet, communities confronting change want to be protected from it even as they are yielding to its lure. Fear of change in private life is at the root of the anxiety which the prospect of change induces when the individual becomes an influential leader in the affairs of the community. Workers are often baffled when confronted by a public figure manifesting such trepidation. More than once, the liaison-consultant wished that his years of experience had better prepared him for this eventuality when he encountered it in Kfar Oranim.

One example of a concerted attempt on a large scale to deal with the hopes and fears that were generated by change on the community level came when community development was first introduced to the Third World. After World War II, pioneering community development workers in economically deprived countries made a determined effort to protect village populations from fundamental social change that was bound to clash with their traditional ways of life. Community participation was geared to be in keeping with the people's readiness to cope with modernity. The community development worker as a supportive agent of change gave villagers the feeling that they were masters of their fate despite the imminence of the industrialization which was sought by the national government of developing countries. There was the terrifying precedent of the Industrial Revolution in the West to be heeded. Community development workers wanted to ward off the great damage which, in its first 50 years of uncontrolled change, industrialism had wrought in the villages of England, referred to by Trevelyan as the country's "principal nursery of the national character". (66)

The effects of the Industrial Revolution warn us that rapid fundamental change exacts a price in pain so high that, to this day, the fear of runaway innovation still haunts the West. A vast body of literature in the arts and sciences bemoans helpless people wallowing in a never-ending identity crisis uncompensated by the material awards of industrialism.

There have been compensating attempts to re-interpret community living to accord with the changes which have come in the wake of industrialism. This major preoccupation in the West is now receiving renewed interest from urbanologists and other social scientists as a result of a trend in the developing countries where massive flocking of rural populations to the cities is creating probems of conurbation and where the creeping uncontrolled growth of the metropolis swallows satellite towns and converts separate urban centers into a megalopolis. Among the various reinterpretations of contemporary community living, an interesting conception has been advanced by Kenneth R. Schneider in "Reconstitution of Community". He says, "Western man has created a new cosmopolitan level of essentially anonymous behavior, including not only bureaucratic organization of business and government, but also cultural and educational activities based largely upon specialization and professionalization. The challenge of community is to establish a worthy intermediate or 'public' range of association of individuals, between the complete intimacy and protection of the family and the awesome anonymity and performance-governed behavior of the cosmopolitan society. The full range of human association may be divided into three quite distinct parts: the family, which is private; the community which is public and the cosmopolitan society which is anonymous." (67)

This foregoing glimpse of self-generating social change as the ruling dynamic which has long since banished the static, pre-industrial view of life (68) provides a useful point of departure for our concern with change, although greatly reduced to the micro gauge of the two distant partners, "twinned" by Project Renewal.

The Steering Committee as a Community Organization from the Vantage Point of the Schneider Formulation

Communities in Israel were not reached by the forces of industrialism that transformed urban life in the West. Yet, the Schneider analysis based on the metamorphosis in the West is applicable to community living in Israel. A comparable development took place after the Six-Day War when Israel moved from a relatively simple society to a modern, industrialized society. While the "social regions" which Schneider discusses can be clearly discerned in Tel Aviv, Jerusalem and Haifa, the different types of relationships corresponding to these developments have not evolved. Israelis have a marked preference for informal, spontaneous associations in the depersonalized metropolitan and community realms, no less than in the close family circle.

This may explain Ariela's concern that the liaison-consultant harbored intentions of changing the natural order of things in Kfar Oranim. Uneasiness pervaded his contact with this important Junius volunteer. She was suspicious of the liaison-consultant's presence in town and distrustful of his motives. At the root of her uneasiness was her feeling that the liaison-consultant was an organization man, biding his time and waiting for an opportunity to introduce change in the intimacy that existed between the Junius volunteers and their neighbors in Kfar Oranim.

Although Ariela was involved in many Kfar Oranim activities, she stayed clear of the Steering Committee except for occasions when the Committee hosted a national figure or when her help was sought to arrange a special event. She had no use for what she considered to be endless committee talk when there was work to be done that could just as well be taken care of without the formalities of committee talkfests.

Her view of committee process as a depersonalized involvement that formalized the friendly relationships existing between helper and helped emerged in her meeting with the two students brought by the liaison-consultant to discuss their assignments. Ariela was not just another Junius volunteer. She was, in fact, the one who, practically speaking, defined voluntarism in an affluent community next to a disadvantaged neighboring town. Her role as the leading volunteer was acknowledged with genuine affection by the people of Kfar Oranim. She was on a first-name basis with the town folk, from the humblest resident to the Mayor. She bore her privileged position as a burden, anxious to be accepted as an equal. At public affairs, she would identify herself as a resident of Kfar Oranim Number Two, as she lightly referred to Junius.

Motivated in part by her husband's political ambitions, Ariela was determined to protect the easygoing mutuality that existed between her and Kfar Oranim. She insisted that the liaison-consultant could enter Kfar Oranim only on her conditions. Her power was manifest whenever the liaison-consultant raised the idea of bringing the two communities closer together. Invariably, the liaison-consultant was told that such ideas had to be discussed with Ariela first, not because the people feared her but because it was the thing to do. It was natural to seek her advice in these matters.

On the other hand, the leaders of Kfar Oranim welcomed Project Renewal programs as God-sent and readily agreed to form the new organization needed to accommodate the "twinning" arrangement with Croydon. Thus, the Steering Committee was established to oversee the Project Renewal program and to assume the bridging function with the distant partner. Unlike Ariela, Kfar Oranim's leaders were never concerned about the loss of primary relationships to some depersonalizing process that might come with the creation of such a central community body. That was because their close-knit intimacy was carried over into the Steering Committee. With it came an array of conflicting interests that frequently served to obscure the Project

Renewal issues under discussion. Among the chief distractions were party affiliations, personal friendships and family ties. The Mayor was always mindful of these collateral interests and took them into account to avoid the risk of rubbing someone the wrong way, turning the meeting into a feuding, squabbling hassle resembling a large family airing long-held, deep-seated grievances.

The only time the Mayor knew that he did not have to worry about these external considerations was during the visits of Croydon's representatives. On these occasions, Kfar Oranim residents invariably fell in with the more formal tone set by the visitors. Just as the Americans left their buddy-buddy familiarity in the coffee shop or the hotel lobby, so did the Kfar Oranim Steering Committee members put aside old crony familiarity and vendettas to address community needs. They joined forces to talk to the visitors about, "Our needs" . . . "We look to Project Renewal to build and repair our day care centers" . . . "Our children are our first priority". . .

But as soon as the visitors left, the formal tone went back on the shelf. To look on this as a regression of some sort or to confuse it with the behavior of simplistic people is a mistake. Informality is in itself a "letting it all hang out" purging experience, a putting oneself on record before all concerned, not to be confused with the informality that breeds contempt. This no-holds-barred frankness is a value Kfar Oranim fully shared with Israeli society, inured to polemics, "often raucous and noisy with the clatter of endless disagreements . . . exacerbated, stifled . . . by tremendous personal rivalries, antagonism and fanatic loyalties." (69) If Steering Committee sessions led to outbursts that got out of control, they were in the style and spirit of public debate, exemplified by the roof-raising verbal flare-ups of Knesset parliamentary exchanges regularly televised on the evening news. This tinder box of incendiary polemics is, like the smaller arena in Kfar Oranim, also susceptible to the influence of visitors in attendance. Who can forget the hushed, respectful hearing President Jimmy Carter received from the Knesset members at the unique session when he spoke about the Camp David agreements?

Observing the different behavior patterns each partner brought to joint meetings of the Steering Committee and the restraining effect of one group upon the other, the liaison-consultant gained a valuable insight. It was one of many that came through inter-cultural comparisons when the twinned communities came together, not only in Steering Committee meetings but also in visits paid by large visiting groups, referred to as missions. Behavior that conveys insight on the level of community is manifest not only through deliberate pronouncements of studied postures by the public figure; things are also said in the heat of the moment that may be forgotten with the next utterance which reveals something about the community no less than spontaneous behavior illuminates essences of an individual's private life. The entire repertoire of roles ranging from the innermost concerns to behavior in the fish bowl of public life is lodged in the one personality. The worker must separate behavior having implications for the community from the individual's private space. Where privacy is under consideration, biography is the clue to individual foibles. The dimension of folklore and history are additional considerations essential to the worker's understanding of community foibles.

The Twinned Communities and Their Distinctive Uses of the Steering Committee

Another feature which distinguishes the two partner communities from each other was the distinctive uses they made of the Steering Committee. For Croydon, the Committee provided a framework of accountability. It was the locus of budget reviews as the basis for deciding on the grants to be made for the ensuing year. It provided a running evaluation of the entire renewal program in its physical and social dimensions and it was the arena for setting priorities.

Beyond that, the Steering Committee served as a vehicle for summoning Kfar Oranim residents to organize community-wide receptions for the visitors with displays of ethnic foods and folk arts. The Croydon visitors found these activities pleasurable as they were brought into direct contact with dimensions of community living that could not be demonstrated at sessions of the Steering Committee. These evocations of Kfar Oranim's culture and traditions gave the representatives of the distant partner a certain agreeable sense of reassurance that otherwise would not have been accessible. Moreover, in the eyes of the visitors, there was an affinity between the folk arts and neighborhood activism in that both arose from the community at its broadest base. More significantly, the sense of shared fate was fed by these displays of community spirit rather than by the functions performed and decisions made at Steering Committee meetings. Another satisfying experience was provided by seeing the social agencies in action. For the visitors, the helping arts were the other side of the folk arts.

Thus, while the Steering Committee provided services to Croydon which, in the aggregate, could be categorized as community organization, Kfar Oranim used the Committee for the additional purpose of summoning the residents to demonstrate community solidarity to the visitors and, no less important, to themselves. The opportunity to display their sense of community in the presence of the Croydon representatives always served to reinforce their inner feelings of pride. However, this function could have been carried out by the Town Council or the Community Center. These two bodies organized civic commemorations such as Independence Day and Remembrance Days for Holocaust victims and for soldiers killed in the Arab-Israeli wars.

What the role of the Steering Committee might have been without Croydon's reliance on it is open to conjecture. The shallowness of the Committee's roots in the organizational framework of Kfar Oranim bcame apparent after Hanoch resigned. During the brief span of several weeks between his leaving and the arrival of his successor, a paralysis set into the work of the Steering Committee while Eitan awaited a signal from Jerusalem that did not come.

Sub-committees met to review budgets and the liaison-consultant tried to help Eitan to get them to focus on presentations by agency representatives. Occasionally, Leah came from the regional office to help. But, without Vered on the scene, the liaison-consultant's efforts were in vain. Gone was the spirit and the skill she brought to budget reviews. Above all, she had kept Eitan alerted to the expectations of Project Renewal, Jerusalem, a matter of great importance to him. Without Vered's guidance, there was a loss of authority in the leadership which Eitan provided to the Steering Committee and its sub-committees. They floundered.

A further indicator of the Steering Committee's decline was the poor performance of Kfar Oranim's representatives at the yearly meeting with the Croydon delegation. Without Vered and Hanoch, the smooth functioning of the previous year was visibly lacking. Considerations crept in that were outside the immediate concern of the Steering Committee. The Mayor and Eitan could not rein in the filibustering principals because they were more worried about the consequences of cutting off the principals than about the reactions of the delegation to the meager quality of the budget review. The principals' uncontrolled oratory produced an emotionally charged situation more in keeping with the type of meetings held when the Croydon delegation was not present. The visitors saw the inability to maintain a semblance of public discusssion appropriate to a central community organization as signifying a sharp drop in the Steering Committee's viability and effectiveness.

The two partners reacted differently to this failure in role play. To the Croydon representatives, it was a breakdown of efficiency both in Kfar Oranim and in Project Renewal, Jerusalem. The Kfar Oranim residents looked at it as a freak accident. The Mayor and Eitan asked the liaison-consultant to intercede after Melvin, the chairman of the Croydon delelgation, having run out of patience, abruptly terminated the meeting. Eitan summarized the Kfar Oranim reaction: "Four individuals made fools of themselves. Does that mean all of Kfar Oranim has to pay the price?"

Conclusion

Improvisation as a Way of Life

Implicit in these annual get-togethers was Croydon's expectation that its distant partners in a modern welfare state (70) would shape up in using the Steering Committee as a planning-coordinating instrumentality. This expectation manifested itself in explicit disappointment by what Croydon deemed to be a collapse in efficiency at the Israeli end. Parenthetically, this reaction is of a piece with the long-standing differences that evoke remonstrations between Diaspora leaders and Israeli spokesmen at international conclaves and joint organizational endeavors.

Differences between the "twinned" communities in checking, clearing and coordinating, though generally underplayed, were a source of tension that often surfaced in connection with travel schedules and other arrangements for overseas missions. At the Kfar Oranim end, as a rule, these complications were taken in stride. Why, the local officials wondered, were such foul-ups looked upon as some sort of betrayal which had to be traced to the source and the culprits held accountable? What was human intelligence for if not to improvise a way out of unforeseen complications? The truth is that Kfar Oranim's approach had to work. What else was there to do but follow this conventional wisdom when an unexpected call came announcing that indivdual visitors or small touring groups had turned up and wanted to visit their "twinned" community?

Improvisation, whether equated with muddling through or pragmatism, goes hand-in-hand with crisis intervention. Crisis wipes the slate clean of standing priorities and standards of efficiency. In the face of the unexpected, improvisation is ethically acceptable. Indeed, reliance on improvisation becomes a necessity as a way of life in a society constantly confronting crises and problems. Steadily facing a spate of burning issues, Israeli decision makers are a harried breed who do not have the luxury of a contemplative planning approach. Improvisation is the admired and preferred method for solving problems, large and small alike. (71)

Informality as a Declared Social Value

Informality in manner and tone is accepted in Israel's public community realm. Improvisation reinforced by informality skirts the ceremonials of decision making with their motions, resolutions, seconds and counting of the ayes and nayes. Eitan was determined to avoid the formality of voting.

He recorded consensus based on his intuitive understanding of how the wind blew. He was careful to avoid reading his own biases into the decisions. An attentive, acute listener with knowledge of each

261

person's hidden agenda, Eitan was very keen at sizing up who was for, who was against and who was undecided. Thus, the Steering Committee made decisions without the ayes being openly separated from the nays by a show of hands. Thanks to Eitan's skill, the will of the majority prevailed. Where there was uncertainty, there was no hesitancy in challenging what Eitan had divined. This informal method of decision making accompanied by a lack of parliamentary procedure was strange to Croydon.

It would be unrealistic to expect the Steering Committee to adopt formal rituals when they related to each other with clan-like intimacy in all other aspects of their lives. The question becomes all the more pertinent in the light of past factors, cherished to this day, which shaped intimacy and informality as handed down by the pioneers who came to Palestine from Eastern Europe in the late 19th century. Sephardim also had close knit relationships, based on the large extended family structure rather than on the isolation imposed on the Ashkenazim when they lived in Europe. Living cheek by jowl in crowded ghettos, East European Jews found intimacy to be an unavoidable way of life.

Supposedly, Emancipation was the end of the ghetto. But, assuring equal rights for the ostracized community turned out to be a false promise. Physical walls were replaced by social barriers, even more difficult to bear. As Cuddihy states, "The failure of Jewish Emancipation was a failure of ritual competence and of social encounter: no social rites of public behavior were reciprocally performed . . . This failure of civility spread shock waves through nineteenth century society . . . since the norms of civility . . . spell out and specify for face to face interaction the more general values of the culture the failure of civility came to define 'Jewish Problem' in the era of social modernity."(72)

The failure of civility was not just a widespread mood of unspecified intolerance. Between 1870 and 1914, no less than 48 openly declared anti-Semitic parties and national organizations arose in Germany, Austria-Hungary, France, Russia, Poland and Rumania. (73) The Jews of Eastern Europe recoiled from the bitter fruits which Emancipation had yielded in Western Europe. Responding to modernity with an inner movement known as Haskala, they defined their own reorientation to the changing world. Universalistic 19th century movements such as socialism and nationalism found their parallels within the Jewish community in the form of the Bund and Zionism.

The first aim of the Zionist settlers on arriving in Palestine was to throw off the dispirited, down-trodden self-image imposed by the nations of Europe. There would be no place for the institutionalized hypocrisy of the kind they left behind. For them, civic culture was nothing more than a veneer of public decorum, a formalized salon elegance that hid the dark side of a bowing, heel-clicking gentry which provoked bloody pogroms.

Little wonder that to these utopian socialists who endowed labor, especially working the land, with sacred meaning, urban civic culture was suspect. Bourgeois formalism was seen as preventing people from engaging in straight-from-the-shoulder, unadorned sincerity. In the pioneering quest for a national ethos, self-assurance, self-reliance and self-defense became the main ingredients of *"hevramaniut"* a hail fellow directness in public no less than among relatives and friends. Built on plain spoken candor, the new self-image was to be modeled on the sabra plant, the fruit of which has a thorny exterior but a sweet inside. This popular explanation was given to the baffled newcomer or visitor who was subjected to aggressive familiarity on first encounter. This characteristic is still part of Israeli culture a century later.

Jews in the United States and Canada had a far different experience from the early Zionist pioneers although both groups came from exclusionist societies. On their paths to integration in the New World, Jews encountered discrimination but not in the lethal forms of persecution which characterized the Old World. The move into the mainstream began with the children of the immigrants and eventually brought them into all sectors of the civic culture, conforming more or less to the description set forth by Schneider. (74)

Observing the two off-shoots of the same parent community, the liaison-consultant noted that their behavior at the point of interaction, though unreflective, was nevertheless influenced by different environments working upon them in different parts of the world. Croydon visitors reached out to Kfar Oranim residents, not only as patrons but also as people sharing the same fate. They somehow managed to convey this emotion but always in the formal tone of people expressing their feelings in the public arena. Kfar Oranim residents sensed this deeply ingrained manner of communicating and responded accordingly. They never attempted to impose the intimacy or informality that existed among themselves.

The Use of the Past as Precedent in Community Work

An interpretation of a problem is not an answer to it. In terms of a solution, we are left with new questions since the comparative approach, as presented, seems too general for any specific ameliorative intervention on the part of the liaison-consultant. Indeed, can the diagnosis of a macro condition affecting an entire society be directly applied to the solution of a micro problem faced by one particular small locality? When a breakdown in committee functioning occurs, docs it matter, in terms of the worker's intervention, whether the disruptive behavior came as a by-product of a sanctioned way of life or as a result of inefficiency?

If the objective were to do something for the expedient purpose of getting the Steering Committee back to its best behavior while the guests were present, then cross-cultural analysis is of little relevance. For purposes of expediency, the problem could be resolved by returning Vered to the job to do her drills with sub-committee members or to run interference for them when things got complicated at budget reviews with the Croydon delegation. If, however, an integrative process were desired to implant the Steering Committee into the vitals of the community, that would necessitate tracing the problem to its roots.

To become impatient with the past because it does not yield clues to immediate intervention is to turn away from the repository of knowledge for understanding the problem at hand. It means facing the future with little other than intuition and its assortment of inscrutable hunches.

From a practical point of view, we know that it is impossible to ignore the past completely. If the practitioner does not heed it in a disciplined way, the past asserts itself operationally as custom, as superstition, as prejudice the unlit pathways of folklore that will frustrate the foolhardy worker who tries head on to "break the community of its bad habits". Such advice is not only for the raw recruit who has only recently entered community work. The liaison-consultant, whose years of experience should have warned him, was lured into a vain quest for a stable group to address the possibility of establishing a cooperative of Kfar Oranim youth to do gardening and and maintenance work at the facililties being enlarged and rebuilt by Project Renewal. Of the reasons which impeded this project, the fear of failure which was at the core of the resistance revealed by many local workers, created a generalized pessimism that could not be overcome.

Very similar was the response of the local professionals to the suggestion of setting up a means of exchanging information about agency programs through regular monthly sessions. This was seen as an added burden to their busy schedules. "Why come together every month to discuss what we already know?" was the unvarying reaction. "After all, we see each other day in and day out. What new things can friends tell each other at these meetings that we haven't previously discussed?" Actually, the information exchanged in these informal, friendly chats was gossip that left the workers uninformed. What was happening to the aging people who were not coming to the agencies? Why did Kurdish immigrants continue a ghettoized existence in Kfar Oranim? What might be done to give more effective help to troubled youth? Such questions were doomed to remain unanswered in the absence of formal interaction among the professionals.

The logical place to pursue the idea of a coordinating body was the Steering Committee. But, without lengthy preparation, the concept would only have baffled its members. If Kfar Oranim were to make the Steering Committee the focus of its human services, the body would have to symbolize the organizational or functional community rather than Kfar Oranim, the natural community. Such a structure would require the Steering Committee to become the storehouse of rules, policies, principles, regulations, and procedures of "community business" conducted over the years.

The accumulation of materials would provide the current leadership and staff with the opportunity of relating to the bygone era as a resource which is capable of feeding the present by way of precedent. By definition, precedents are set in the past but, as used by the legal profession, for example, they exert a powerful binding influence on the present. While precedent does not carry the same force in community work as in law, it can provide important guidelines to decision making in the present. Mustering a precedent can be helpful to the worker who is trying to function as a change agent. Precedent used as concrete example may succeed when bare logic has been of no avail.

In 1983, the Steering Committee was not within hailing distance of such a central role. The only sign that its members had the potential to transcend their assigned bundle of tasks was the ability which the Committee had to bring out among the residents collective enthusiasm when they received visiting groups from Croydon. Otherwise, they stuck to the job description prescribed by Project Renewal. Interestingly enough, they related in the same literal way to the assignments identified by the national housing agency for the neighborhood leaders. Members of the Steering Committee insisted that the grass roots activists limit themselves to the role of maintaining and beautifying apartment blocks. The activists sought a wider role and openly opposed attempts to restrain their constant efforts to enlarge their authority.

This self-restraining thrust by the Steering Committee was an unique departure from the usual tendency of organizations to aggrandize their scope and influence. The opposite course taken by the Steering Committee might be explained by the fact that the Mayor and members of the Town Council who served on the Steering Committee were concerned about keeping the Steering Committee within its boundaries in order to make sure that the Town Council's primacy was maintained in the affairs of Kfar Oranim. This may also be the reason why Eitan gave the impression that the Steering Committee and his job as its executive secretary were only passing phases in the framework of Kfar Oranim.

Voluntarism and Social Statesmanship

Ventures launched on the scale of Project Renewal are always faced with unexpected shortcomings. Like random errors, they are virtually unavoidable. So, happily, are the unanticipated achievements that arise to gratify initiators of large scale projects, compensating for the burdened awareness that the success of their undertaking was incomplete. From what we know, it is clear that Project Renewal did not identify community participation as one of its declared objectives. Nevertheless, participatory democracy advanced within the framework of Project Renewal. This element of reform can be counted as a welcome gain even though it was neither planned nor anticipated. It is a gain that must be considered tentative since it still remains to be integrated as a permanent feature of community work in Israel.

In the older welfare societies of England, the United States and Canada, reform has long been a proclaimed goal. In those countries, social welfare reforms seem to come in two-stage cycles that may not closely parallel the evolving situation in Israel but which still have meaning for a country whose approach to social welfare has been greatly influenced by the West.

During the initial phase of the cycle, constituencies arise to alert the general population to pressing social needs which are ignored or left unattended. This is the era that produces charismatic leaders (75) who invest their roles with social statesmanship in the spirit of voluntarism. Under energetic and forceful leadership, the organized group progressively enlarges its influence as it moves from the identification of need to press for the establishment of voluntaristic institutions or social service agencies to meet this need. The militant voluntarism reaches its height when it acquires sufficient public support to pressure government to accept responsibility for the agency originally established under voluntary sponsorship.

One test of electoral democracy is its capacity for allowing new centers of influence and power to arise and to pressure undeterred for specific changes. Such dynamism is core participatory democracy which allows the community to exercise control over its elites — what Almond and Verba refer to as civic competence. (76) The capacity of the organized constituencies and their leaders to create the changes they sought is borne out by the large number of social welfare programs which had their origin in the voluntary sectors of England, the United States and Canada and which are now provided by their governments.

The second stage is one in which change becomes routinized and volunteers assume roles as helpers. Change oriented voluntarism shifts to service volunteering — big brothers, meals on wheels deliverers, gray ladies, etc. The helping role, having acquired expertise based on specialized knowledge, tested skills and ethical codes is entrusted to professionals. These qualified practitioners take responsibillity for

Conclusion

teaching and socializing volunteers to their roles as aides. The training is designed to orient the volunteers to their distinct and separate duties and status.

In this stage, there is inherent tension between the professional and the volunteer, especially in functions where professionals have not attained the clear definition of role which prevails, for example, between physicians and volunteer hospital aides. This is an inevitable part of the shift from the first stage to the second.

The reforms which fundamentally altered life in England started early in the 19th century and then extended to North America where they lasted into the post-World War II era. In nearly every case, these reforms, whether in public health, prisons, child welfare, mental health, services to the aged, or fighting poverty came as a result of the leadership each cause received from volunteer leaders. Their achievements were bound to move succeeding volunteers into static maintenance roles in institutions created by their forebears.

Every new era brings new problems and needs. The challenge of meeting current need requires leaders capable of restoring the restlessness and quest for change that characterized voluntarism in earlier eras. Beyond that, volunteers as change agents need a compelling thrust from the era itself. The 1930's, afflicted by the Great Depression, provided such an atmosphere of urgency. The 1960's vividly exemplified a turbulent period that promised more than it delivered. An enduring contribution of the 1960's is the new meaning of voluntarism. Disadvantaged populations heretofore expected to leave social action to board members and other influential leaders assumed roles in community leadership together with members of the middle class who had been the main campaigners for reform on behalf of poor people.

Israel has its share of men and women who brought statesmanship to efforts to creating organizations to answer human need. However, they were not buttressed by constituencies exerting influence to advance the interest of participatory democracy. Nor did they become mediating forces between the government and the community at large. This is not to suggest that Israelis are passive or indifferent. Politics constitute the monopolizing passion and the primary outlet for feelings.

As Wolfsfeld indicates, "the attitudes of the ordinary citizens . . . pointed to a political culture in which protest is the first course of . . . action . . . one reason for the politics of provocation is that many Israelis feel locked out of institutional paths of influence and find mobilized action an alternative . . ." (77)

There have been desultory attempts to generate social action aimed, among other things, at giving the disadvantaged a bigger stake in the affairs of their communities. Mention has been made of the Black Panthers, a confrontation which was interrupted by the Yom Kippur War of 1973. When community participation again became an issue

Distant Partners: Community Change Through Project Renewal

in the 1980's, many Israeli officials began to worry even though the circumstances were quite different. This time, the thrust for change came not from indigenous disadvantaged people but rather from affluent communities reaching out from afar as partners in a comprehensive renewal effort. Whether their influence will become part of a passing experience recorded under the name of Project Renewal or a permanent feature of the community workers' continuing role on the Israeli scene is up to those who will decide on where to take community participation from here.

From Aid to Interdependence

Finally, it is important to underline the significance of Project Renewal as an illustration of innovation in international assistance. Troubled relationships between have and have-not nations call for a new outlook on international aid. Willy Brandt claims that in order to survive, mankind must heed the need for change from chaos to order. He sees international aid as the cohesive element which will transform the world into a community of global interdependence. To achieve international cooperation, Brandt insists that we cannot ignore the consequences of conflicts and tensions in our time-uprooted millions of refugees, death camps of Europe, the Hiroshima bomb, the carnage in Indochina and Cambodia. (78) Brandt reminds us that mass annihilation is the alternative to aid and cooperation.

Project Renewal is a tiny example in the vast scheme of international aid but its symbolism is significant. Evaluations of achievements and shortcomings must give way to a different yardstick. First and foremost, Project Renewal is an expression of partnership in rehabilitation and development by a people who paid a heavy price to the genocidal forces of destruction that Brandt warned us not to ignore. This deep sense of partnership was always present even if Croydon visitors did no more than traipse around the town with their Kfar Oranim hosts or dropped by a new day care center in the final stages of completion or sat in a class of youngsters learning mathematics with the aid of computers or watched old-timers play backgammon or drew up two teams for an impromptu soccer game. These mundane activities symbolized two communities distant partners interdependent in their moral commitment to survival. This was and is the heart and soul of Project Renewal.

268

FOOTNOTES

1. Parsons, Talcott. *Essays in Social Theory.* Glencoe, Illinois: The Free Press, 1958. See "The Professions and Social Structure." Pp. 34-49

2. Hughes, Everett C. *Men and Their Work.* Glencoe, Illinois: The Free Press, 1958. See "Institutional Office and the Person." Pp. 56-67

3. Ross, Murray G. *Community Organization: Theory and Principles.* New York: Harper and Row, 1955. P. 210

4. Homans, George G. "Status Disparity Among Clerical Workers." *Modern Sociology.* Edited by Alvin W. Gouldner and Helen P. Gouldner, New York: Harcourt, Brace and World, 1963. Pp. 230-243

5. Lipsky, Michale. *Street-Level Bureaucracy.* New York: Russell Sage Foundation, 1980. P. 160

6. Andron, Saul. "Program and Fiscal Accountability from Afar: The Project Renewal Experience." Presented at the International Conference on Urban Revitalization. Jerusalem, March, 1986

7. Hoffman, Charles. *Project Renewal: Community and Change In Israel.* Jerusalem: Renewal Department, Jewish Agency for Israel, 1986. See Chapter 2, "Setting the Stage." Pp. 21-46

8. Ibid., P. 39

9. Stock, Ernest. "Grassroots Politics — Israel Style." *Midstream,* June-July, 1966. Pp. 65-66

10. Lappin, Ben. "Poverty in Israel and Community Work: Involvement or Marginality." Presented to the Association of Community Workers in Israel. Spring, 1980

11. Carmon, Naomi. "Israel's Project Renewal. History, Principles, Goals and Scope." Based on the introductory chapter of *Comprehensive Evaluation of Project Renewal.* By R. Alterman, N. Carmon and M. Hill. Haifa: The Samuel Institute for Advanced Studies in Sciences and Technology, Technion — Israel Institute of Technology. In press.

12. Pardes, Yoseph. "Schools for the Development of Local Community Leaders". Jerusalem: Ministry of Labor and Social Affairs, Services for Community Work, June, 1985. P.2

13. Carmon, Naomi. Op. cit. P. 2

14. Jesse Steiner, a pioneer American theorist in community organization, traced the first instances of federated fund-raising

in North America to the Cincinnati Jewish community. In 1896, the Jewish agencies in that city launched a joint drive to provide unified funding for their services. Steiner claims that this venture showed the larger community the value of unified fund-raising and joint budgeting. He asserts that it was the precedent for the Cleveland Chamber of Commerce decision in 1908 to study the problem of funding the social agencies in that city. The study led to the establishment five years later of the Cleveland Federation for Charity and Philanthropy. See *Community Organization: A Study of its Theory and Current Practice.* By Jesse F. Steiner. New York: Century Company, 1925. P. 178

15. Kramer, Ralph M. "Voluntary Agencies and Social Change in Israel, 1972-1982." Jerusalem: Israel Social Science Research, 1986. P. 57

16. Elazar, Daniel et al. *The Extent, Focus and Impact of Diaspora Involvement in Project Renewal. Part II: Six Case Studies of Diaspora-Neighborhood Linkage.* Jerusalem: International Evaluation Committee for Project Renewal, May, 1983, Pp. 21-24

17. Ibid. P. 21

18. Steiner, Jesse F. Op. cit. Pp. 114-118

19. Writings on community organization and community development from a comparative perspective begin to appear in the early 1950's when community development was adapted for application in industrially developed nations. One example is the book edited by Dan A. Chekki, *Community Development: Theory and Method of Planned Change.* New Delhi: Vikas Publishing House, 1979. A number of writers contributed chapters, synthesizing the two approaches to community work. See, for example, "Concepts of Community Work — A British View" by Muriel Smith, Pp. 47-59. An earlier endeavor to study the relationship between the two methods came at a workshop at Brandeis University in 1960. See "Community Development and Community Organization: An International Workshop." New York: National Association of Social Workers, 1961.

20. Roberts, Robert W. and Robert H. Nee. *Theories of Social Casework.* Chicago: University of Chicago Press, 1972. See "The Functional Approach To Casework Practice" by Ruth Smalley.

21. Coser, Lewis. *The Functions of Social Conflict.* Glencoe, Illinois: The Free Press, 1964. Chapter VIII, Pp. 134-149

22. Teicher, Morton I. "Social Casework — Science or Art?" *Child Welfare,* July, 1967, Pp. 393-396

23. Medawar, Peter B. *Induction and Intuition in Scientific Thought.* London: Methuen & Co., 1970. Pp. 56-57. See also *Essays on Creativity in the Sciences* edited by Myron A. Coler. New York: New York University Press, 1963.

24. Perlman, Robert and Arnold Gurin. *Community Organization and Social Planning.* New York: John Wiley & Sons, 1972. See "A Problem-Solving Model." Pp. 61-75

25. Halmos, Paul. *The Personal and the Political: Social Work and Political Action.* London, Hutchinson, 1978. P. 15

26. Perlman, Robert and Arnold Gurin. Op. cit. P. 74

27. Coser, Lewis. Op. cit. P. 31

28. Torcyzner,Jim. "Dynamics of Strategic Relationships." in *Readings in Community Organization Practice.* Edited by Ralph M. Kramer and Harry Specht. Englewood Cliffs, New Jersey: Prentice-Hall, Inc., 1983. Pp. 168-180

29. Schermerhorn, Richard A. *Society and Power.* New York: Random House, 1965. 1965. P. 108

30. Woodroofe, Kathleen. *From Charity to Social Work in England and the United States.* Toronto: University of Toronto Press, 1966. P. 42

31. Plant, Ramond. *Social and Moral Theory in Casework.* London: Routledge and Kegan Paul, 1970. See "Casework: Its Moral, Social and Political Engagement." Pp. 89-90

32. Brager, George A. "Advocacy and Political Behavior." *Social Work*, April, 1963. Pp. 5-15

33. Wolff, Kurt H., Editor. *The Sociology of Georg Simmel.* Glencoe, Illinois: The Free Press, 1964. Pp. 183-185. Simmel's distinction between prestige and authority deals with role-taking in social situations. Although he does not take into account ethical restraints on roles in the helping professions, Simmel's views on prestige and authority in superordinate-subordinate relationships throw light on the interaction between helper and helped in the worker-client framework. In her evaluation of Project Renewal, Naomi Carmon deals with another aspect of power and prestige resources in the distressed communities. See "Directed Social Change, An Evaluation of Project Renewal in Israel." Presented at the International Symposium on Neighborhood Policy, Massachusetts Institute of Technology, May 1-2, 1986. Pp. 24-25

34. Johnson, Arlien. "Methods and Skills in Community Organization." in *Community Organization in Action.* Edited by Ernest B. Harper and Arthur Dunham. New York: Association Press, 1959. Pp.

81-85

35. Ibid.

36. Bolan, Richard S. "Community Decision Behavior: The Culture of Planning." in *Readings in Community Organization Practice.* Edited by Ralph M. Kramer and Harry Specht. Englewood Cliffs, New Jersey: Prentice-Hall, Inc. Pp. 209-224

37. Rodgers, Barbara with Abraham Doron and Michael Jones. *The Study of Social Policy: A Comparative Approach.* London: George Allen and Unwin, 1979. P. 192

38. Bailey, Roy and Mike Brake, Editors. *Radical Social Work.* London: Edward Arnold (Publishers), 1975. See "Community Development: A Radical Alternative?" Pp. 129-143

39. Heschel, Abraham. *A Passion for Truth.* New York: Straus and Giroux, 1973, P. 105

40. Hoffman, Charles. Op. cit.

41. Elazar, Daniel and Paul E. King. *The Extent, Focus and Impact of Diaspora Involvement in Project Renewal. Interim Report.* Jerusalem: Center for Public Affairs, August 11, 1982. Pp. 49-55

42. Jaffe, Eliezer. "Entering a New Era After Project Renewal." *Jerusalem Post,* January 16, 1987

43. Elazar, Daniel et al. *The Extent, Focus and Impact of Diaspora Involvement in Project Renewal. Part II: Six Case Studies of Diaspora-Neighborhood Linkage.* Jerusalem: International Evaluation Committee for Project Renewal, May, 1983. "Israel-Diaspora Relations in the Pre-Renewal Era." P. 1

44. Jaffe, Eliezer. Op. cit.

45. Mannheim, Karl. *Man and Society in an Age of Reconstruction.* New York: Harcourt, Brace and World, 1949. P. 378

46. Bernstein, Irving. "Reluctant Consensus." *Jerusalem Post,* July 1, 1986

47. Elazar, Daniel et al. Op. cit.

48. Ya'acobi, Gad. "Ya'acobi Warns Likud Not to Hurt Jewish Unity." *Jerusalem Post*, July 29, 1987

49. Carmon, Naomi. Op. cit.

50. Gilbert, Neil. *Capitalism and the Welfare State.* New Haven: Yale University Press, 1983. P. 4

51. Once considered a crowning achievement, the welfare state has

been roundly criticized in a number of books and articles in the 1980's. For example, in 1981, George Gilder examined welfarism as "The Crisis of Policy". The Organization for Economic Cooperation and Development in 1981 and Ramesh Mishra in 1984 brought out their studies under the same title, "The Welfare State in Crisis".

52. Well-known American educators have played important roles in establishing Israeli schools of social work. For example, Eileen Blackey brought her experience in curriculum planning to the creation of the Paul Baerwald School of Social Work, Hebrew University, serving as its first dean. Morton I. Teicher used his expertise in founding schools of social work (Wurzweiler School of Social Work, Yeshiva University and Oppenheimer College of Social Services, Lusaka, Northern Rhodesia, now Zambia) to help establish the School of Social Work, Bar Ilan University. Joseph Eaton was active in the early stages of the Haifa University School of Social Work.

53. *North-South: A Programme for Survival.* Report of the Independent Commission on International Development Issues. Chairman, Willy Brandt. London: Pan Books, 1980. P. 73

54. Ibid. P. 291

55. Ibid. Pp. 261-262

56. Bugnicourt, Jacques. "Popular Participation in Development in Africa." *Assignment Children.* Geneva: United Nations Children's Fund, 1982. P. 98

57. Ibid.

58. Ibid.

59. Hayes, Carlton J.H. *A Political and Cultural History of Europe.* Volume I, New York: Macmillan Co., 1945. P. 537

60. For meanings of "good", see Ewing, A.C. *The Definition of Good.* New York: Macmillan Co., 1947. Chapter IV, Pp. 112-144. The meaning of "good" in its various nuances is not discussed herein. It is conveyed in its common usage by people to describe how they feel about "good" in relation to the phenomenon of power in possession of those who use it to pursue political and professional aims.

61. Taylor, Samuel H. "Community Work and Social Work: The Community Liaison Approach" in *Theory and Practice of Community Social Work*, edited by Samuel H. Taylor and Robert W. Roberts. New York: Columbia University Press, 1985, Pp. 179-214

62. Terrel, Paul. "The Social Worker as Radical: Roles of Advocacy" in *Perspectives on Social Welfare*, edited by Paul E. Weinberger. New York: Macmillan Co., 1971. Pp. 355-364

63. Specht, Harry. "Disruptive Tactics" in *Readings in Community Organization Practice*, edited by Ralph M. Kramer and Harry Specht. Englewood Cliffs, New Jersey: Prentice-Hall, 1969. Pp. 372-386

64. Grosser, Charles F. *New Directions in Community Organization from Enabling to Advocacy.* New York: Praeger Publishers, 1973. P. 199

65. Guttman, Michal. *The Rationale of Violence in Social Welfare Bureaux: A Conceptual Empirical Study.* Submitted in partial fulfillment of the requirements for a Master's degree. Department of Social Work, Ramat Gan, Israel, June, 1977. P. 153

66. Trevelyan, George M. *British History in the Nineteenth Century and After (1782-1919).* London: Longmans, Green and Co., 1948. P. 2

67. Schneider, Kenneth R. "Reconstruction of Community" *International Review of Community Development,* New Series 15, 16, 1966. Pp. 19-42

68. Trevelyan, George M. op. cit. P. 5

69. Elon, Amos. *The Israelis - Founders and Sons.* London: Wiedenfeld and Nicolson, 1971. P. 303

70. Doron, Abraham. *The Study of Social Policy: A Comparative Approach.* London: George Allen and Unwin, 1979. Pp. 112-148

71. Teicher, Morton I. "Social Planning in Israel". *Journal of Jewish Communal Service,* Summer, 1976. Pp. 374-383

72. Cuddihy, John M. *The Ordeal of Civility.* New York: Delta Publishing Co., 1976. P. 3

73. *Encyclopedia Judaica.* Jerusalem: Keter Publishing House, 1971. Volume 3, Pp. 79-86

74. Schneider, Kenneth R. Op. cit.

75. Grosser, Charles F. Op. cit. P. 119

76. Almond, Gabriel A. and Sidney Verba. *The Civic Culture.* Boston: Little, Brown and Co., 1963. Pp. 136-167

77. Wolfsfeld, Gadi. *The Politics of Provocation: Participation and Protest in Israel.* New York: State University of New York Press, 1988. P. 163

78. *North-South: A Programme for Survival.* Op. cit. P.13,18

Conclusion

Appendix
Participants in the Documentary

Croydon

Phillip	Community Leader, National Chairman, Project Renewal, United States
Solomon	Community Leader
Melvin	Community Leader, Chairman Project Renewal Committee
Edith	Community Leader
Mark	Senior Staff Member, Jewish Federation
Charles	Dentist, Volunteer

Israel Government

Reuven	Deputy Minister of Housing
Zipporah	Supervisor, Government Housing Corporation
Amit	Staff Member, Government Housing Corporation
Ranan	Supervisor, Ministry of Labor and Social Affairs
Giora	Supervisor, Ministry of Labor and Social Affairs
Ari	Supervisor, Ministry of Labor and Social Affairs
Yosef	Supervisor, Ministry of Housing

Junius

Ariela	Volunteer in Kfar Oranim
Noam	Husband of Ariela; Israeli Political Leader
Adah	Volunteer in Kfar Oranim
Myron	Husband of Adah
Dalia	Volunteer in Kfar Oranim
Phyllis	Volunteer in Kfar Oranim
Deena	Hotel Manager
Shmuel	Director, Golf Club
Morris	Business Man
Stella	Wife of Morris
Nadav	Attorney, representing Morris and Stella
Percy	Business Man

Project Renewal

Roger	Director, United States Office
Hanoch	Senior Executive, Jewish Agency, Jerusalem
Marek	Successor to Hanoch
Marcus	Senior Executive, Inter-Ministerial Committee

Ofir   Staff Member
Leah   Staff Member, Regional Office
Vered   Staff Member, Regional Office
Shimon   Staff Member, Regional Office
Jared   Staff Member, Regional Office
Judith   Staff Member, Jerusalem
Menashe   Staff Member, Jerusalem
Yonaton   Staff Member, Jerusalem
Stephen   Staff Member, Jerusalem
Rolf   Staff Member, Jerusalem

Kfar Oranim
Shaul   Mayor
Eitan   Executive Secretary, Steering Committee
Amos   Deputy Mayor
Yehuda   Town Council Member, Candidate for Mayor
Rani   Town Clerk; Secretary, Town Council
Uri   Director, Welfare Department
Yoram   Social Worker, Welfare Department
Chaya   Social Worker, Welfare Department
Dan   Director, Community Center
Ilan   Youth Worker, Community Center
Ovadiah   Director of Physical Planning
Rafael   Director, Youth Orchestra
Yuval   Director, School System
Meron   Successor to Yuval
Ephraim   Director, Labor Party Branch
Mordecai   Secretary, Labor Party Branch
Shulamith   Representative of Na'mat (Pioneer Women)
Ralph   Director of Volunteers
Aaron   Director of Youth Work
Shimon   Successor to Aaron
Yishai   Chairman, Trustees of Educational Institutions and
                Cultural Organizations Committee
Tamar   Community Worker
Aryeh   Community Worker, Para-professional
Yael   Community Worker, Volunteer
Martha   Community Worker, Volunteer
Micha   Volunteer, Member of Neighboring Kibbutz
Zalman   Owner of Scopus Manufacturing Company,
                Member of Knesset (Israeli Legislature)
Avram   Principal, Malachti School
Richard   University Student, Assigned to Kfar Oranim for
                Field Experience
Ehud   University Student, Assigned to Kfar Oranim for

	Field Experience
Motti	Resident
Dorit	Resident, Teen-ager
Shula	Resident; Teen-ager

Other

Rabbi Cohen	Director, High School in Israel
Oren	Staff member, High School in Israel
Zev	Staff member, construction company
Ruth	Liaison-consultant, Jerusalem slum area
Dennis	Director, Keren Malka Tennis Center
Naomi	Director of Public Relations, Keren Malka Tennis Center
Gil	Staff Member, "Eighteen-Plus', Youth-serving Organization
Martin	Director, Jerusalem Research Institute, Convenor of Liaison-consultant meetings

About the Authors

Ben W. Lappin is former Director and Professor Emeritus, School of Social Work, Bar Ilan University, Ramat Gan, Israel. Before settling in Israel in 1970, he served as Professor, Faculty of Social Work, University of Toronto. He earned his Ph.D. in social work at the University of Toronto in 1965. Dr. Lappin practiced community work in Canada and has written extensively on the subject.

Morton I. Teicher is the founding dean of the Wurzweiler School of Social Work, Yeshiva University and Dean Emeritus, School of Social Work, University of North Carolina at Chapel Hill. He has been involved in community work in the United States, Canada, Israel, Egypt and Northern Rhodesia (Zambia). Dr. Teicher earned his master's degree in social work at the University of Pennsylvania and his Ph.D. in anthropology at the University of Toronto.